BAKEMONOGATARI

OH!GREAT
ORIGINAL STORY:
NISIOISIN

ORIGINAL CHARACTER
DESIGN: VOFAN

15

MAIN CHARACTERS

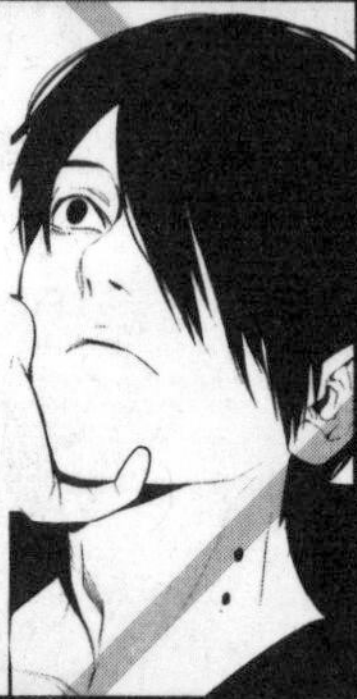

Koyomi Araragi

A boy who became Kiss-Shot's thrall after saving her. He decides to fight Kiss-Shot, his master, and ultimately wins, but now...

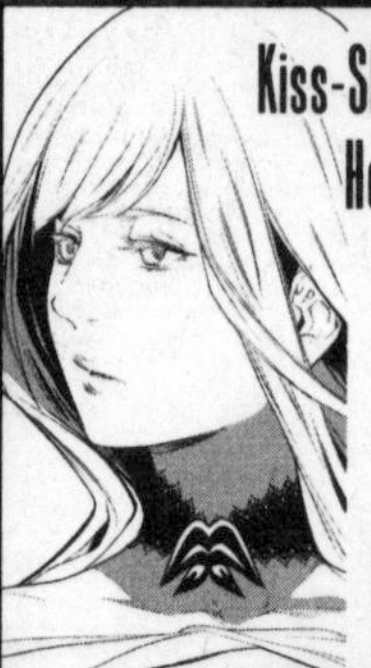

Kiss-Shot Acerola-Orion Heart-Under-Blade

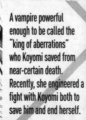

A vampire powerful enough to be called the "king of aberrations" who Koyomi saved from near-certain death. Recently, she engineered a fight with Koyomi both to save him and end herself.

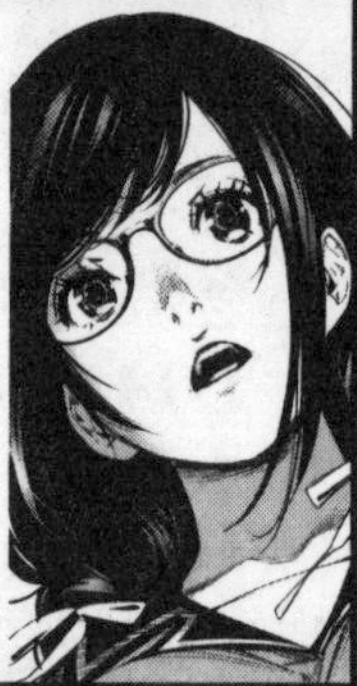

Tsubasa Hanekawa

Koyomi's friend who goes to the same school as him, and an honor student that few honors could sufficiently describe. She saw through Kiss-Shot's plan.

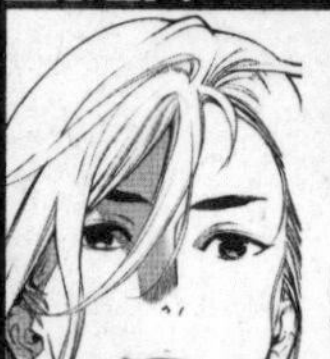

Seishiro Shishirui

Kiss-Shot's first thrall. Though they fought alongside each other at one point, their relationship broke down and he took his own life.

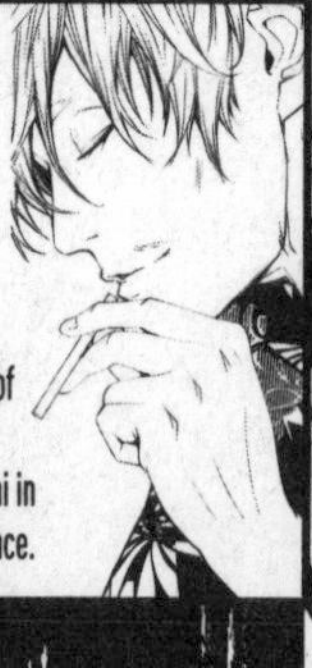

Mèmè Oshino

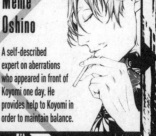

A self-described expert on aberrations who appeared in front of Koyomi one day. He provides help to Koyomi in order to maintain balance.

THE STORY SO FAR

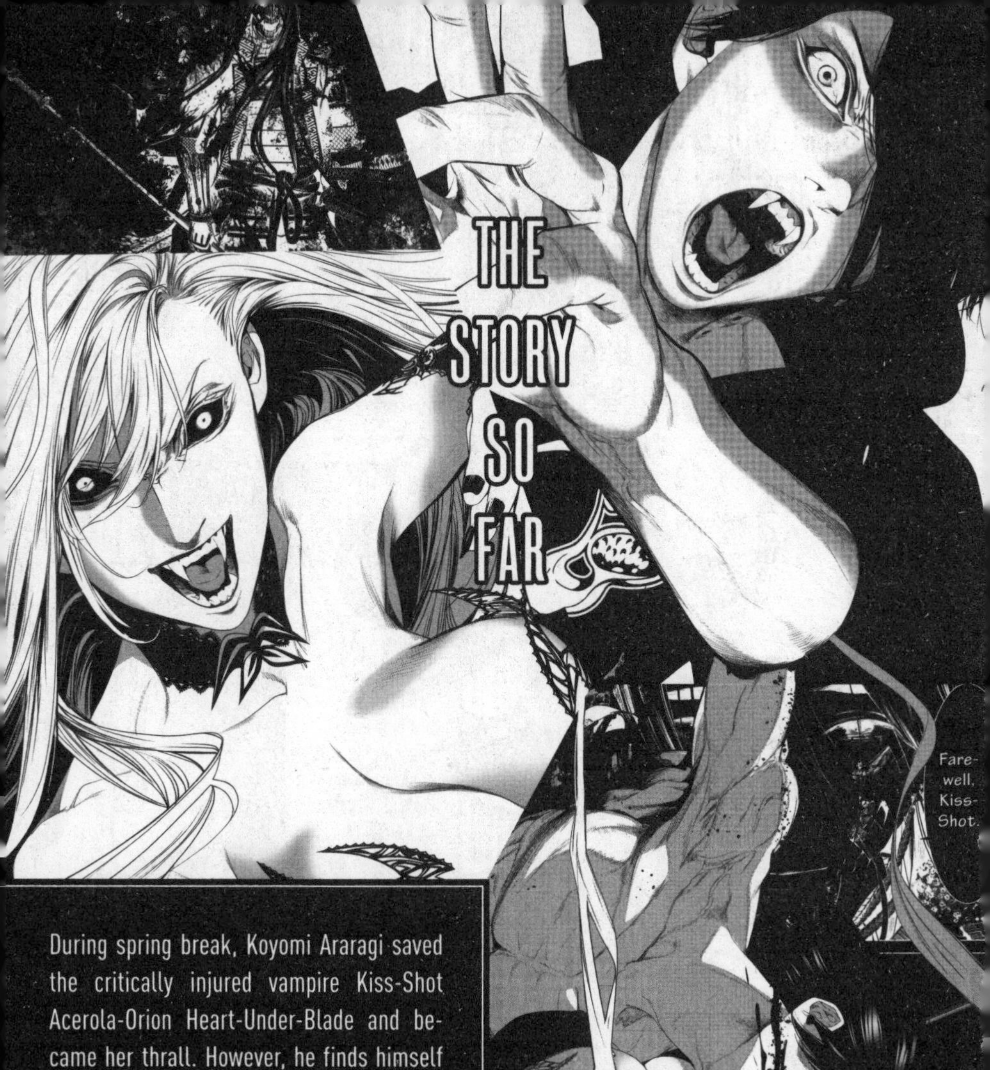
Farewell, Kiss-Shot.

During spring break, Koyomi Araragi saved the critically injured vampire Kiss-Shot Acerola-Orion Heart-Under-Blade and became her thrall. However, he finds himself fighting against his master and defeating her to stop the aberration she is. But upon doing so, he learns that Kiss-Shot had actually set up the situation so she could die and save Koyomi in the process. What will Koyomi do now that he has had a glimpse into the past and emotions of the king of aberrations...?

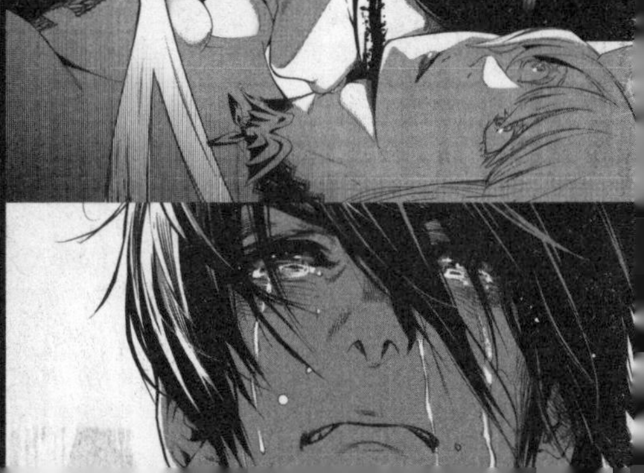

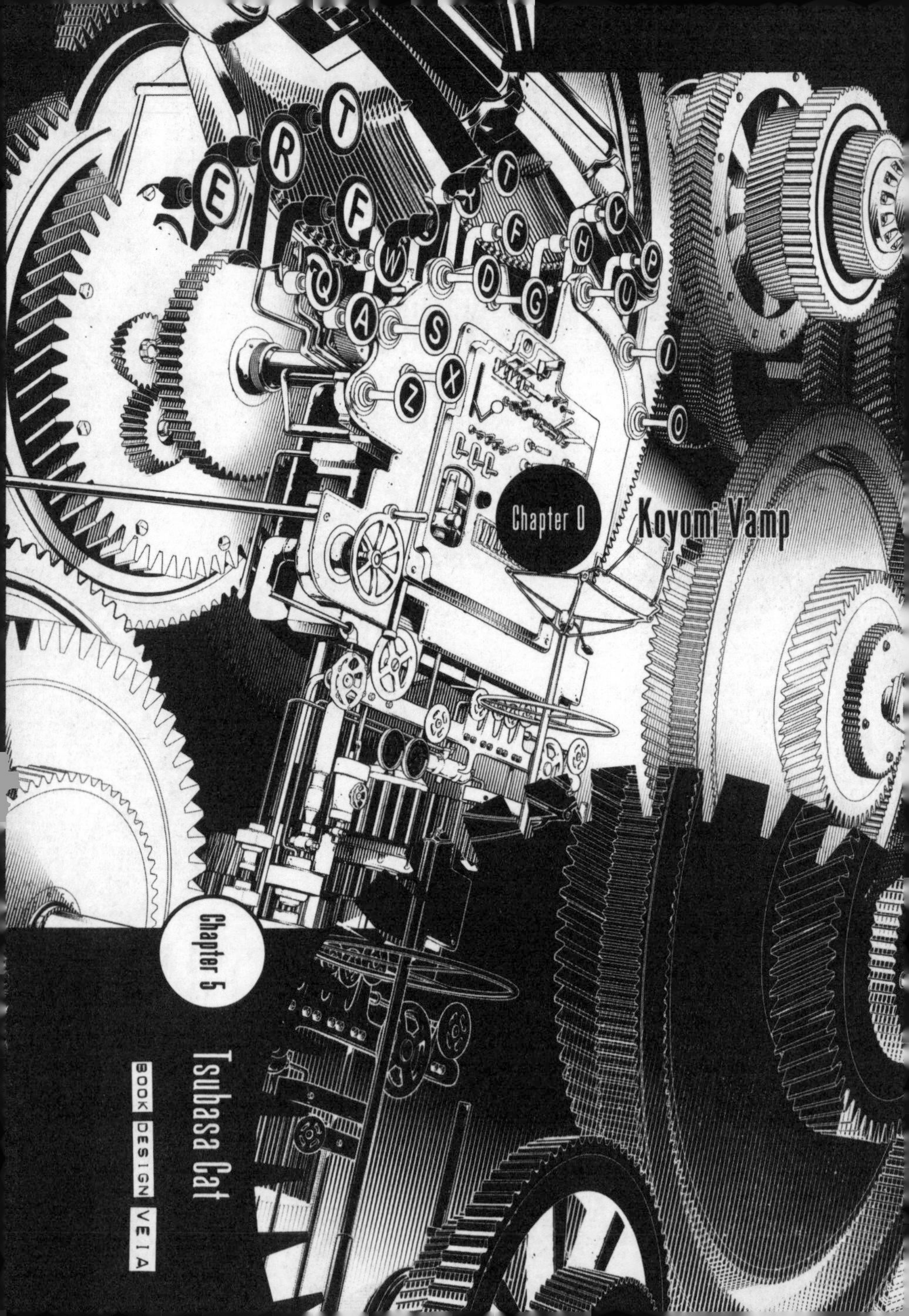
Chapter 0
Koyomi Vamp
Chapter 5
Tsubasa Cat
BOOK DESIGN VEIA

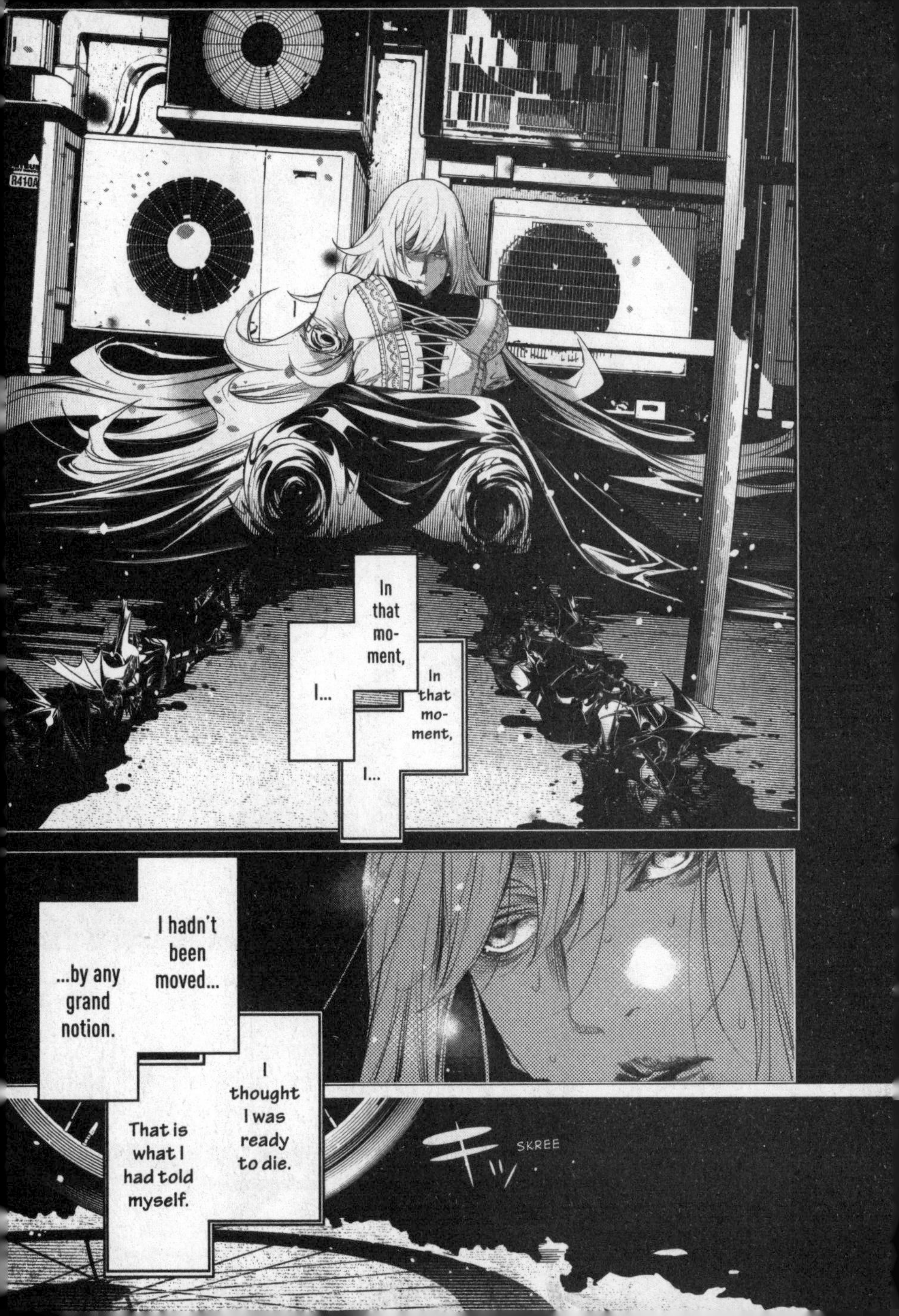
In that mo-ment, I...
In that mo-ment, I...
I hadn't been moved...
...by any grand notion.
I thought I was ready to die.
That is what I had told myself.
SKREE

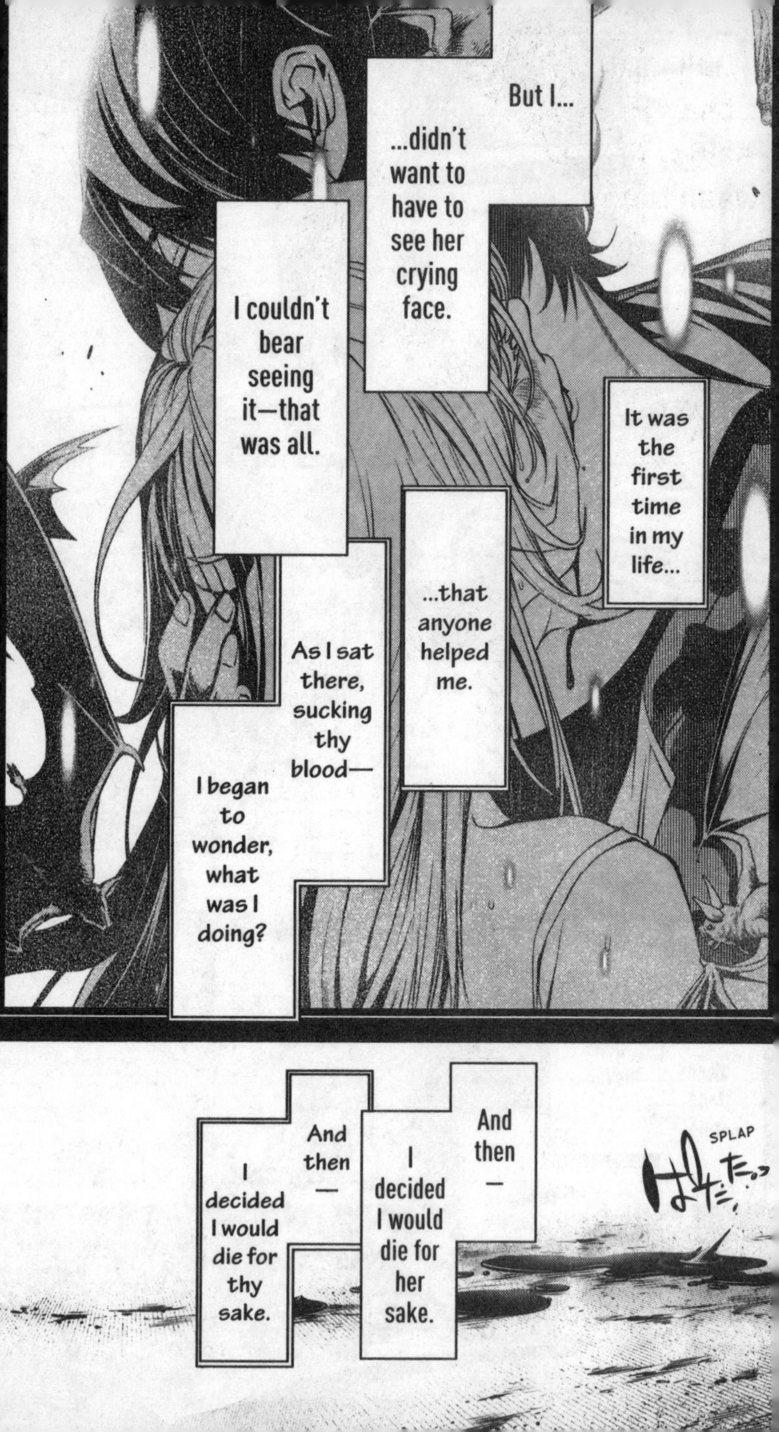
But I...
...didn't want to have to see her crying face.
I couldn't bear seeing it—that was all.
It was the first time in my life...
...that anyone helped me.
As I sat there, sucking thy blood—
I began to wonder, what was I doing?
SPLAP
And then—
I decided I would die for her sake.
And then—
I decided I would die for thy sake.

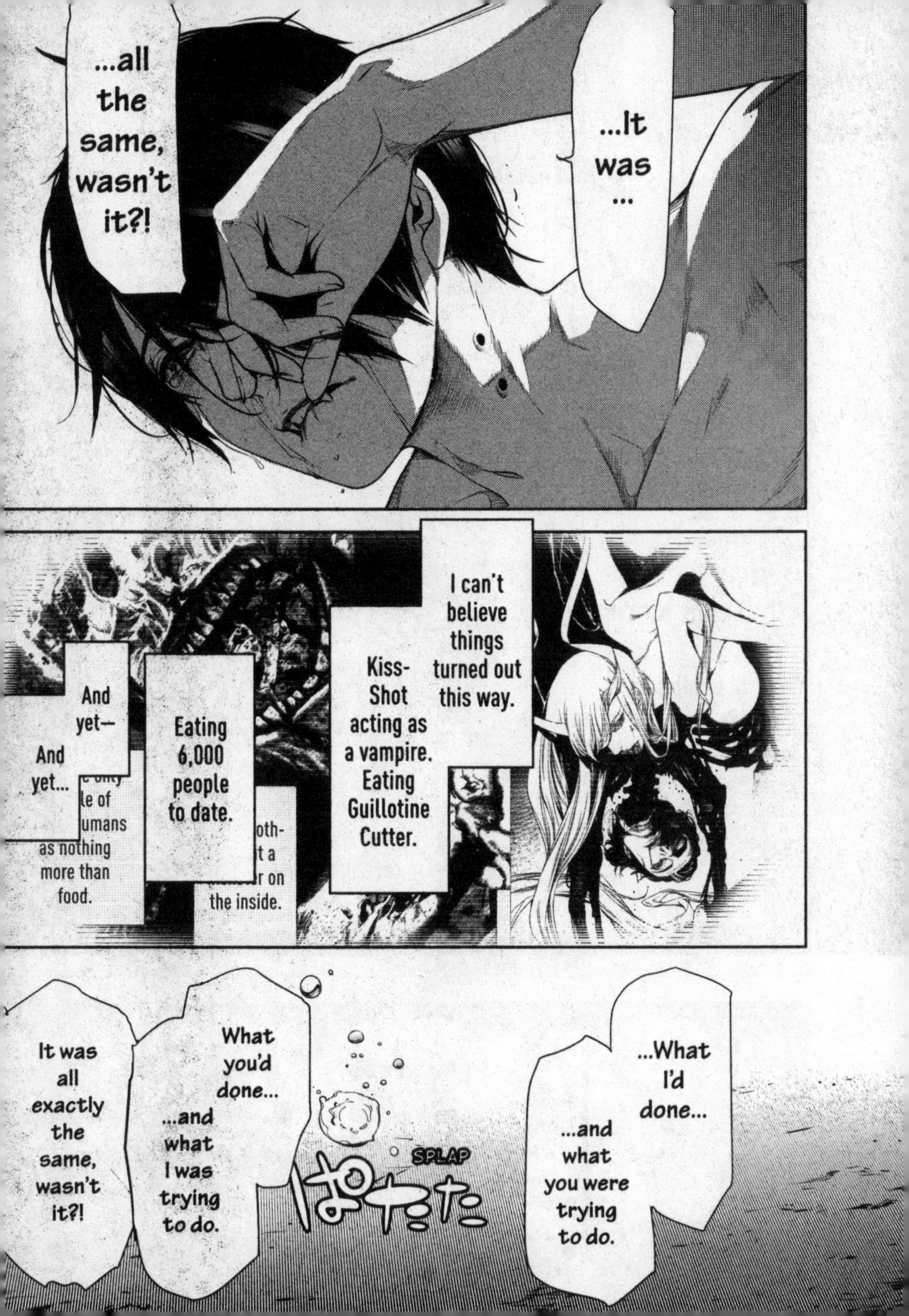
...It was...
...all the same, wasn't it?!
I can't believe things turned out this way.
Kiss-Shot acting as a vampire. Eating Guillotine Cutter.
Eating 6,000 people to date.
the inside.
And yet—
And yet...
as nothing more than food.
...What I'd done...
...and what you were trying to do.
SPLAP
What you'd done...
...and what I was trying to do.
It was all exactly the same, wasn't it?!

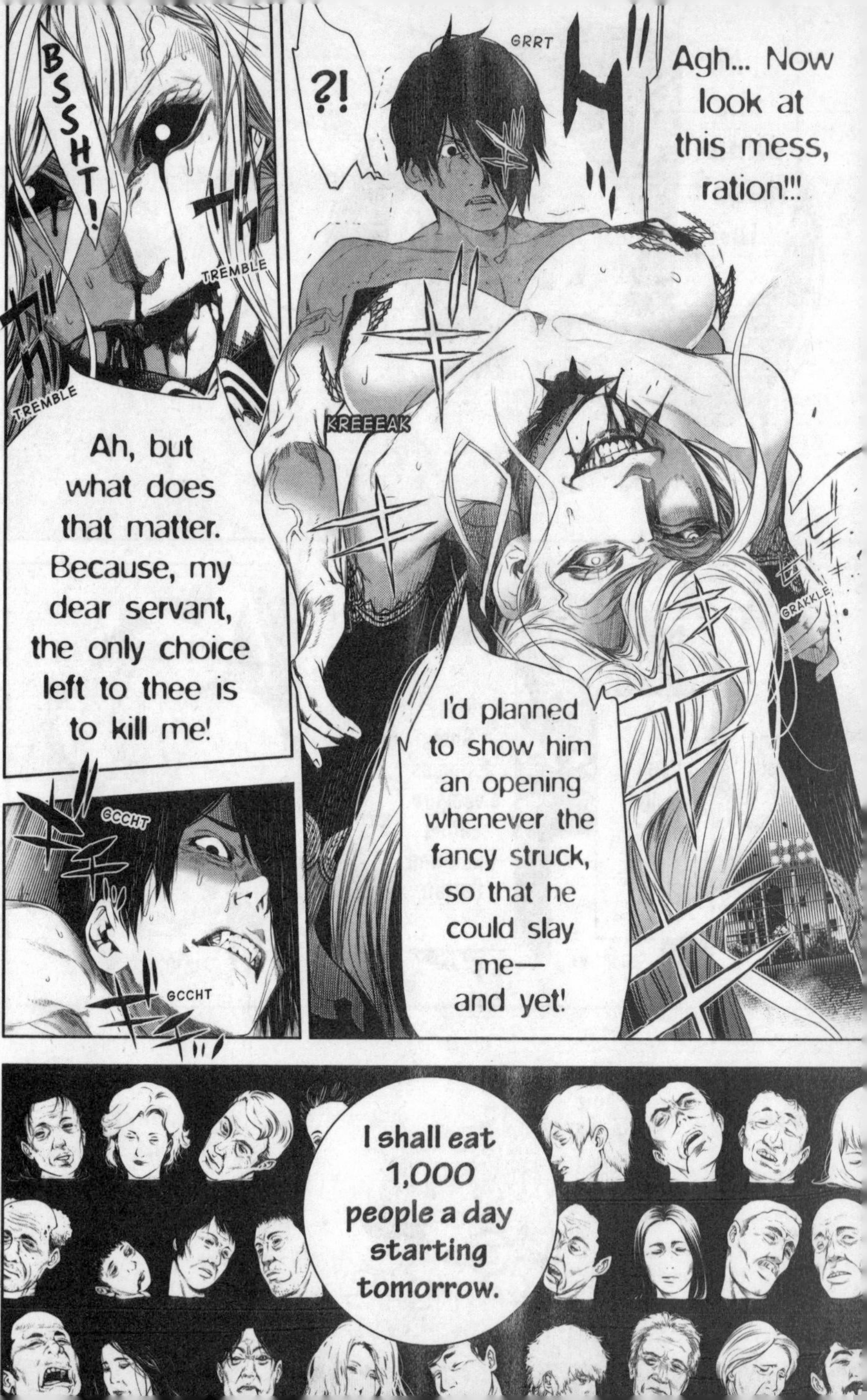
Agh... Now look at this mess, ration!!!
GRRT
?!
GRAKKLE
KREEEAK
I'd planned to show him an opening whenever the fancy struck, so that he could slay me— and yet!
BSSHT!
TREMBLE
TREMBLE
Ah, but what does that matter. Because, my dear servant, the only choice left to thee is to kill me!
GCCHT
GCCHT
I shall eat 1,000 people a day starting tomorrow.

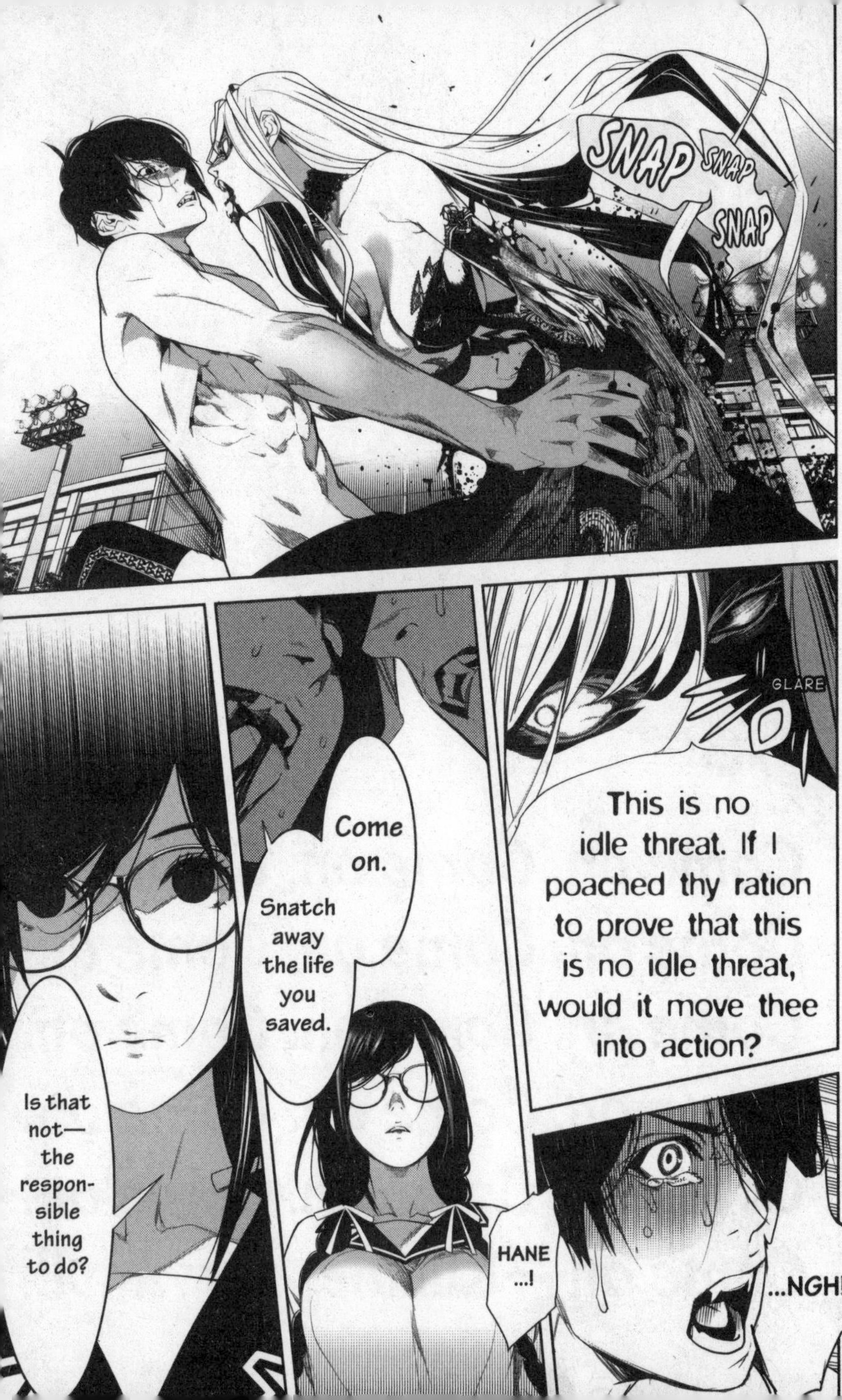

SNAP
SNAP
SNAP
GLARE
This is no idle threat. If I poached thy ration to prove that this is no idle threat, would it move thee into action?
Come on.
Snatch away the life you saved.
Is that not— the responsible thing to do?
...NGH!
HANE ...!

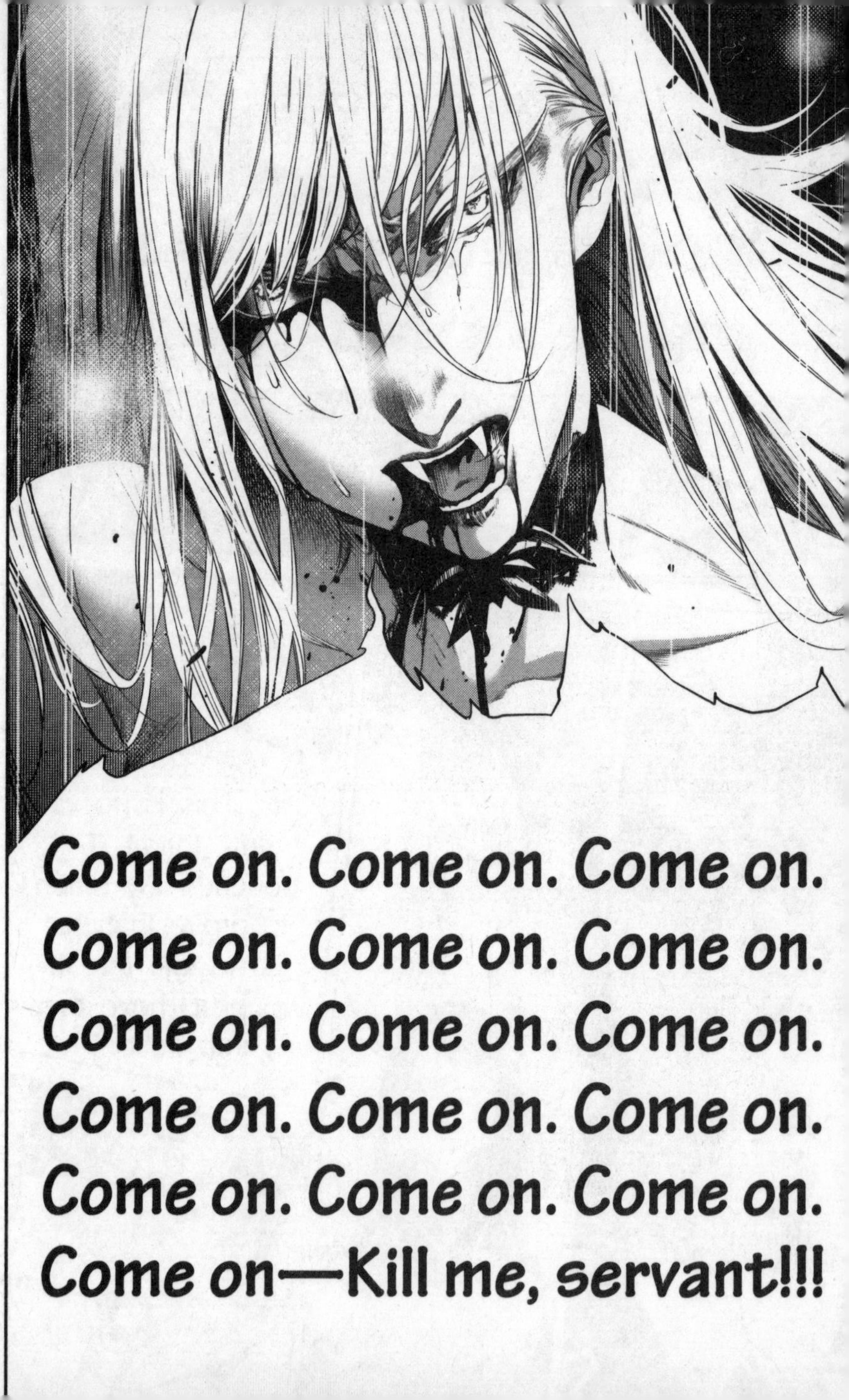
Come on. Come on. Come on.
Come on. Come on. Come on.
Come on. Come on. Come on.
Come on. Come on. Come on.
Come on. Come on. Come on.
Come on—Kill me, servant!!!

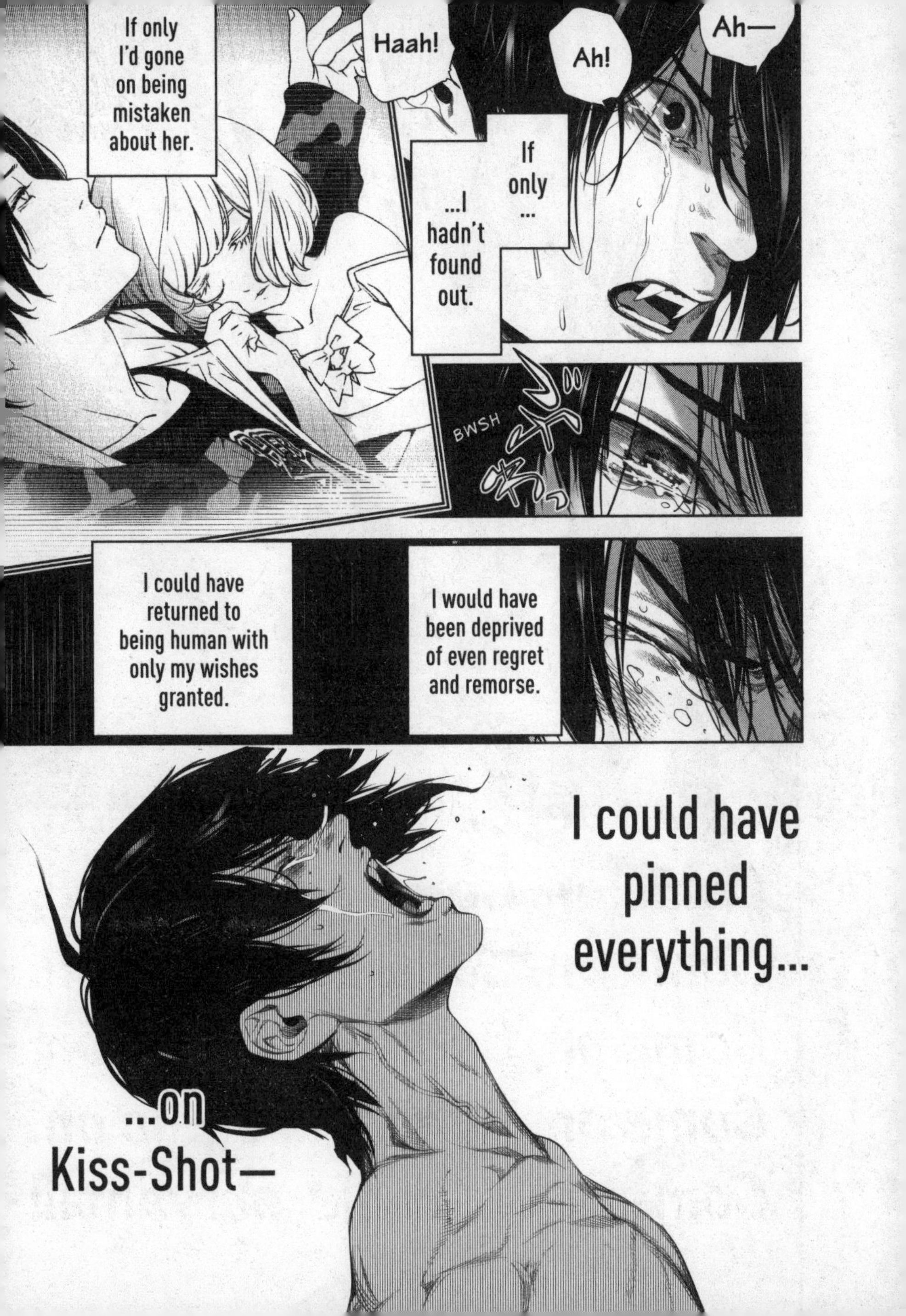
Ah—
Ah!
If only ...
...I hadn't found out.
Haah!
If only I'd gone on being mistaken about her.
BWSH
I would have been deprived of even regret and remorse.
I could have returned to being human with only my wishes granted.
I could have pinned everything...
...on Kiss-Shot—

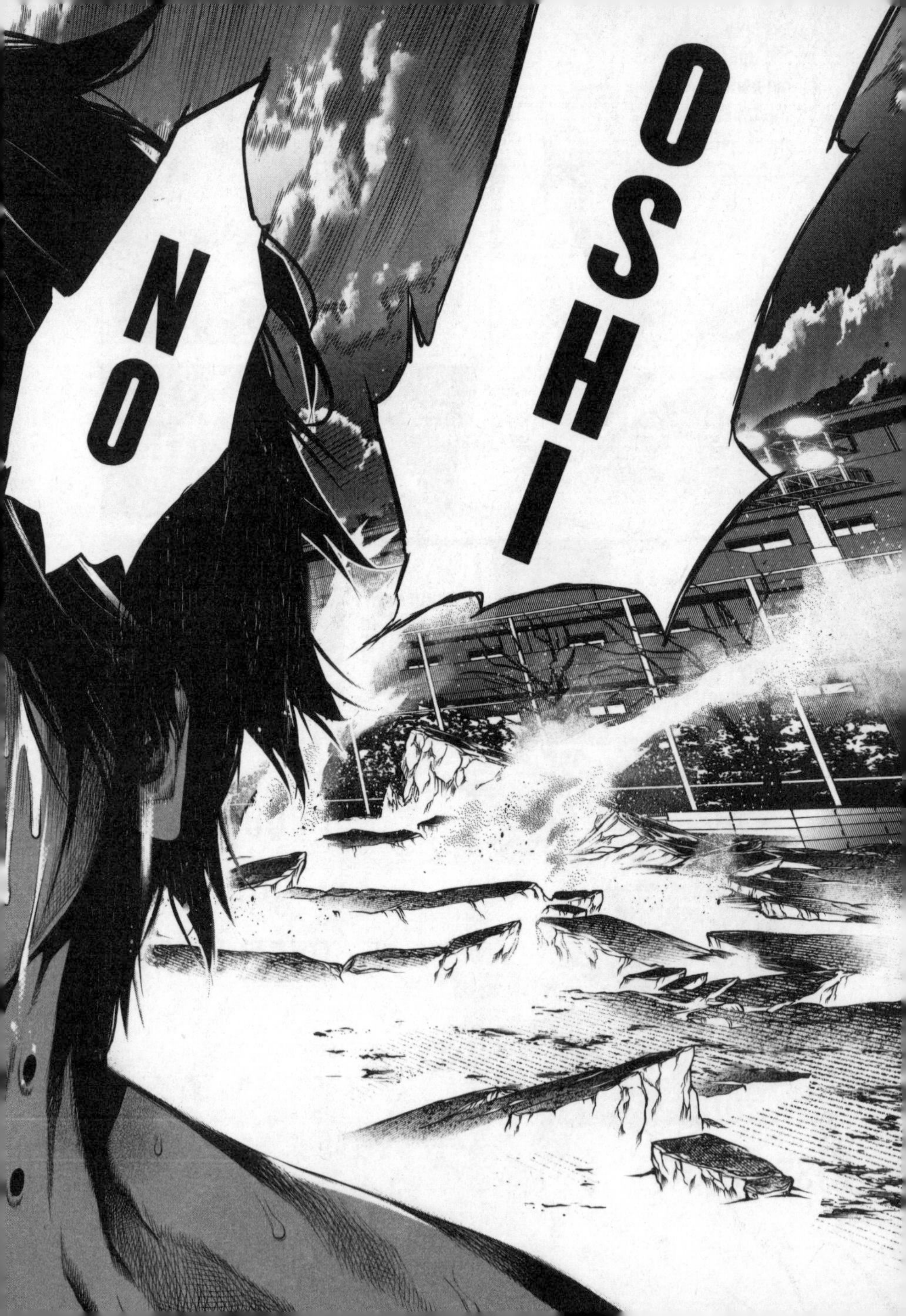
OSHI
NO

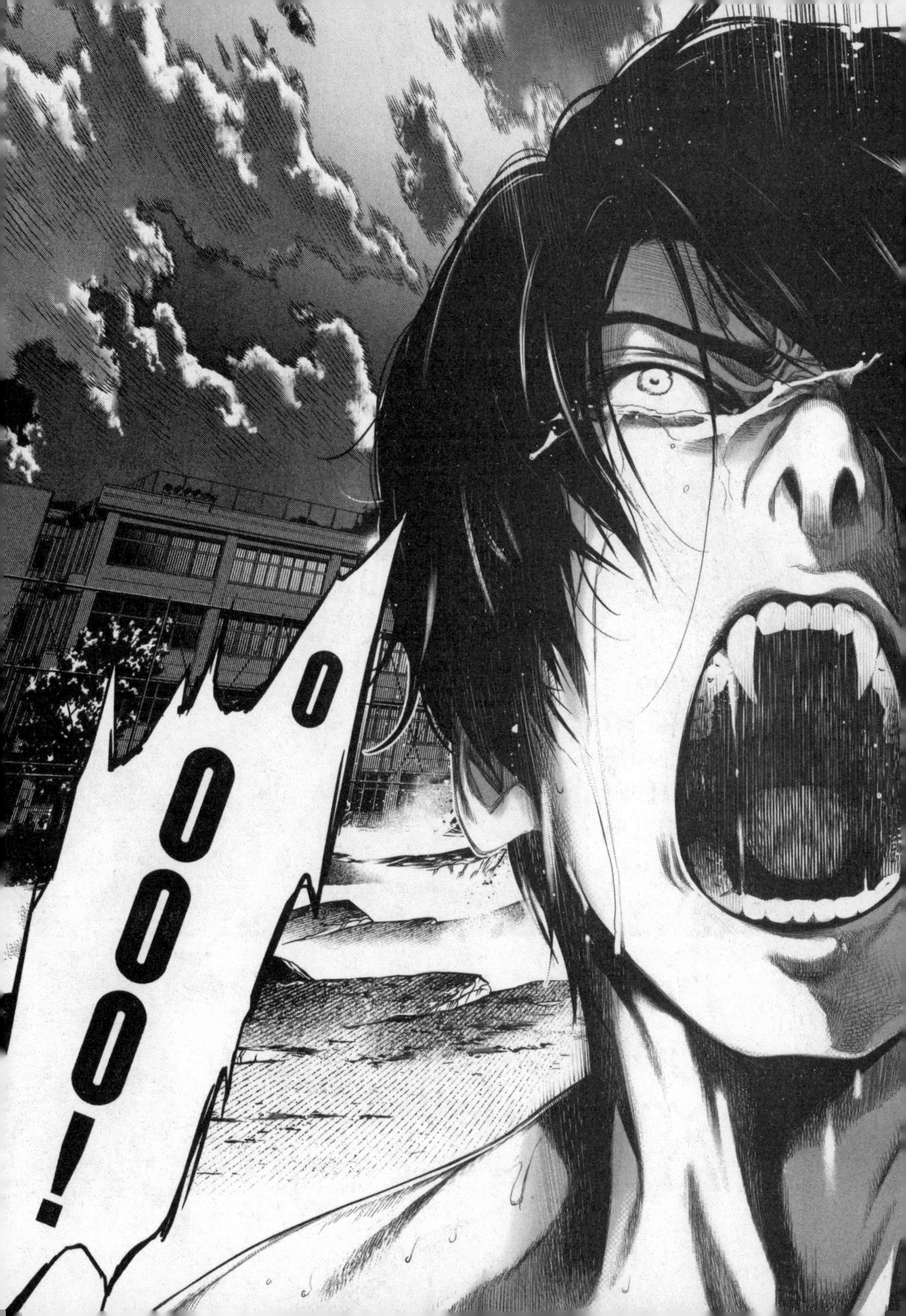

NOOOOOO!!

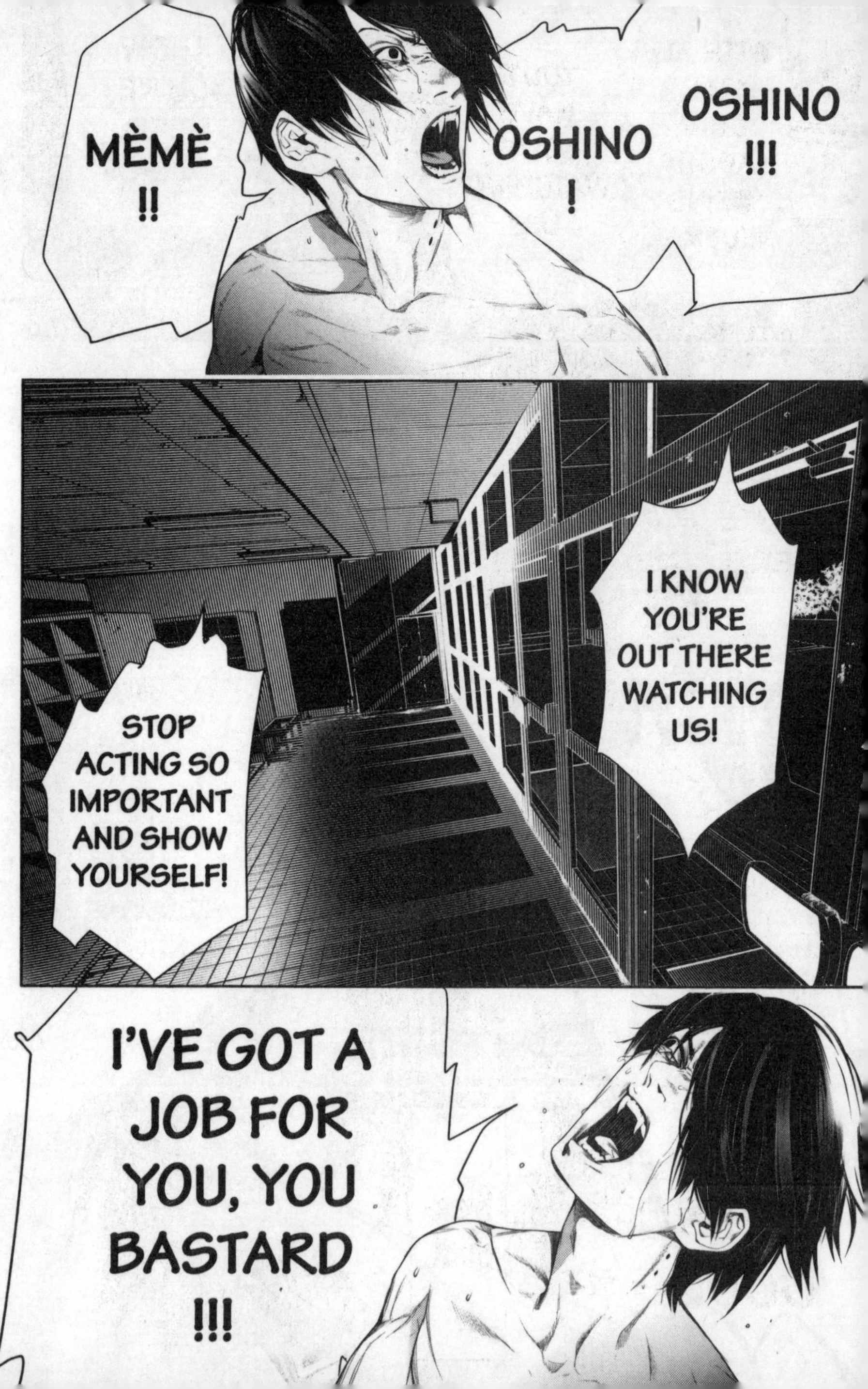
OSHINO !!!
OSHINO !
MÈMÈ !!
I KNOW YOU'RE OUT THERE WATCHING US!
STOP ACTING SO IMPORTANT AND SHOW YOURSELF!
I'VE GOT A JOB FOR YOU, YOU BASTARD !!!

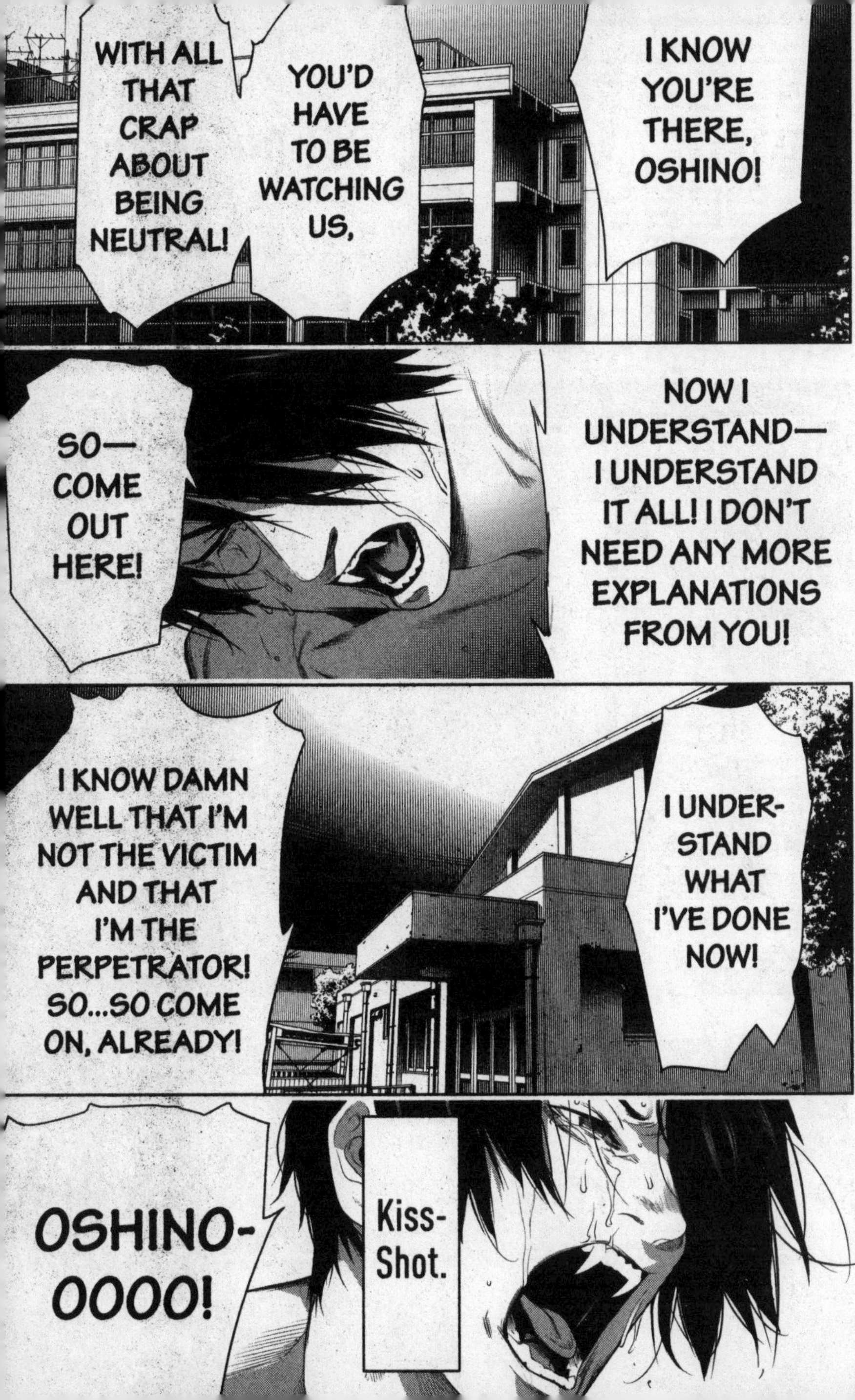
I KNOW YOU'RE THERE, OSHINO!
YOU'D HAVE TO BE WATCHING US,
WITH ALL THAT CRAP ABOUT BEING NEUTRAL!
NOW I UNDERSTAND—I UNDERSTAND IT ALL! I DON'T NEED ANY MORE EXPLANATIONS FROM YOU!
SO—COME OUT HERE!
I UNDER-STAND WHAT I'VE DONE NOW!
I KNOW DAMN WELL THAT I'M NOT THE VICTIM AND THAT I'M THE PERPETRATOR! SO...SO COME ON, ALREADY!
Kiss-Shot.
OSHINO-OOOO!

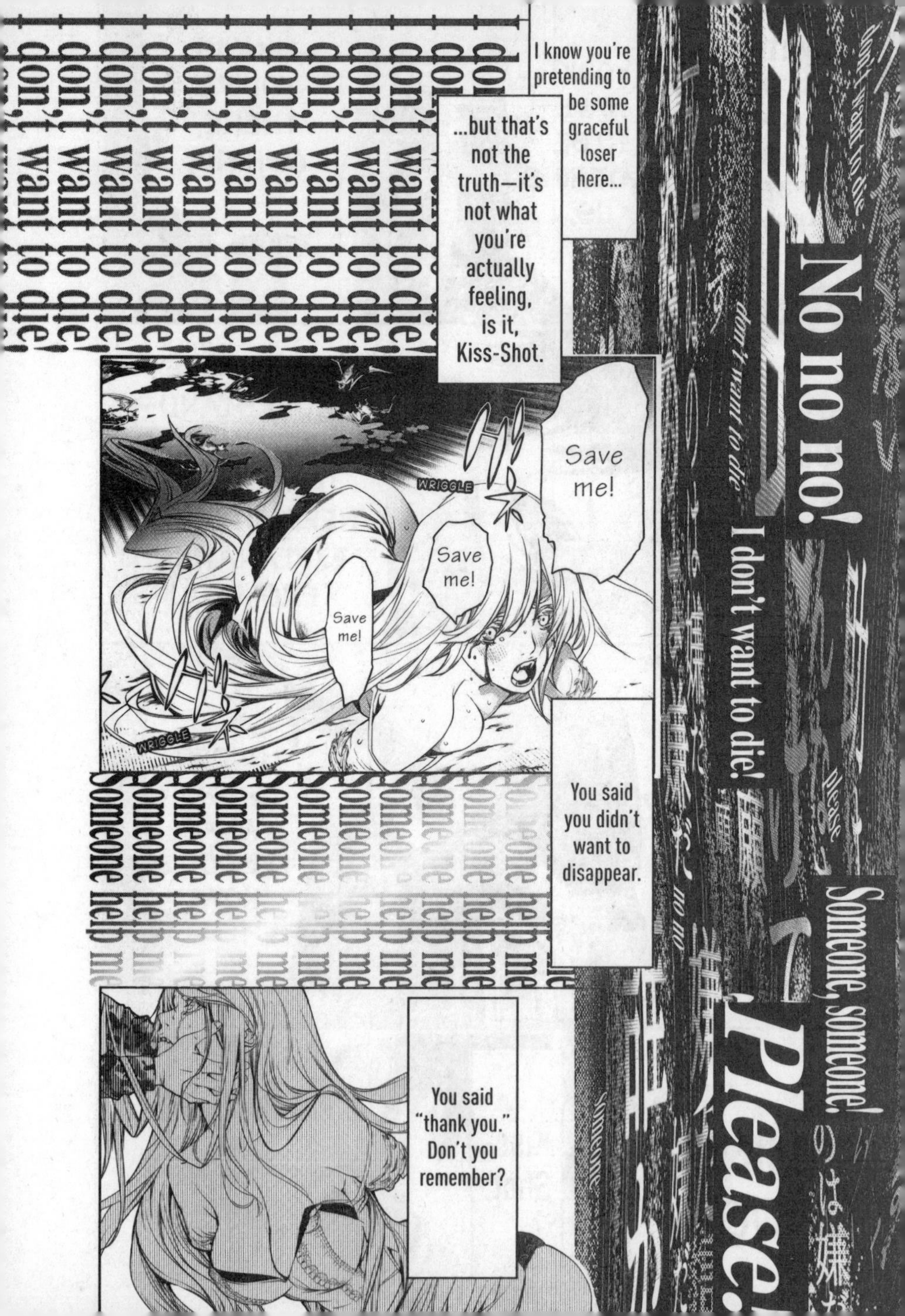
No no no!
I don't want to die!
don't want to die
Someone, someone, someone!
Please!
I know you're pretending to be some graceful loser here...
...but that's not the truth—it's not what you're actually feeling, is it, Kiss-Shot.
don't want to die!
don't want to die!
don't want to die!
don't want to die!
don't want to die!
don't want to die!
Save me!
WRIGGLE
Save me!
Save me!
WRIGGLE
You said you didn't want to disappear.
Someone help me
Someone help me
Someone help me
Someone help me
Someone help me
Someone help me
Someone help me
You said "thank you." Don't you remember?

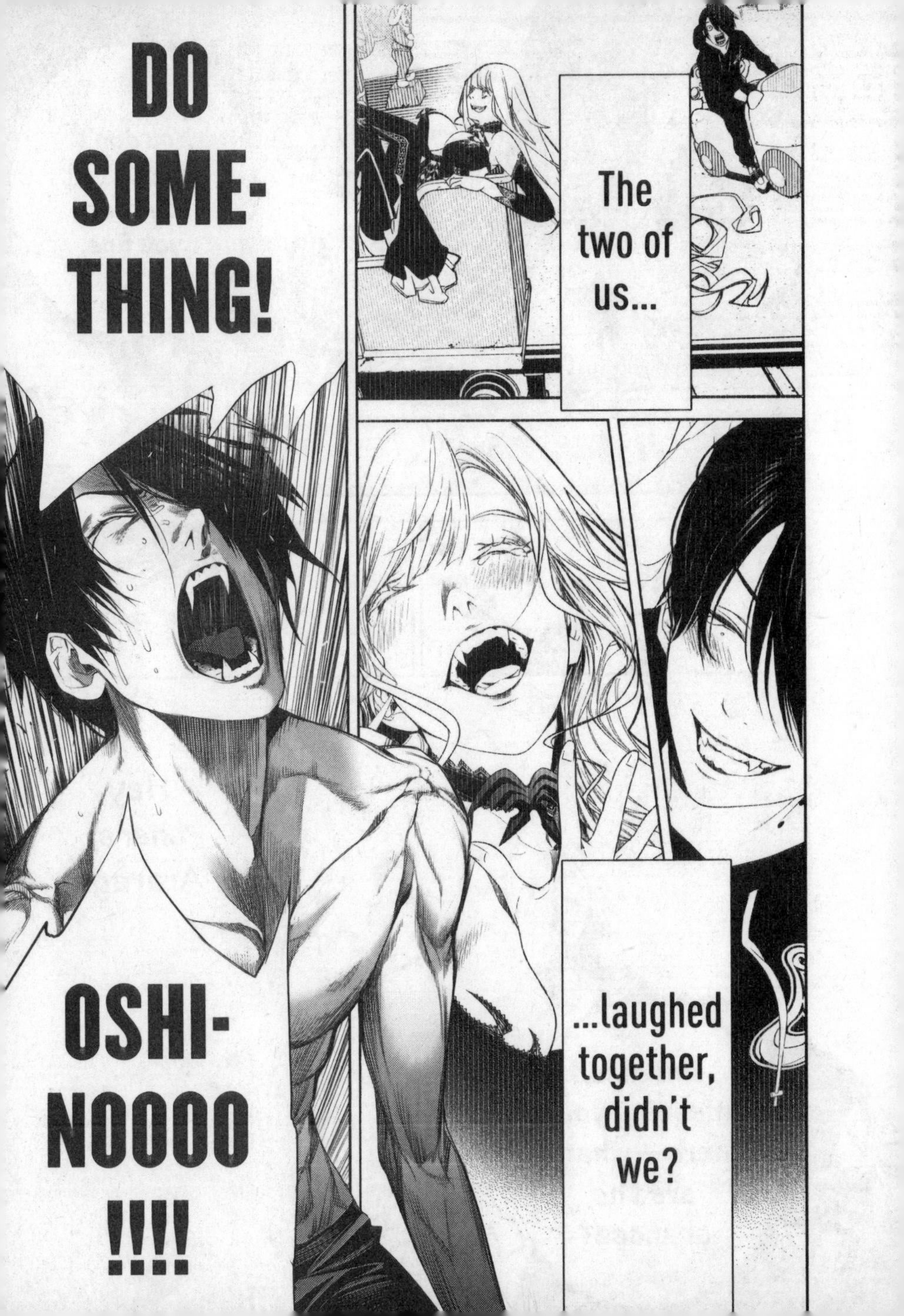
The two of us...
...laughed together, didn't we?
DO SOME-THING!
OSHI-NOOOO!!!!

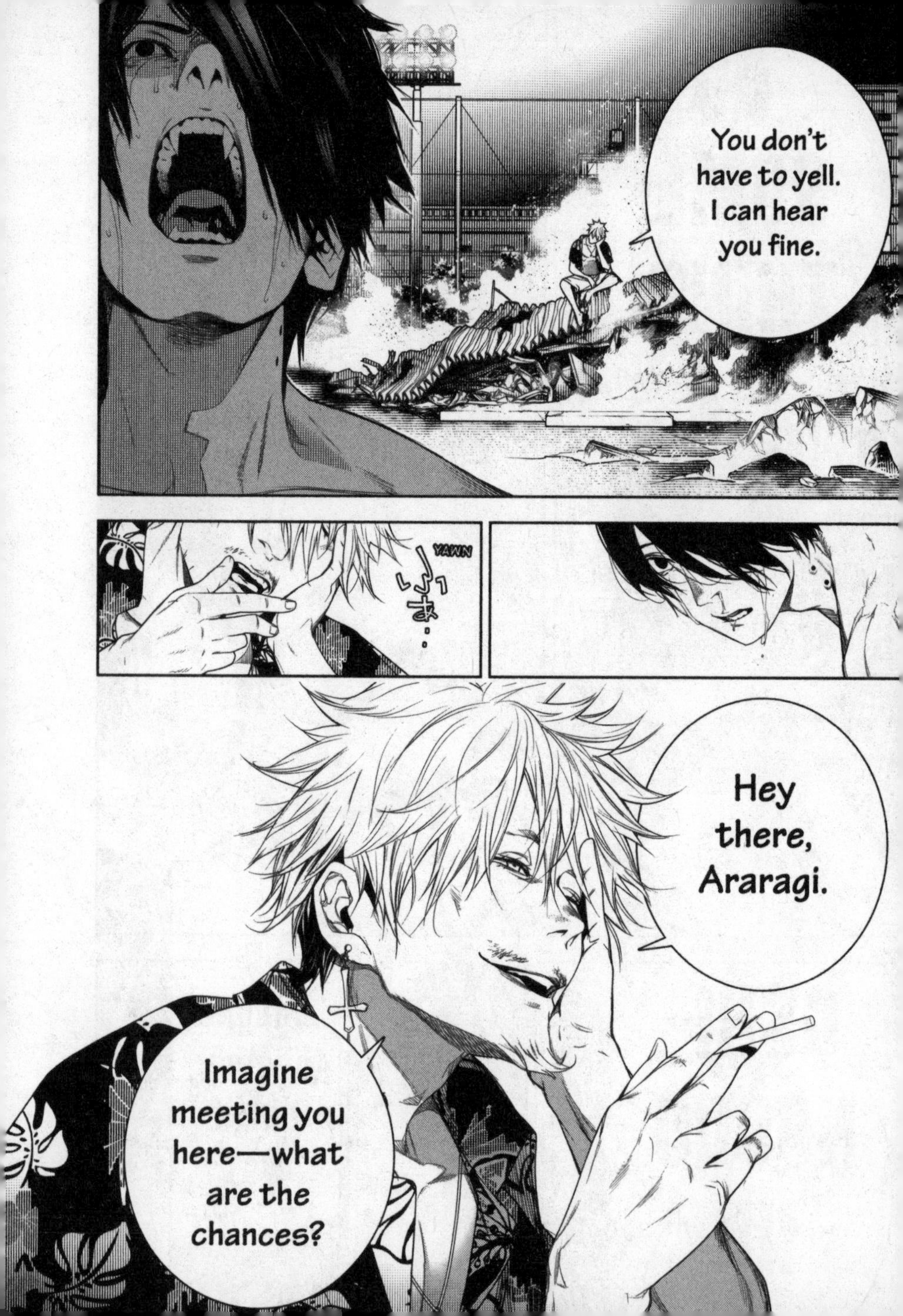
You don't have to yell. I can hear you fine.
YAWN
Hey there, Araragi.
Imagine meeting you here—what are the chances?

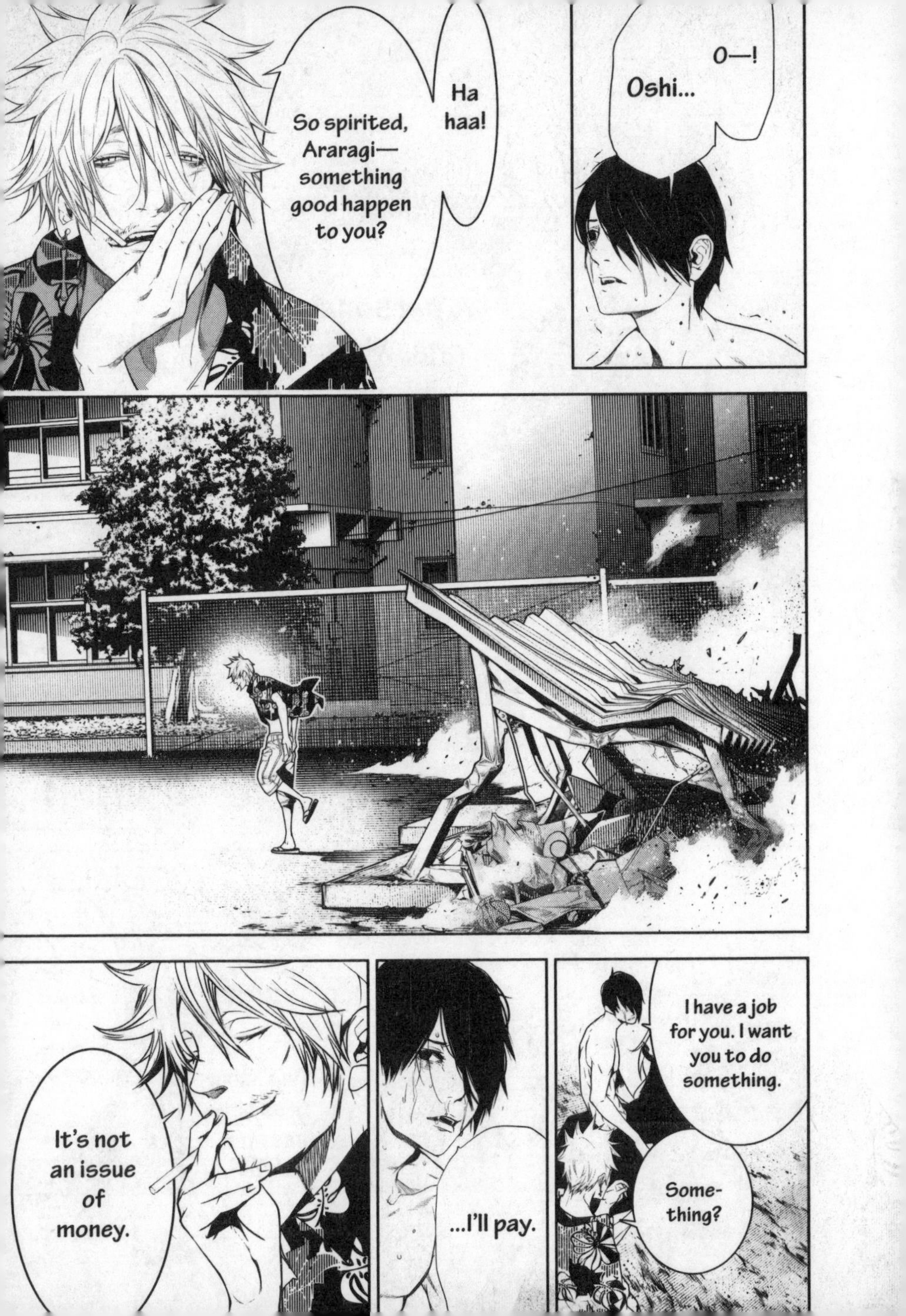
O—!
Oshi...
Ha haa!
So spirited, Araragi—something good happen to you?
I have a job for you. I want you to do something.
Some-thing?
...I'll pay.
It's not an issue of money.

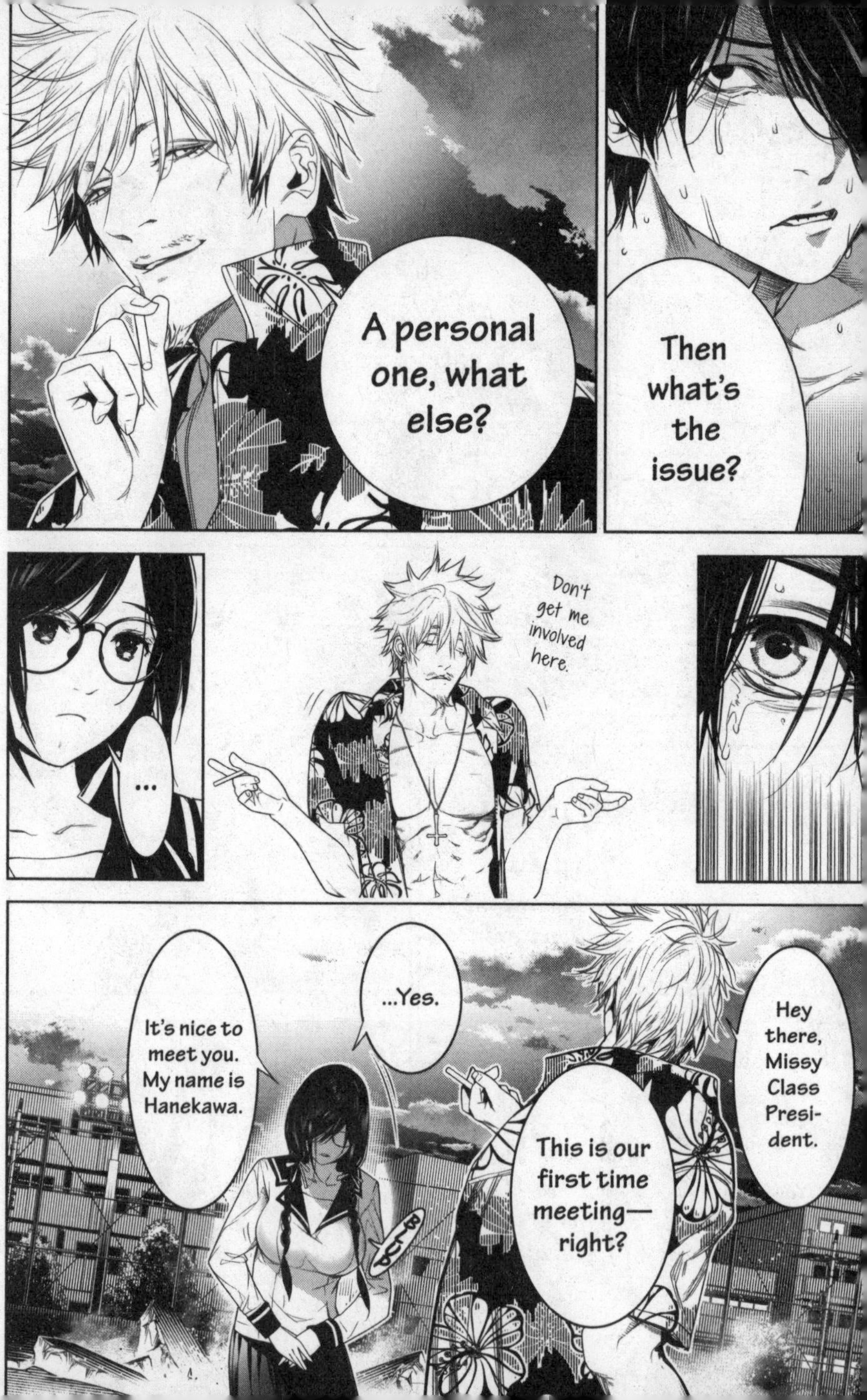
Then what's the issue?
A personal one, what else?
Don't get me involved here.
...
Hey there, Missy Class President.
This is our first time meeting—right?
...Yes.
It's nice to meet you. My name is Hanekawa.

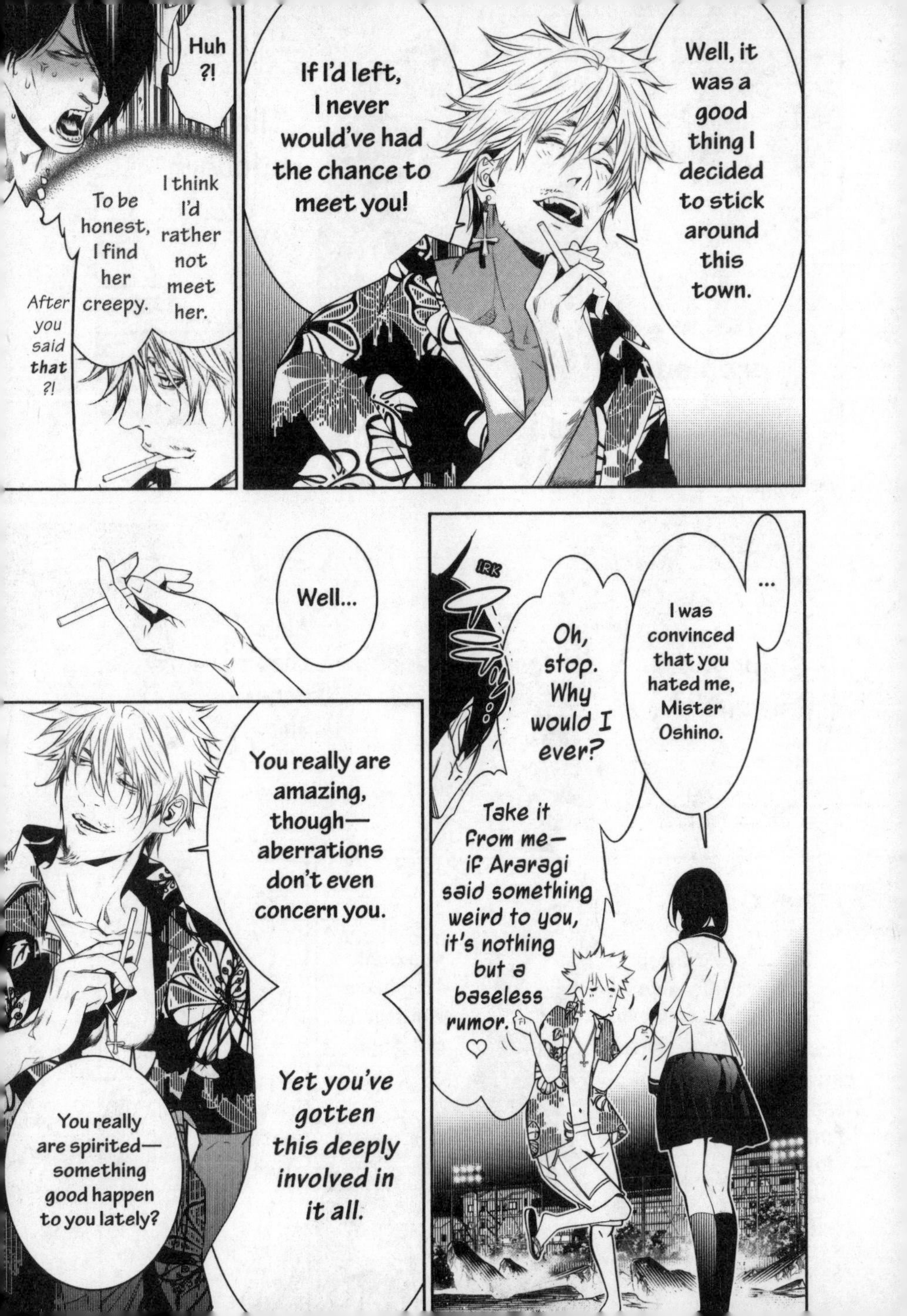
Well, it was a good thing I decided to stick around this town.
If I'd left, I never would've had the chance to meet you!
Huh ?!
I think I'd rather not meet her.
To be honest, I find her creepy.
After you said that ?!
...
I was convinced that you hated me, Mister Oshino.
IRK
Oh, stop. Why would I ever?
Take it from me— if Araragi said something weird to you, it's nothing but a baseless rumor. ♡
Well...
You really are amazing, though— aberrations don't even concern you.
Yet you've gotten this deeply involved in it all.
You really are spirited— something good happen to you lately?

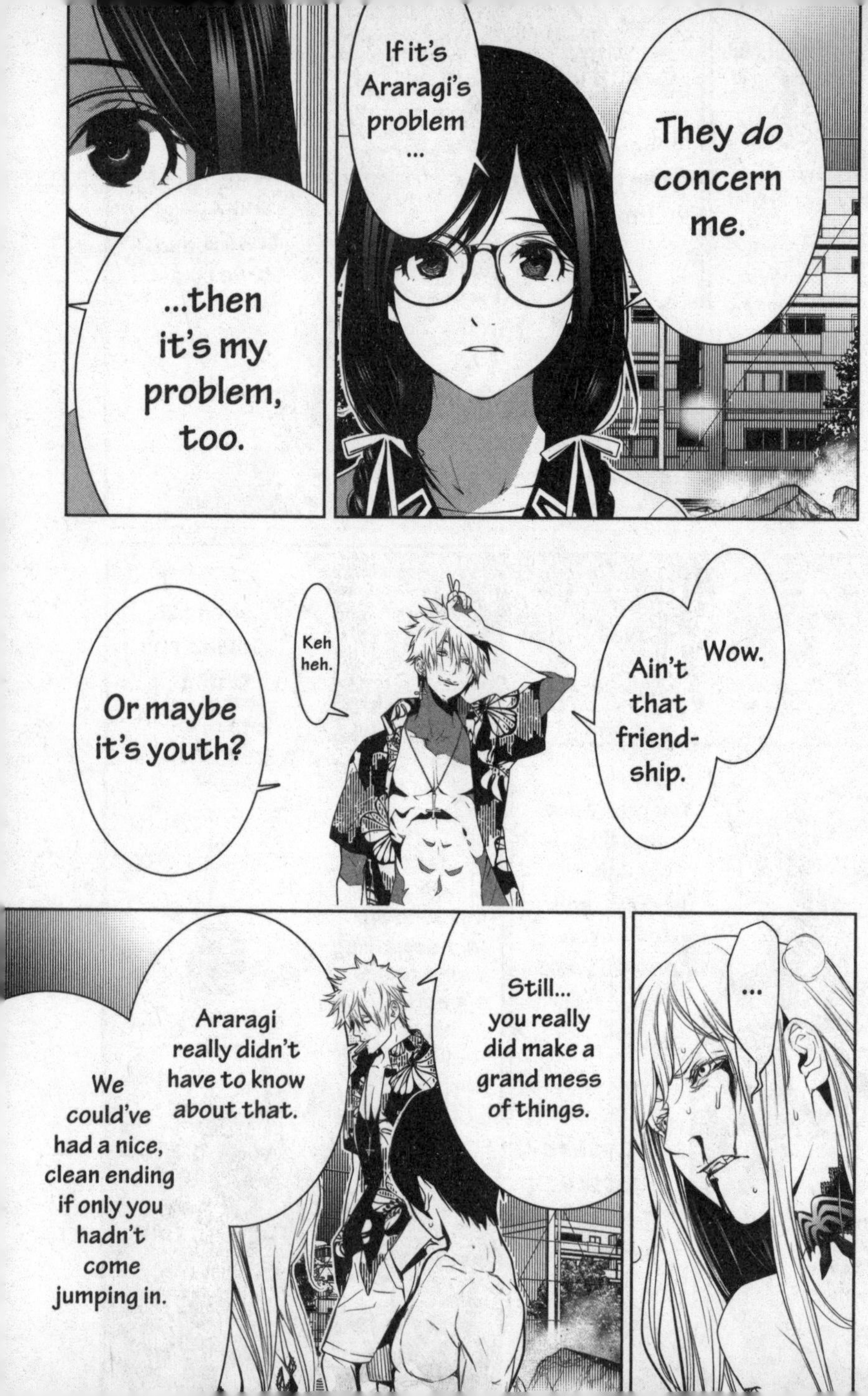
They *do* concern me.
If it's Araragi's problem ...
...then it's my problem, too.
Wow. Ain't that friendship.
Keh heh.
Or maybe it's youth?
...
Still... you really did make a grand mess of things.
Araragi really didn't have to know about that.
We could've had a nice, clean ending if only you hadn't come jumping in.

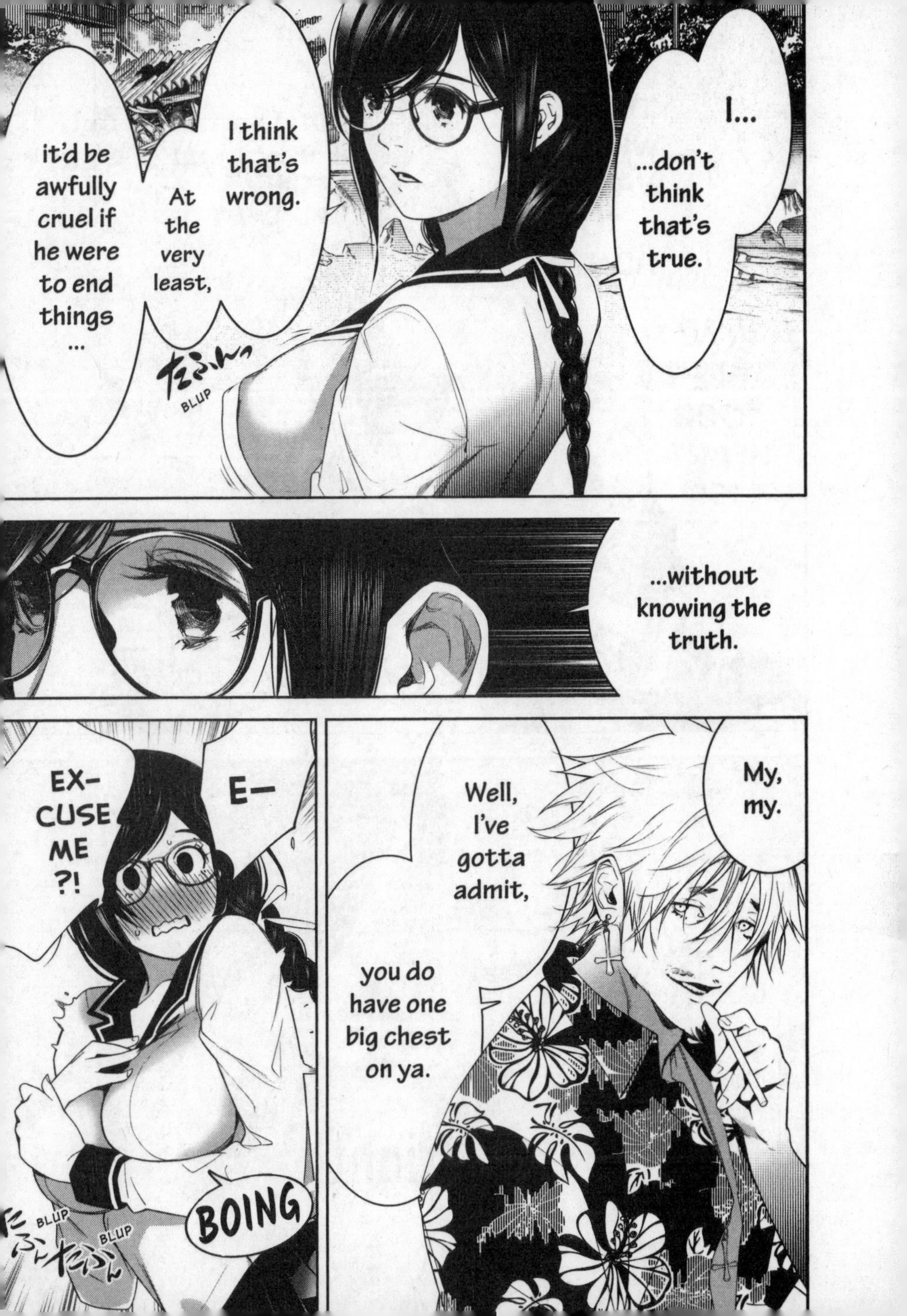
I...
...don't think that's true.
I think that's wrong.
At the very least,
it'd be awfully cruel if he were to end things ...
たぷんっ
BLUP
...without knowing the truth.
My, my.
Well, I've gotta admit,
you do have one big chest on ya.
E—
EX-CUSE ME ?!
BOING
たぷん
BLUP
たぷん
BLUP

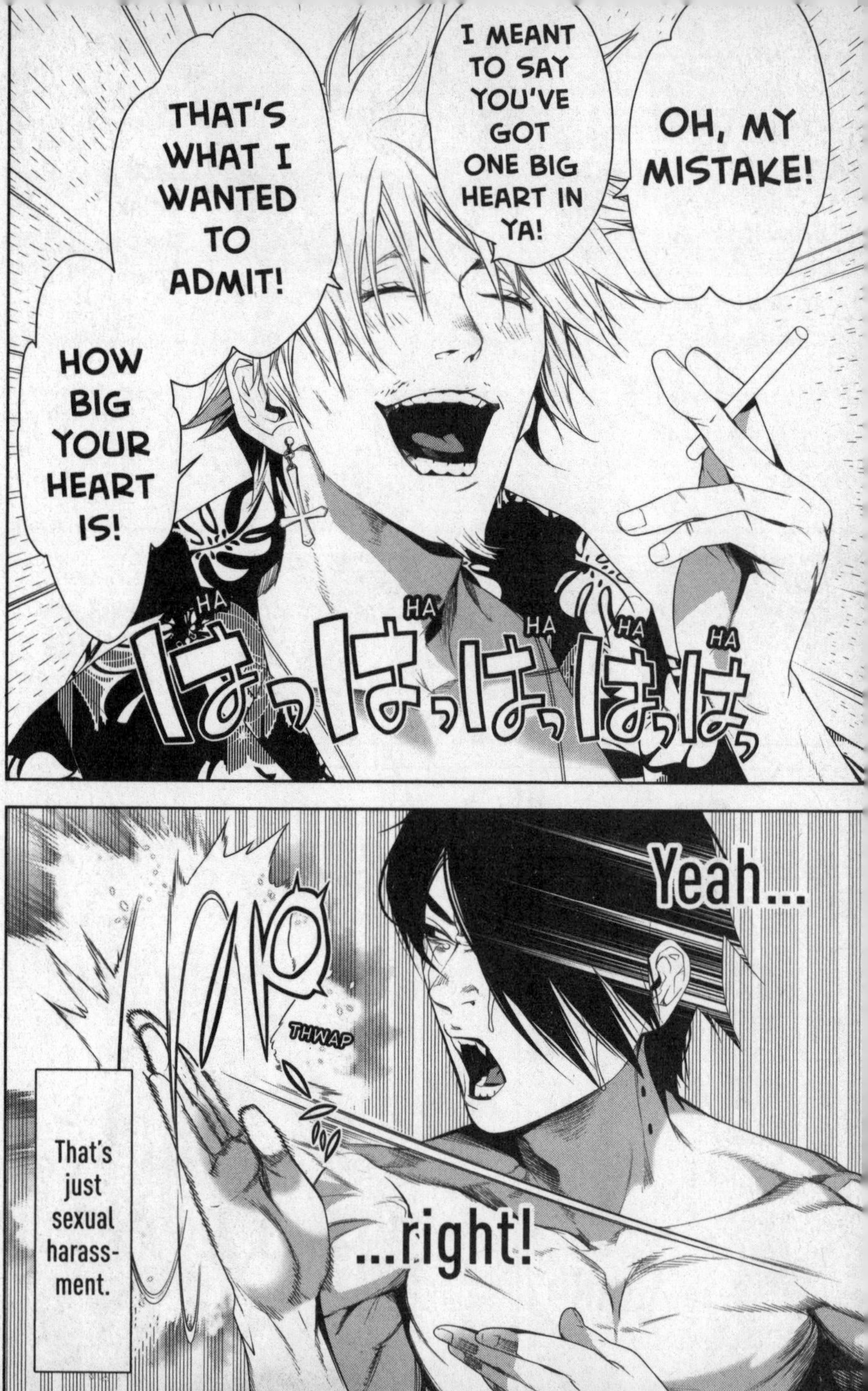
OH, MY MISTAKE!
I MEANT TO SAY YOU'VE GOT ONE BIG HEART IN YA!
THAT'S WHAT I WANTED TO ADMIT!
HOW BIG YOUR HEART IS!
HA HA HA HA HA
Yeah...
...right!
THWAP
That's just sexual harass-ment.

物語 *gatari*

物 *mono*
KOYOMIVamp
15

化 *bake*

bake

mono

KOYOMIvamp
15

語 gatari

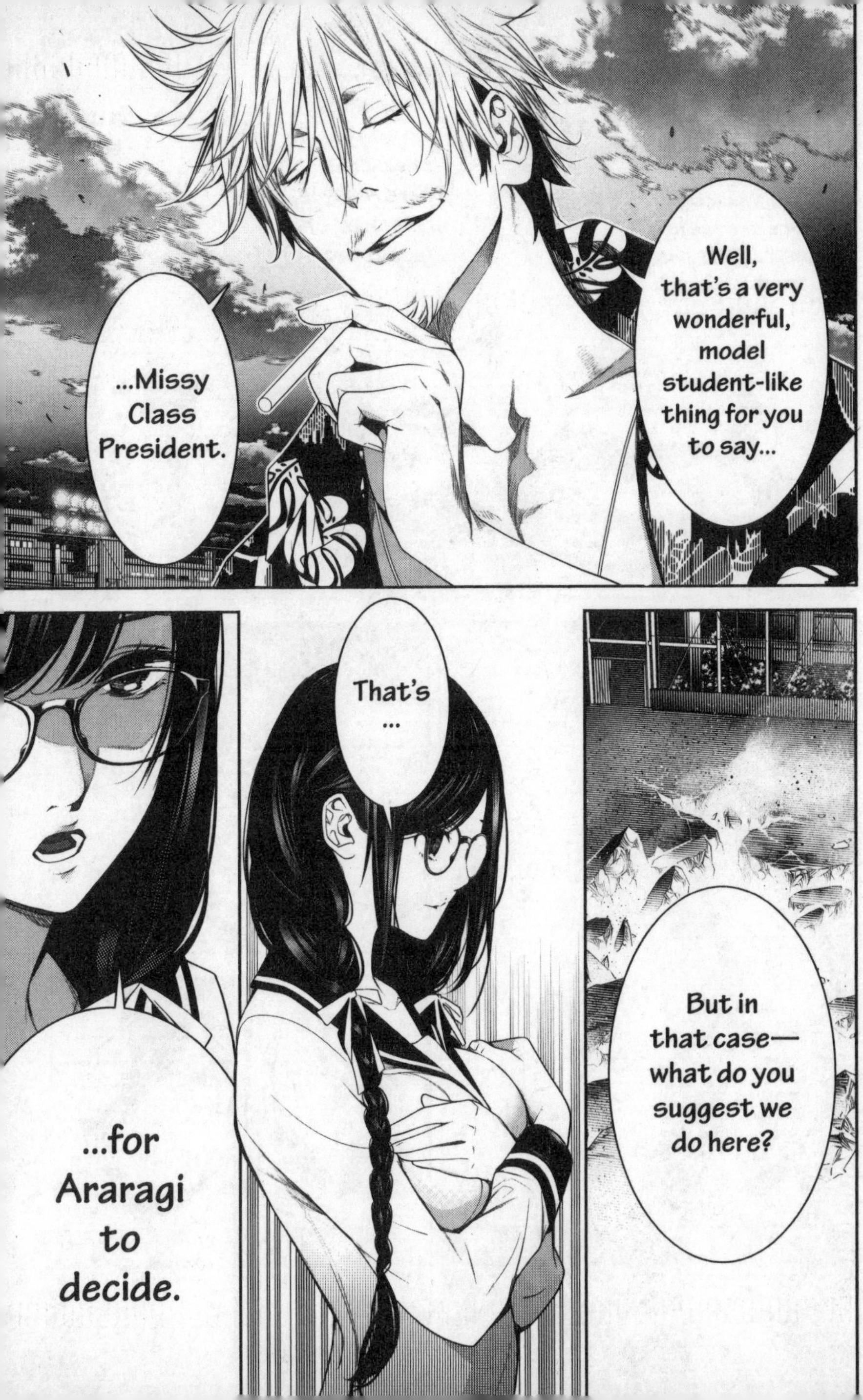
Well, that's a very wonderful, model student-like thing for you to say...
...Missy Class President.
But in that case— what do you suggest we do here?
That's ...
...for Araragi to decide.

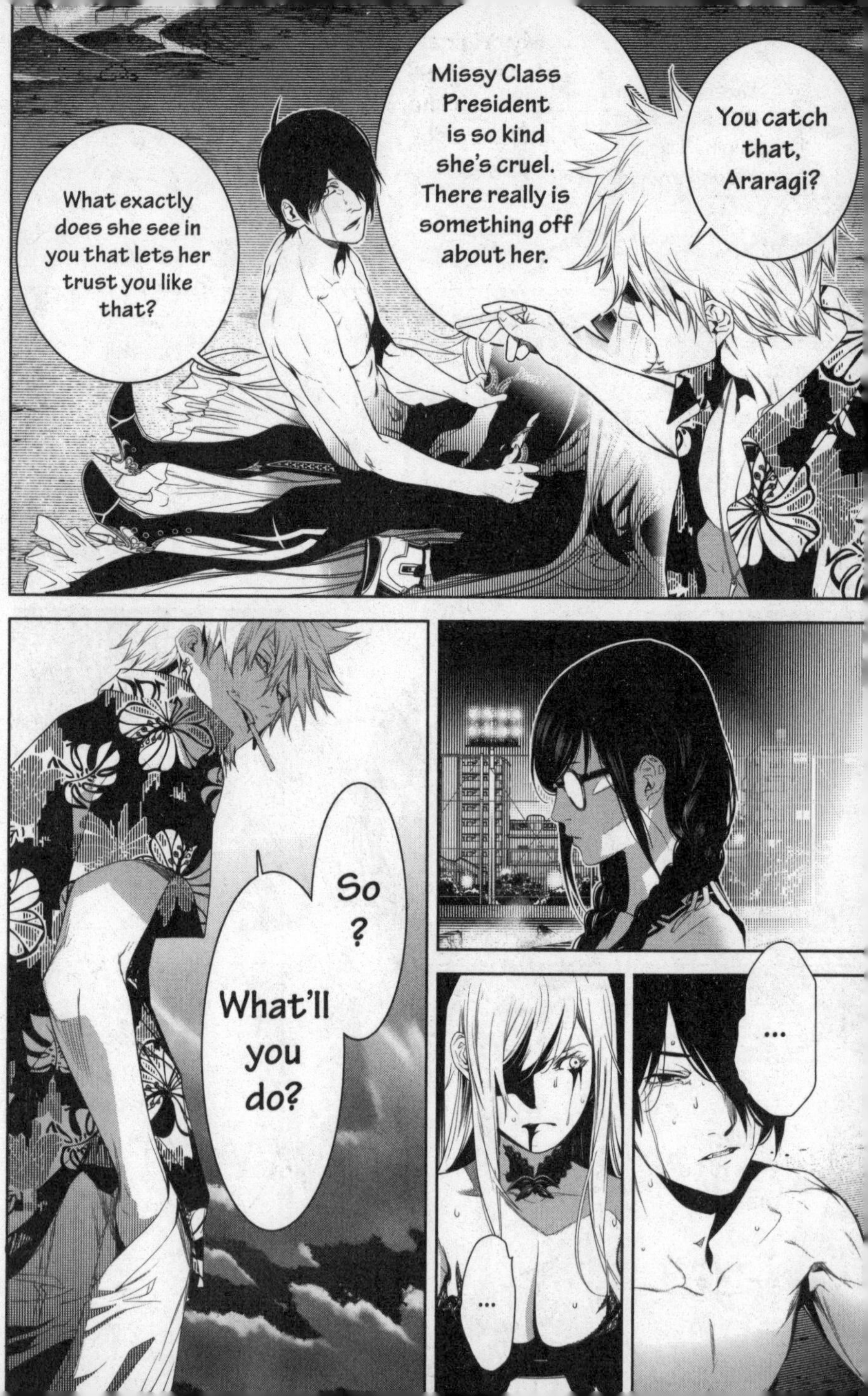
You catch that, Araragi?
Missy Class President is so kind she's cruel. There really is something off about her.
What exactly does she see in you that lets her trust you like that?
...
...
So?
What'll you do?

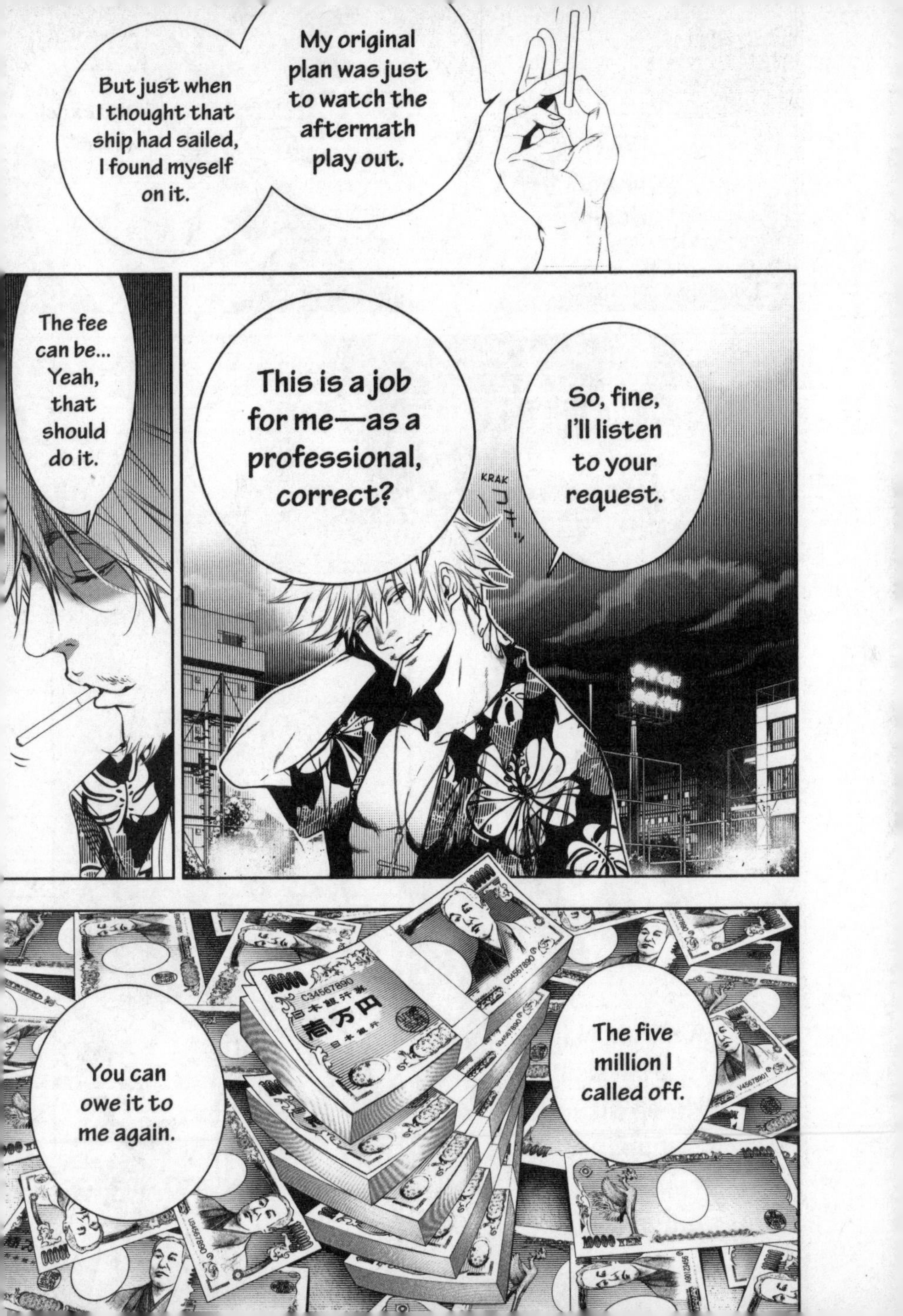
My original plan was just to watch the aftermath play out.
But just when I thought that ship had sailed, I found myself on it.
So, fine, I'll listen to your request.
KRAK
This is a job for me—as a professional, correct?
The fee can be... Yeah, that should do it.
The five million I called off.
You can owe it to me again.

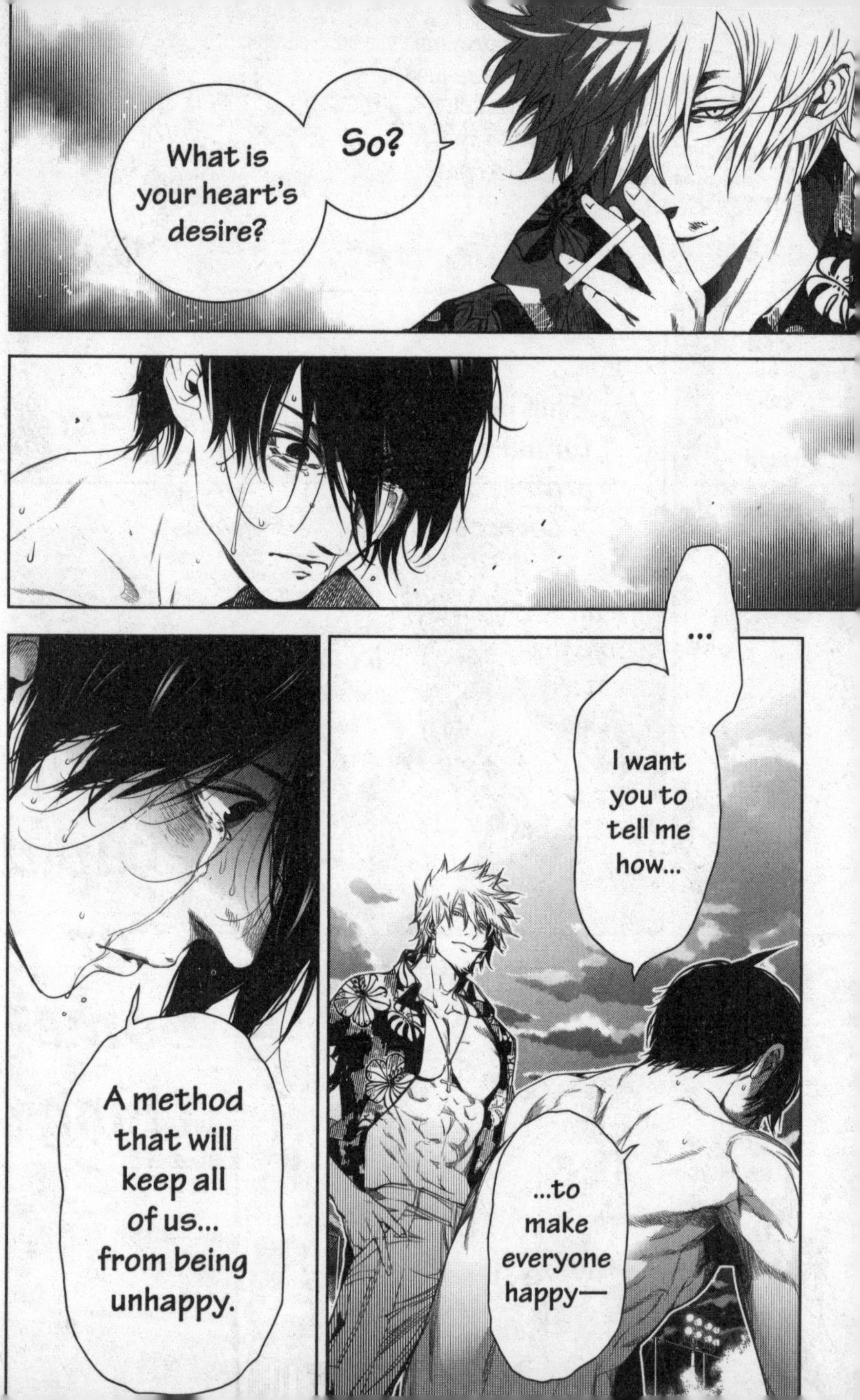
So?
What is your heart's desire?
...
I want you to tell me how...
...to make everyone happy—
A method that will keep all of us... from being unhappy.

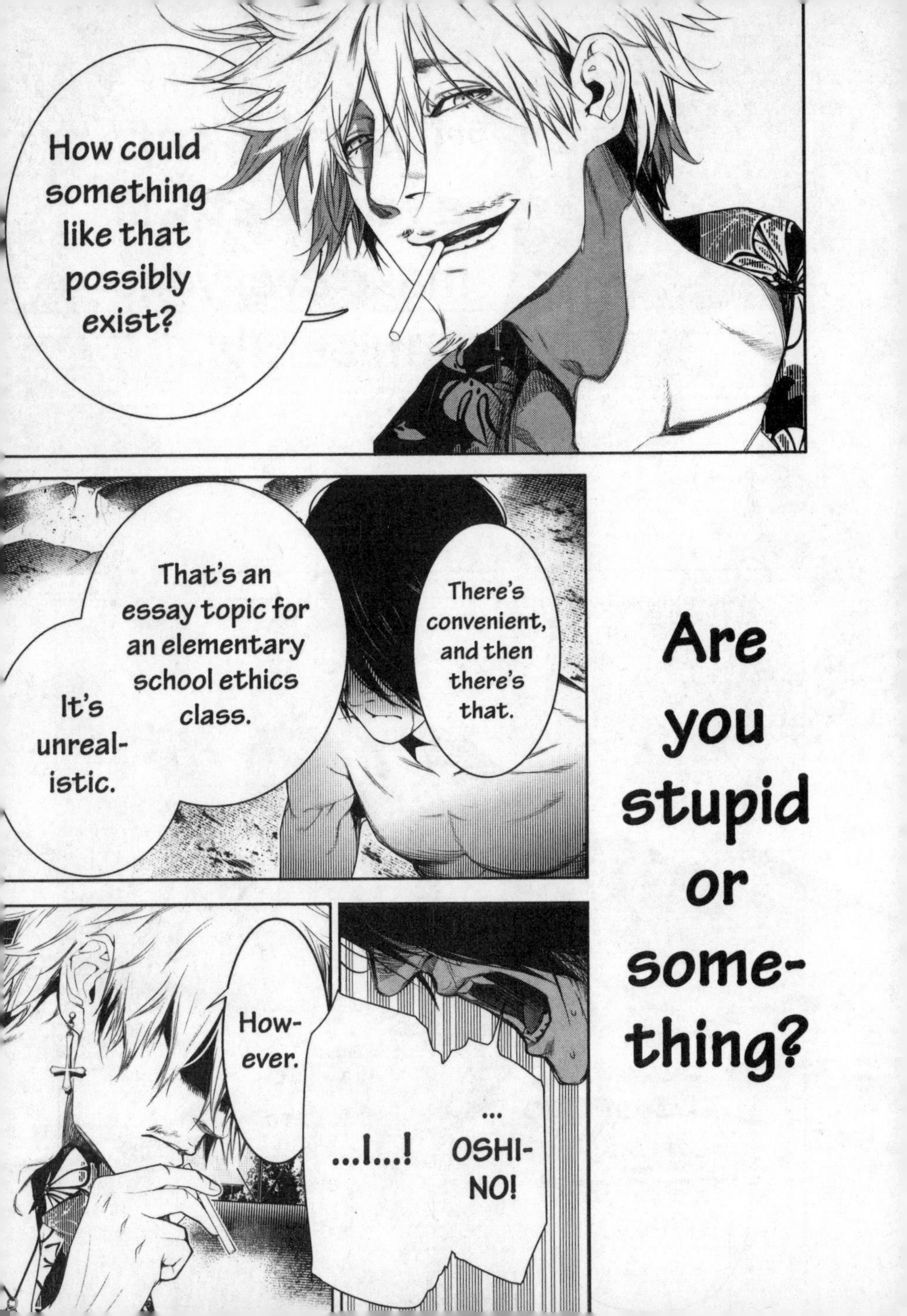
How could something like that possibly exist?
Are you stupid or something?
There's convenient, and then there's that.
That's an essay topic for an elementary school ethics class.
It's unreal-istic.
... OSHI-NO!
...I...!
How-ever.

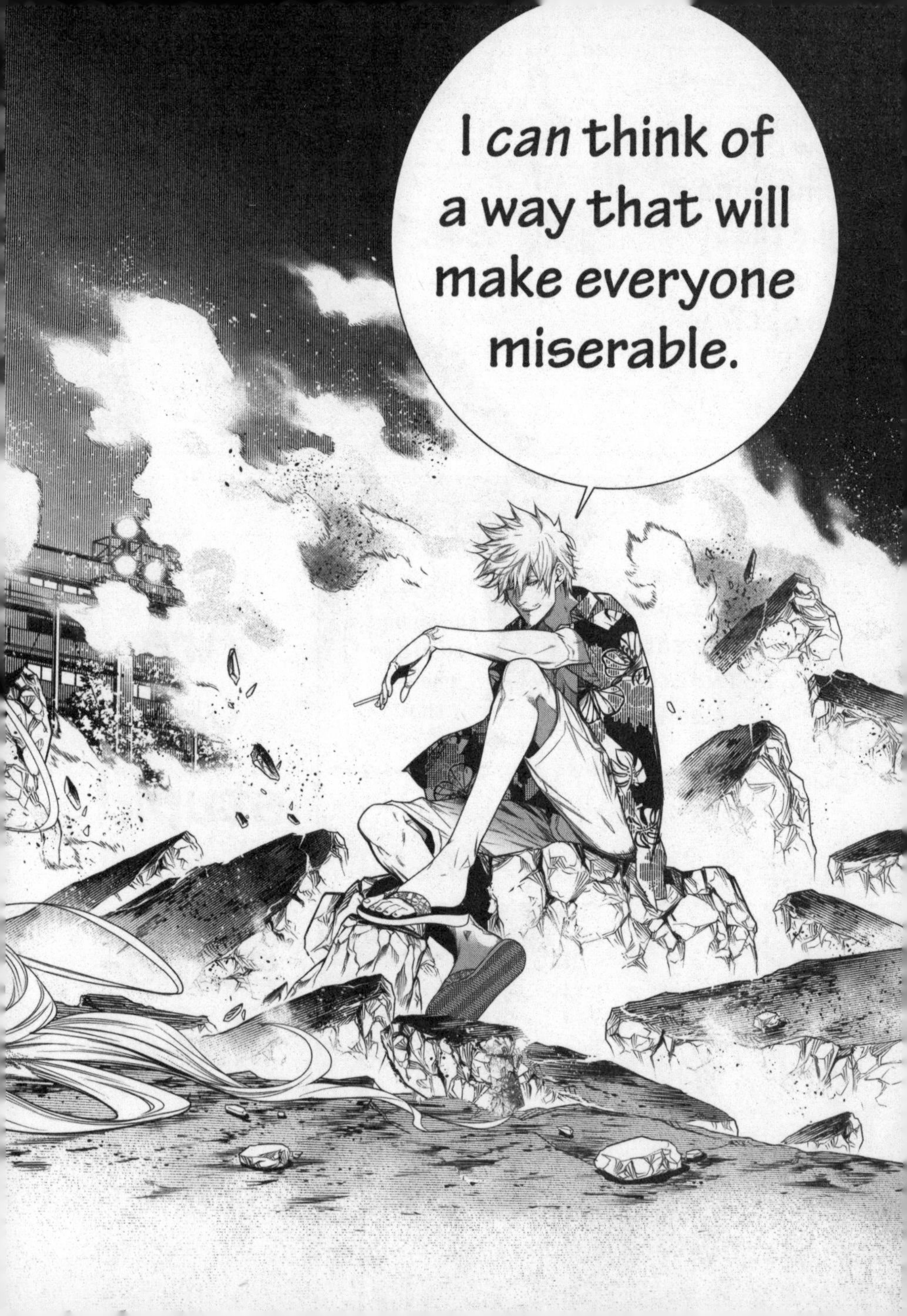
I *can* think of a way that will make *everyone* miserable.

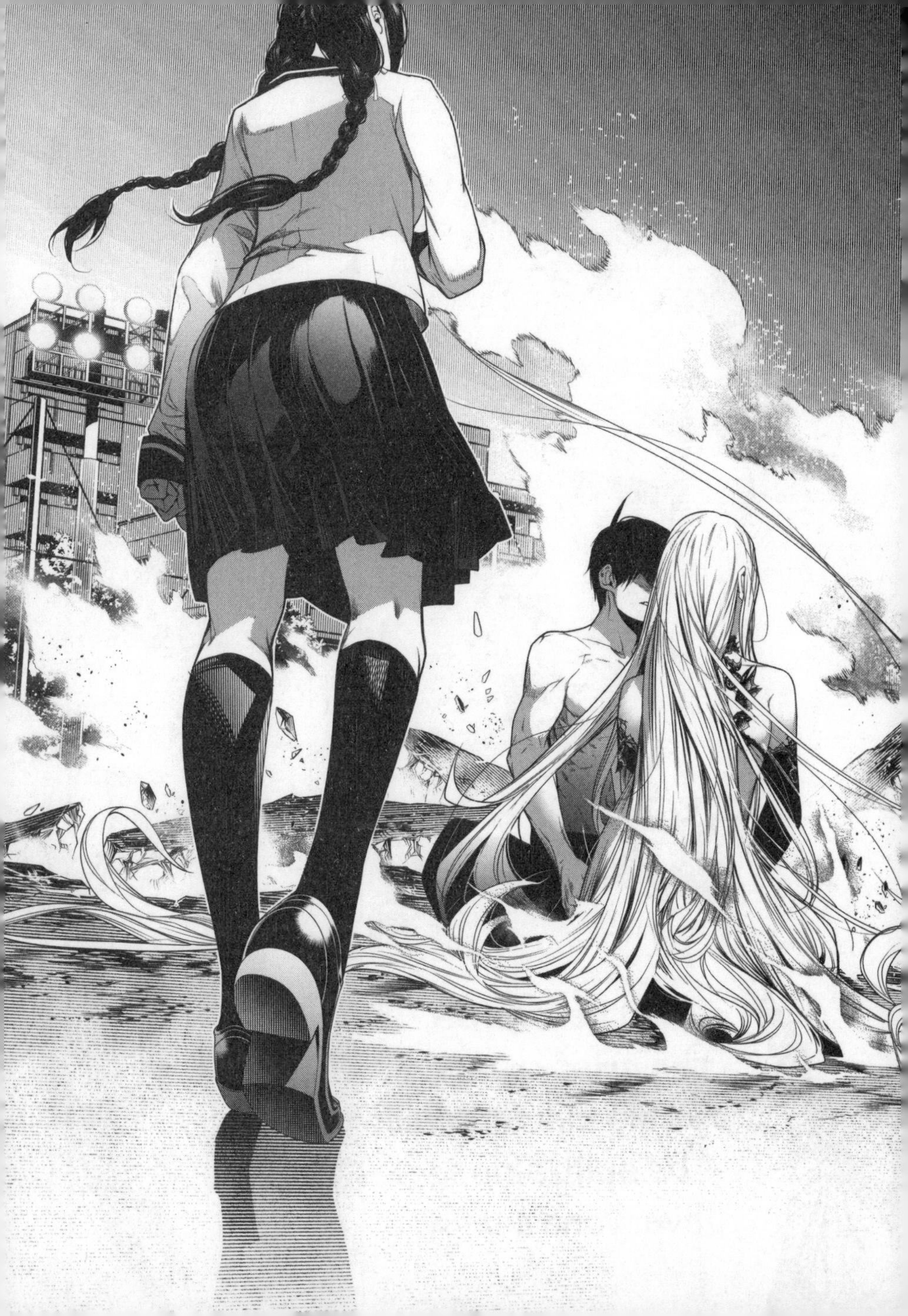

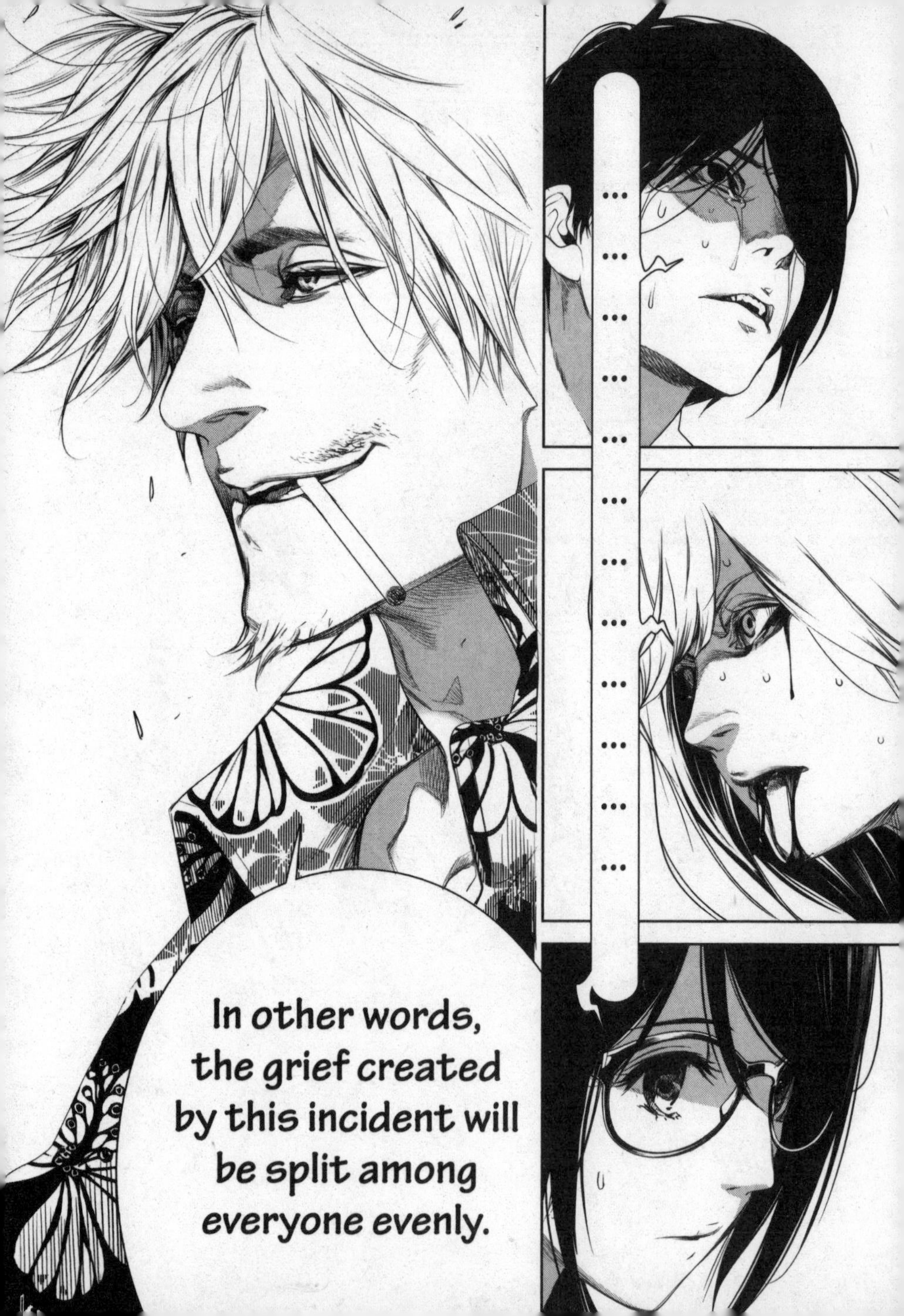
......
In other words, the grief created by this incident will be split among everyone evenly.

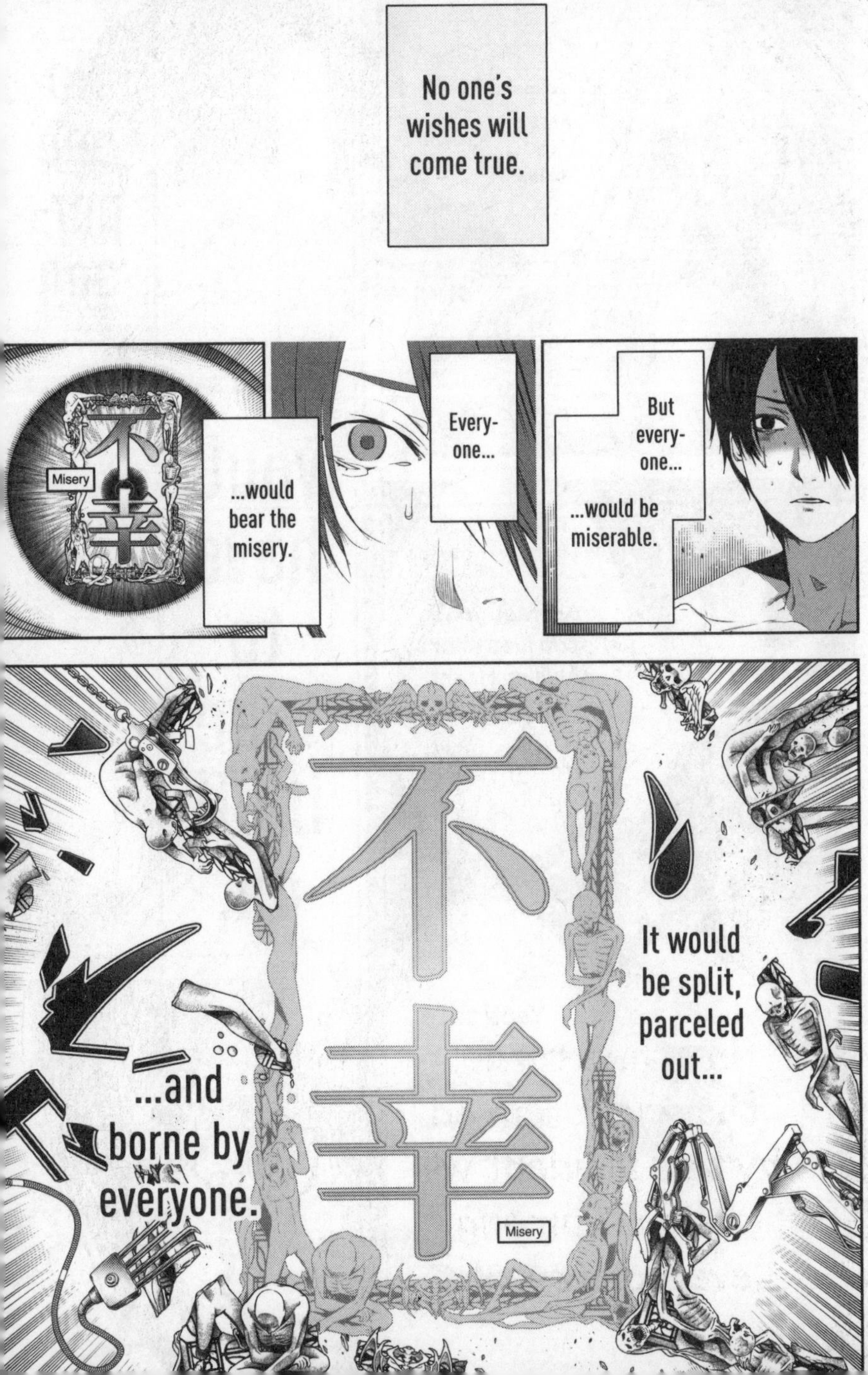
No one's wishes will come true.
But every-one...
...would be miserable.
Every-one...
Misery
...would bear the misery.
It would be split, parceled out...
Misery
...and borne by everyone.

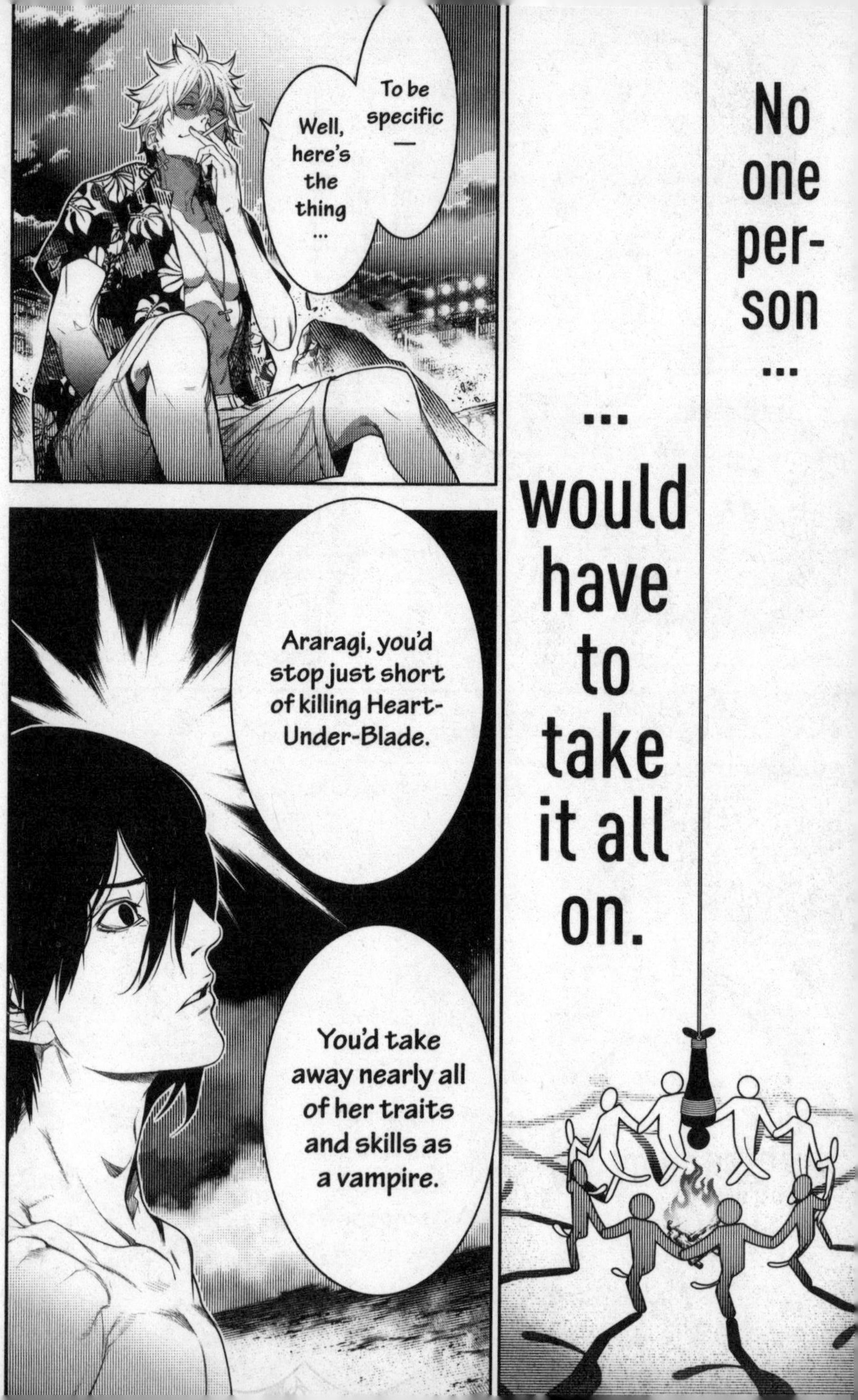
No one per-son ...
... would have to take it all on.
Well, here's the thing ...
To be specific —
Araragi, you'd stop just short of killing Heart-Under-Blade.
You'd take away nearly all of her traits and skills as a vampire.

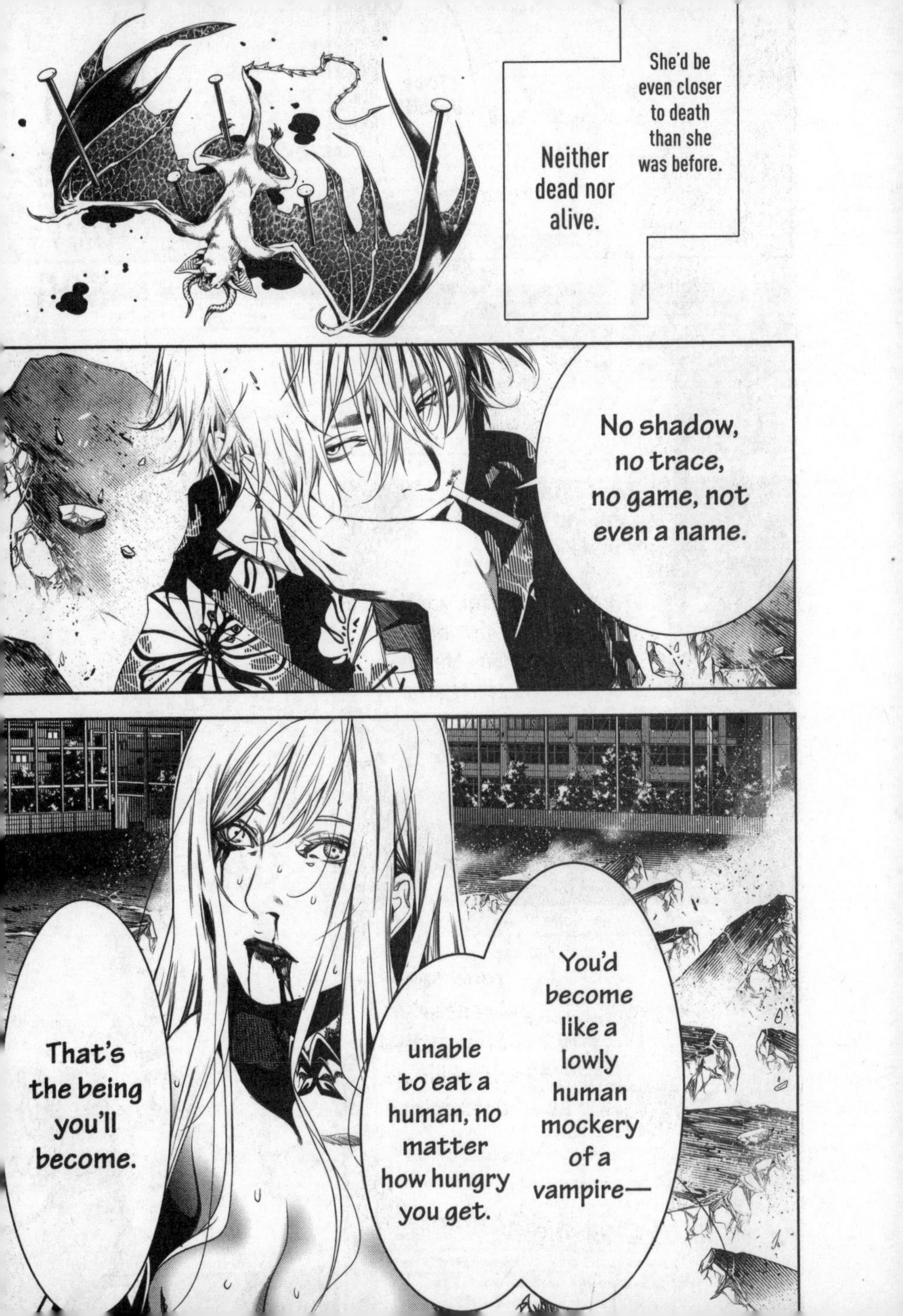
She'd be even closer to death than she was before.
Neither dead nor alive.
No shadow, no trace, no game, not even a name.
You'd become like a lowly human mockery of a vampire—
unable to eat a human, no matter how hungry you get.
That's the being you'll become.

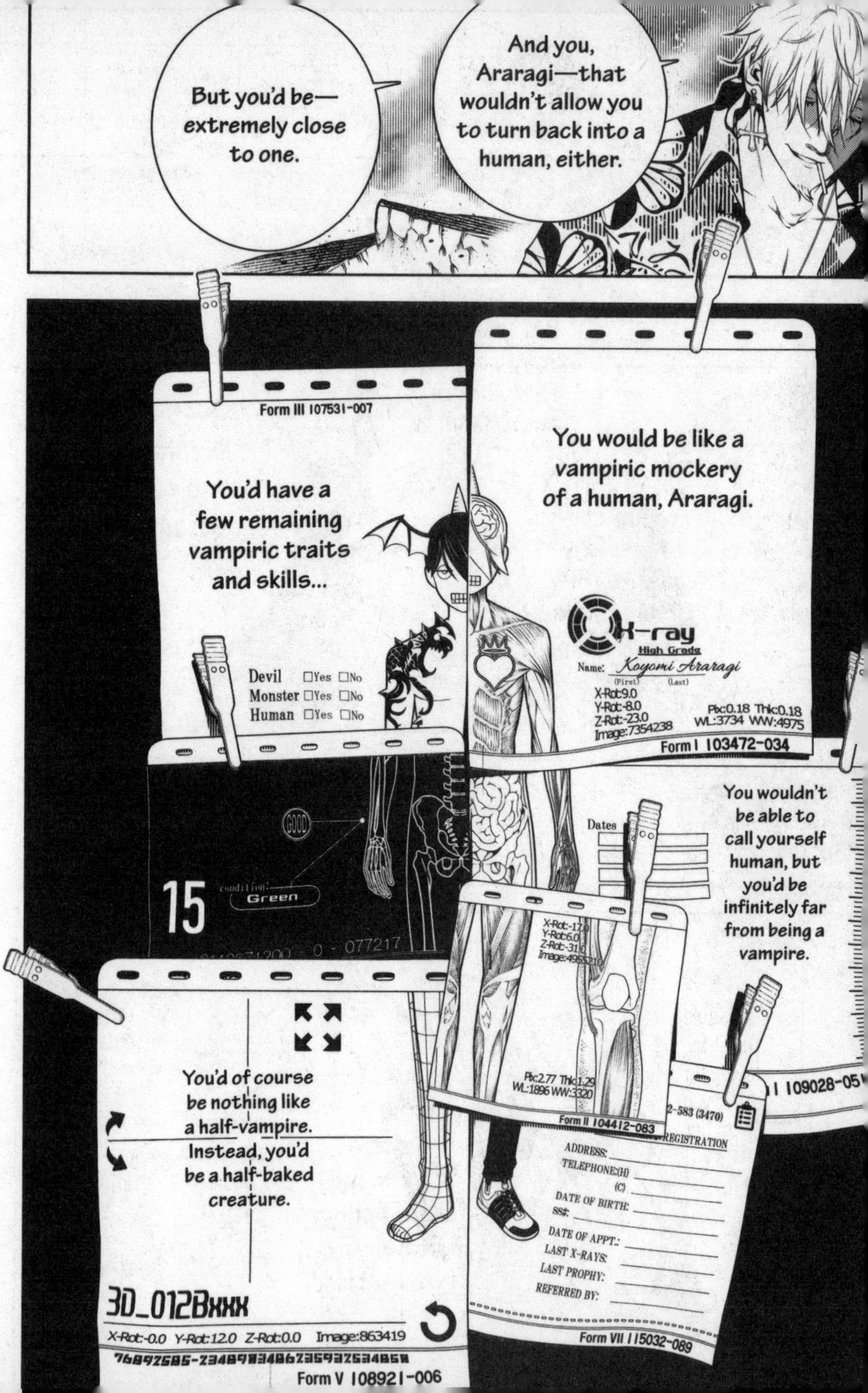
And you, Araragi—that wouldn't allow you to turn back into a human, either.
But you'd be—extremely close to one.
Form I 103472-034
You would be like a vampiric mockery of a human, Araragi.
X-ray
High Grade
Name: Koyomi Araragi
(First) (Last)
X-Rot:9.0
Y-Rot:-8.0
Z-Rot:-23.0
Image:7354238
Pix:0.18 Thk:0.18
WL:3734 WW:4975
Form III 107531-007
You'd have a few remaining vampiric traits and skills...
Devil ☐Yes ☐No
Monster ☐Yes ☐No
Human ☐Yes ☐No
GOOD
15
condition:
Green
You wouldn't be able to call yourself human, but you'd be infinitely far from being a vampire.
Dates
X-Rot:-17.0
Y-Rot:6.0
Z-Rot:-31.0
Image:4955210
Pix:2.77 Thk:1.29
WL:1896 WW:3320
Form II 104412-083
109028-05
REGISTRATION
ADDRESS:
TELEPHONE:(H)
(C)
DATE OF BIRTH:
SS#:
DATE OF APPT.:
LAST X-RAYS:
LAST PROPHY:
REFERRED BY:
Form VII 115032-089
You'd of course be nothing like a half-vampire. Instead, you'd be a half-baked creature.
3D_012Bxxx
X-Rot:-0.0 Y-Rot:12.0 Z-Rot:0.0 Image:863419
Form V 108921-006

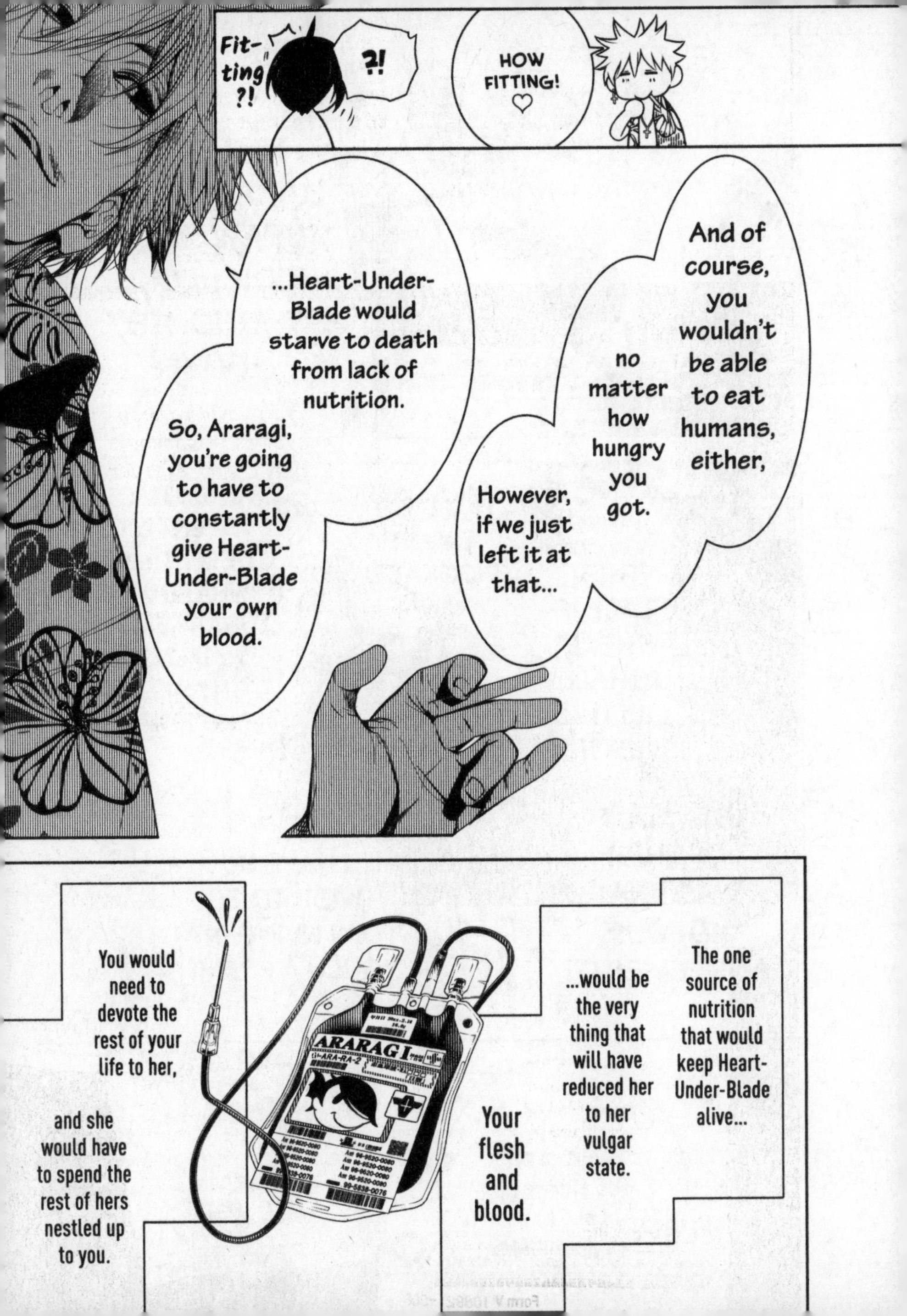
HOW FITTING! ♡
?!
Fit-ting?!
And of course, you wouldn't be able to eat humans, either,
no matter how hungry you got.
However, if we just left it at that...
...Heart-Under-Blade would starve to death from lack of nutrition.
So, Araragi, you're going to have to constantly give Heart-Under-Blade your own blood.
The one source of nutrition that would keep Heart-Under-Blade alive...
...would be the very thing that will have reduced her to her vulgar state.
Your flesh and blood.
ARARAGI
You would need to devote the rest of your life to her,
and she would have to spend the rest of hers nestled up to you.

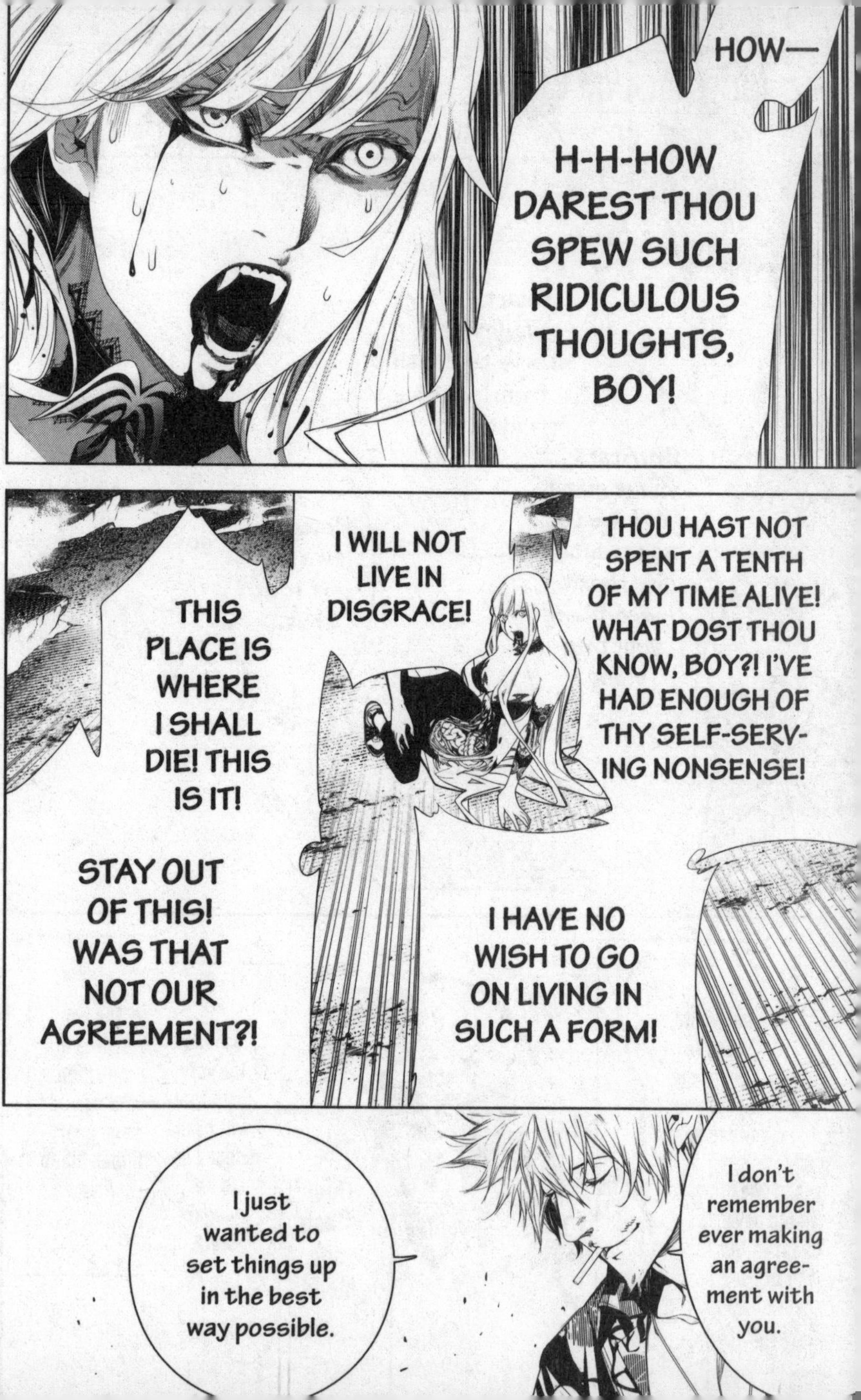
HOW—
H-H-HOW DAREST THOU SPEW SUCH RIDICULOUS THOUGHTS, BOY!
THOU HAST NOT SPENT A TENTH OF MY TIME ALIVE! WHAT DOST THOU KNOW, BOY?! I'VE HAD ENOUGH OF THY SELF-SERVING NONSENSE!
I WILL NOT LIVE IN DISGRACE!
THIS PLACE IS WHERE I SHALL DIE! THIS IS IT!
I HAVE NO WISH TO GO ON LIVING IN SUCH A FORM!
STAY OUT OF THIS! WAS THAT NOT OUR AGREEMENT?!
I don't remember ever making an agreement with you.
I just wanted to set things up in the best way possible.

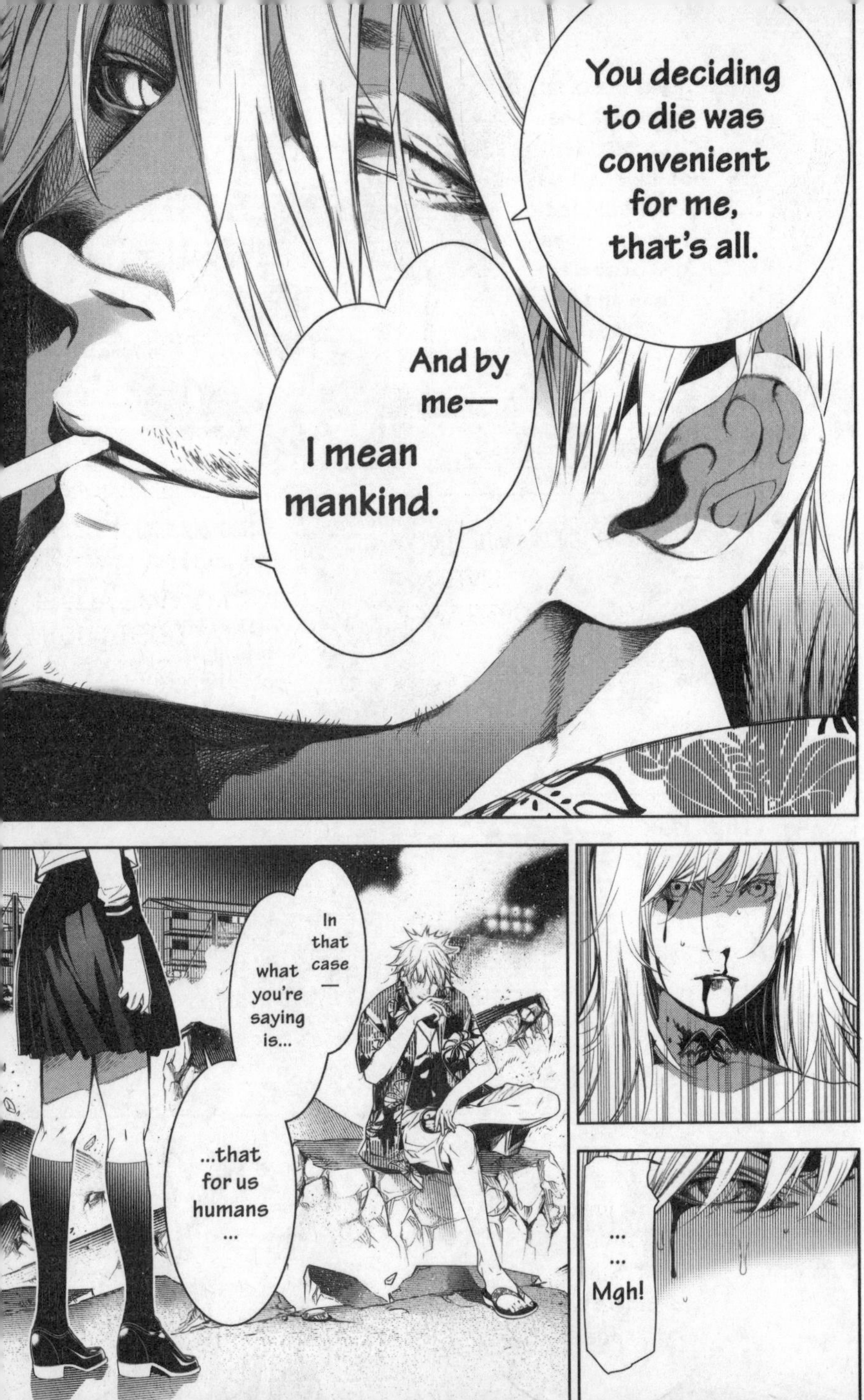
You deciding to die was convenient for me, that's all.
And by me—
I mean mankind.
... ... Mgh!
In that case—
what you're saying is...
...that for us humans ...

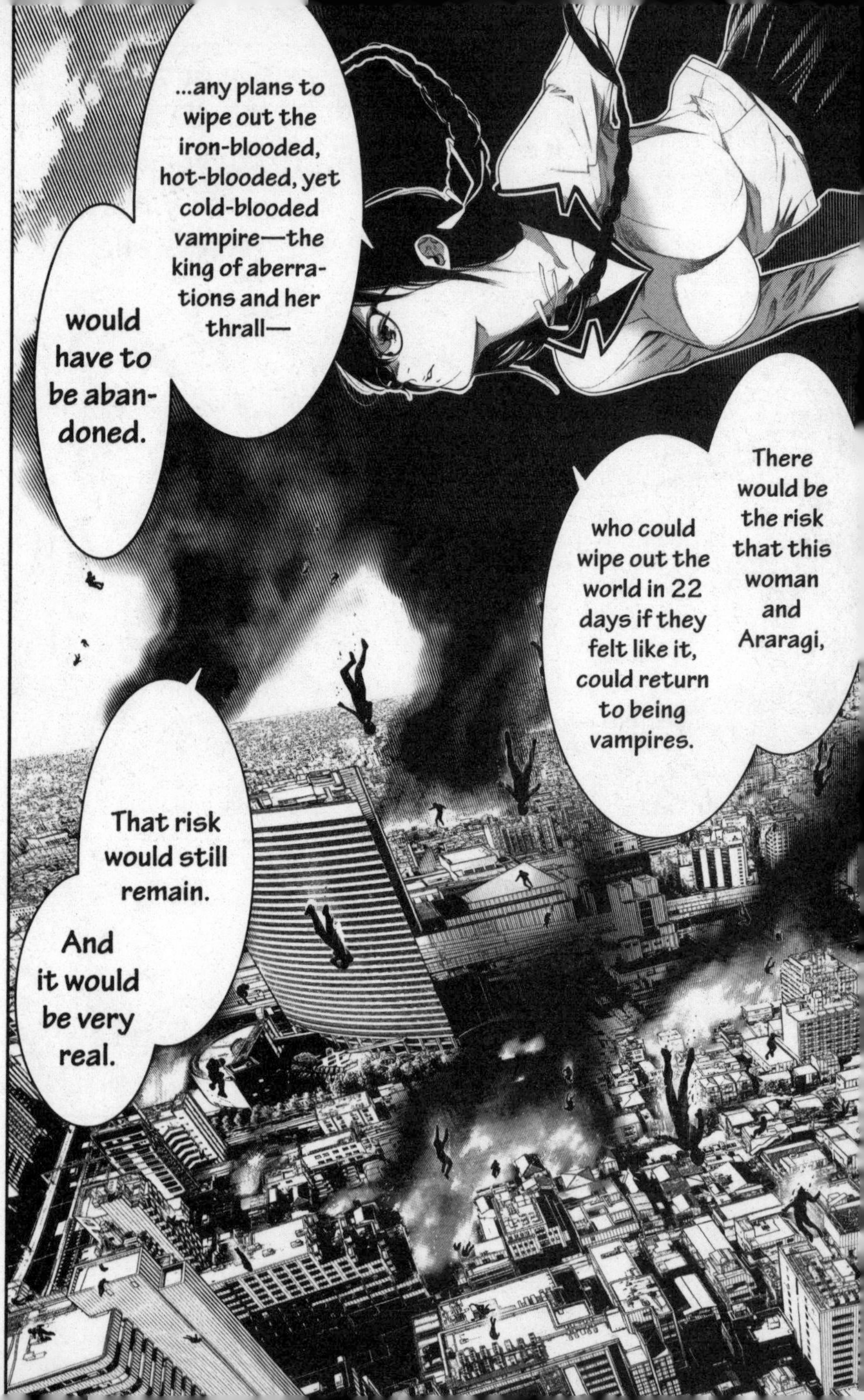
...any plans to wipe out the iron-blooded, hot-blooded, yet cold-blooded vampire—the king of aberrations and her thrall—
would have to be abandoned.
There would be the risk that this woman and Araragi,
who could wipe out the world in 22 days if they felt like it, could return to being vampires.
That risk would still remain.
And it would be very real.

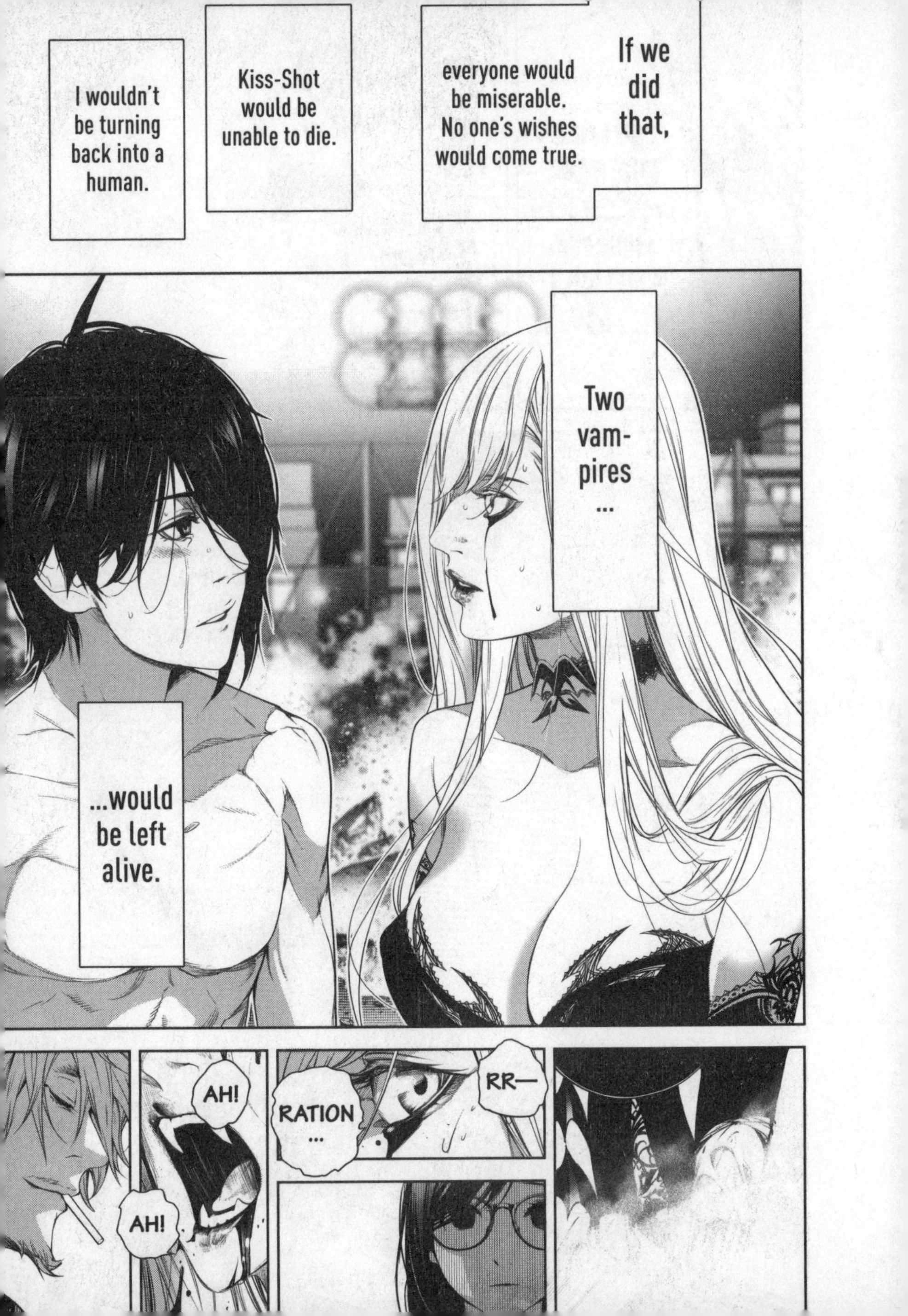
If we did that,
everyone would be miserable. No one's wishes would come true.
Kiss-Shot would be unable to die.
I wouldn't be turning back into a human.
Two vam-pires ...
...would be left alive.
RR—
RATION ...
AH!
AH!

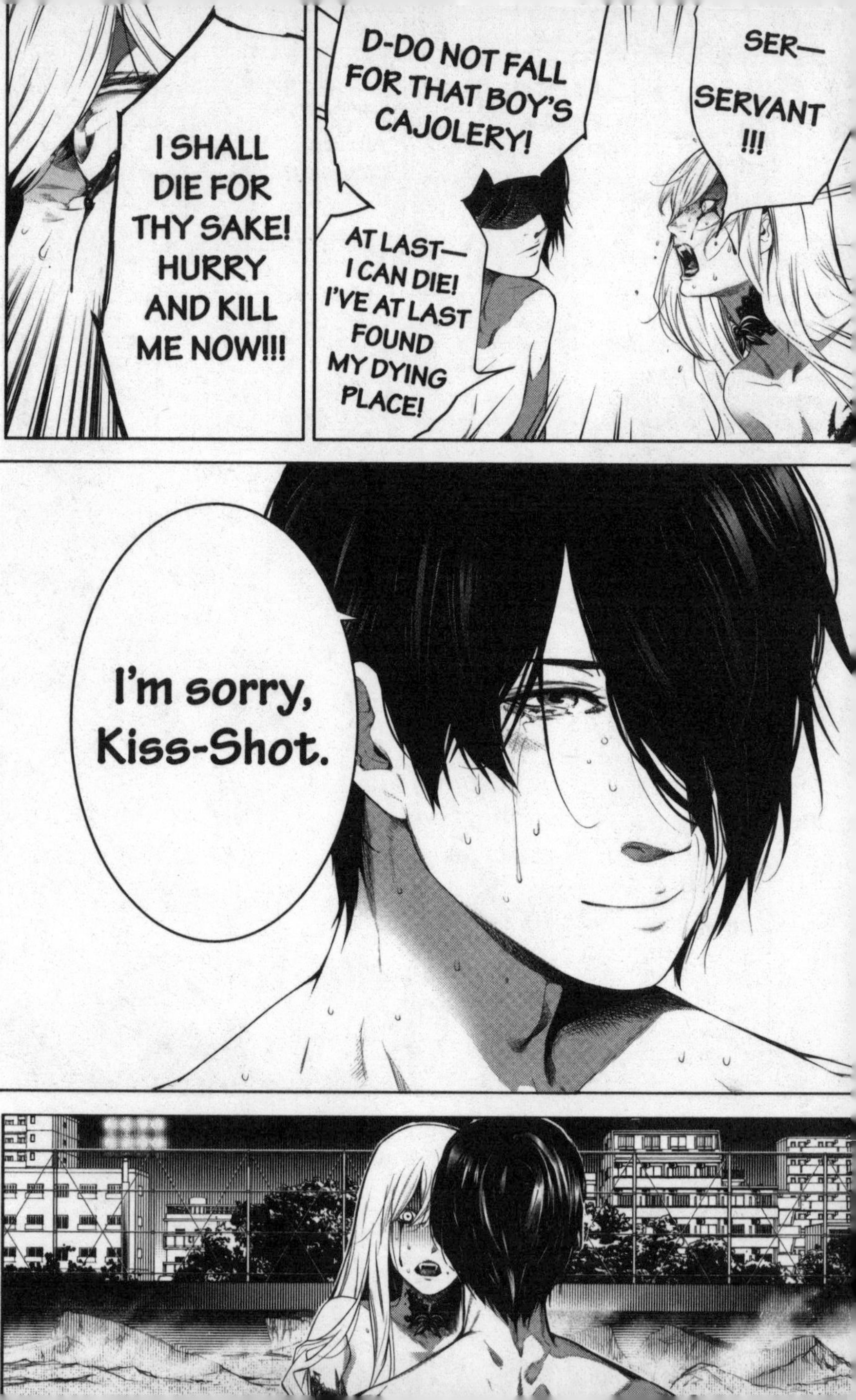
SER— SERVANT!!!
D-DO NOT FALL FOR THAT BOY'S CAJOLERY!
AT LAST— I CAN DIE! I'VE AT LAST FOUND MY DYING PLACE!
I SHALL DIE FOR THY SAKE! HURRY AND KILL ME NOW!!!
I'm sorry, Kiss-Shot.

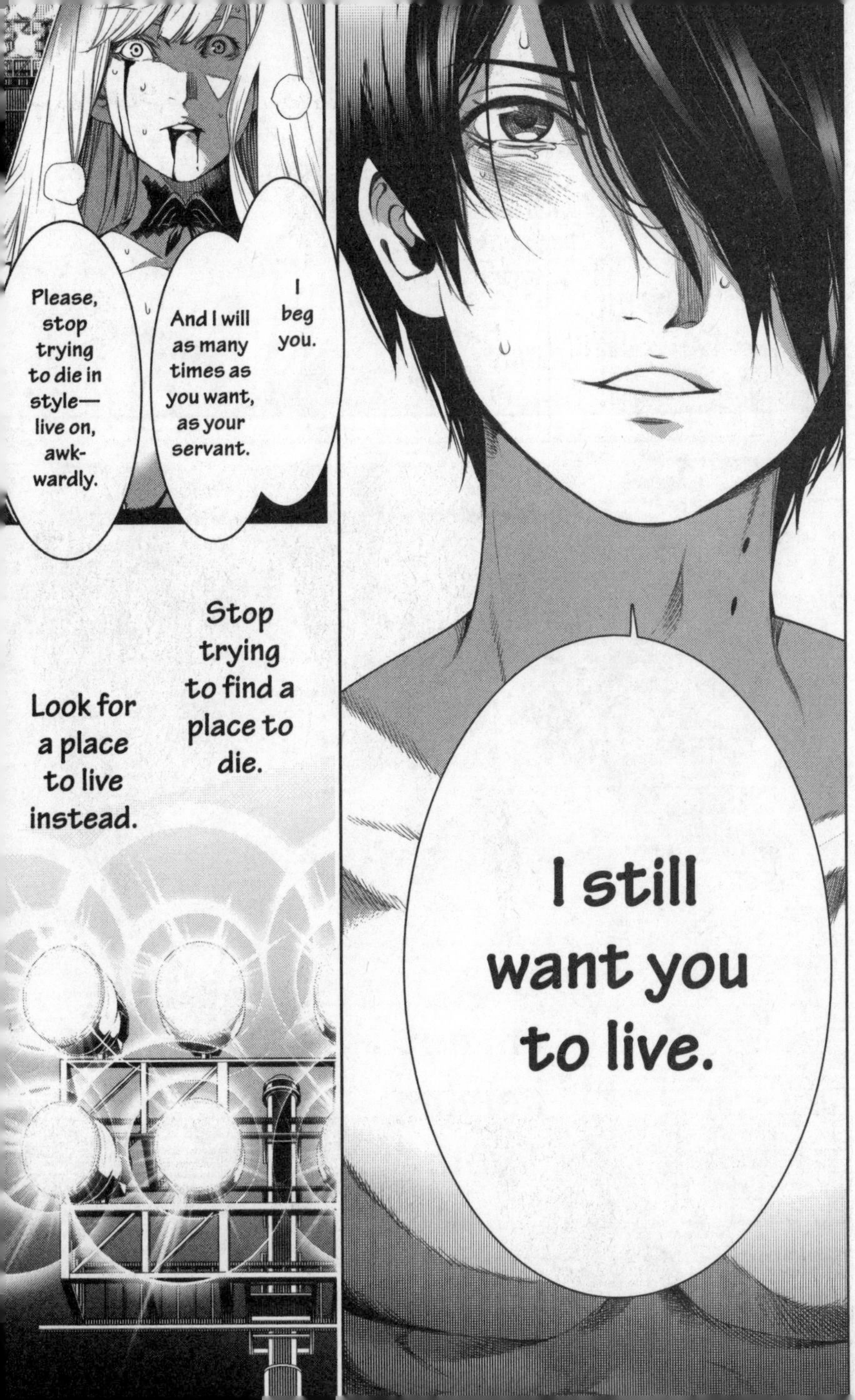
I still want you to live.
I beg you.
And I will as many times as you want, as your servant.
Please, stop trying to die in style—live on, awkwardly.
Stop trying to find a place to die.
Look for a place to live instead.

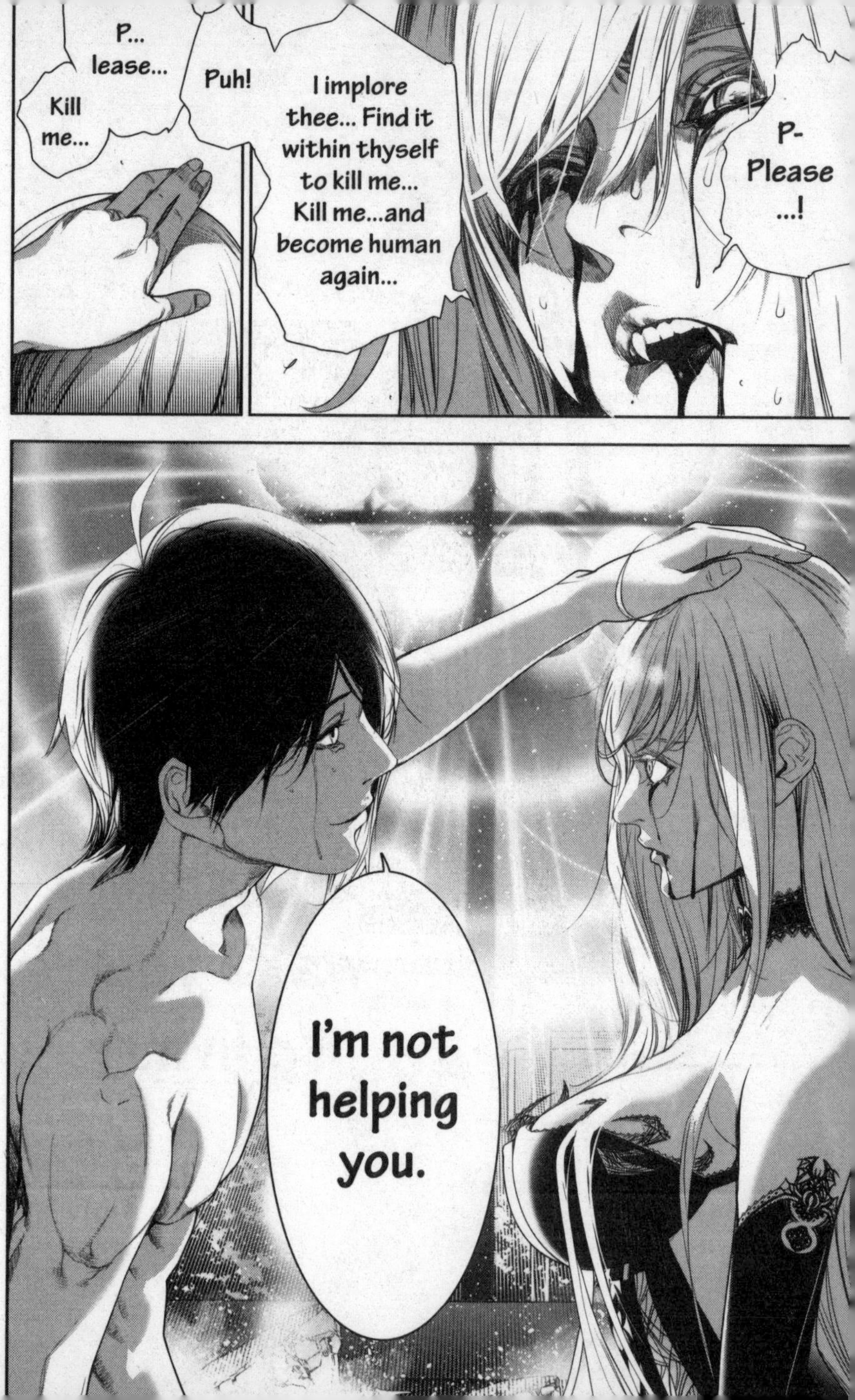
P- Please ...!
I implore thee... Find it within thyself to kill me... Kill me...and become human again...
Puh!
P... lease...
Kill me...
I'm not helping you.

GOOD
15
condition:
Green
30_012Bxxx

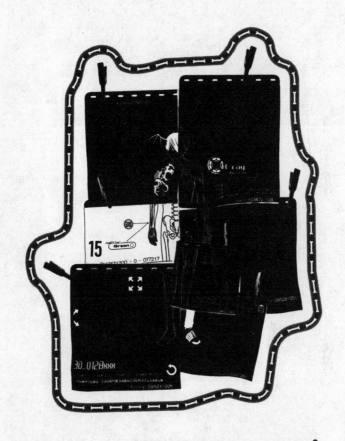

BAKEMONOGATARI
15

Form III 107531-007
Devil Yes No
Monster Yes No
Human Yes No
X-ray
High Grade
Name: Koyomi Araragi
X-Rot:9.0
Y-Rot:-8.0
Z-Rot:-23.0
Image:7354238
Pic:0.18 Thk:0.18
WL:3734 WW:4975
Form I 103472-034
15
Green
Dates
I 109028-051
Form II 104412-083
ADDRESS:
TELEPHONE(H)
DATE OF BIRTH
DATE OF APPT.:
LAST X-RAYS:
LAST PROPHY:
REFERRED BY:
Form VII 115032-089
3D_012Bxxx
X-Rot:-0.0 Y-Rot:12.0 Z-Rot:0.0 Image:863419
Form V 108921-006

BAKEMONOGATARI
15

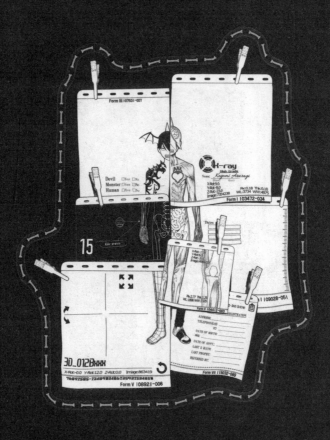

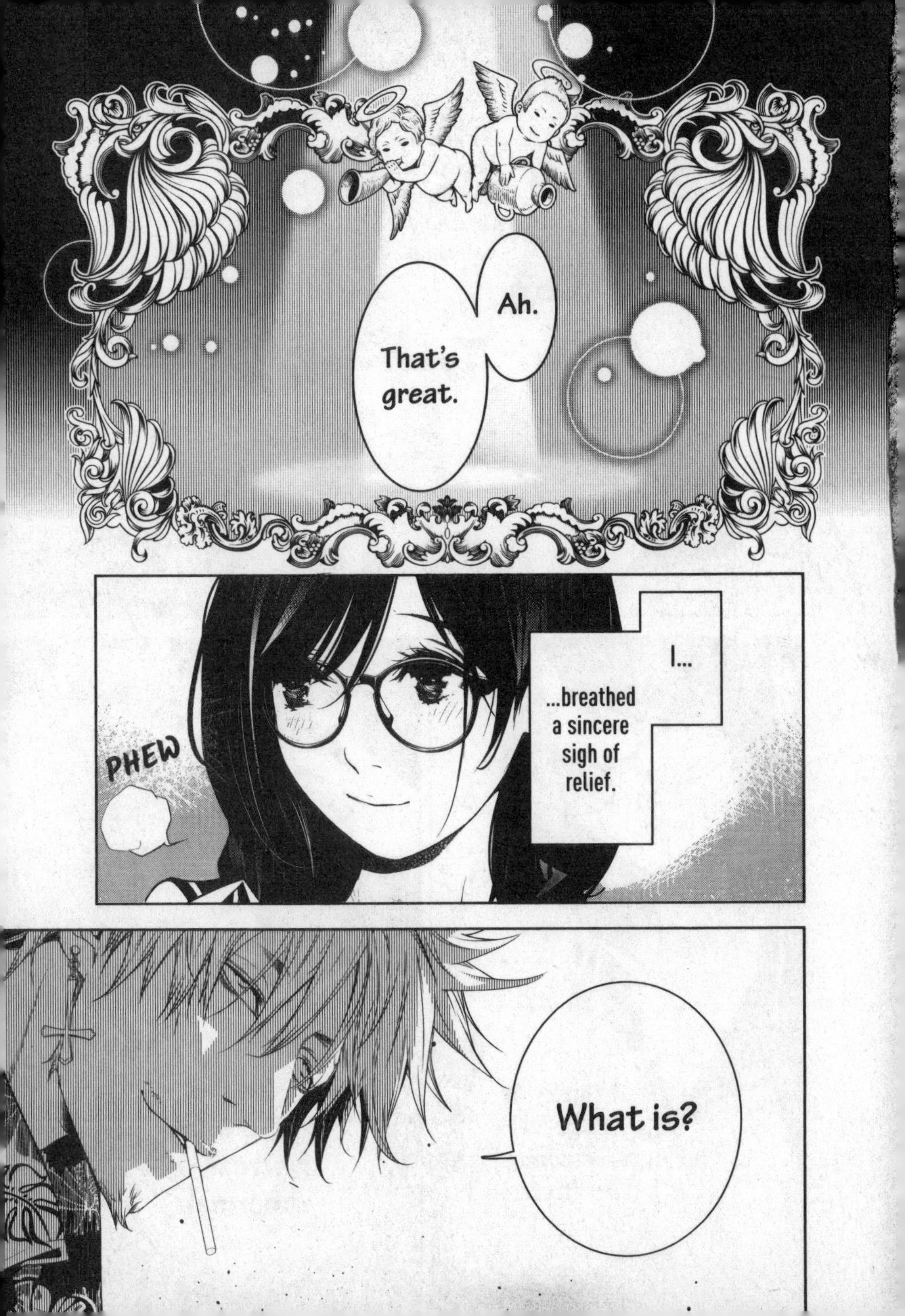
Ah.
That's great.
I...
...breathed a sincere sigh of relief.
PHEW
What is?

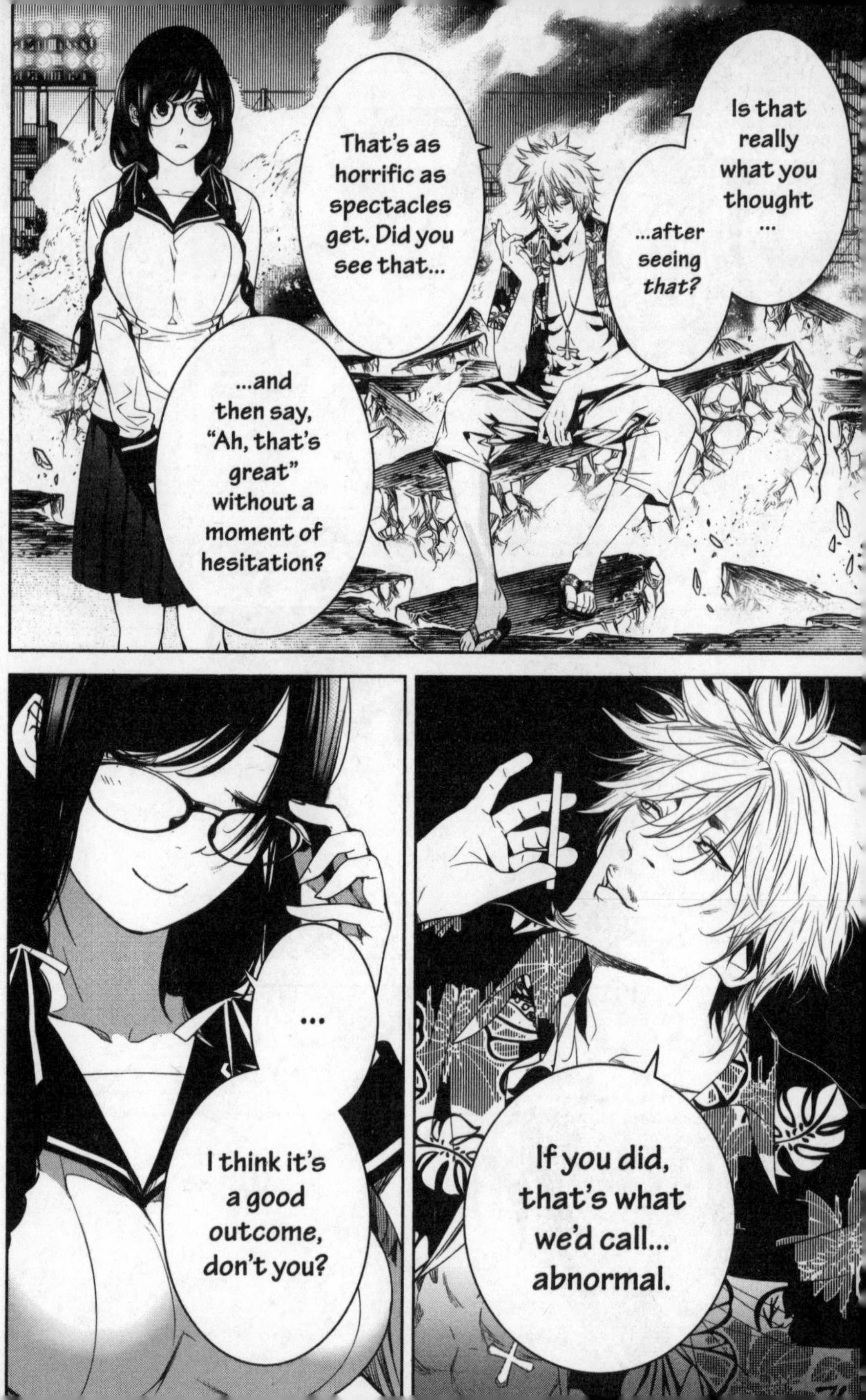
Is that really what you thought ...
...after seeing *that*?
That's as horrific as spectacles get. Did you see that...
...and then say, "Ah, that's great" without a moment of hesitation?
If you did, that's what we'd call... abnormal.
...
I think it's a good outcome, don't you?

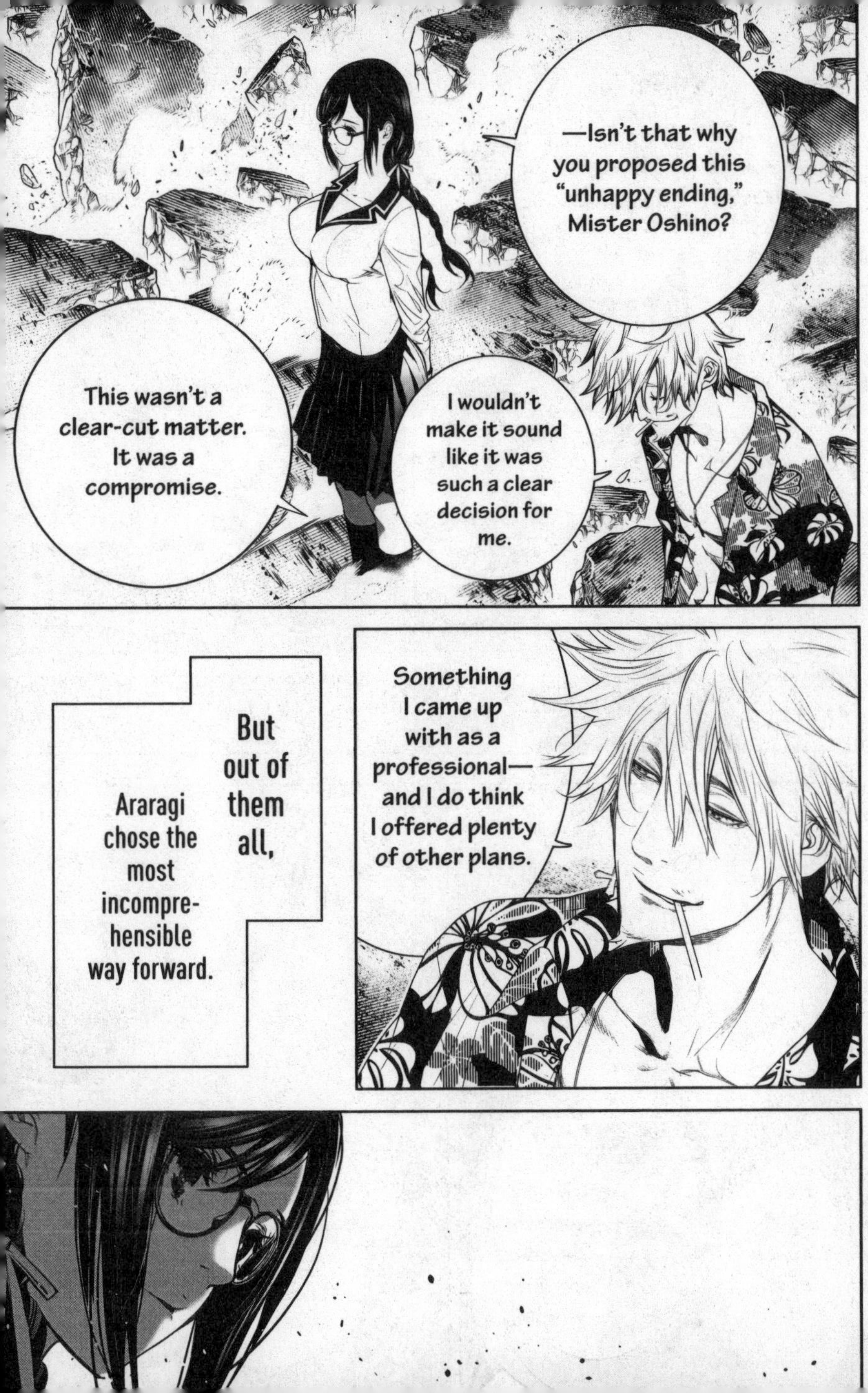
—Isn't that why you proposed this "unhappy ending," Mister Oshino?
I wouldn't make it sound like it was such a clear decision for me.
This wasn't a clear-cut matter. It was a compromise.
Something I came up with as a professional—and I do think I offered plenty of other plans.
But out of them all,
Araragi chose the most incompre-hensible way forward.

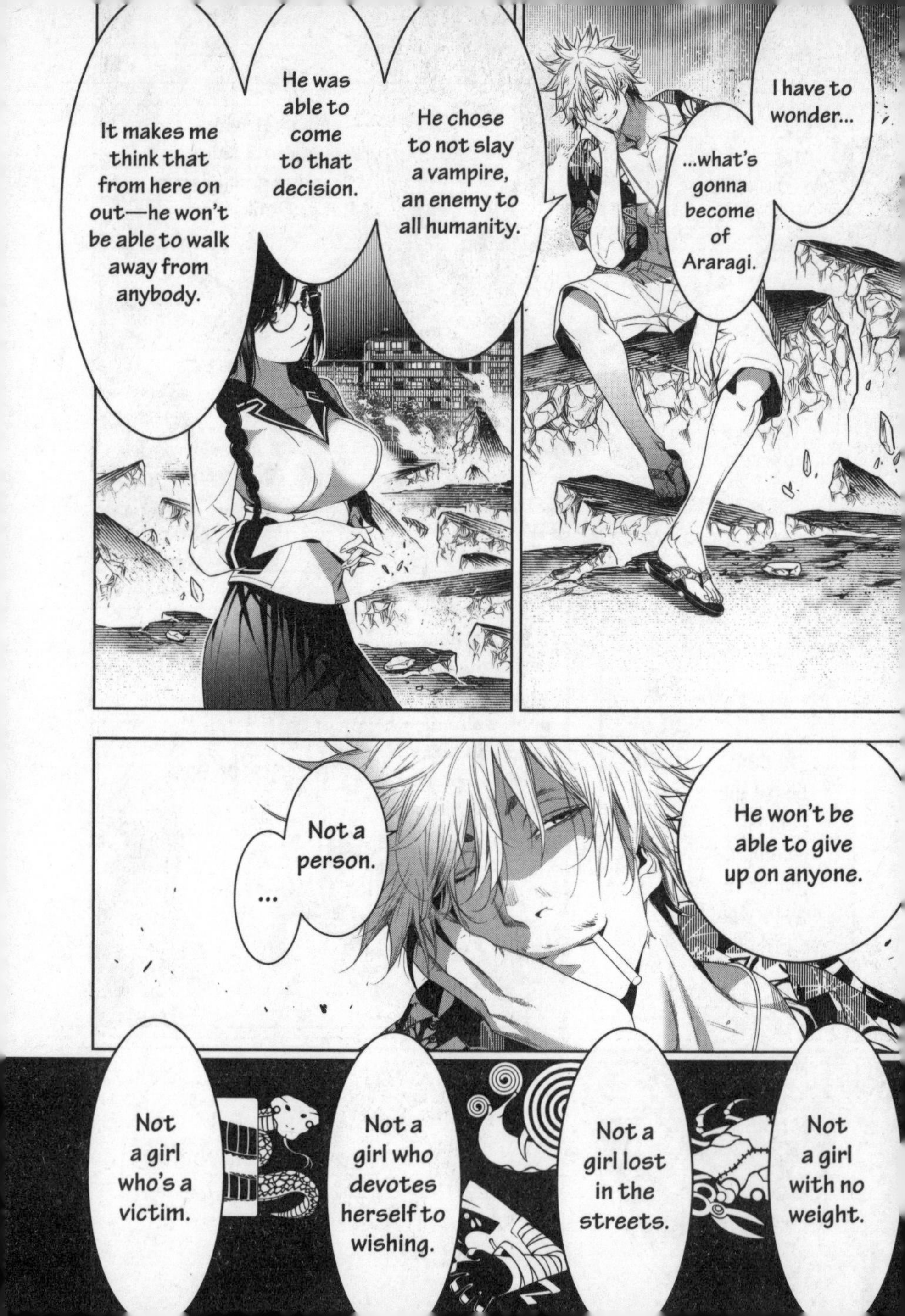
I have to wonder...
...what's gonna become of Araragi.
He chose to not slay a vampire, an enemy to all humanity.
He was able to come to that decision.
It makes me think that from here on out—he won't be able to walk away from anybody.
He won't be able to give up on anyone.
Not a person.
...
Not a girl with no weight.
Not a girl lost in the streets.
Not a girl who devotes herself to wishing.
Not a girl who's a victim.

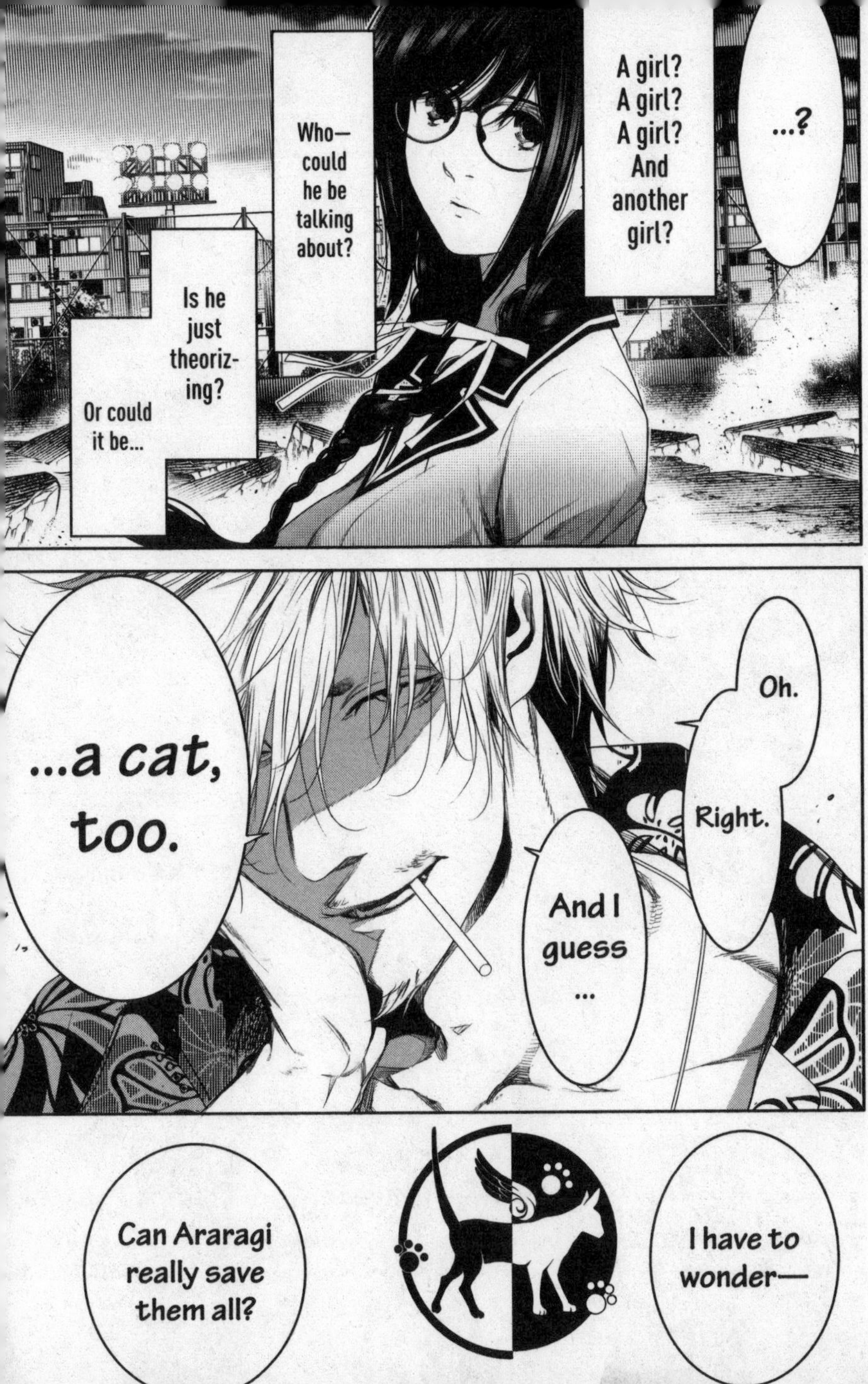
...?
A girl? A girl? A girl? And another girl?
Who—could he be talking about?
Is he just theorizing?
Or could it be...
Oh.
Right.
And I guess ...
...a cat, too.
I have to wonder—
Can Araragi really save them all?

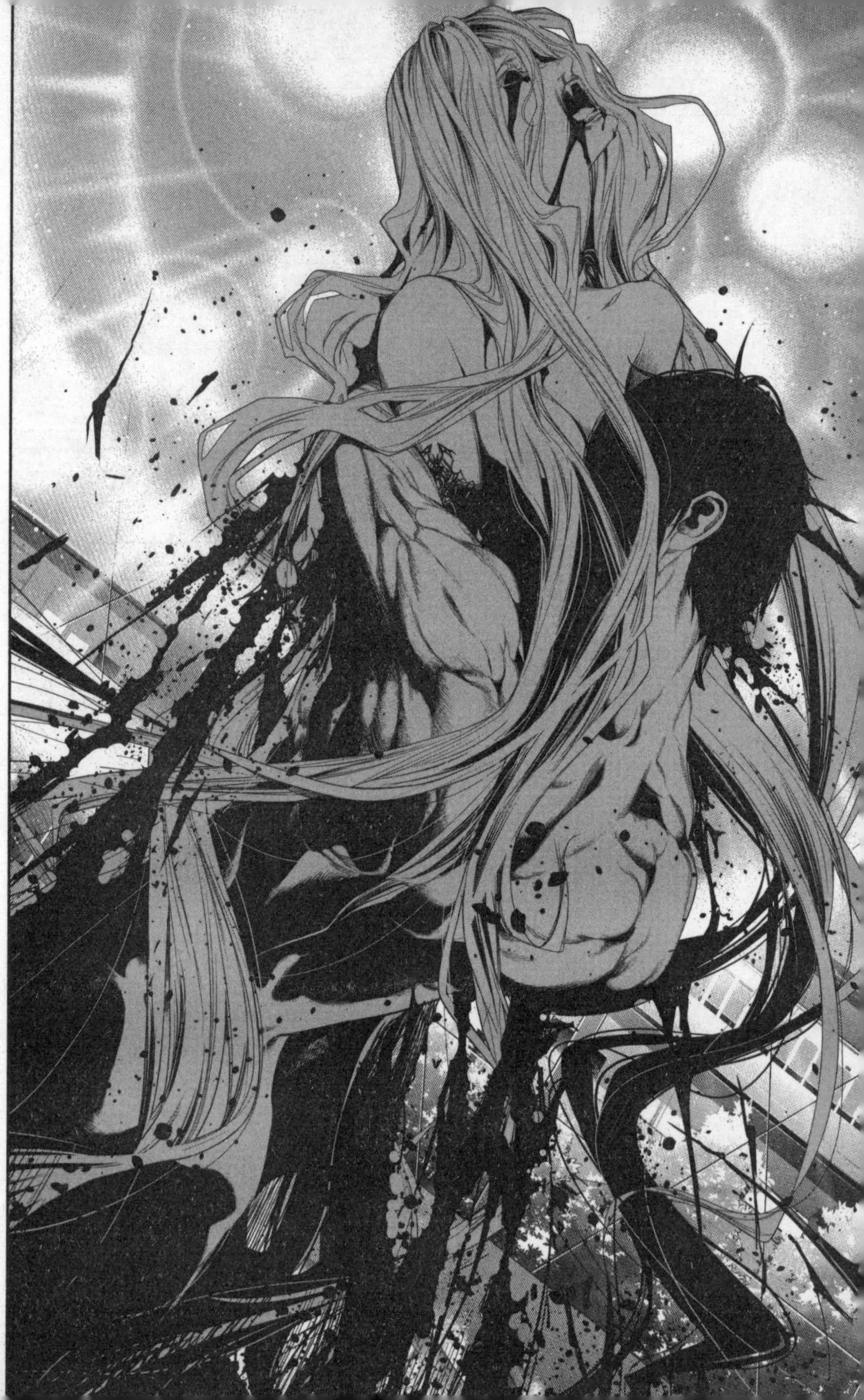

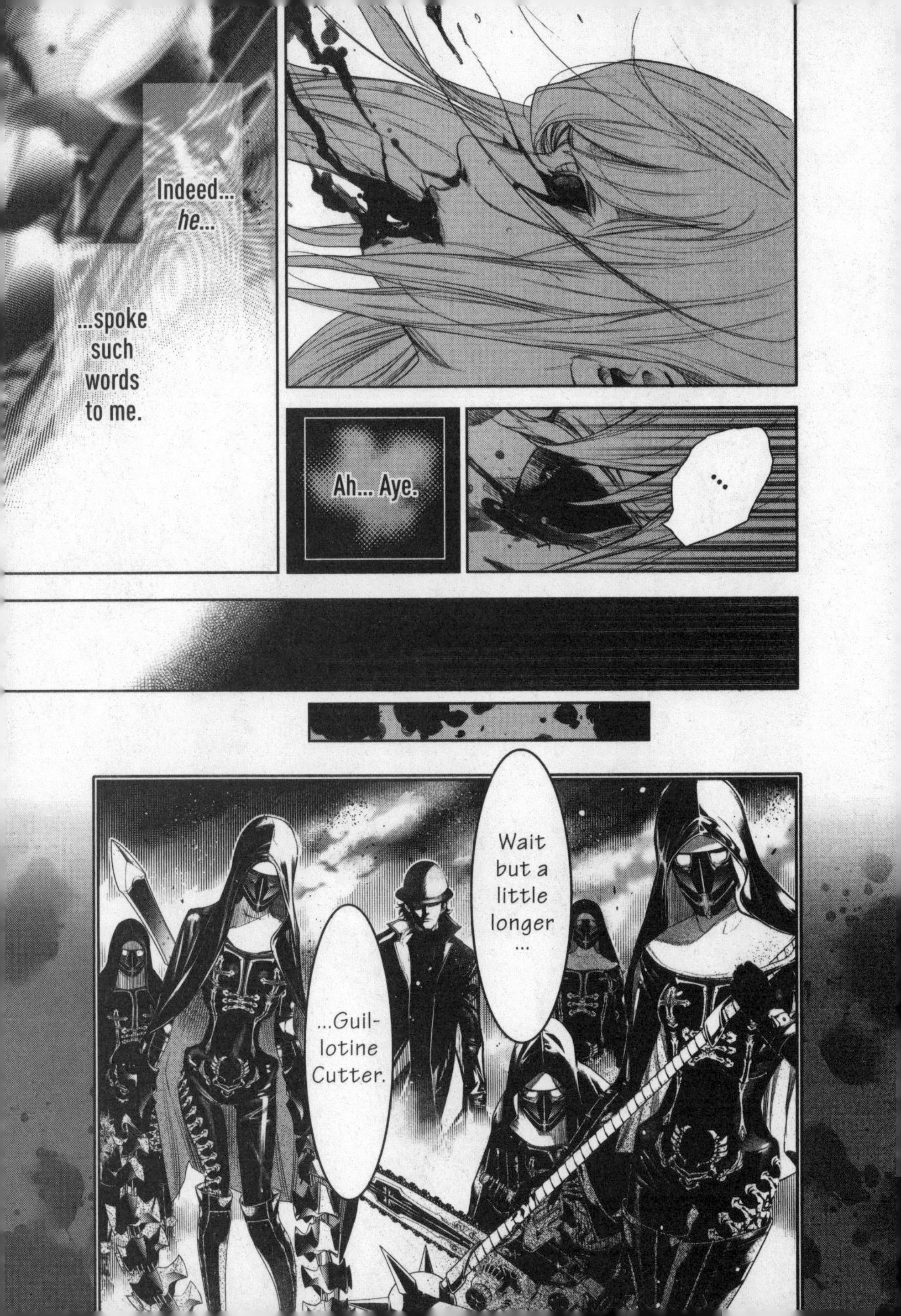
...
Ah... Aye.
Indeed... he...
...spoke such words to me.
Wait but a little longer ...
...Guil-lotine Cutter.

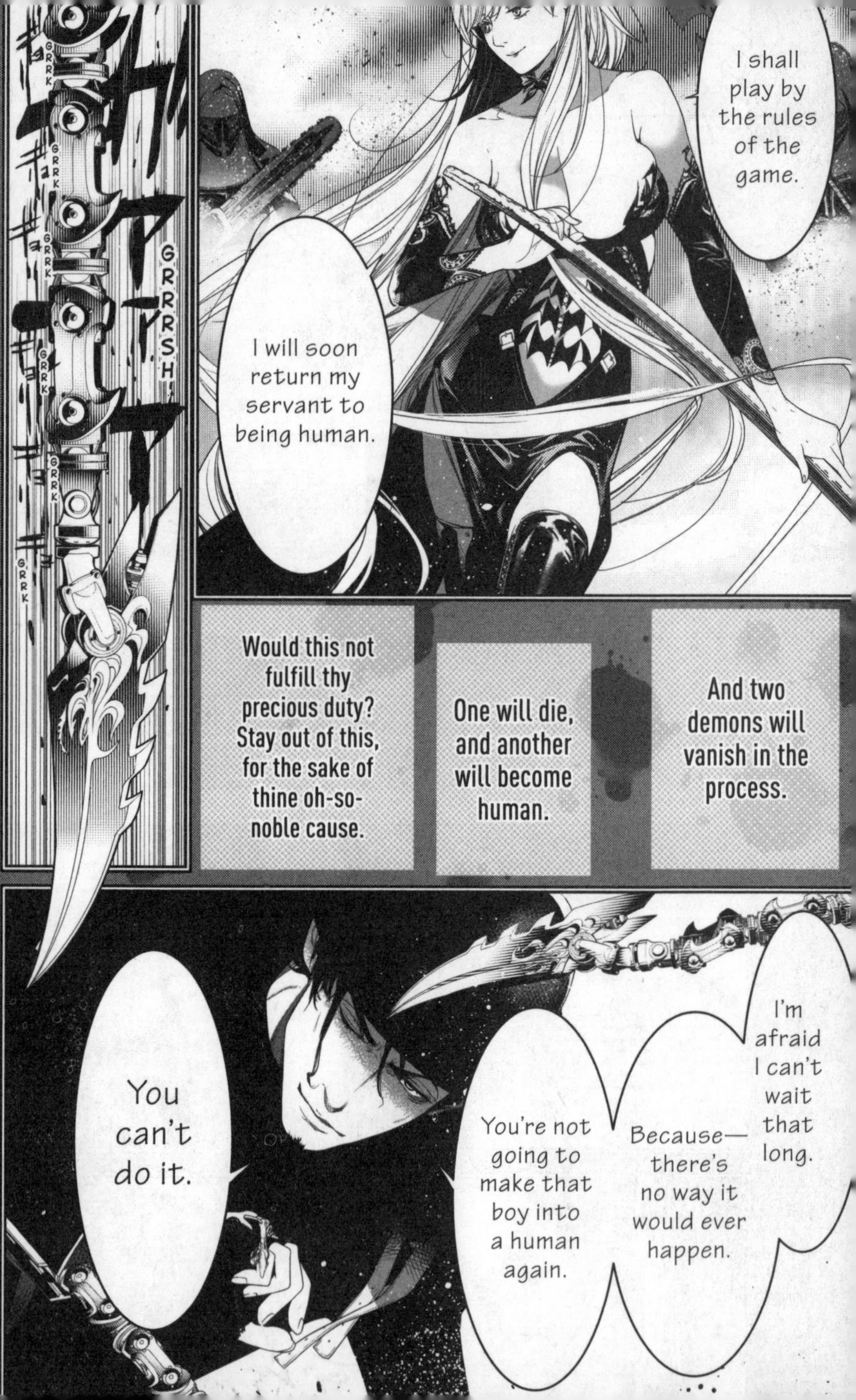
I shall play by the rules of the game.
I will soon return my servant to being human.
And two demons will vanish in the process.
One will die, and another will become human.
Would this not fulfill thy precious duty? Stay out of this, for the sake of thine oh-so-noble cause.
GRRK
GRRK
GRRK
GRRRSH
GRRK
GRRK
GRRK
I'm afraid I can't wait that long.
Because— there's no way it would ever happen.
You're not going to make that boy into a human again.
You can't do it.

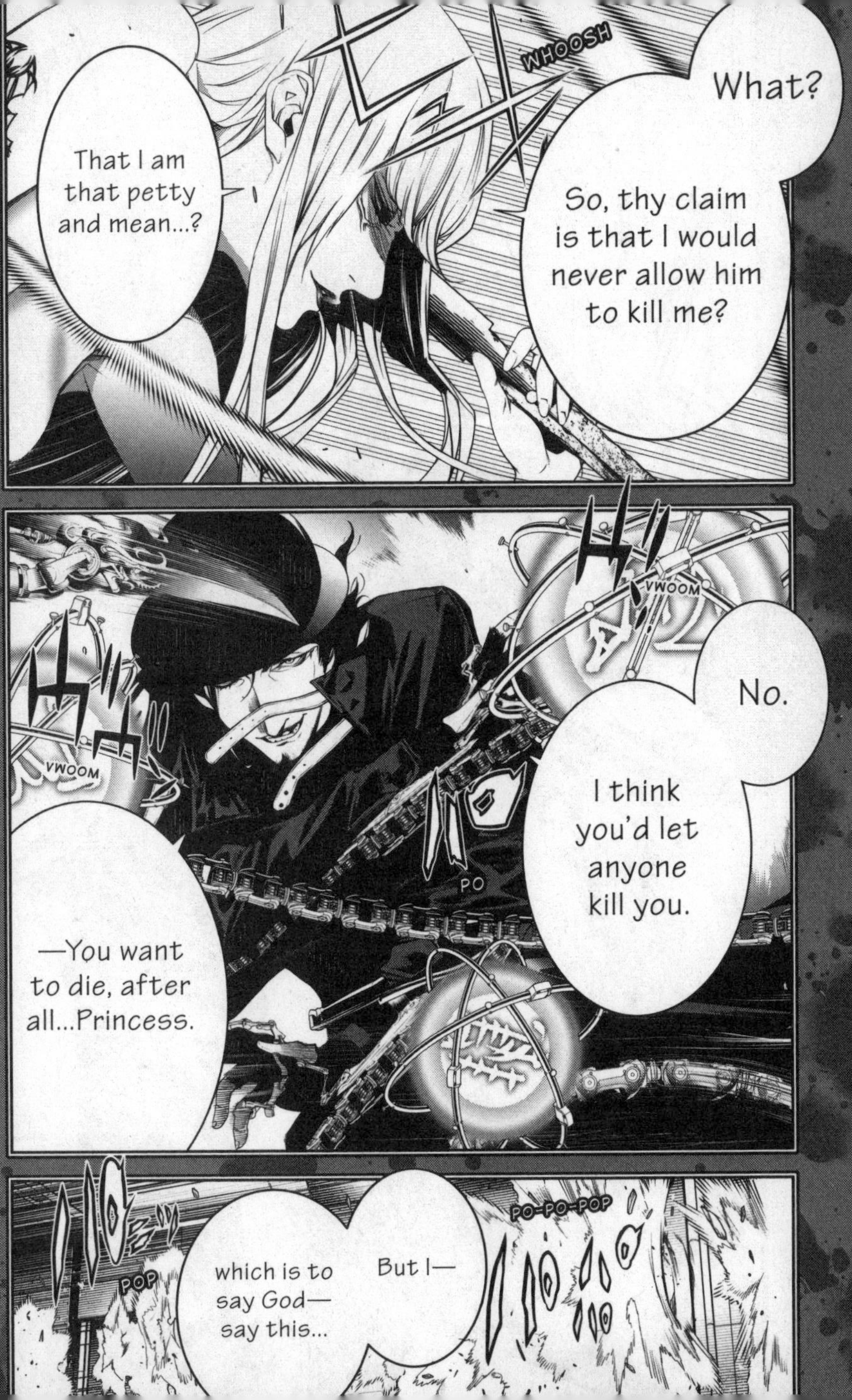
WHOOSH
What?
So, thy claim is that I would never allow him to kill me?
That I am that petty and mean...?
VWOOM
No.
I think you'd let anyone kill you.
PO
VWOOM
—You want to die, after all...Princess.
PO-PO-POP
But I—
which is to say God—say this...
POP

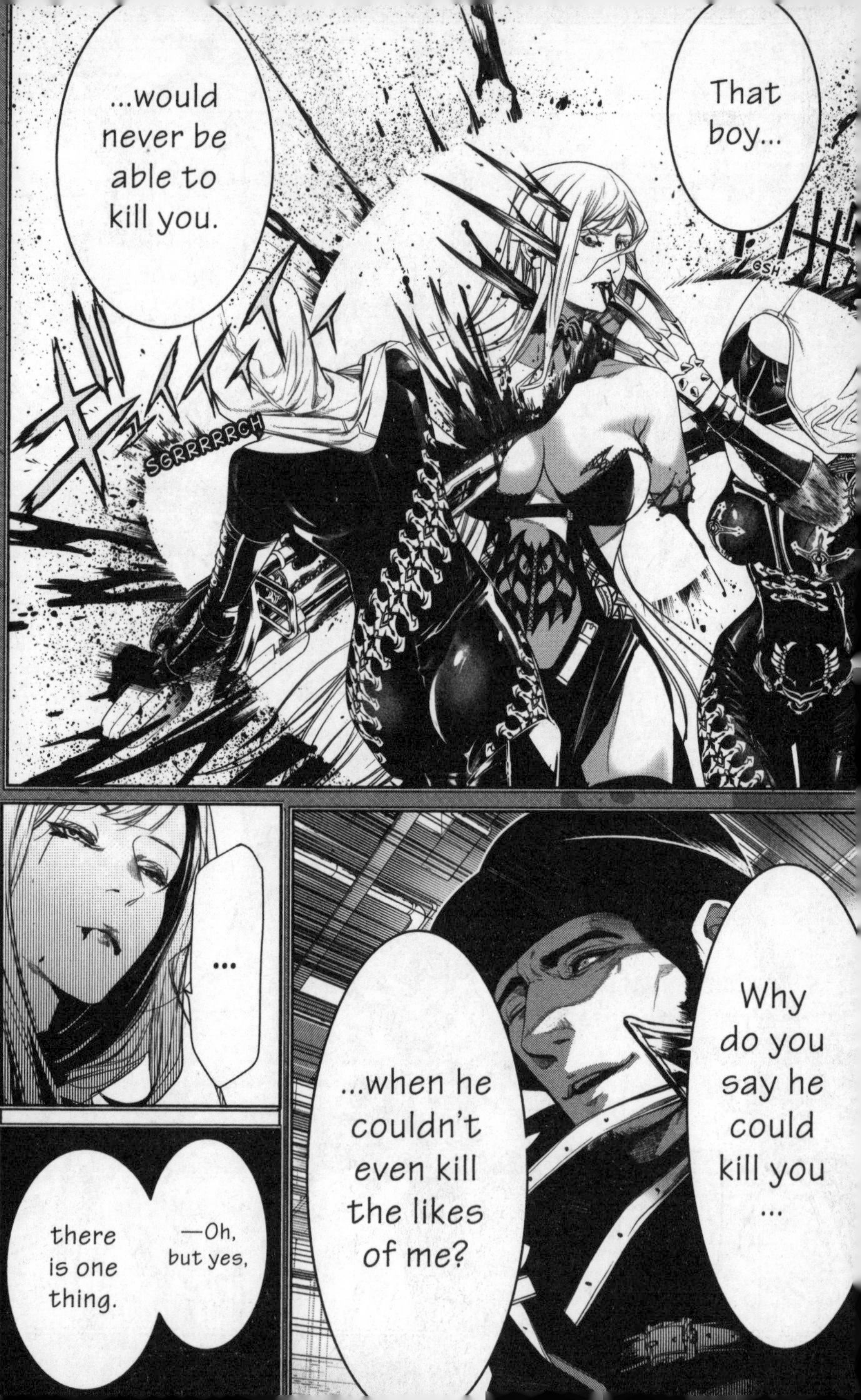
That boy...
GSH
...would never be able to kill you.
SGRRRRRCH
Why do you say he could kill you ...
...when he couldn't even kill the likes of me?
...
—Oh, but yes,
there is one thing.

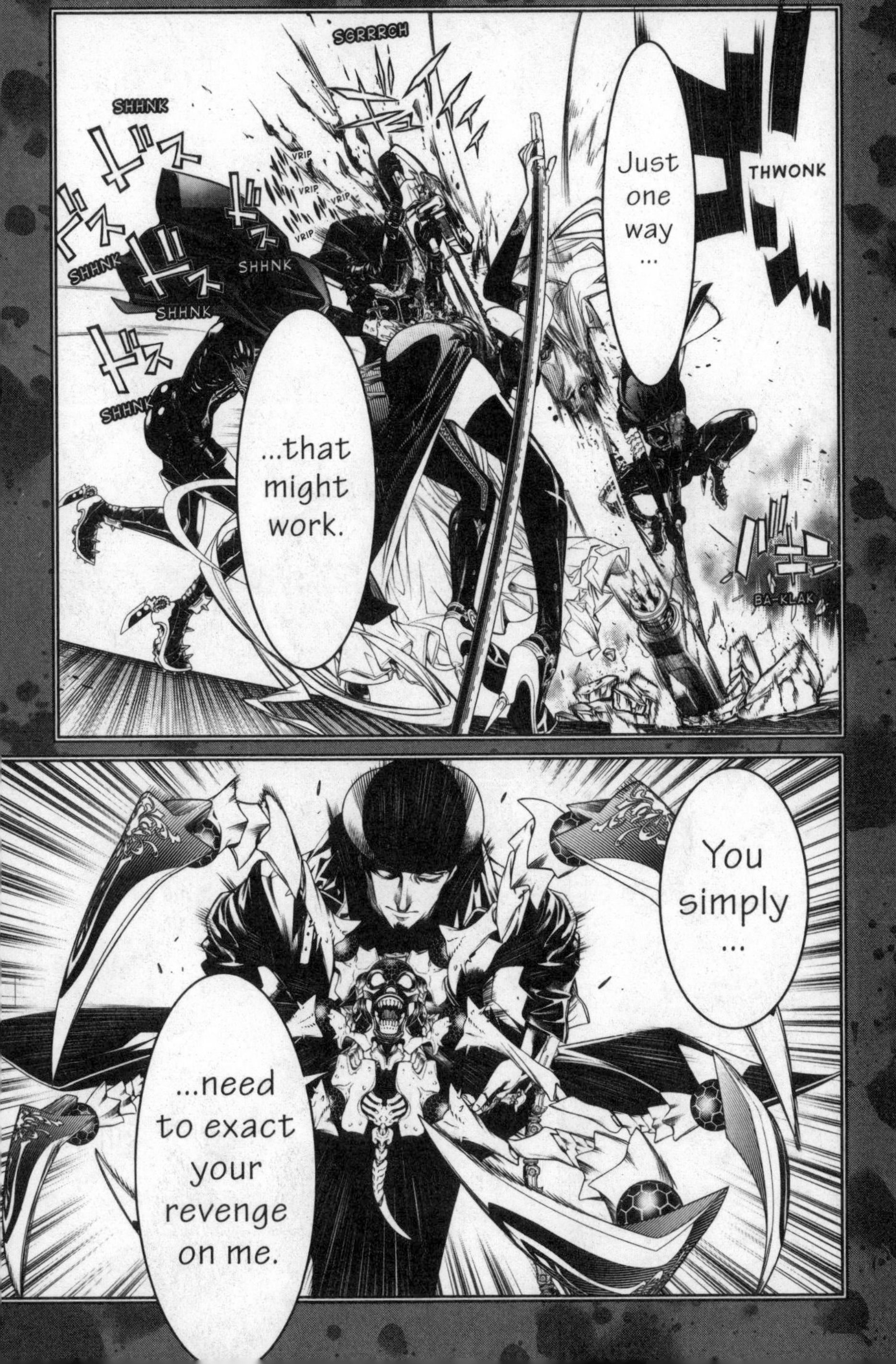
THWONK
Just one way ...
SGRRRCH
VRIP
VRIP
VRIP
VRIP
SHHNK
...that might work.
SHHNK
SHHNK
SHHNK
SHHNK
BA-KLAK
You simply ...
...need to exact your revenge on me.

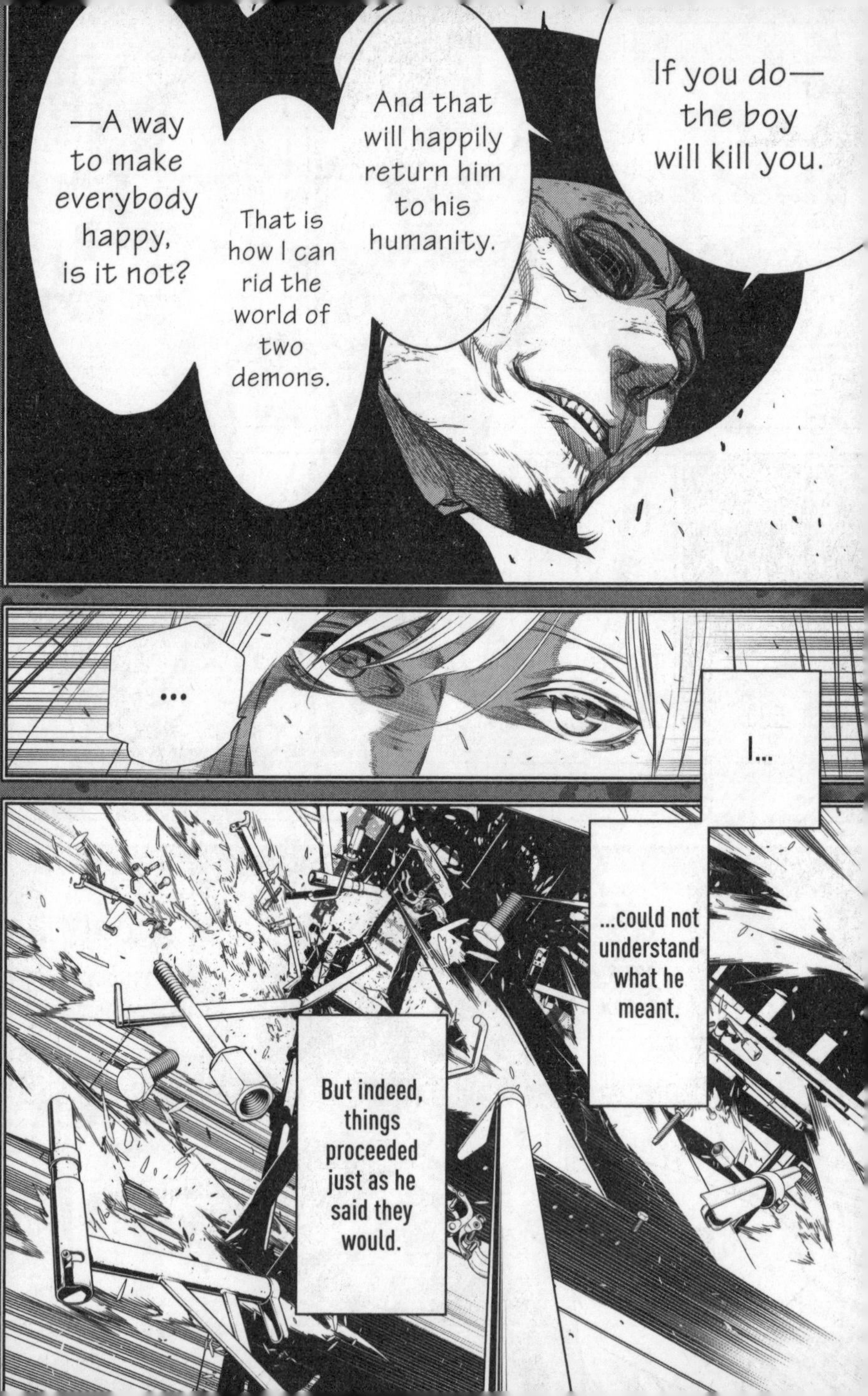
If you do— the boy will kill you.
And that will happily return him to his humanity.
That is how I can rid the world of two demons.
—A way to make everybody happy, is it not?
I...
...
...could not understand what he meant.
But indeed, things proceeded just as he said they would.

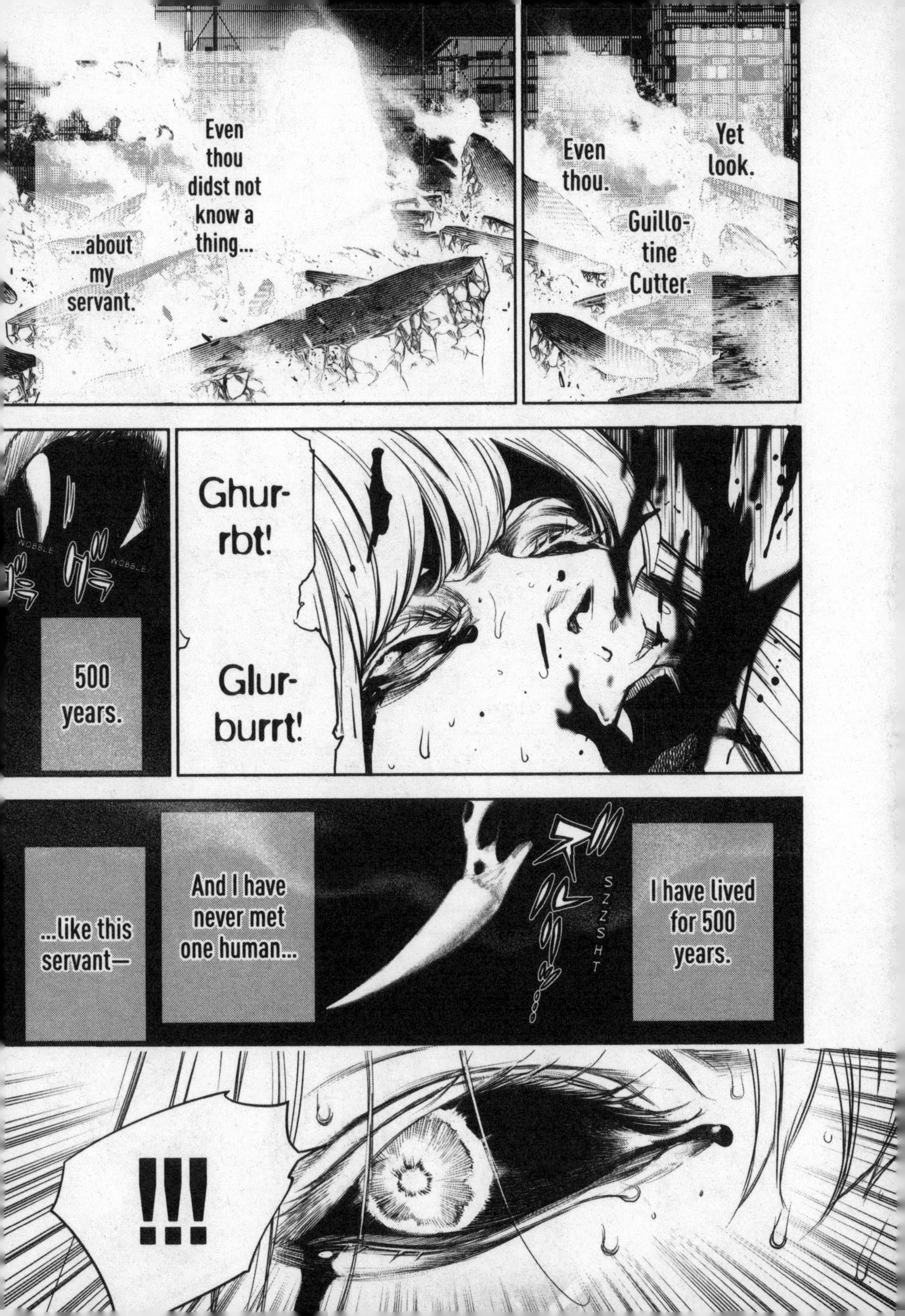
Yet look.
Even thou.
Guillo-tine Cutter.
Even thou didst not know a thing...
...about my servant.
Ghur-rbt!
Glur-burrt!
WOBBLE
WOBBLE
500 years.
I have lived for 500 years.
SZZSHT
And I have never met one human...
...like this servant—
!!!

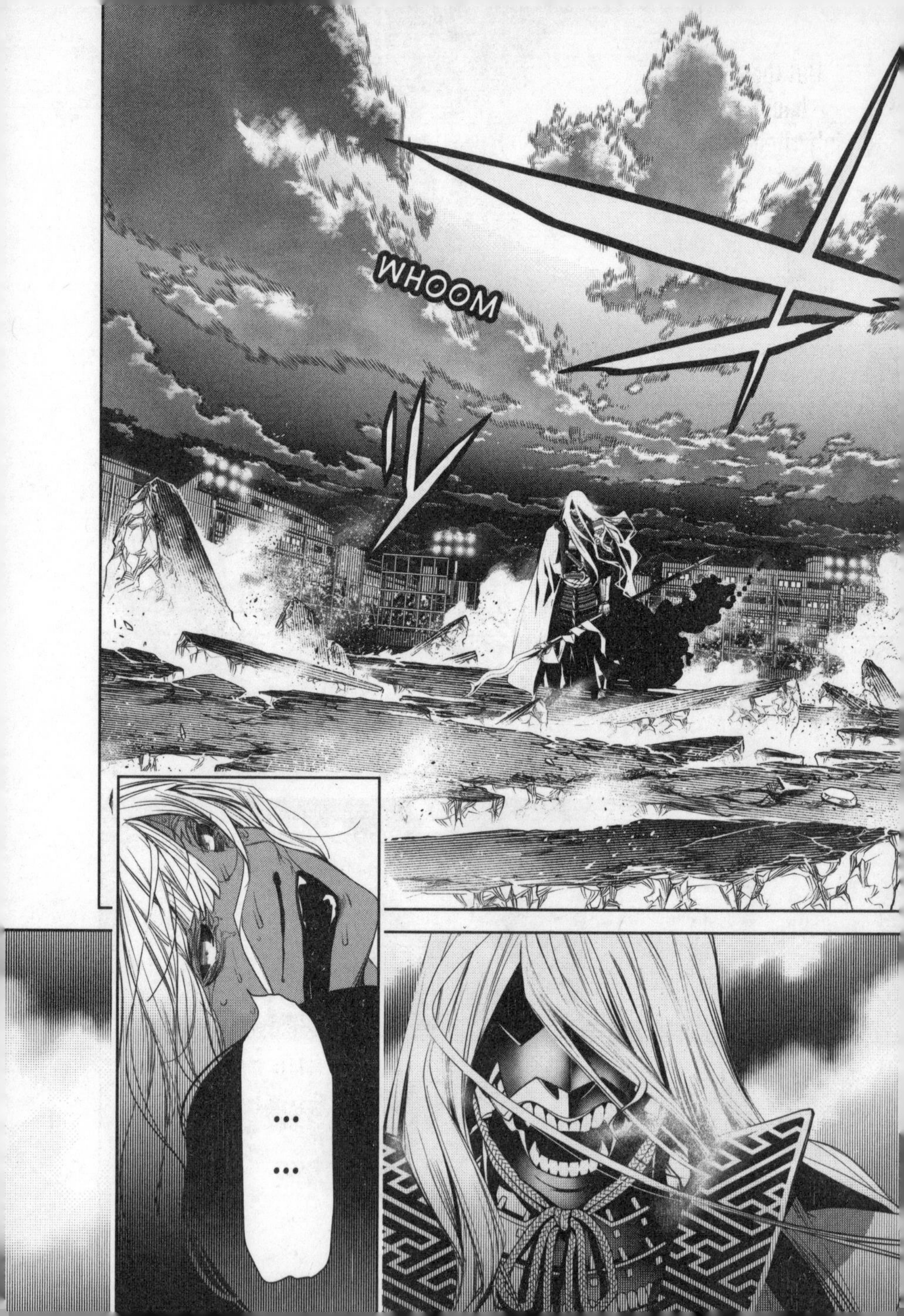
WHOOM
...
...

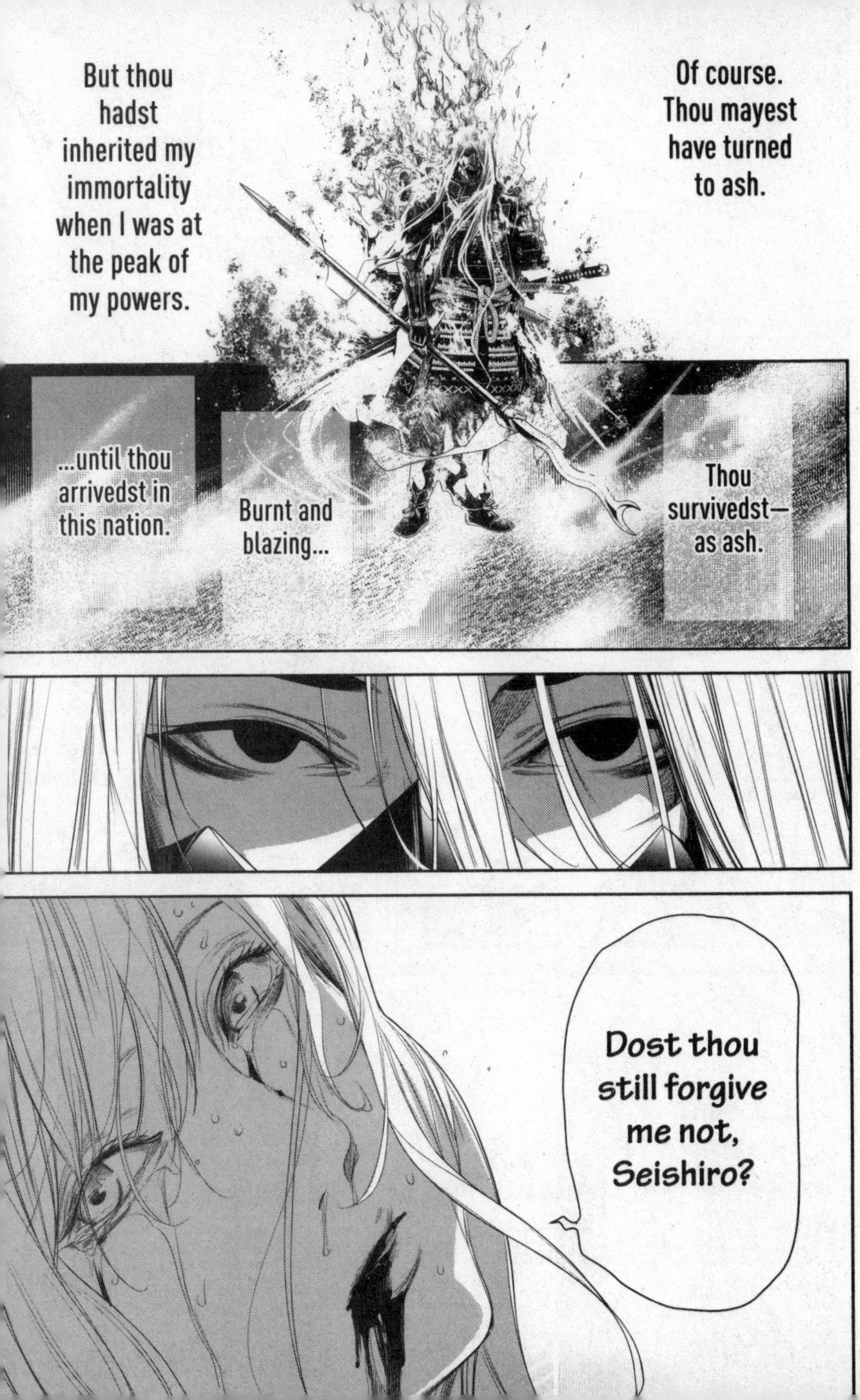
Of course. Thou mayest have turned to ash.
But thou hadst inherited my immortality when I was at the peak of my powers.
Thou survivedst— as ash.
Burnt and blazing...
...until thou arrivedst in this nation.
Dost thou still forgive me not, Seishiro?

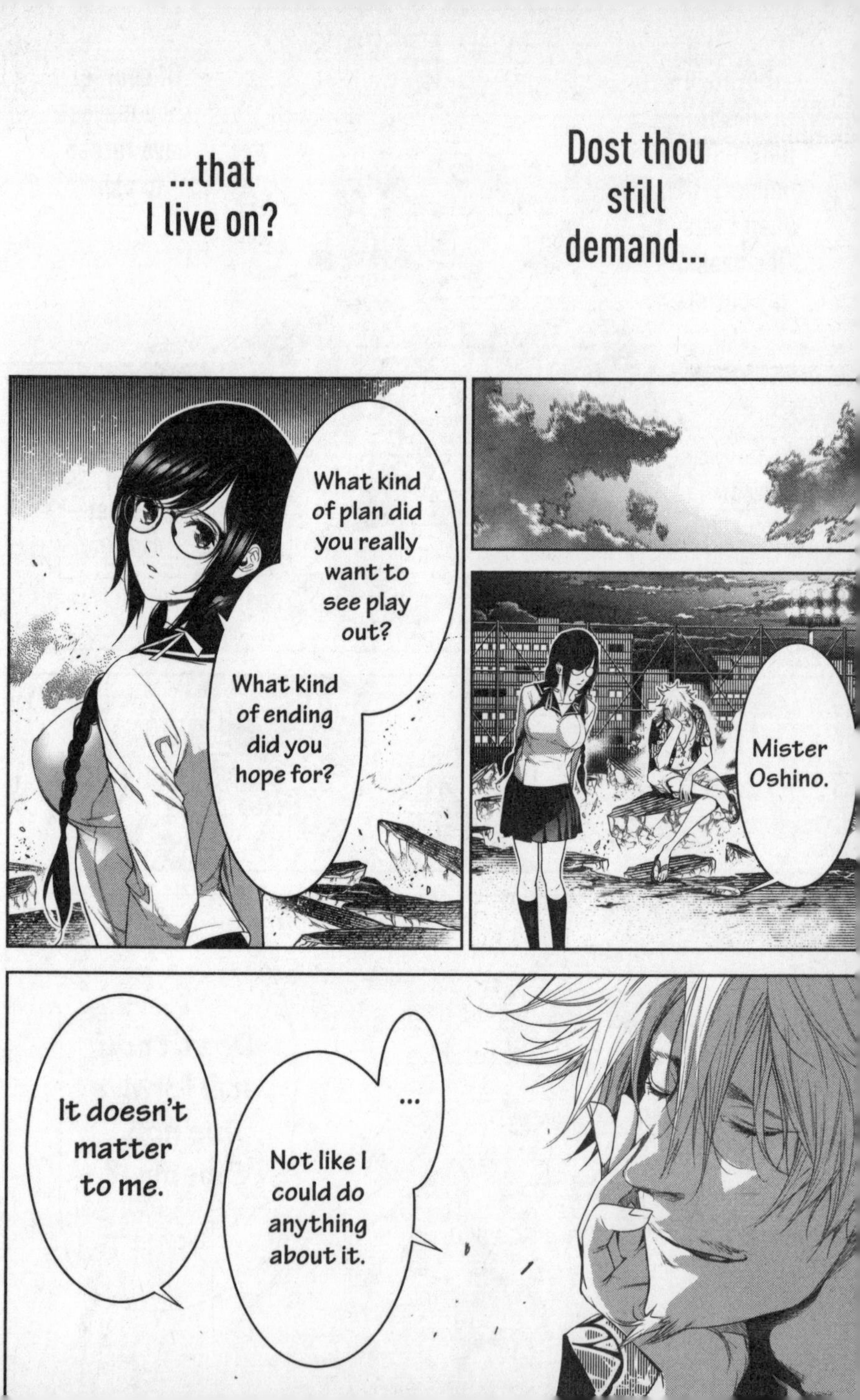
Dost thou still demand...
...that I live on?
Mister Oshino.
What kind of plan did you really want to see play out?
What kind of ending did you hope for?
... Not like I could do anything about it.
It doesn't matter to me.

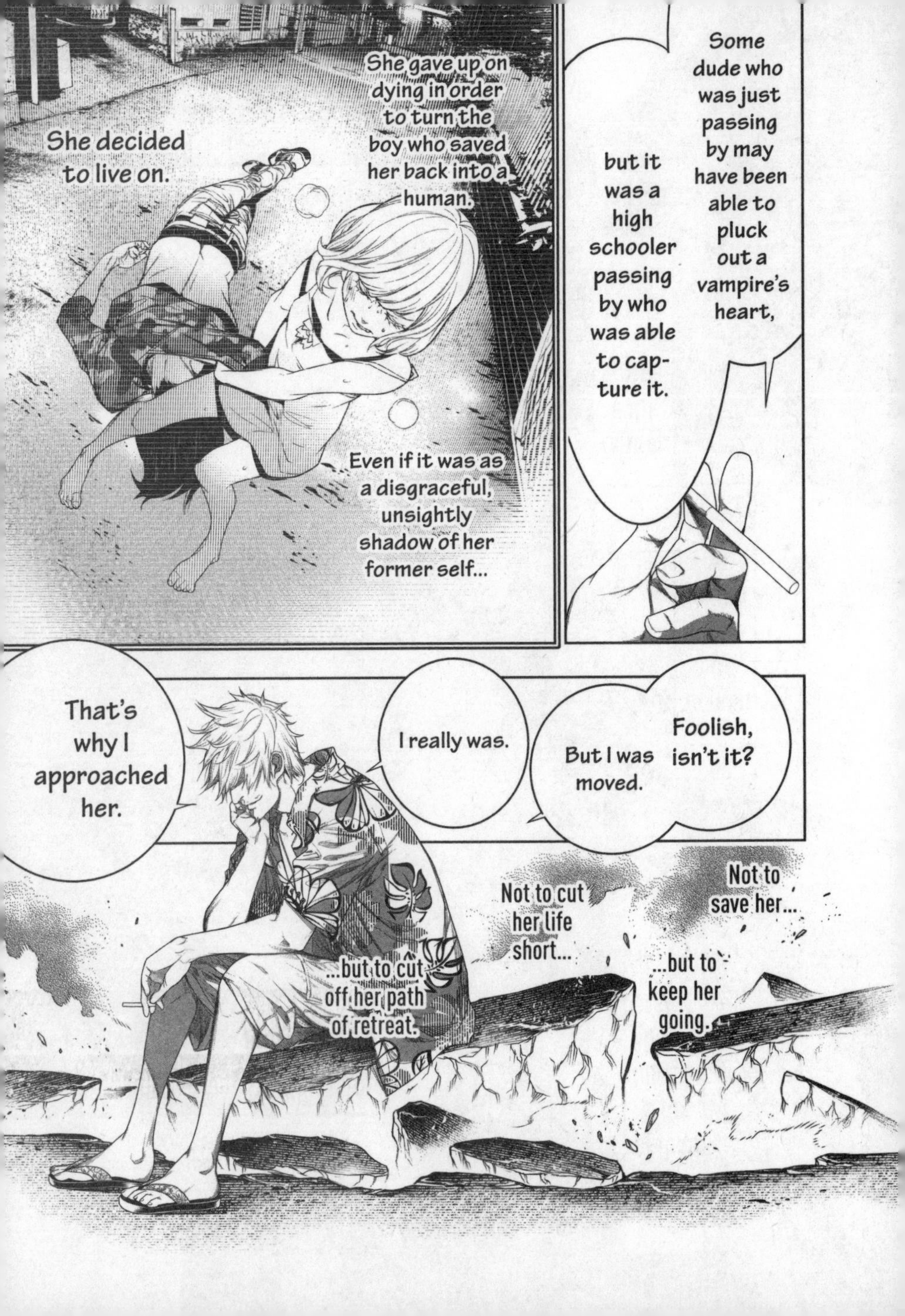
Some dude who was just passing by may have been able to pluck out a vampire's heart,
but it was a high schooler passing by who was able to capture it.
She gave up on dying in order to turn the boy who saved her back into a human.
She decided to live on.
Even if it was as a disgraceful, unsightly shadow of her former self...
Foolish, isn't it?
But I was moved.
I really was.
That's why I approached her.
Not to save her...
...but to keep her going.
Not to cut her life short...
...but to cut off her path of retreat.

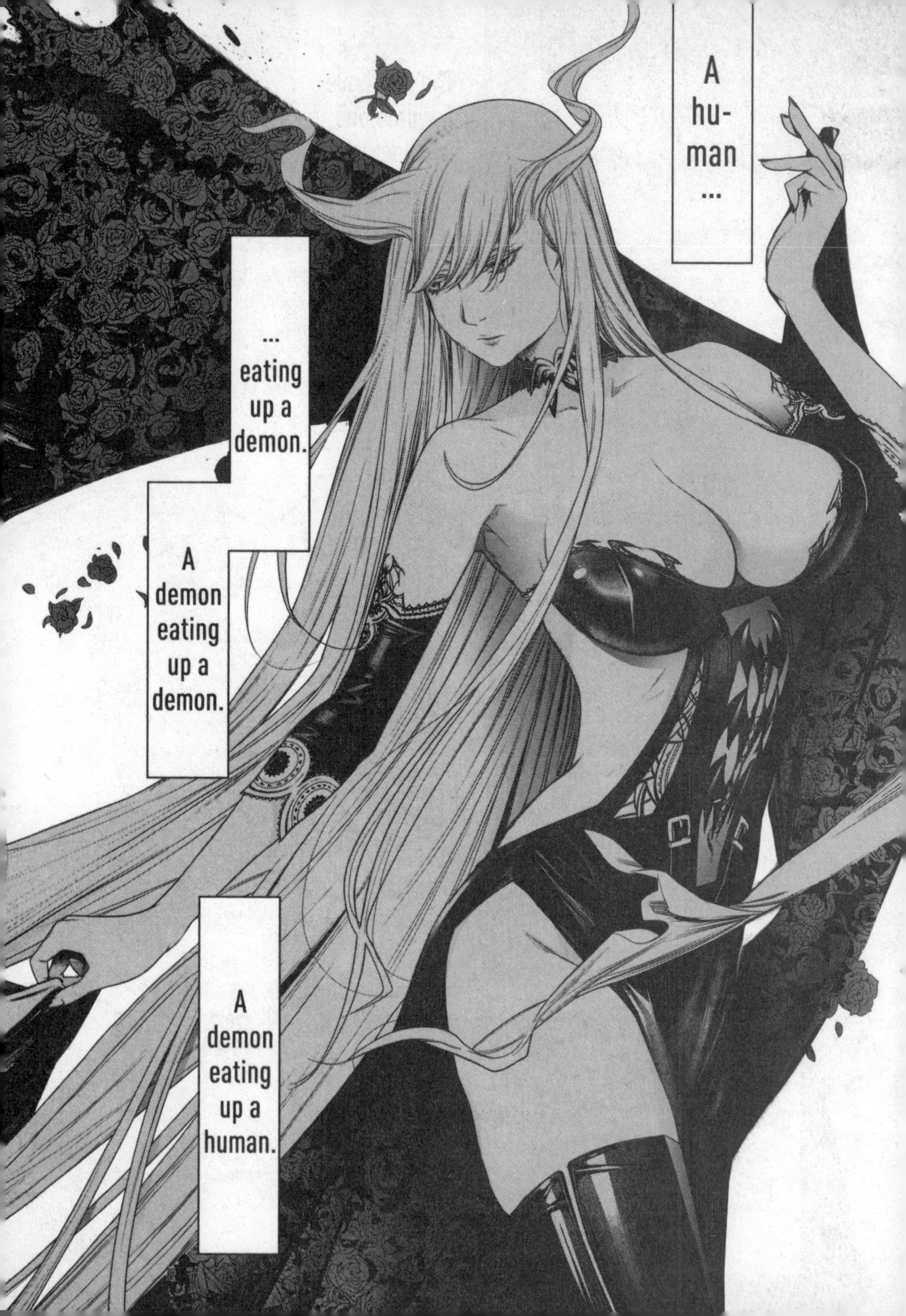
A human...
...eating up a demon.
A demon eating up a demon.
A demon eating up a human.

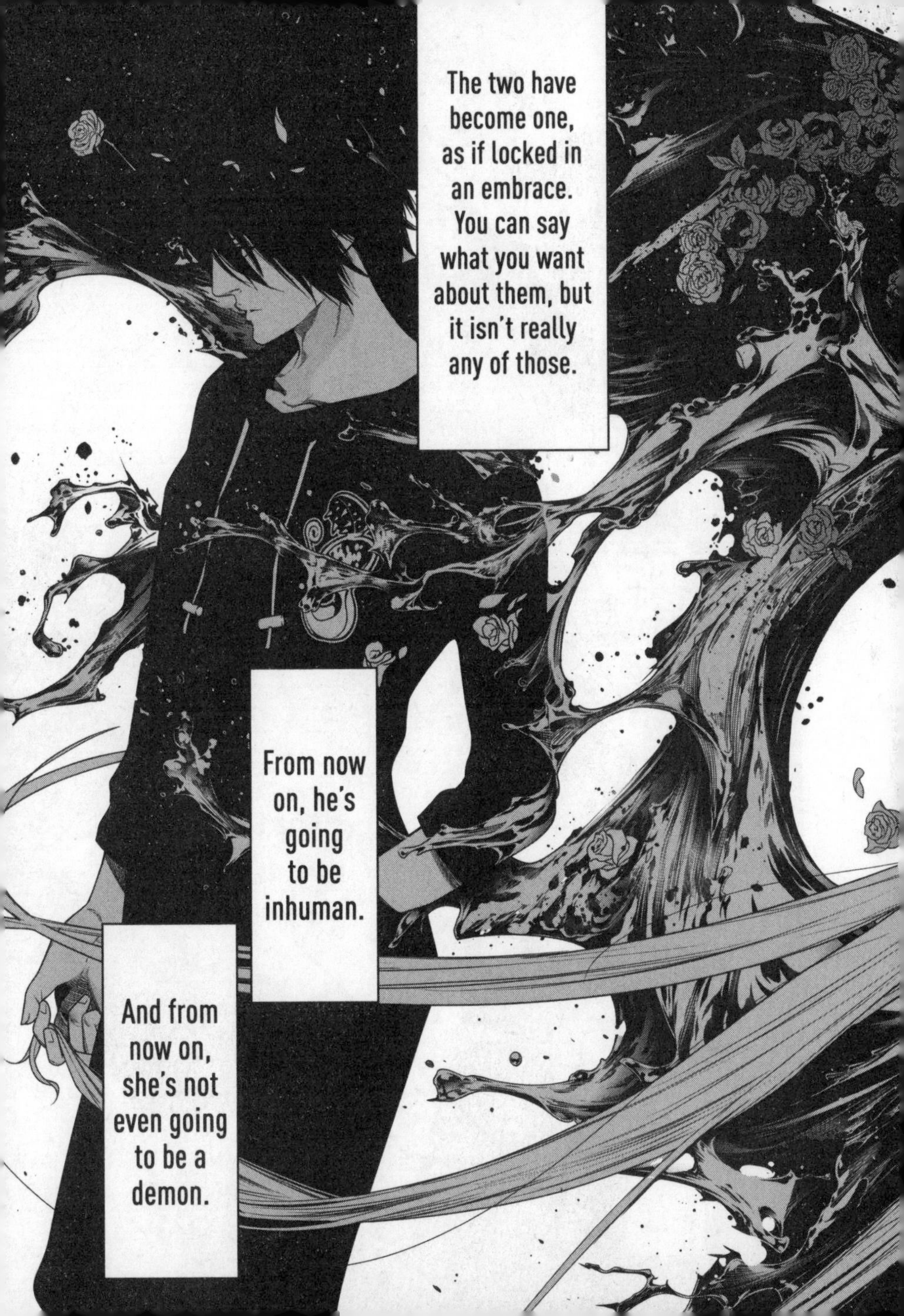
The two have become one, as if locked in an embrace. You can say what you want about them, but it isn't really any of those.
From now on, he's going to be inhuman.
And from now on, she's not even going to be a demon.

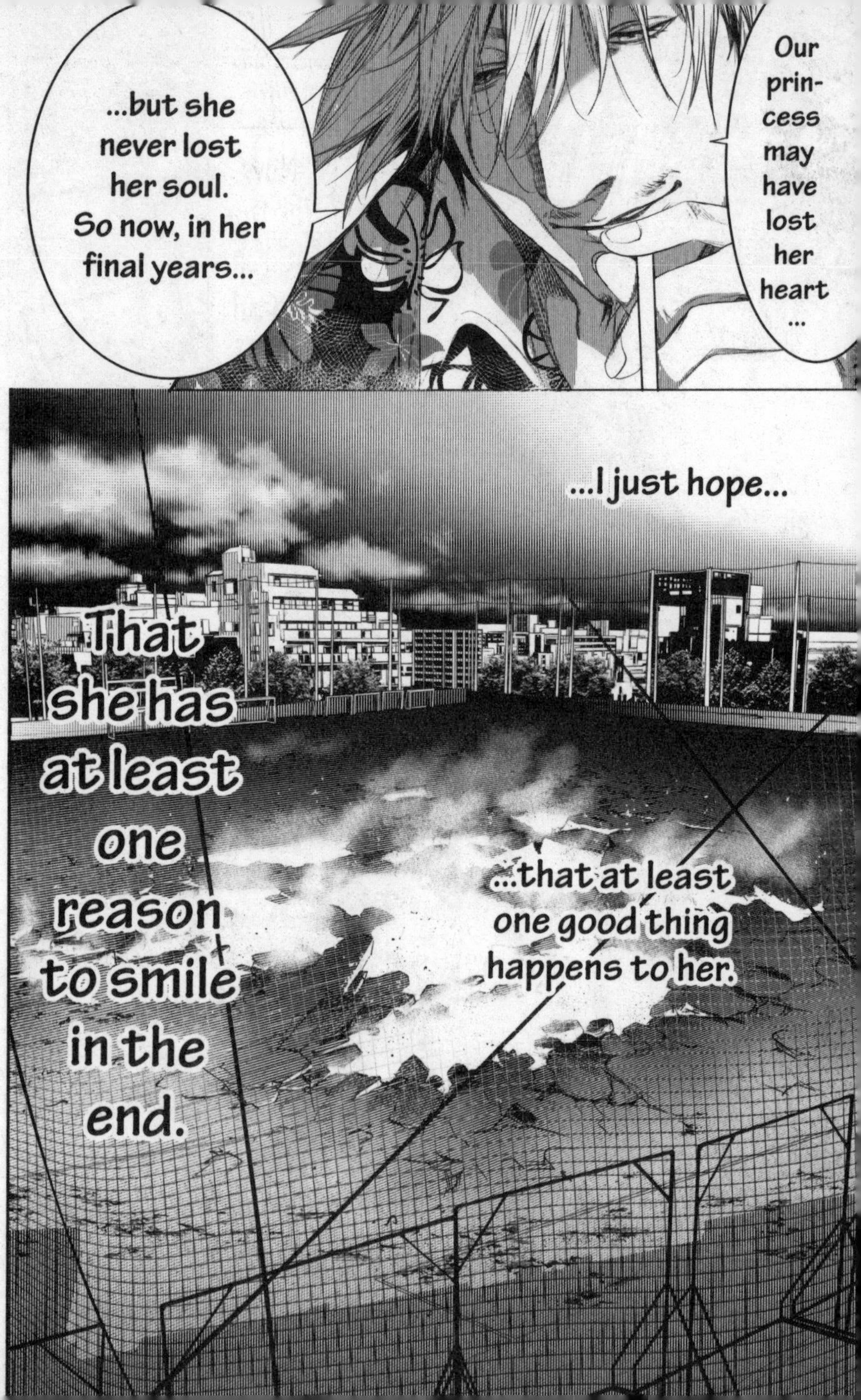
Our princess may have lost her heart...
...but she never lost her soul. So now, in her final years...
...I just hope...
...that at least one good thing happens to her.
That she has at least one reason to smile in the end.

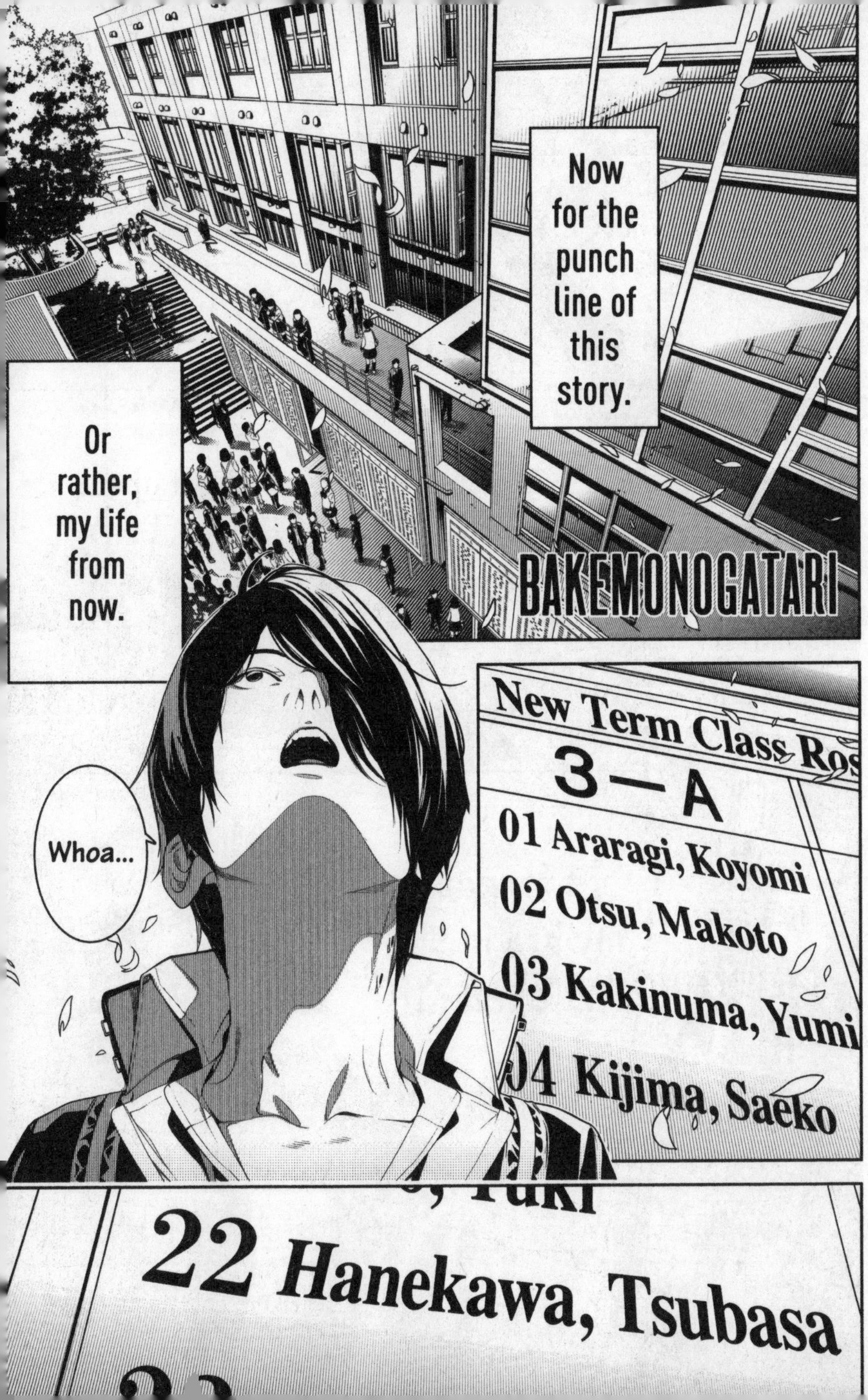
Now for the punch line of this story.
Or rather, my life from now.
BAKEMONOGATARI
New Term Class Ros
3—A
01 Araragi, Koyomi
02 Otsu, Makoto
03 Kakinuma, Yumi
04 Kijima, Saeko
Whoa...
22 Hanekawa, Tsubasa

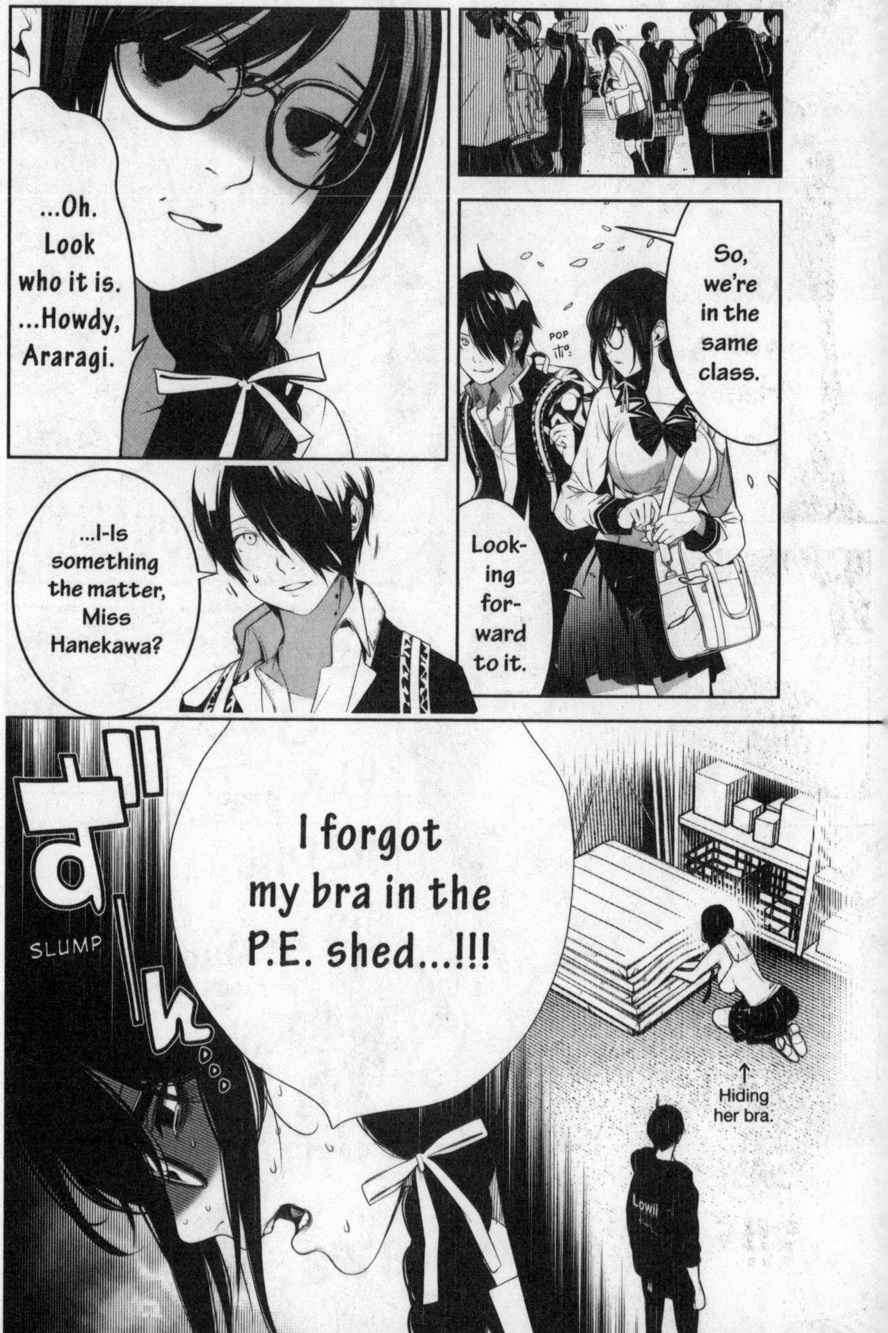

POP
So, we're in the same class.
Looking-ing for-ward to it.
...Oh. Look who it is. ...Howdy, Araragi.
...I-Is something the matter, Miss Hanekawa?
I forgot my bra in the P.E. shed...!!!
SLUMP
Hiding her bra.

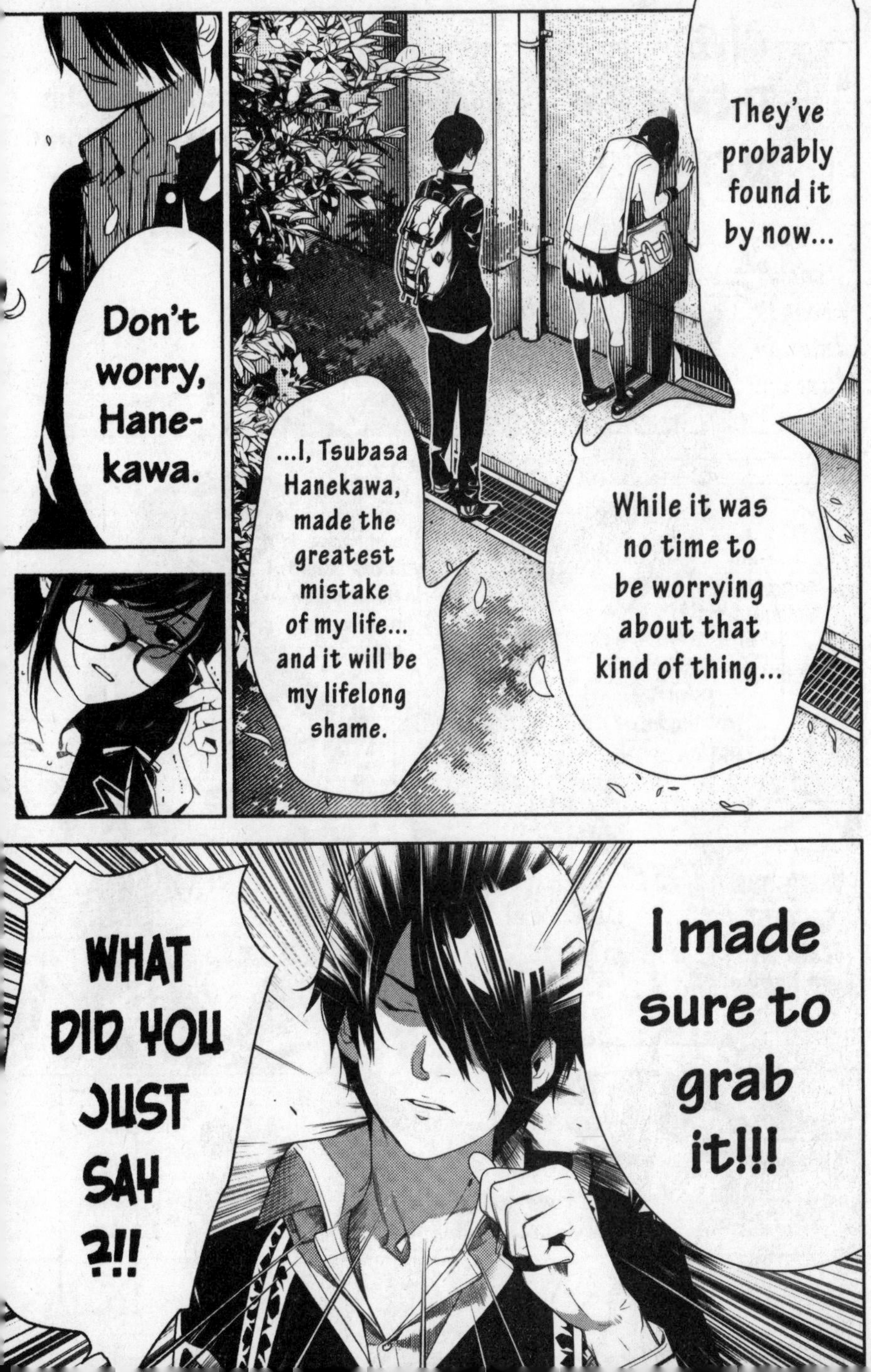
They've probably found it by now...
While it was no time to be worrying about that kind of thing...
...I, Tsubasa Hanekawa, made the greatest mistake of my life... and it will be my lifelong shame.
Don't worry, Hanekawa.
I made sure to grab it!!!
WHAT DID YOU JUST SAY ?!!

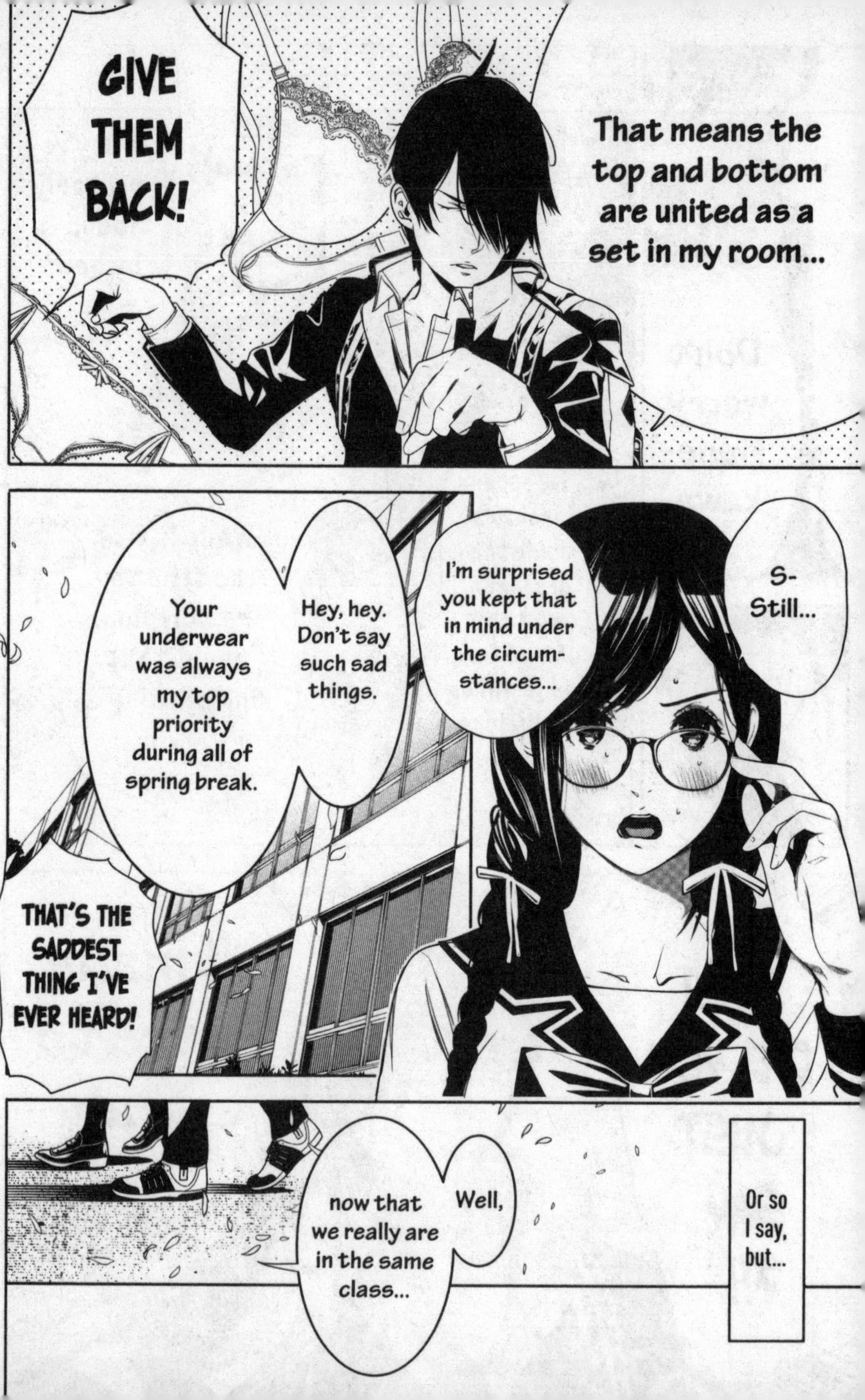
That means the top and bottom are united as a set in my room...
GIVE THEM BACK!
S- Still...
I'm surprised you kept that in mind under the circumstances...
Hey, hey. Don't say such sad things.
Your underwear was always my top priority during all of spring break.
THAT'S THE SADDEST THING I'VE EVER HEARD!
Or so I say, but...
Well, now that we really are in the same class...

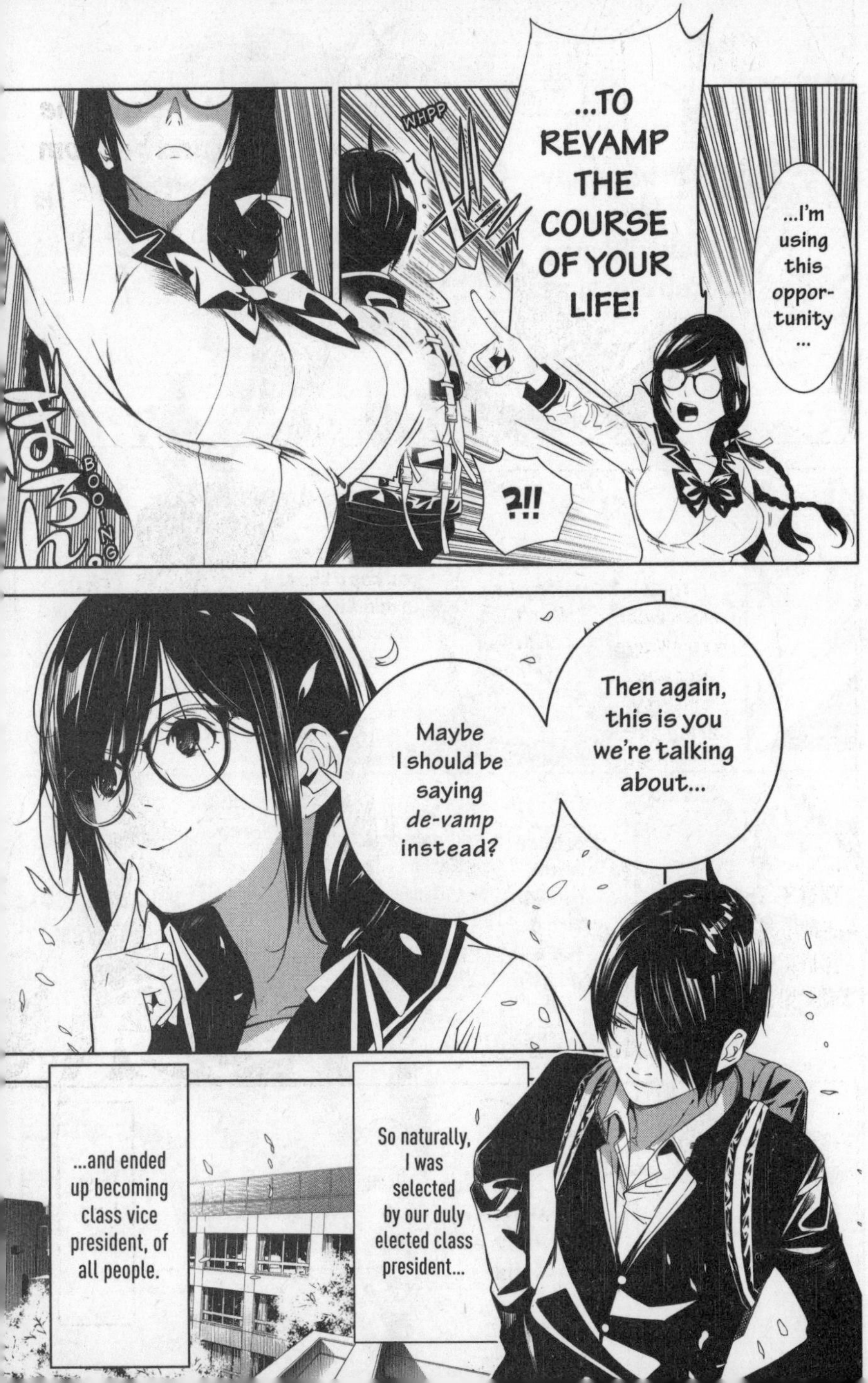
...I'm using this opportunity...
...TO REVAMP THE COURSE OF YOUR LIFE!
WHPP
?!!
BOOING
まろん
Then again, this is you we're talking about...
Maybe I should be saying *de-vamp* instead?
So naturally, I was selected by our duly elected class president...
...and ended up becoming class vice president, of all people.

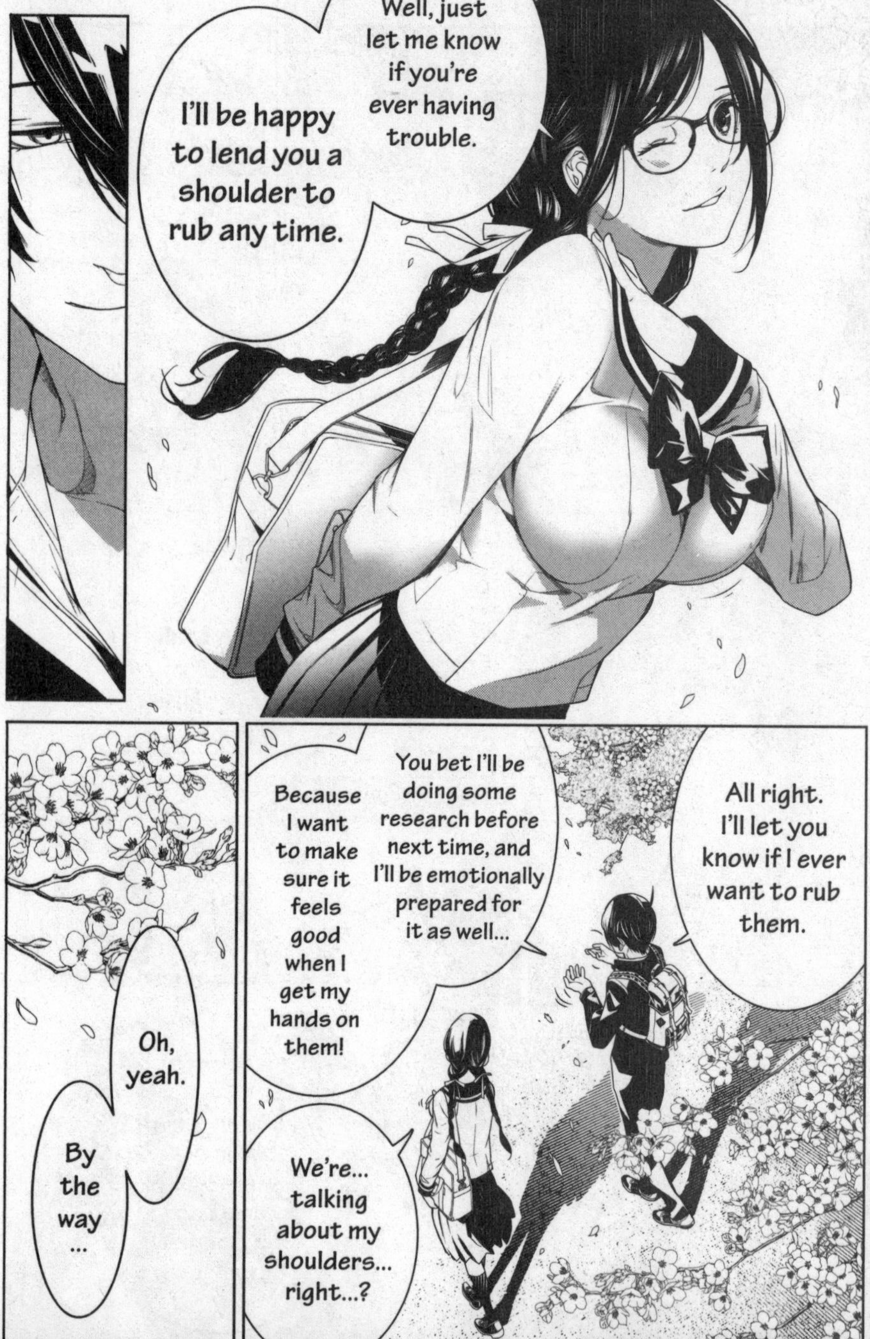
Well, just let me know if you're ever having trouble.
I'll be happy to lend you a shoulder to rub any time.
All right. I'll let you know if I ever want to rub them.
You bet I'll be doing some research before next time, and I'll be emotionally prepared for it as well...
Because I want to make sure it feels good when I get my hands on them!
We're... talking about my shoulders... right...?
Oh, yeah.
By the way ...

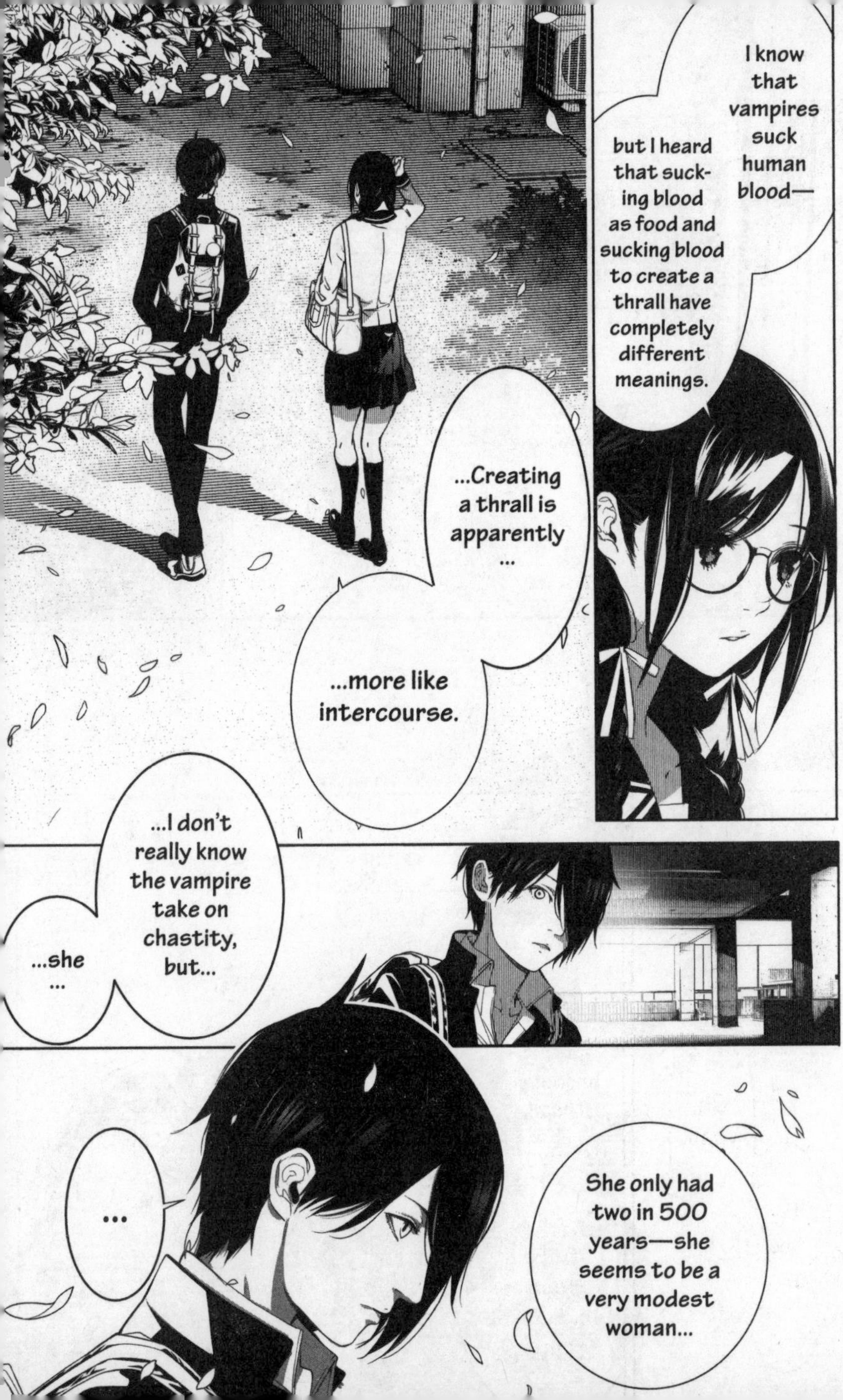
I know that vampires suck human blood—
but I heard that sucking blood as food and sucking blood to create a thrall have completely different meanings.
...Creating a thrall is apparently ...
...more like intercourse.
...I don't really know the vampire take on chastity, but...
...she ...
She only had two in 500 years—she seems to be a very modest woman...
...

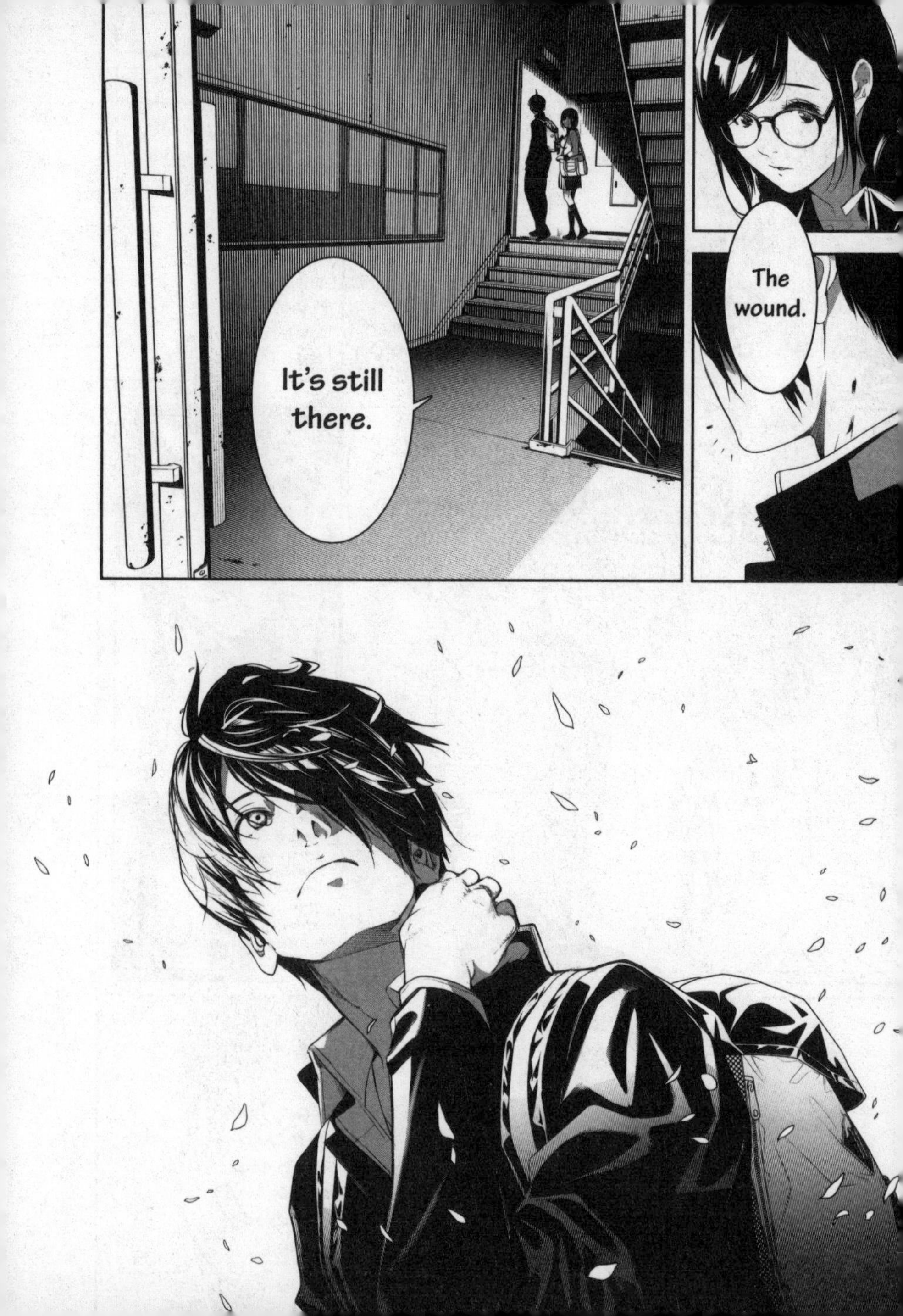
The wound.
It's still there.

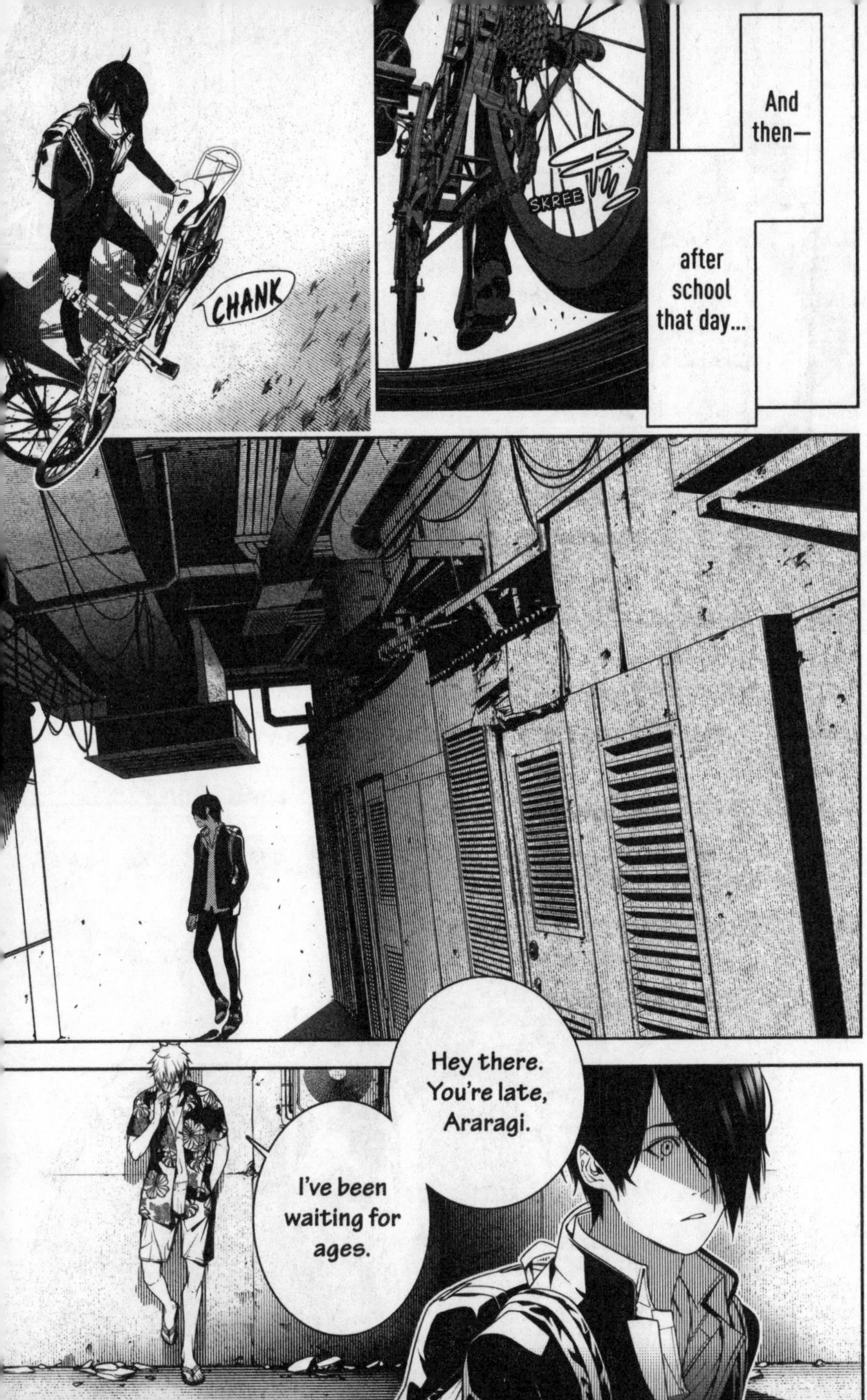
And then—
after school that day...
SKREE
CHANK
Hey there. You're late, Araragi.
I've been waiting for ages.

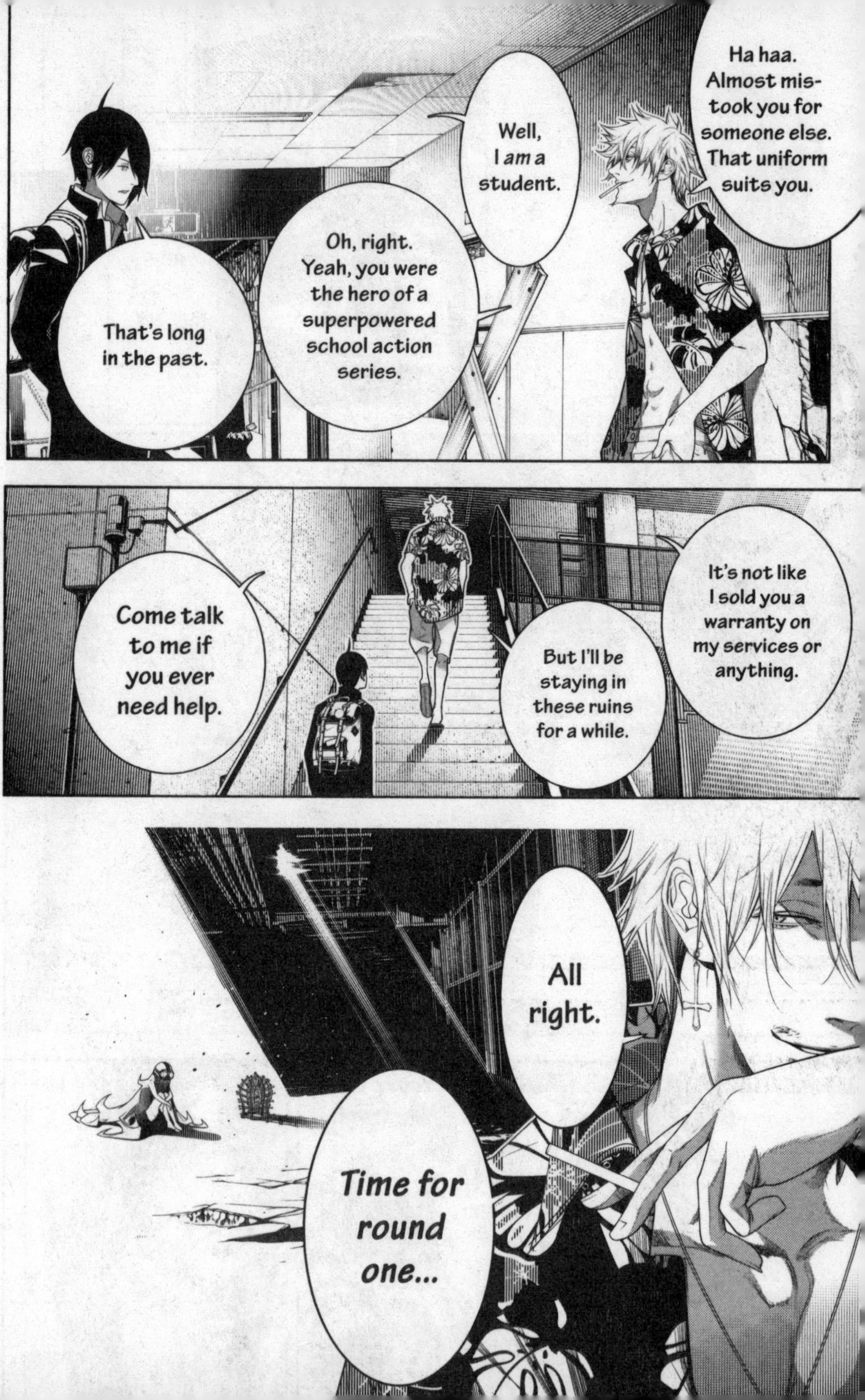
Ha haa. Almost mis-took you for someone else. That uniform suits you.
Well, I *am* a student.
Oh, right. Yeah, you were the hero of a superpowered school action series.
That's long in the past.
It's not like I sold you a warranty on my services or anything.
But I'll be staying in these ruins for a while.
Come talk to me if you ever need help.
All right.
Time for round one...

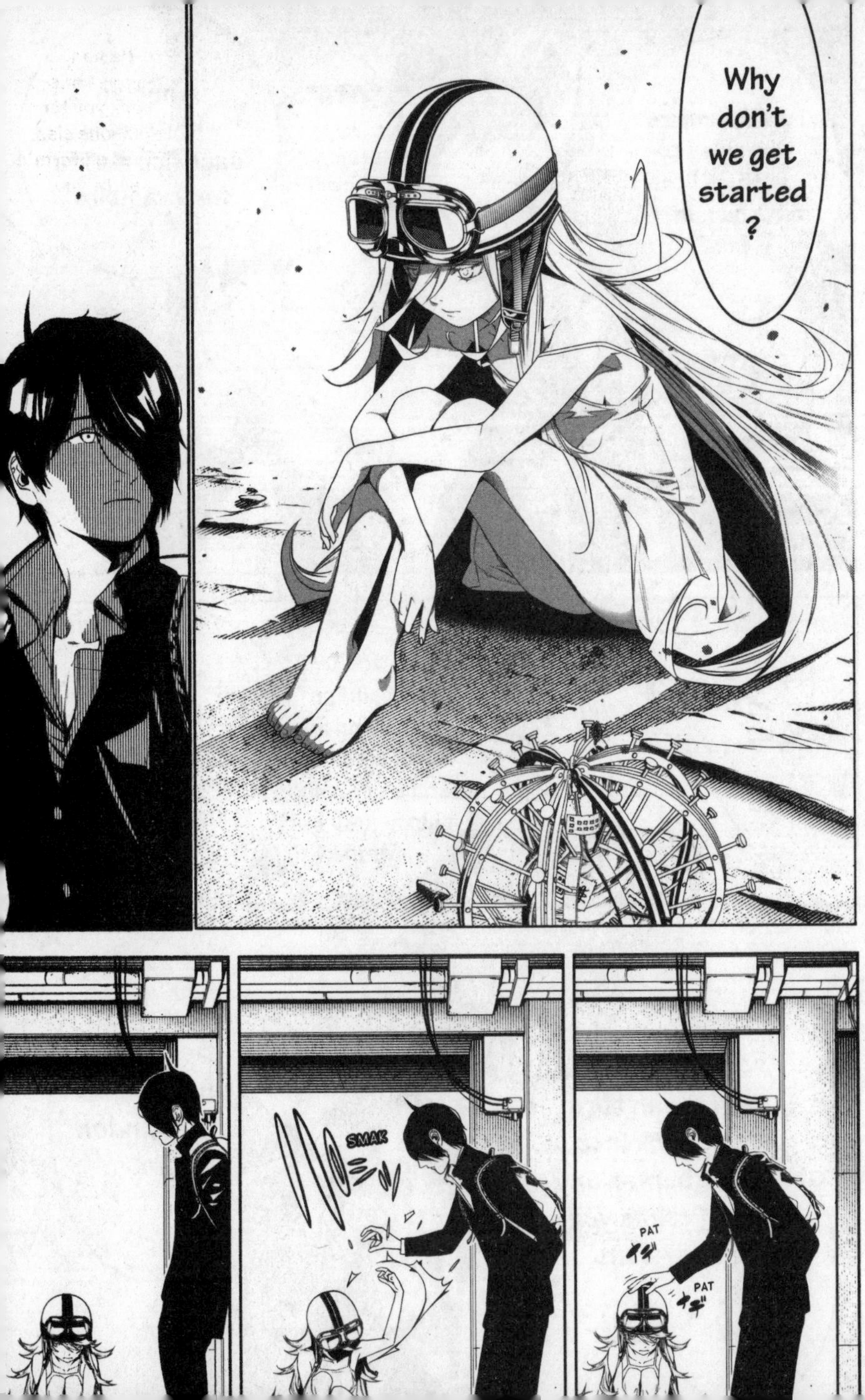
Why don't we get started ?
PAT
PAT
SMAK

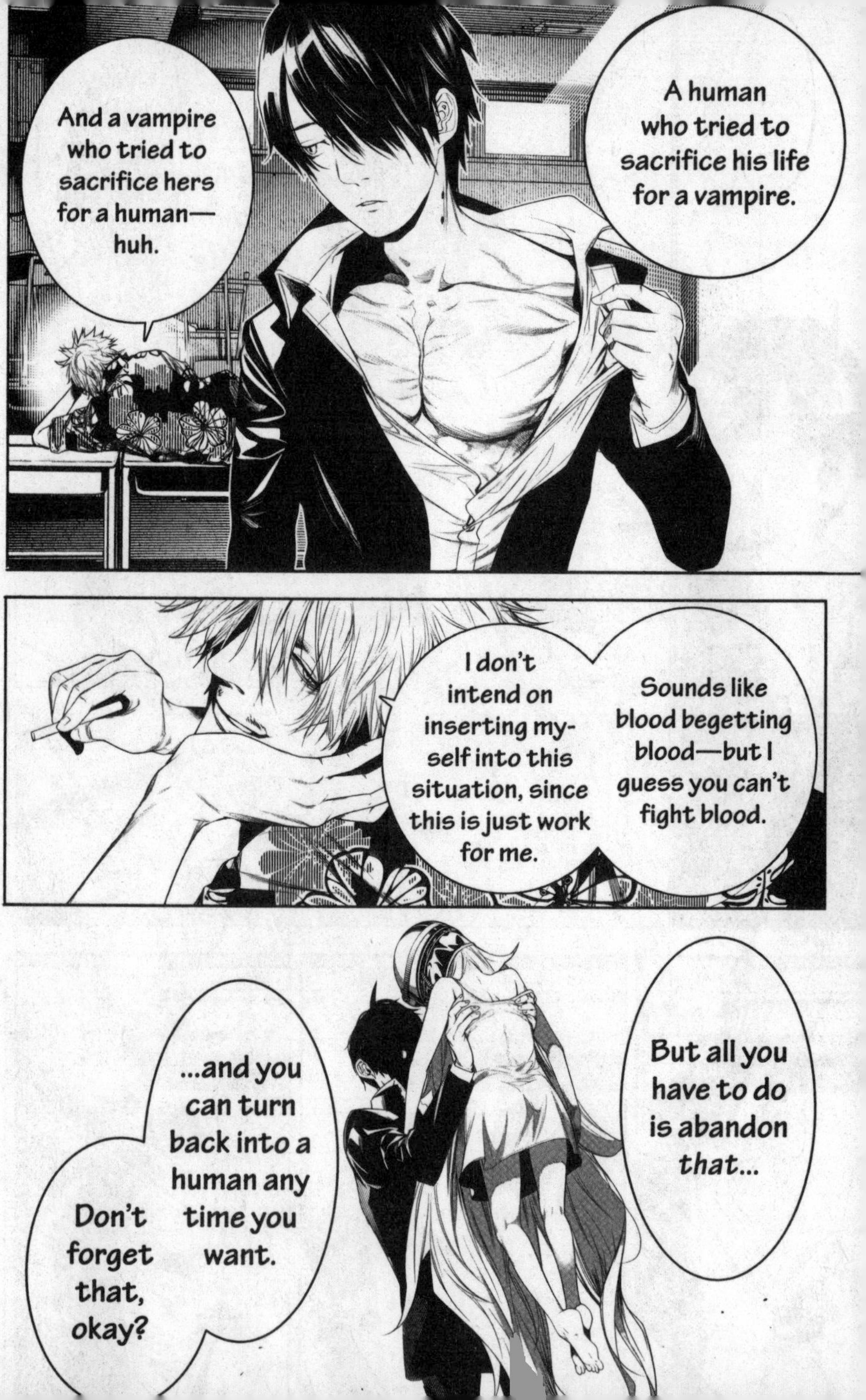
A human who tried to sacrifice his life for a vampire.
And a vampire who tried to sacrifice hers for a human—huh.
Sounds like blood begetting blood—but I guess you can't fight blood.
I don't intend on inserting my-self into this situation, since this is just work for me.
But all you have to do is abandon *that*...
...and you can turn back into a human any time you want.
Don't forget that, okay?

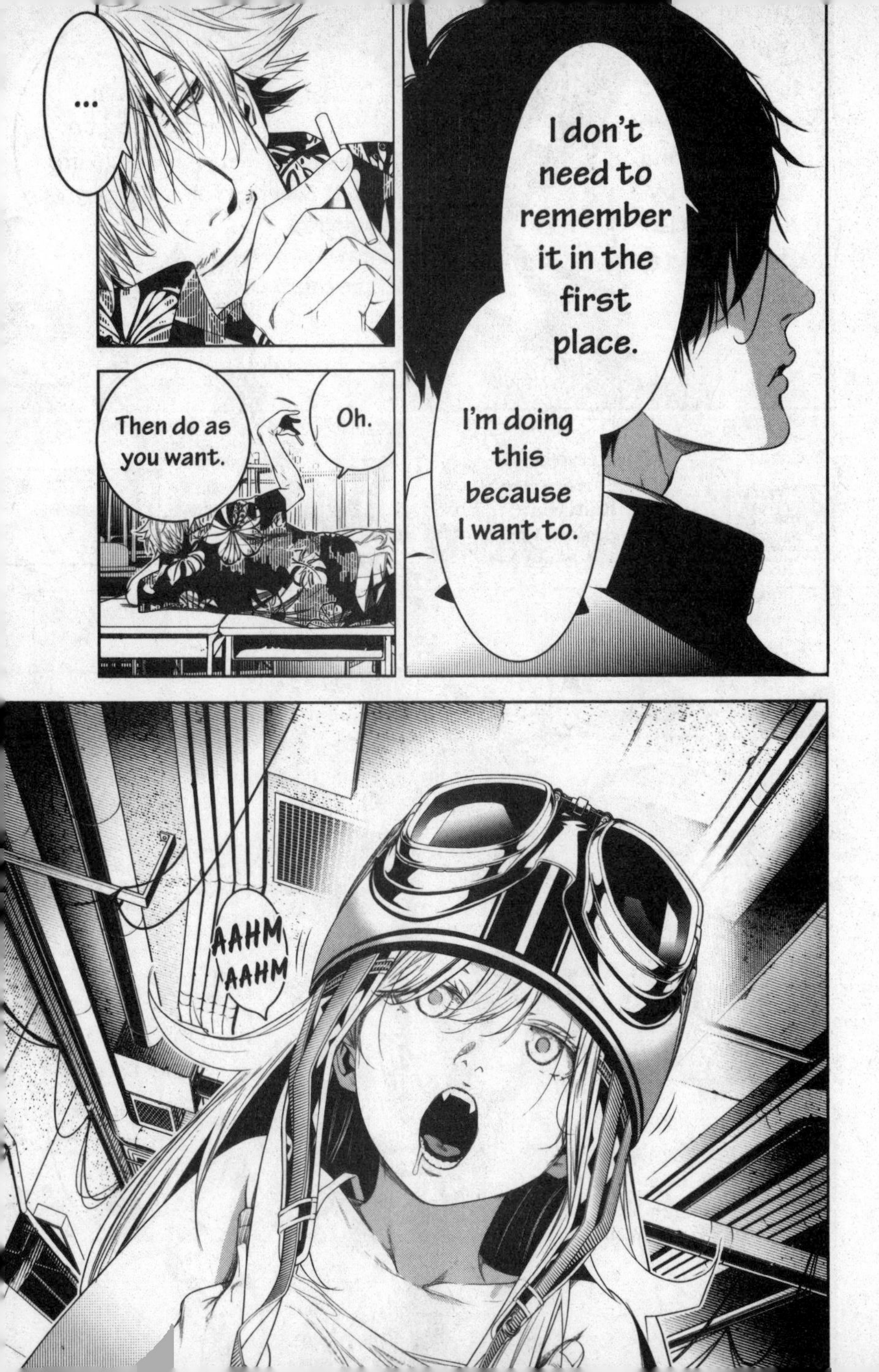
I don't need to remember it in the first place.
I'm doing this because I want to.
...
Oh.
Then do as you want.
AAHM AAHM

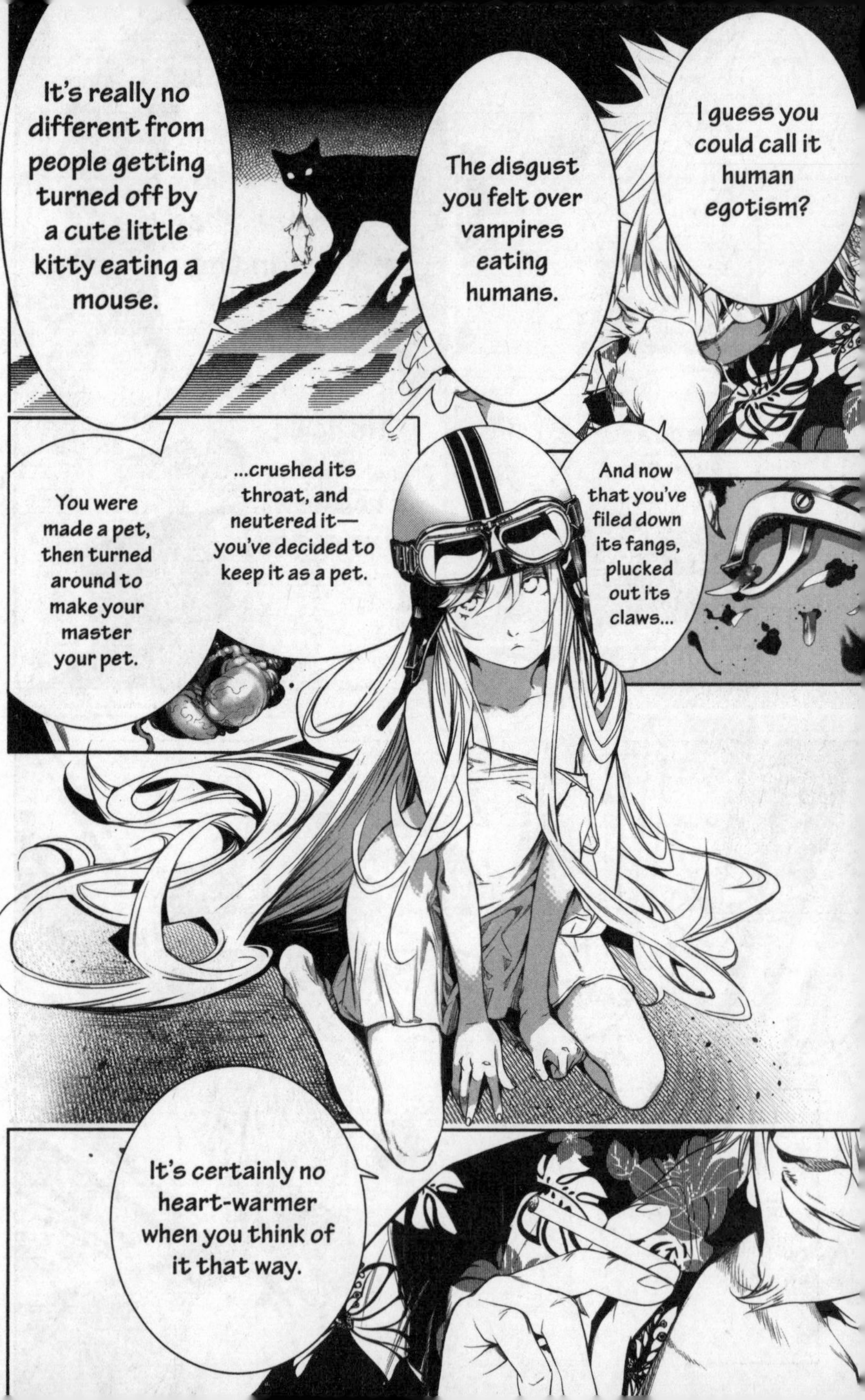
I guess you could call it human egotism?
The disgust you felt over vampires eating humans.
It's really no different from people getting turned off by a cute little kitty eating a mouse.
And now that you've filed down its fangs, plucked out its claws...
...crushed its throat, and neutered it—you've decided to keep it as a pet.
You were made a pet, then turned around to make your master your pet.
It's certainly no heart-warmer when you think of it that way.

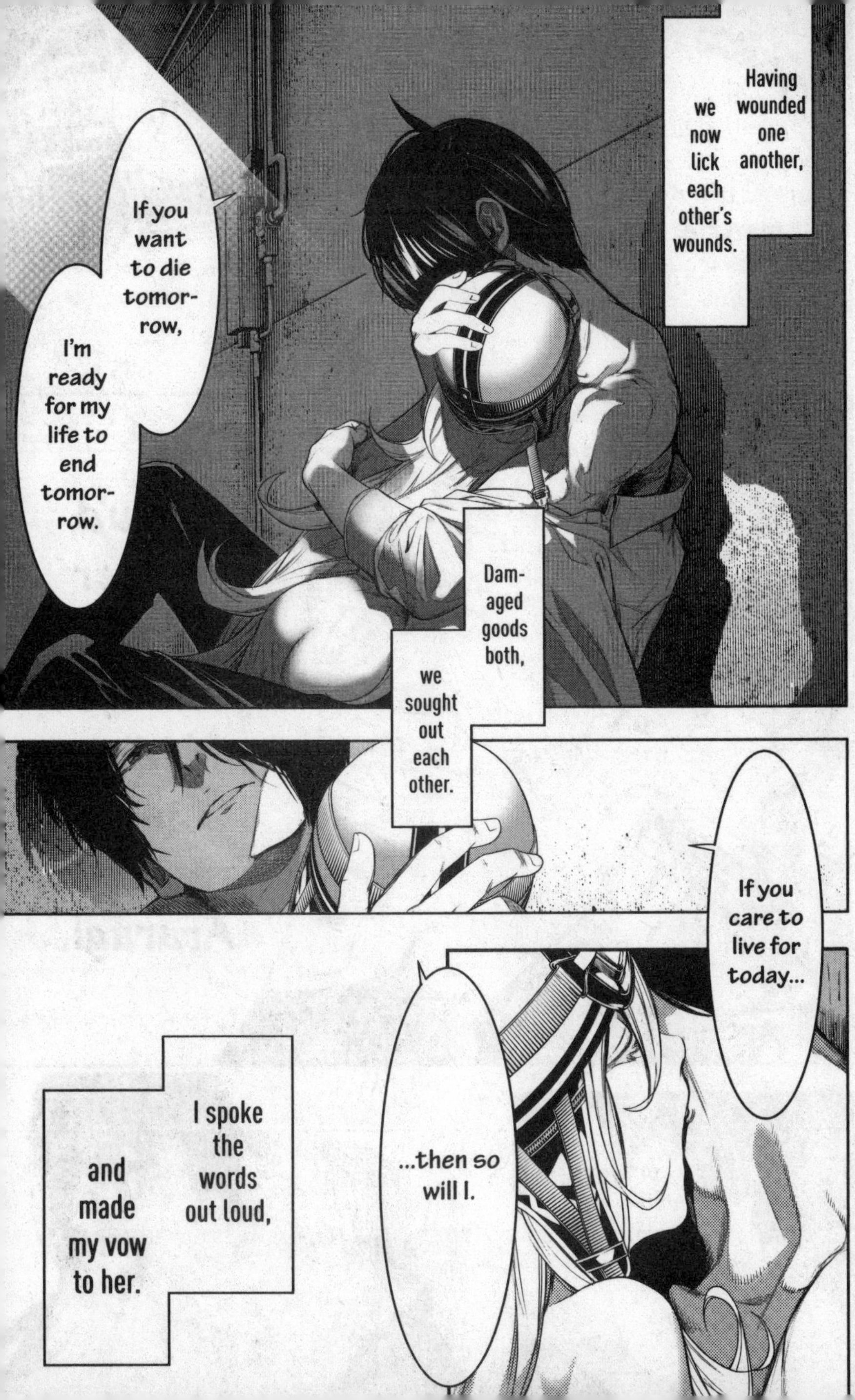
Having wounded one another, we now lick each other's wounds.
If you want to die tomor-row, I'm ready for my life to end tomor-row.
Dam-aged goods both, we sought out each other.
If you care to live for today...
...then so will I.
I spoke the words out loud, and made my vow to her.

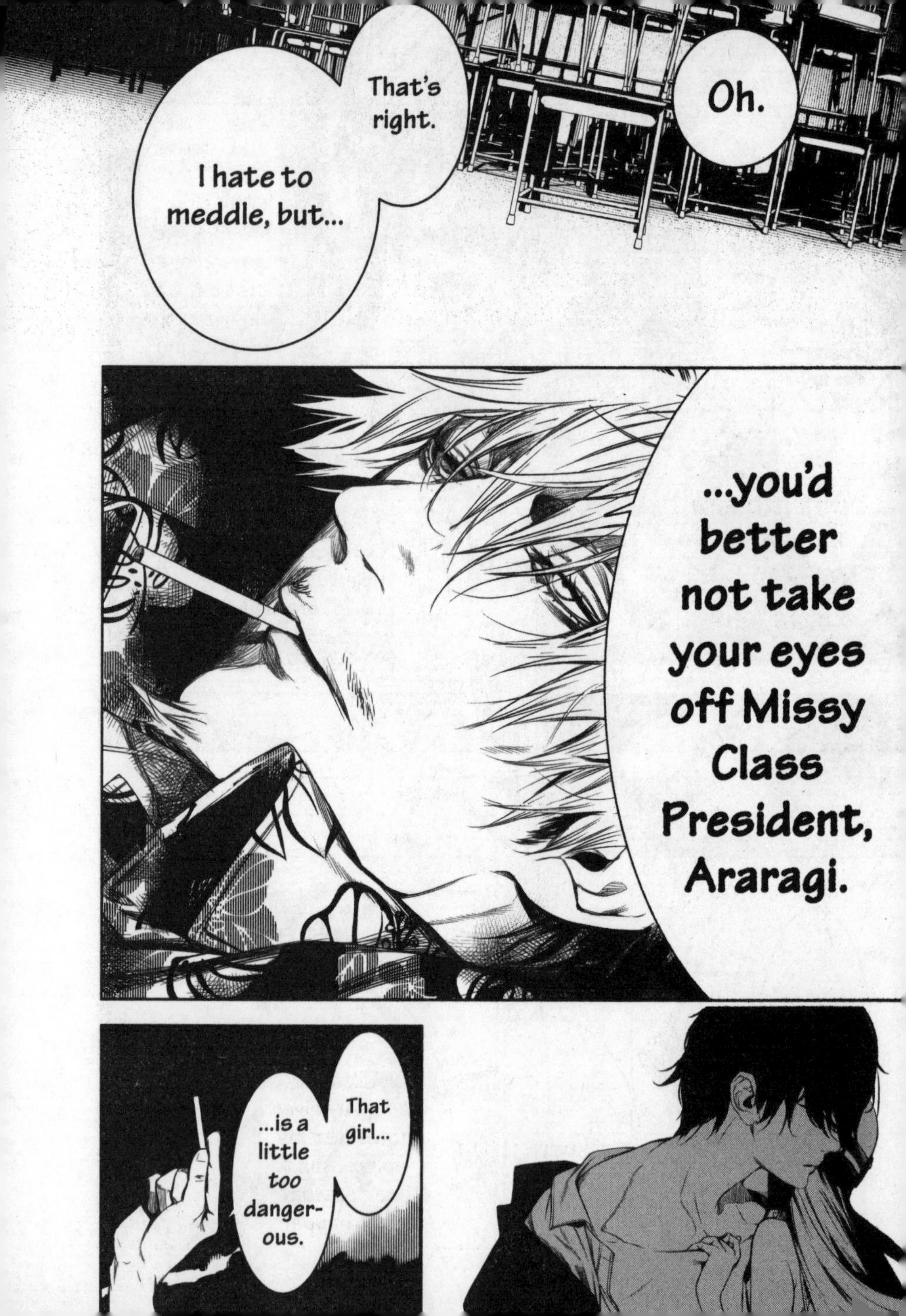
Oh.
That's right.
I hate to meddle, but...
...you'd better not take your eyes off Missy Class President, Araragi.
That girl...
...is a little too dangerous.

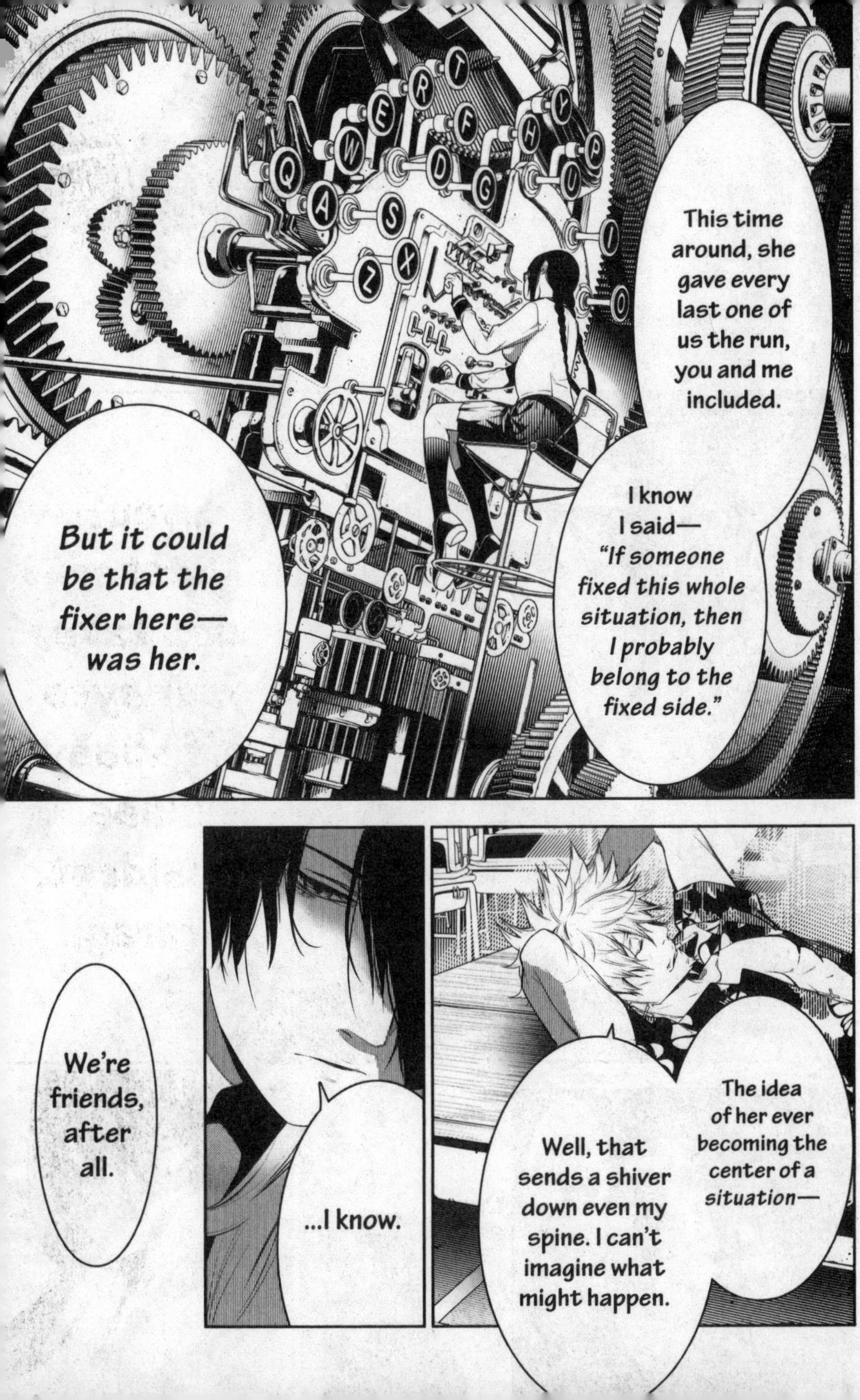
This time around, she gave every last one of us the run, you and me included.
I know I said— "If someone fixed this whole situation, then I probably belong to the fixed side."
But it could be that the fixer here— was her.
The idea of her ever becoming the center of a *situation*—
Well, that sends a shiver down even my spine. I can't imagine what might happen.
...I know.
We're friends, after all.

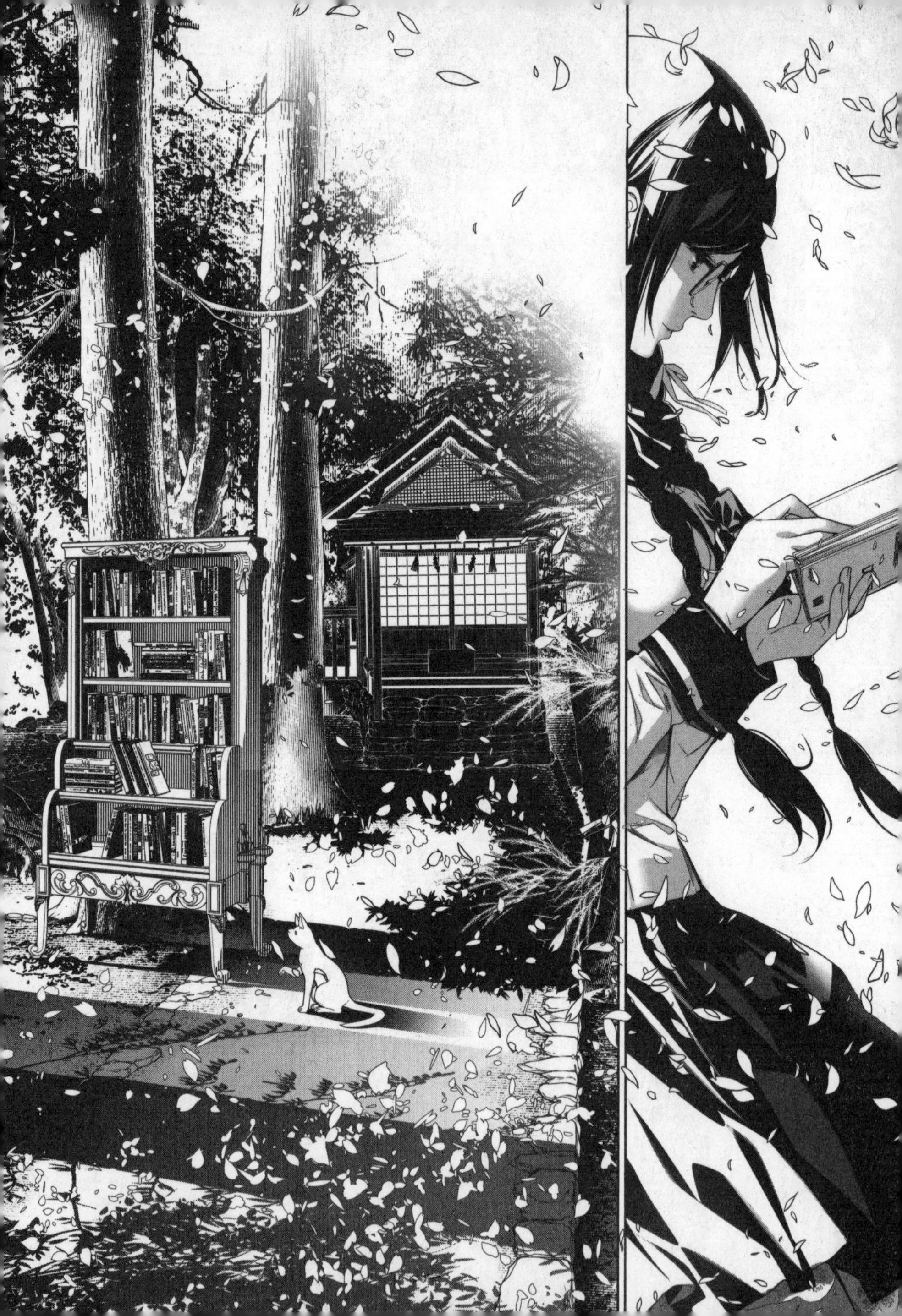

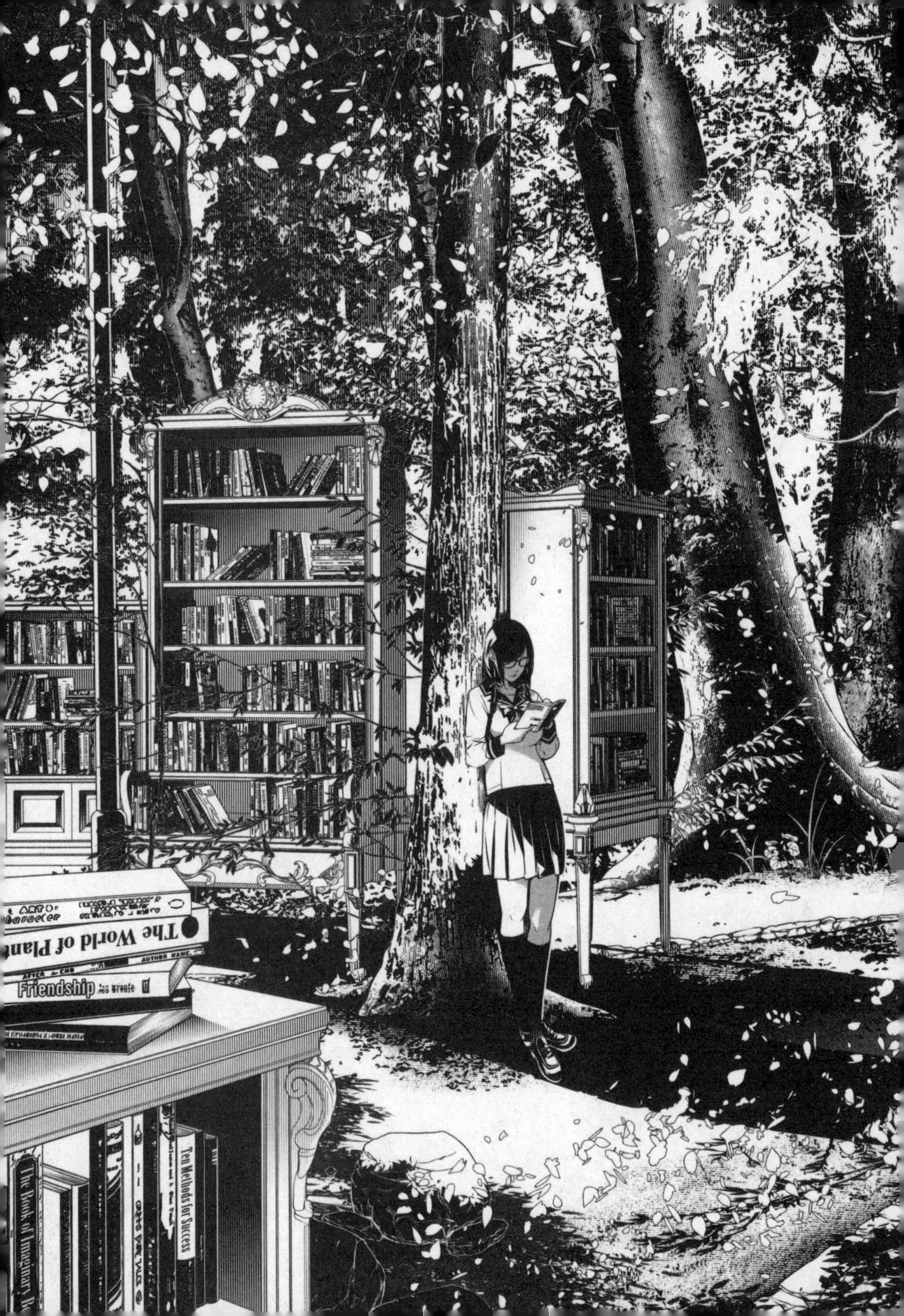

The World of Plan
AUTHOR NAME
Friendship
Ten Methods for Success
The Book of Imaginary B

BAKEMONOGATARI

0 5 : Tsubasa Cat

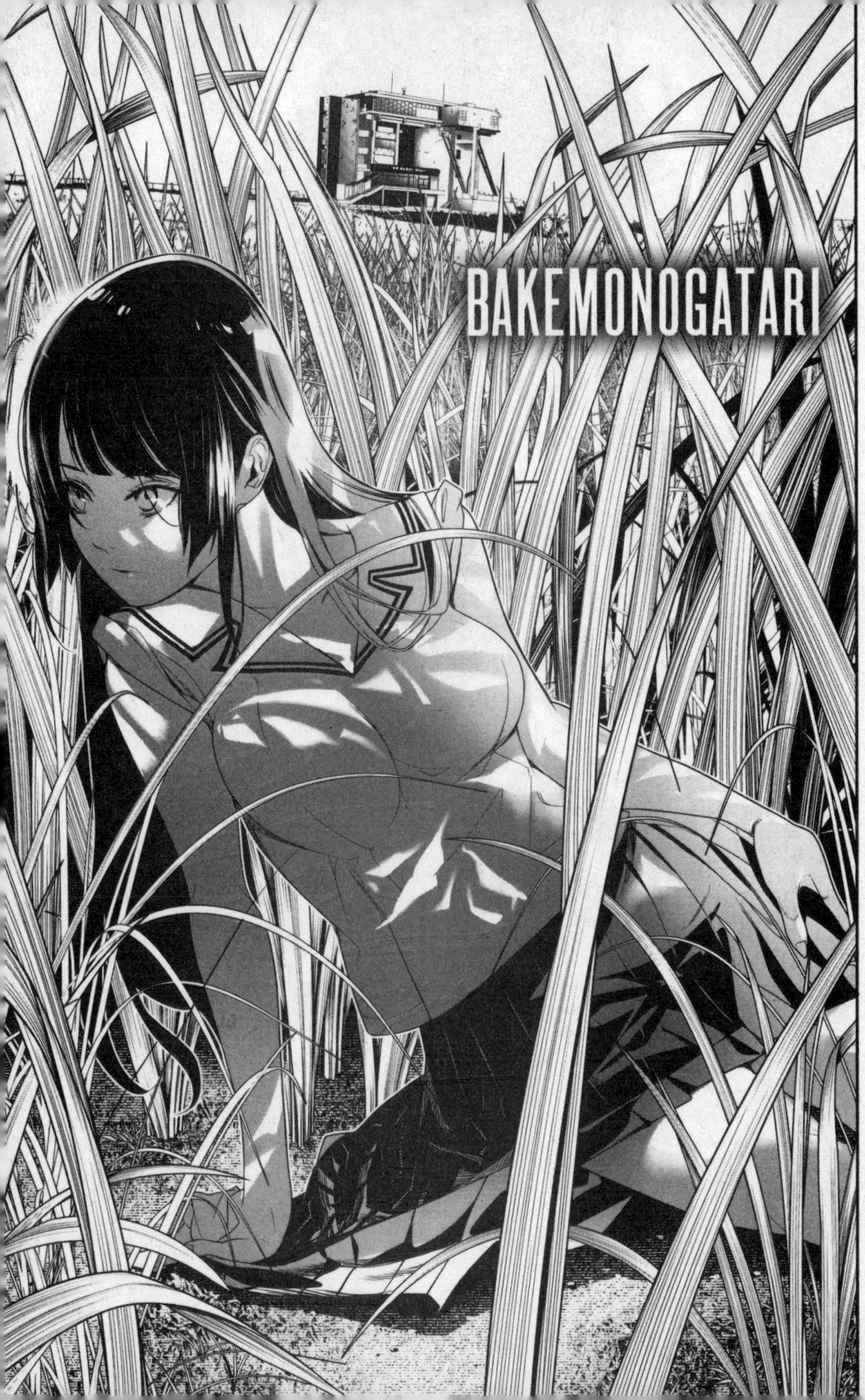
BAKEMONOGATARI

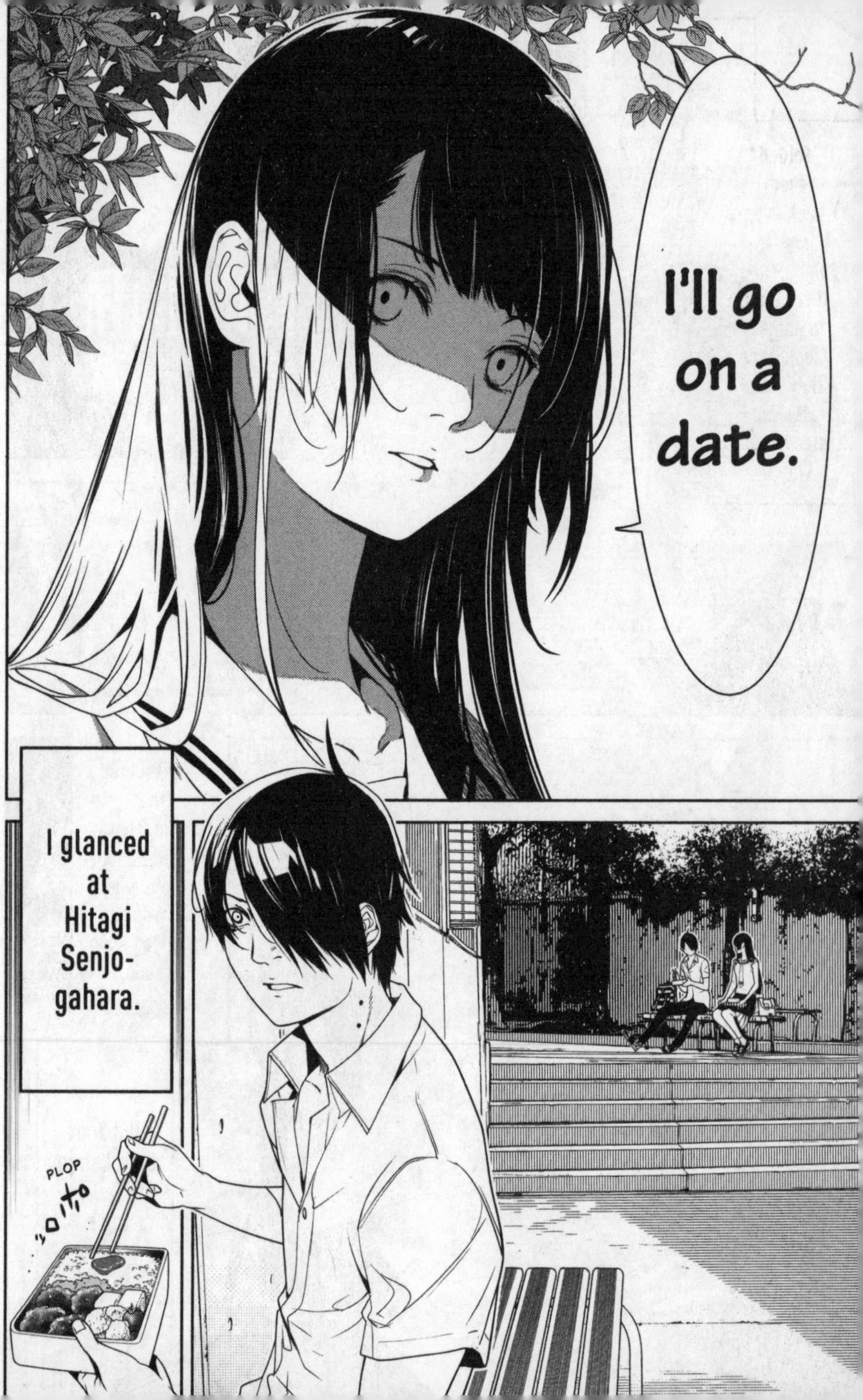
I'll go on a date.
I glanced at Hitagi Senjo-gahara.
PLOP

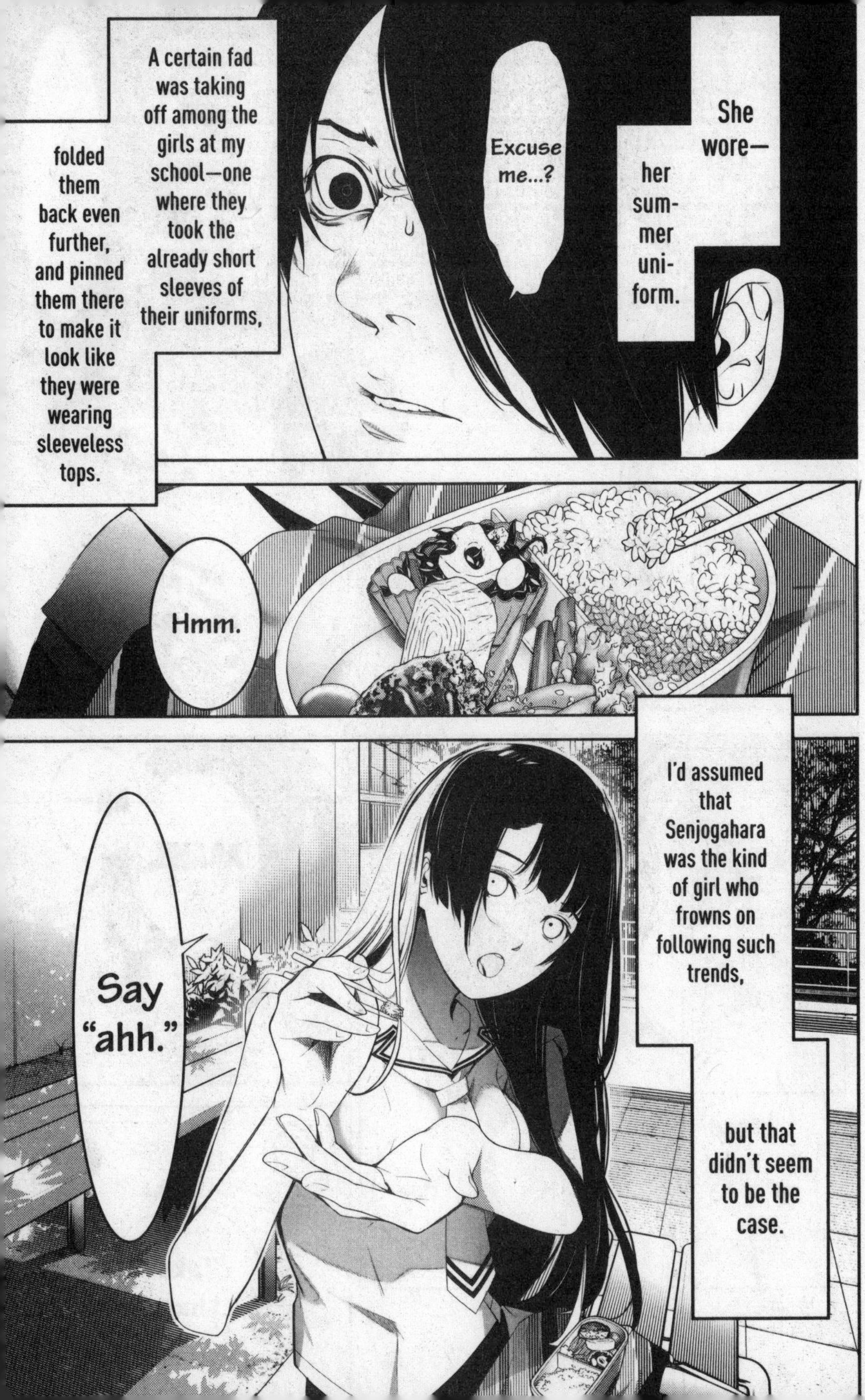
She wore—
her summer uniform.
Excuse me...?
A certain fad was taking off among the girls at my school—one where they took the already short sleeves of their uniforms,
folded them back even further, and pinned them there to make it look like they were wearing sleeveless tops.
Hmm.
I'd assumed that Senjogahara was the kind of girl who frowns on following such trends,
but that didn't seem to be the case.
Say "ahh."

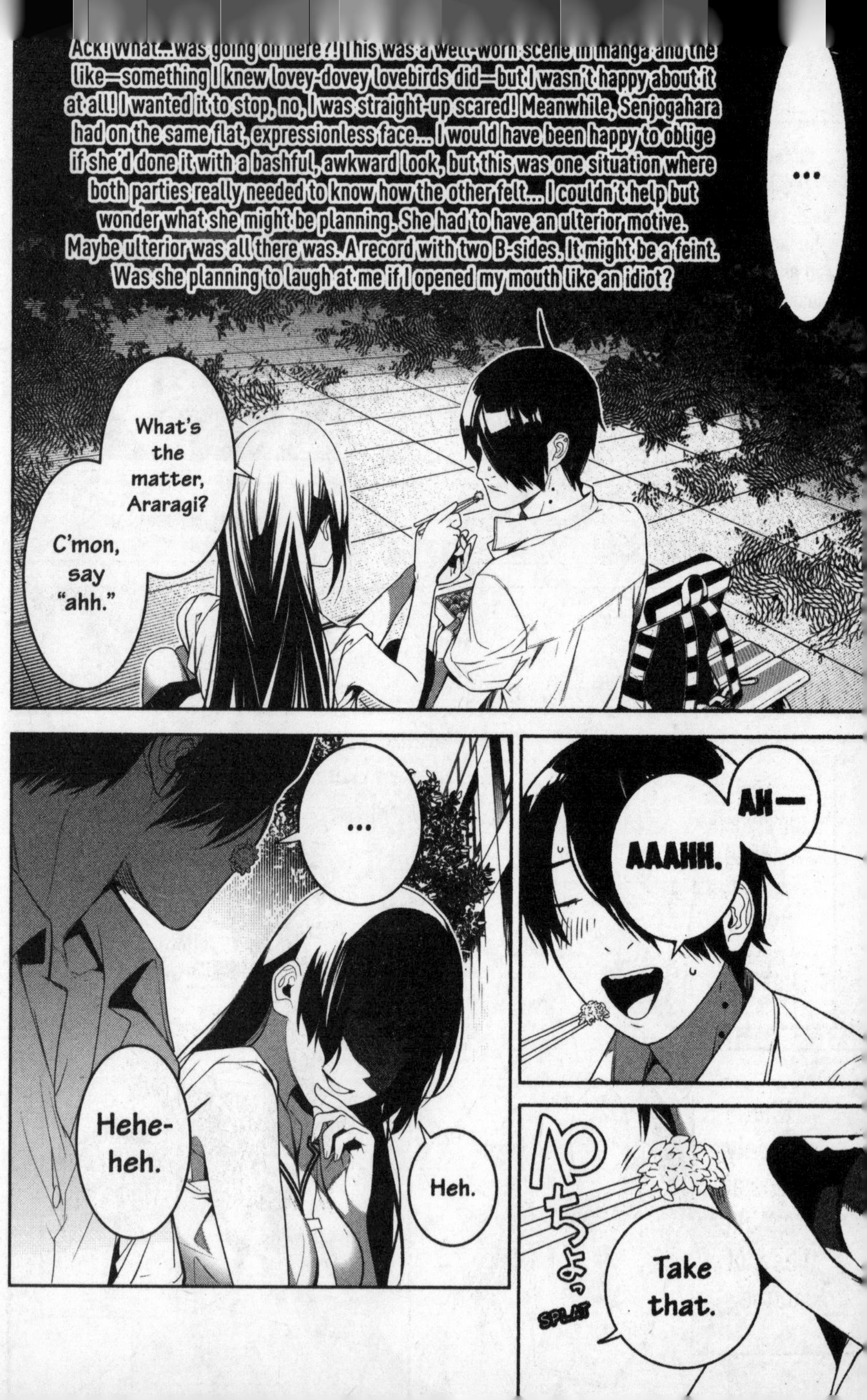
...
Ack! What...was going on here?! This was a well-worn scene in manga and the like—something I knew lovey-dovey lovebirds did—but I wasn't happy about it at all! I wanted it to stop, no, I was straight-up scared! Meanwhile, Senjogahara had on the same flat, expressionless face... I would have been happy to oblige if she'd done it with a bashful, awkward look, but this was one situation where both parties really needed to know how the other felt... I couldn't help but wonder what she might be planning. She had to have an ulterior motive. Maybe ulterior was all there was. A record with two B-sides. It might be a feint. Was she planning to laugh at me if I opened my mouth like an idiot?
What's the matter, Araragi?
C'mon, say "ahh."
AH— AAAHH.
Take that.
SPLAT
...
Heh.
Hehe-heh.

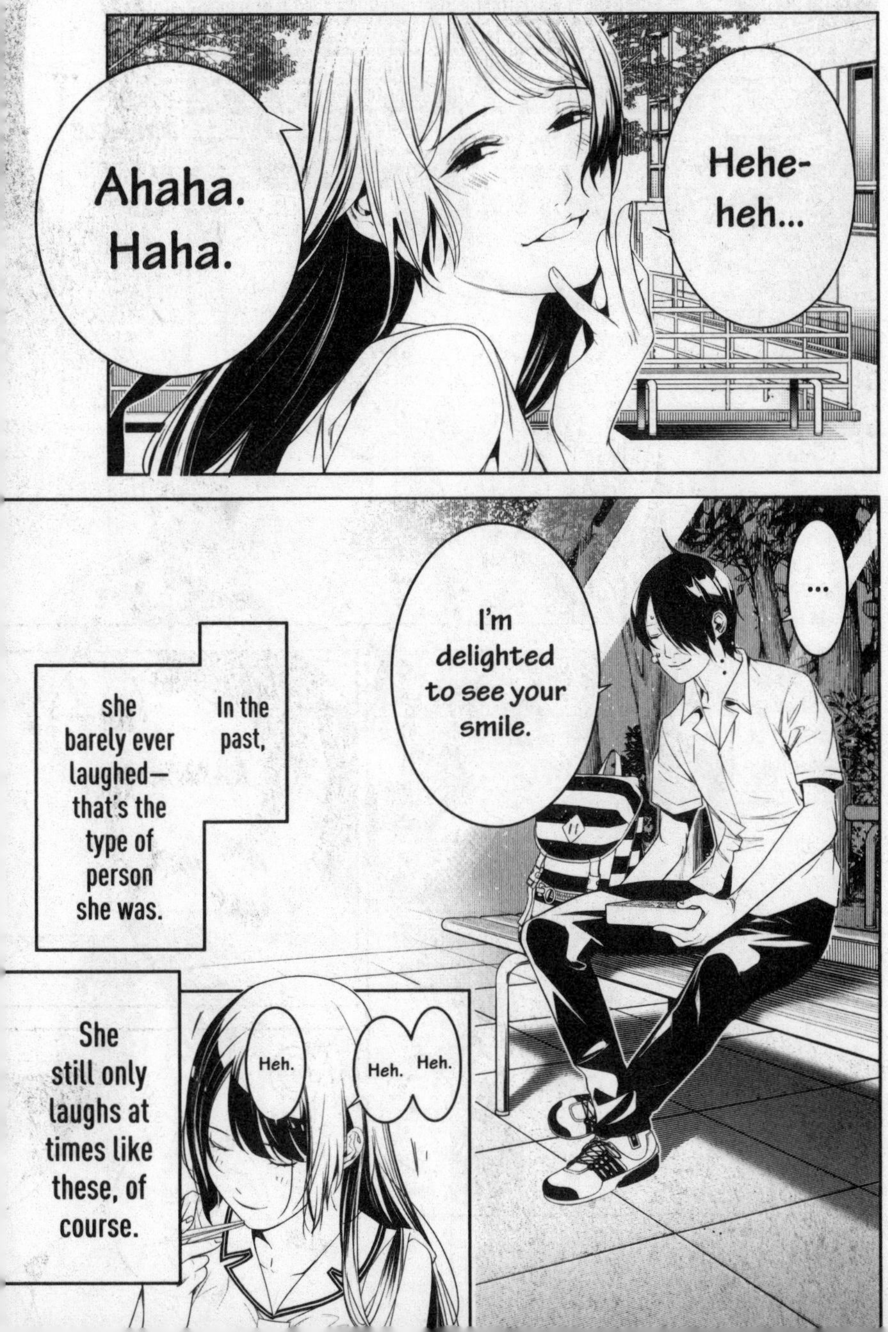

Hehe-heh...
Ahaha. Haha.
...
I'm delighted to see your smile.
In the past, she barely ever laughed—that's the type of person she was.
Heh. Heh.
Heh.
She still only laughs at times like these, of course.

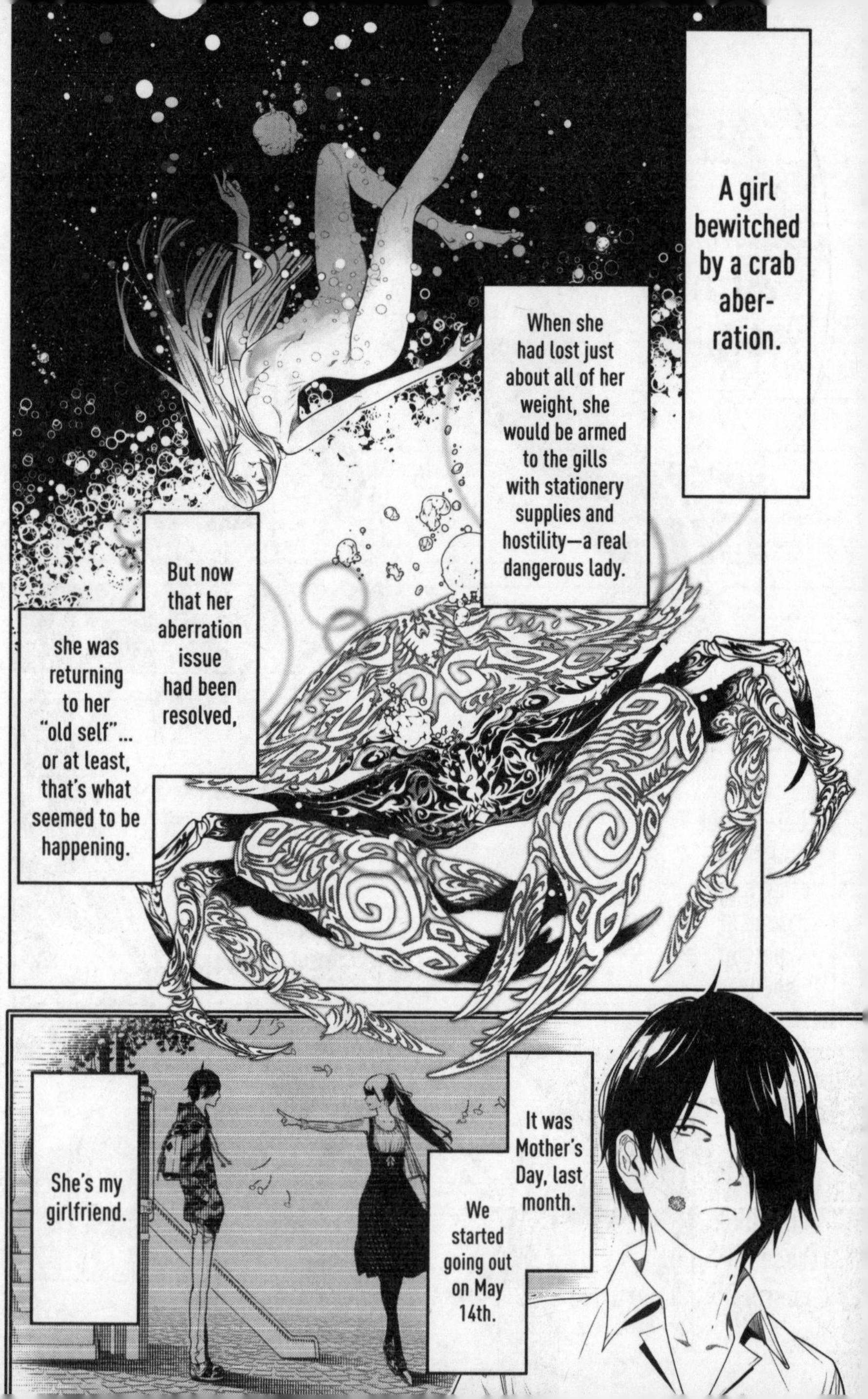
A girl bewitched by a crab aber-ration.
When she had lost just about all of her weight, she would be armed to the gills with stationery supplies and hostility—a real dangerous lady.
But now that her aberration issue had been resolved,
she was returning to her "old self"... or at least, that's what seemed to be happening.
It was Mother's Day, last month.
We started going out on May 14th.
She's my girlfriend.

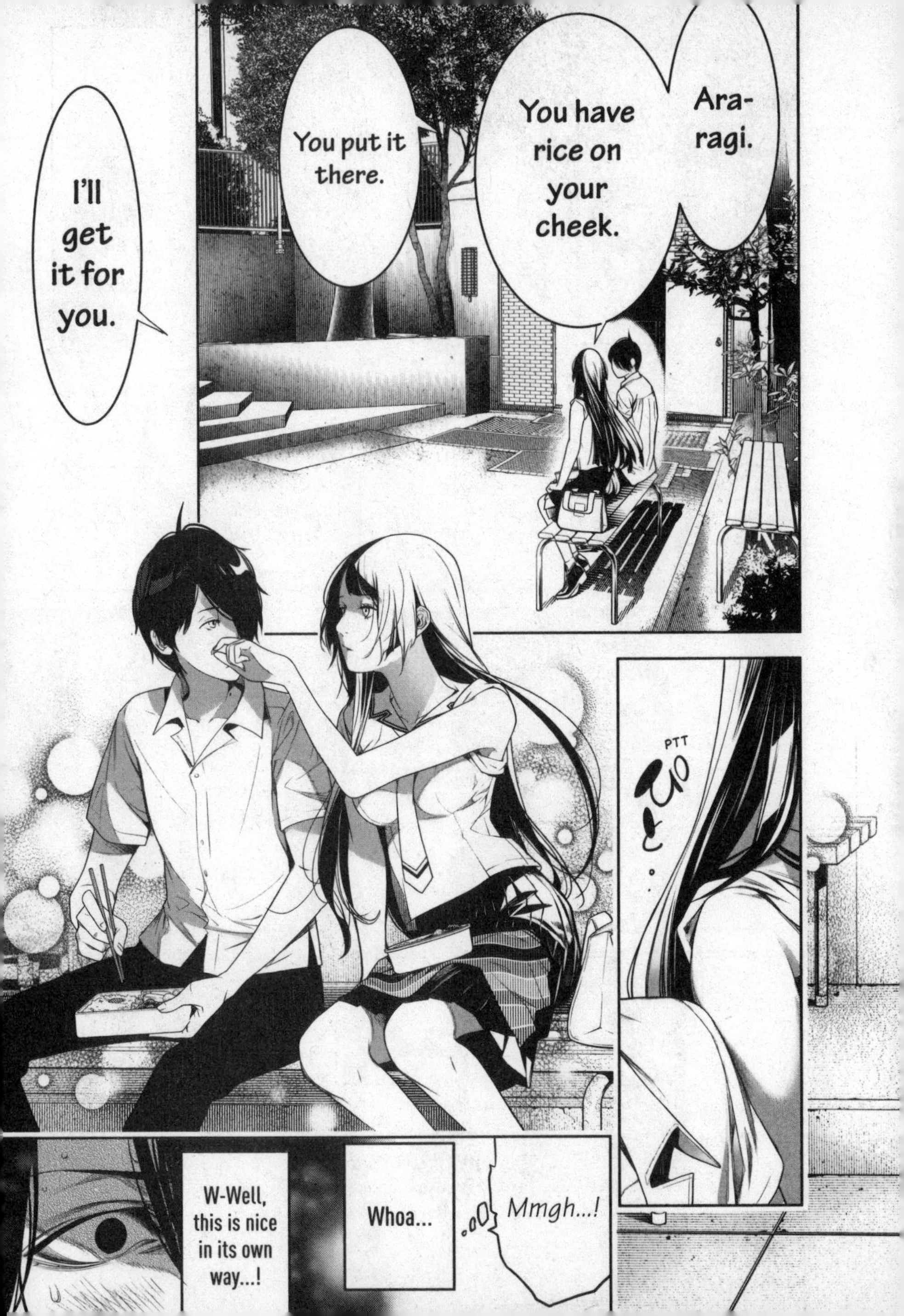
Ara-ragi.
You have rice on your cheek.
You put it there.
I'll get it for you.
PTT
Mmgh...!
Whoa...
W-Well, this is nice in its own way...!

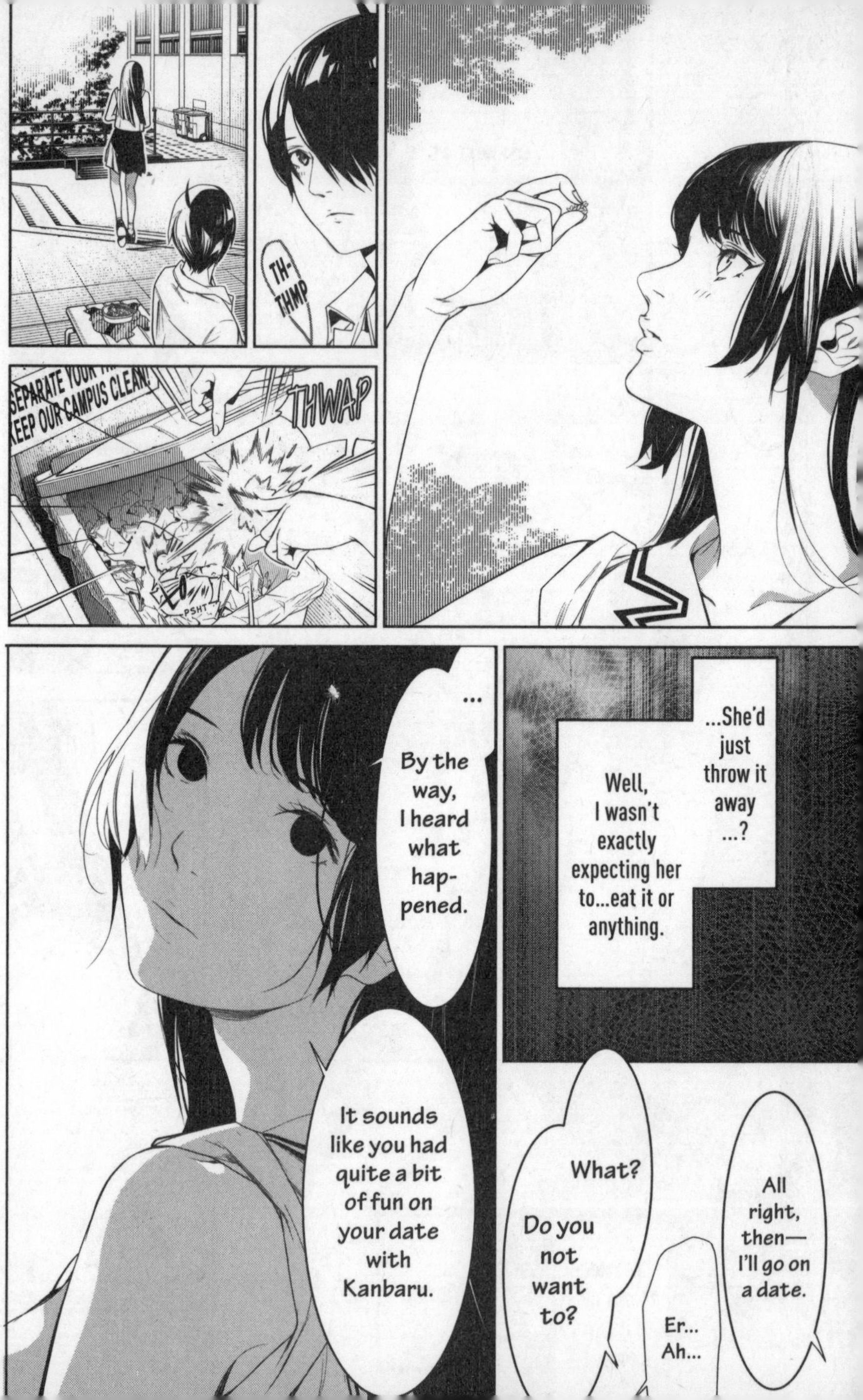
TH-THMP
SEPARATE YOUR
KEEP OUR CAMPUS CLEAN!
THWAP
PSHT
...She'd just throw it away...?
Well, I wasn't exactly expecting her to...eat it or anything.
All right, then— I'll go on a date.
Er... Ah...
What?
Do you not want to?
...
By the way, I heard what happened.
It sounds like you had quite a bit of fun on your date with Kanbaru.

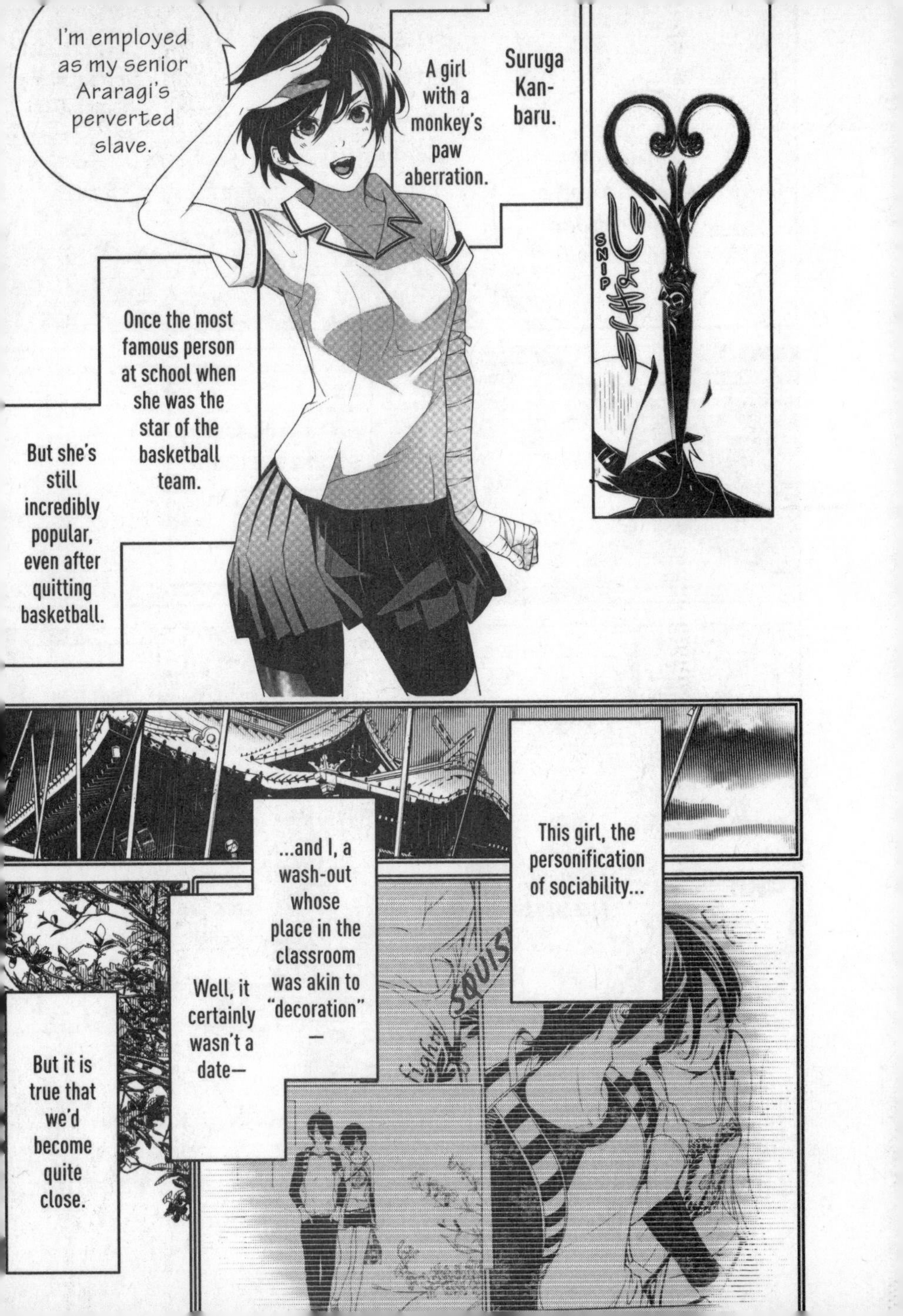
SNIP
Suruga Kan-baru.
A girl with a monkey's paw aberration.
I'm employed as my senior Araragi's perverted slave.
Once the most famous person at school when she was the star of the basketball team.
But she's still incredibly popular, even after quitting basketball.
This girl, the personification of sociability...
...and I, a wash-out whose place in the classroom was akin to "decoration" —
SQUIS
Well, it certainly wasn't a date—
But it is true that we'd become quite close.

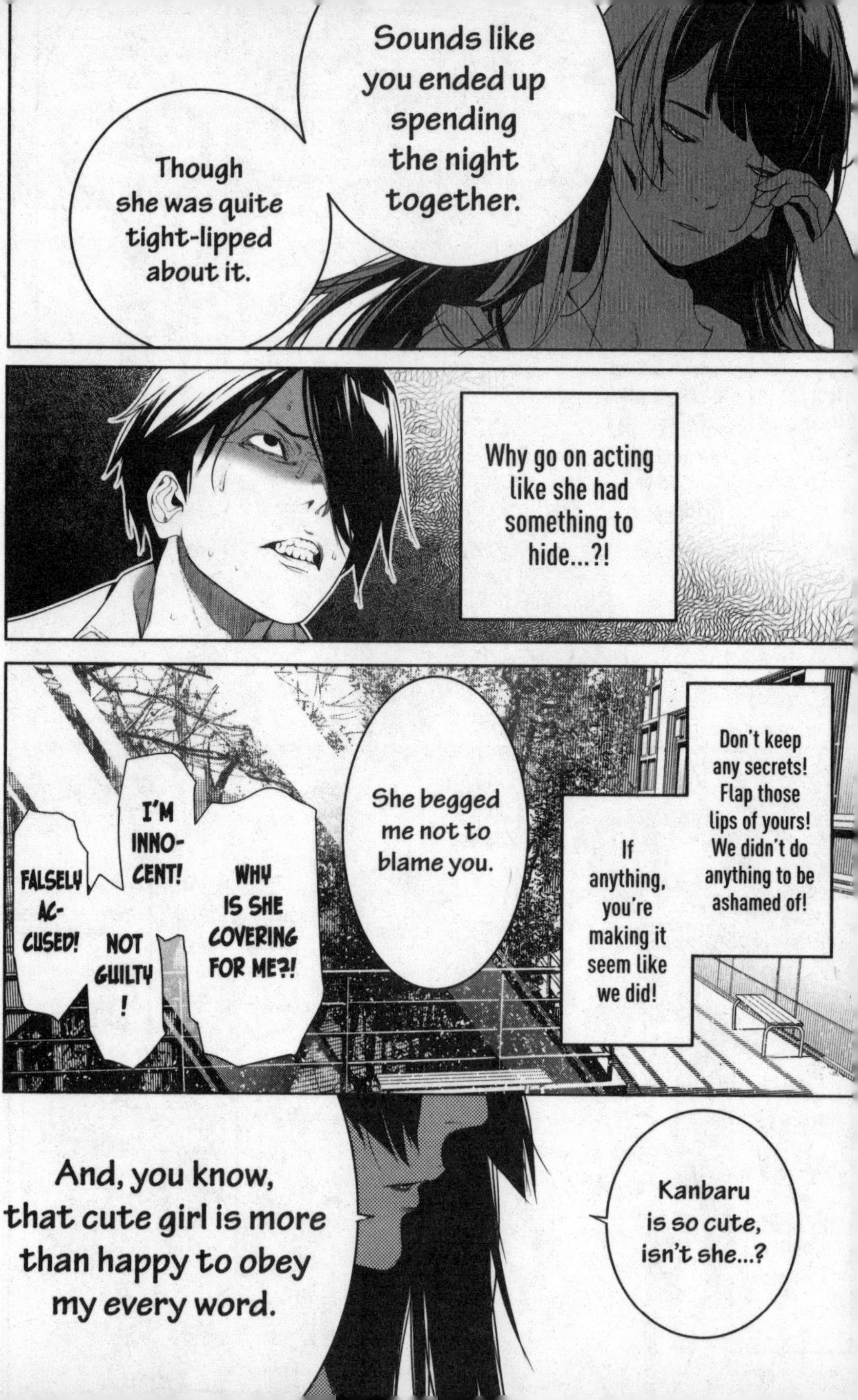
Sounds like you ended up spending the night together.
Though she was quite tight-lipped about it.
Why go on acting like she had something to hide...?!
Don't keep any secrets! Flap those lips of yours! We didn't do anything to be ashamed of!
If anything, you're making it seem like we did!
She begged me not to blame you.
WHY IS SHE COVERING FOR ME?!
I'M INNO-CENT!
NOT GUILTY!
FALSELY AC-CUSED!
Kanbaru is so cute, isn't she...?
And, you know, that cute girl is more than happy to obey my every word.

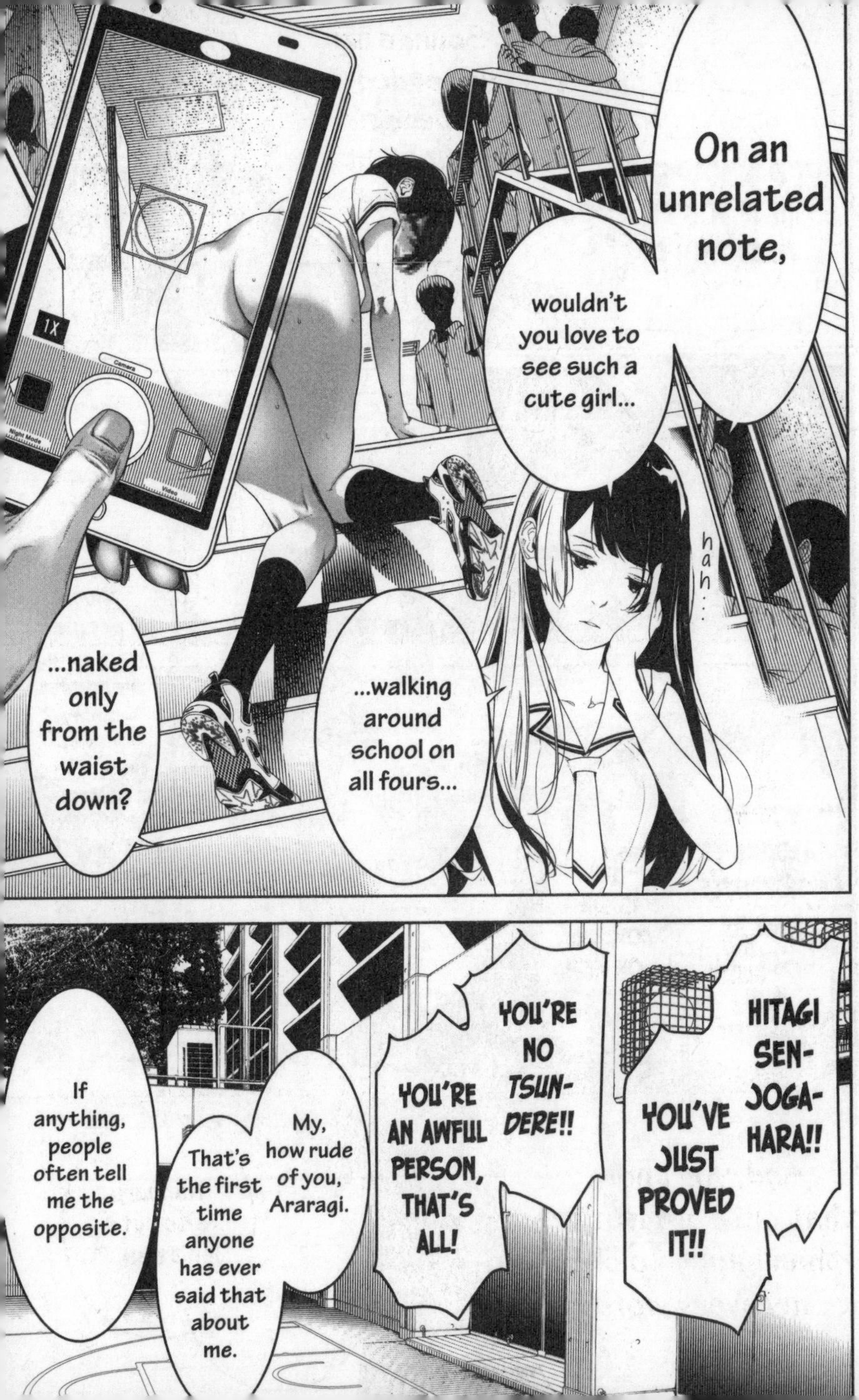
On an unrelated note,
wouldn't you love to see such a cute girl...
hah...
...walking around school on all fours...
...naked only from the waist down?
HITAGI SENJOGAHARA!!
YOU'VE JUST PROVED IT!!
YOU'RE NO TSUNDERE!!
YOU'RE AN AWFUL PERSON, THAT'S ALL!
My, how rude of you, Araragi.
That's the first time anyone has ever said that about me.
If anything, people often tell me the opposite.

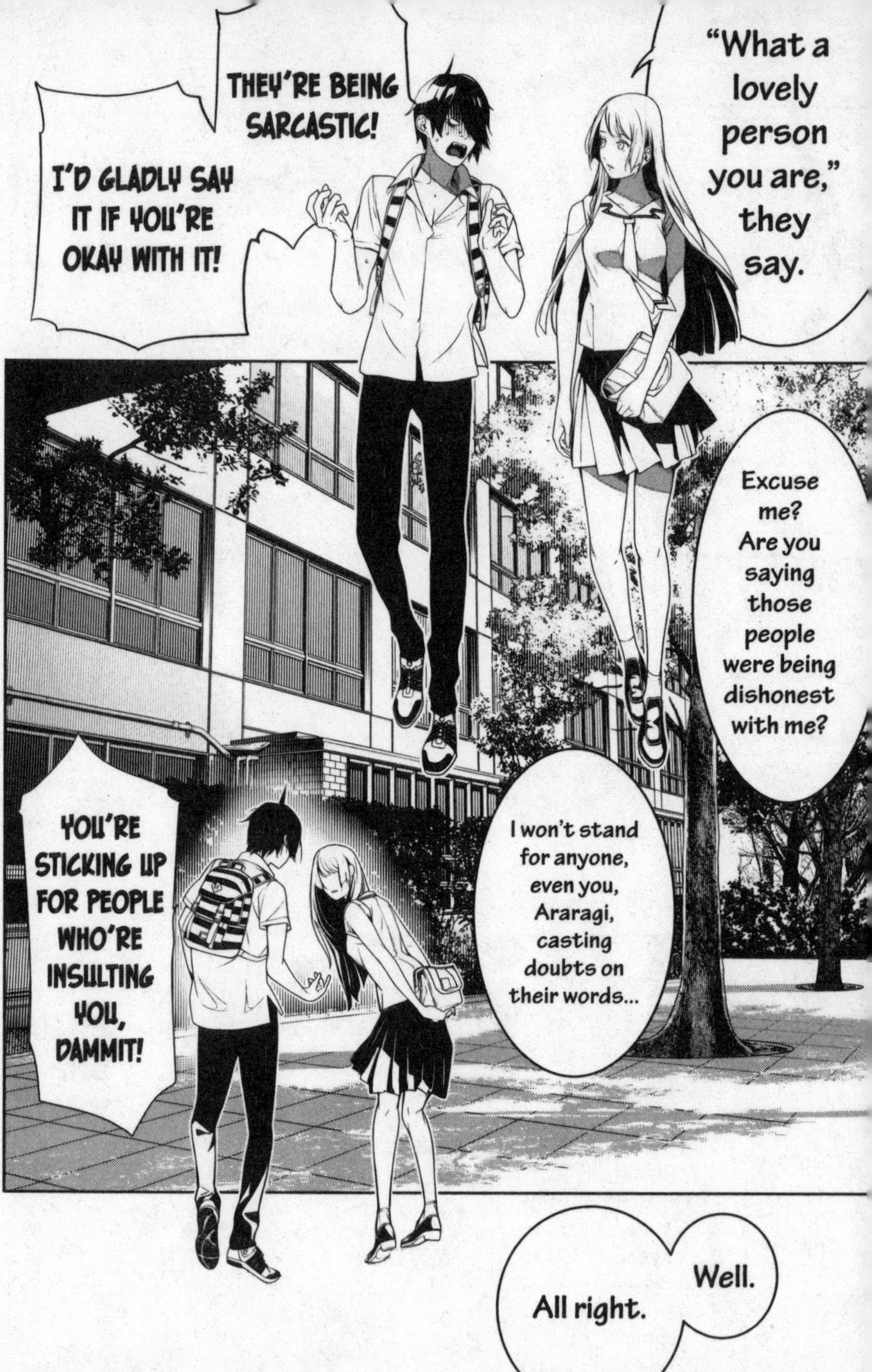
"What a lovely person you are," they say.
THEY'RE BEING SARCASTIC!
I'D GLADLY SAY IT IF YOU'RE OKAY WITH IT!
Excuse me? Are you saying those people were being dishonest with me?
I won't stand for anyone, even you, Araragi, casting doubts on their words...
YOU'RE STICKING UP FOR PEOPLE WHO'RE INSULTING YOU, DAMMIT!
Well.
All right.

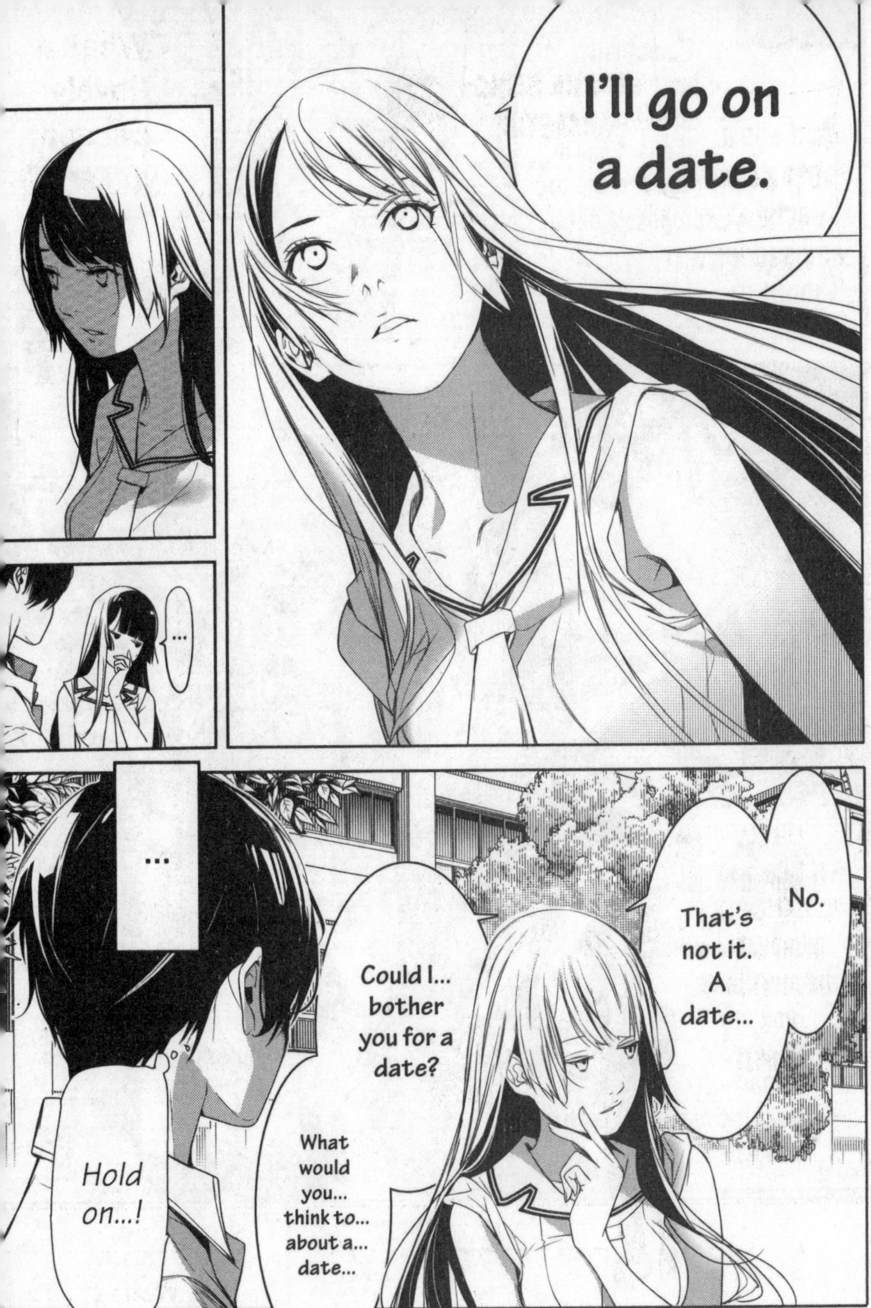
I'll go on a date.
...
No.
That's not it. A date...
Could I... bother you for a date?
What would you... think to... about a... date...
...
Hold on...!

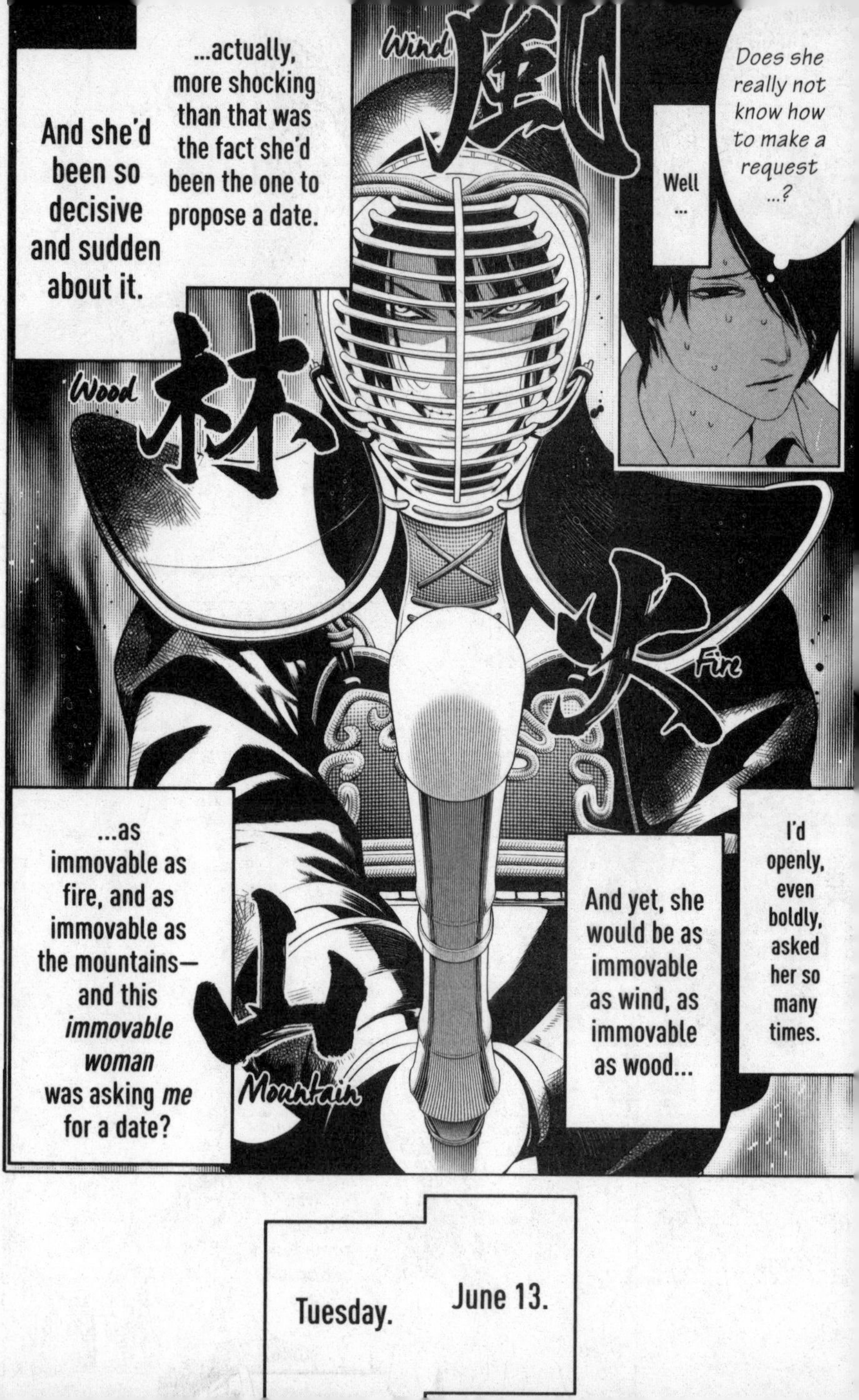

Does she really not know how to make a request ...?
Well ...
And she'd been so decisive and sudden about it.
...actually, more shocking than that was the fact she'd been the one to propose a date.
Wind
Wood
Fire
Mountain
I'd openly, even boldly, asked her so many times.
And yet, she would be as immovable as wind, as immovable as wood...
...as immovable as fire, and as immovable as the mountains—and this *immovable woman* was asking *me* for a date?
June 13.
Tuesday.

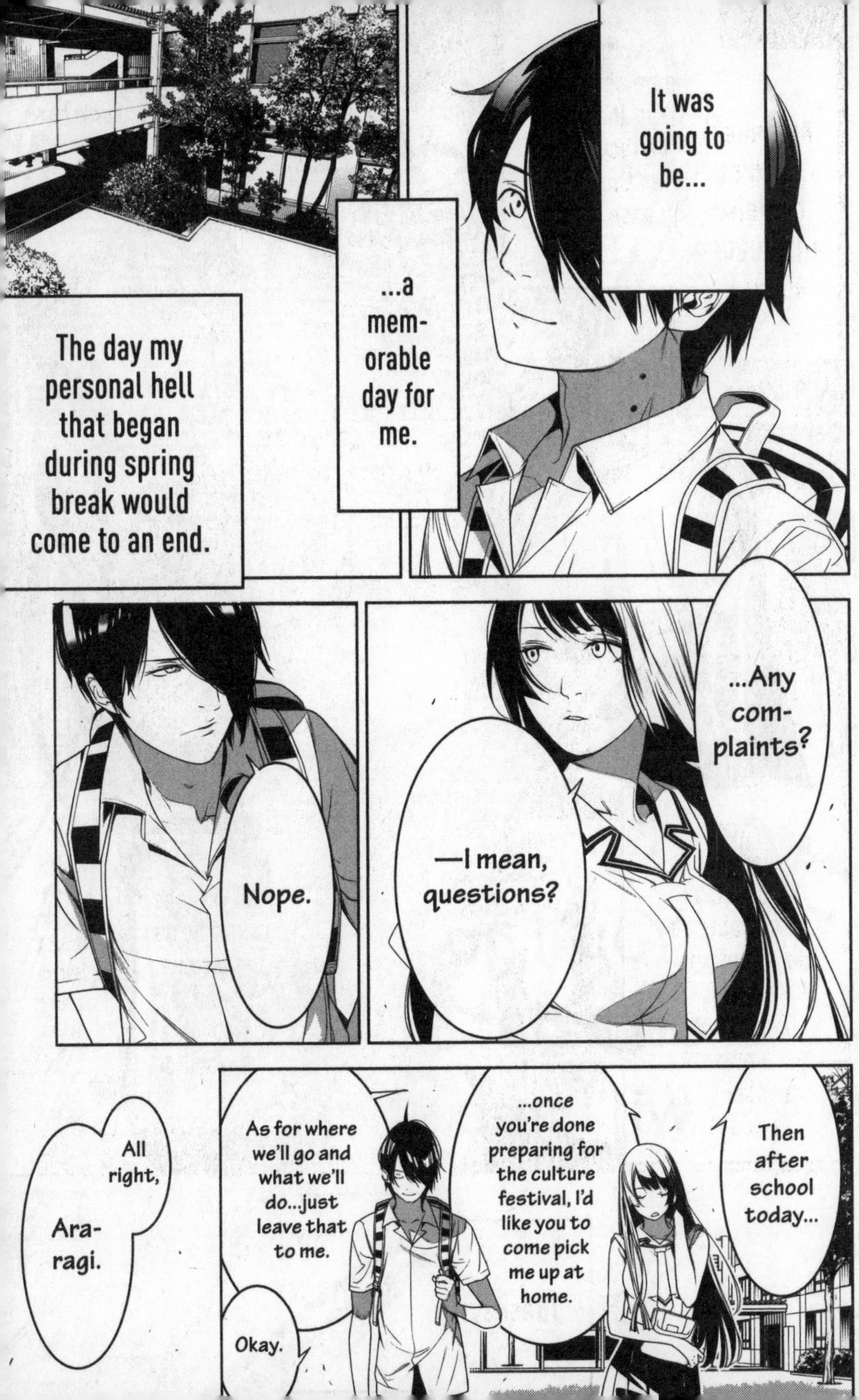

It was going to be...
...a mem-orable day for me.
The day my personal hell that began during spring break would come to an end.
...Any com-plaints?
—I mean, questions?
Nope.
Then after school today...
...once you're done preparing for the culture festival, I'd like you to come pick me up at home.
As for where we'll go and what we'll do...just leave that to me.
Okay.
All right, Ara-ragi.

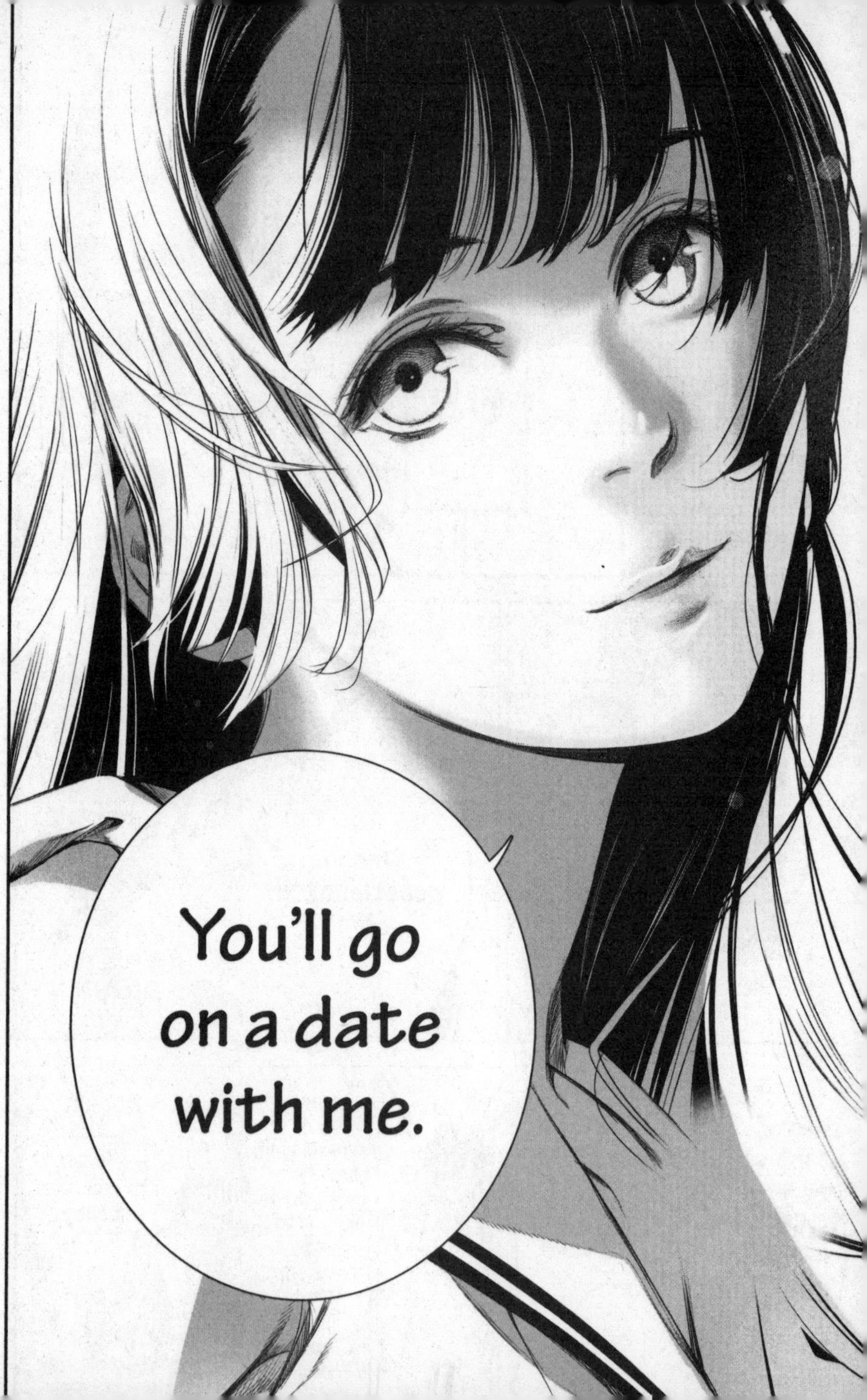
You'll go on a date with me.

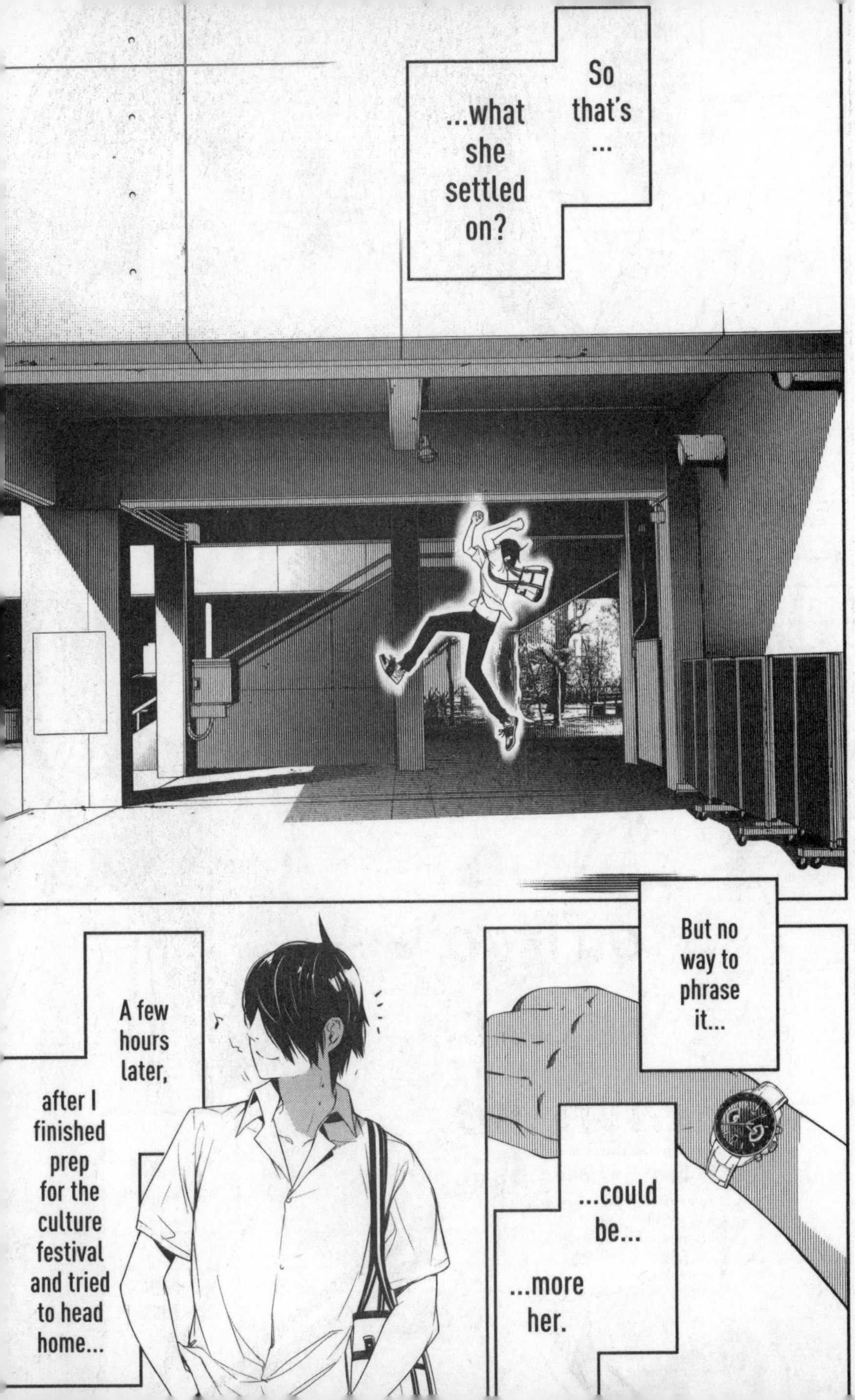
So that's...
...what she settled on?
But no way to phrase it...
...could be...
...more her.
A few hours later,
after I finished prep for the culture festival and tried to head home...

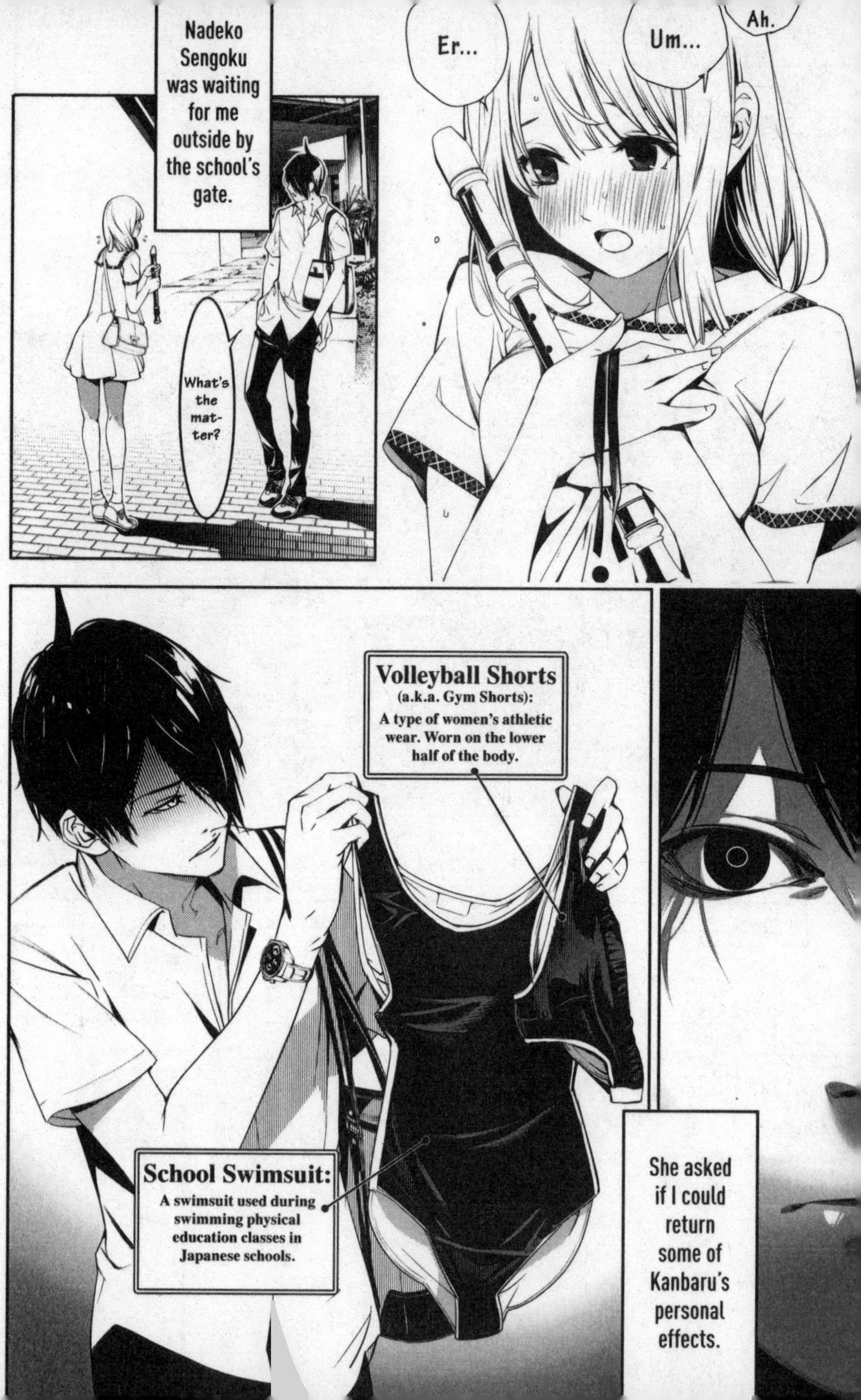
Ah.
Um...
Er...
Nadeko Sengoku was waiting for me outside by the school's gate.
What's the mat-ter?
She asked if I could return some of Kanbaru's personal effects.
Volleyball Shorts
(a.k.a. Gym Shorts):
A type of women's athletic wear. Worn on the lower half of the body.
School Swimsuit:
A swimsuit used during swimming physical education classes in Japanese schools.

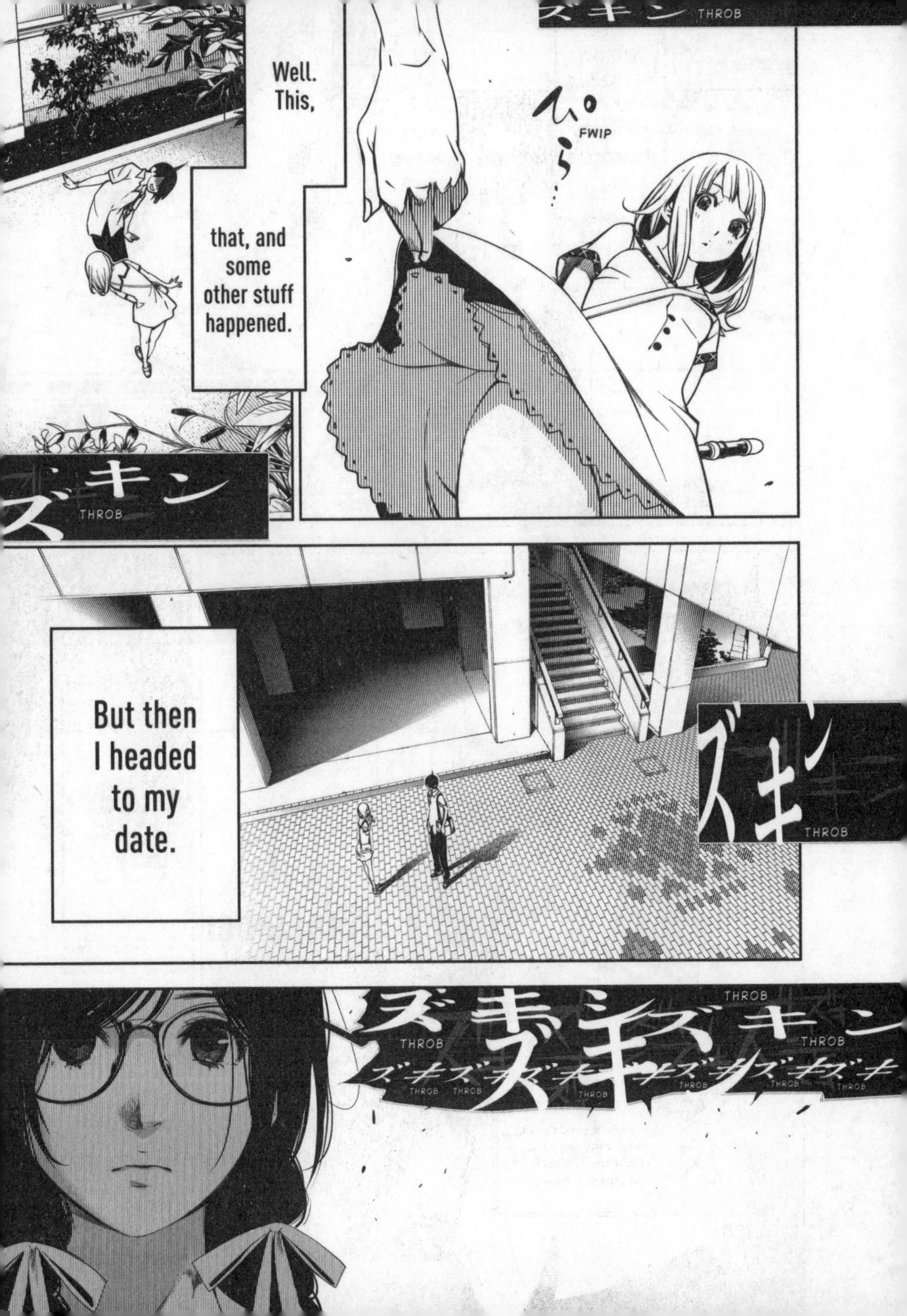
ズキン
THROB
ひら
FWIP
Well. This,
that, and some other stuff happened.
ズキン
THROB
But then I headed to my date.
ズキン
THROB
ズキン
THROB
THROB
ズキ
THROB
ズキズキズキズキズキズキズキ
THROB THROB THROB THROB THROB THROB

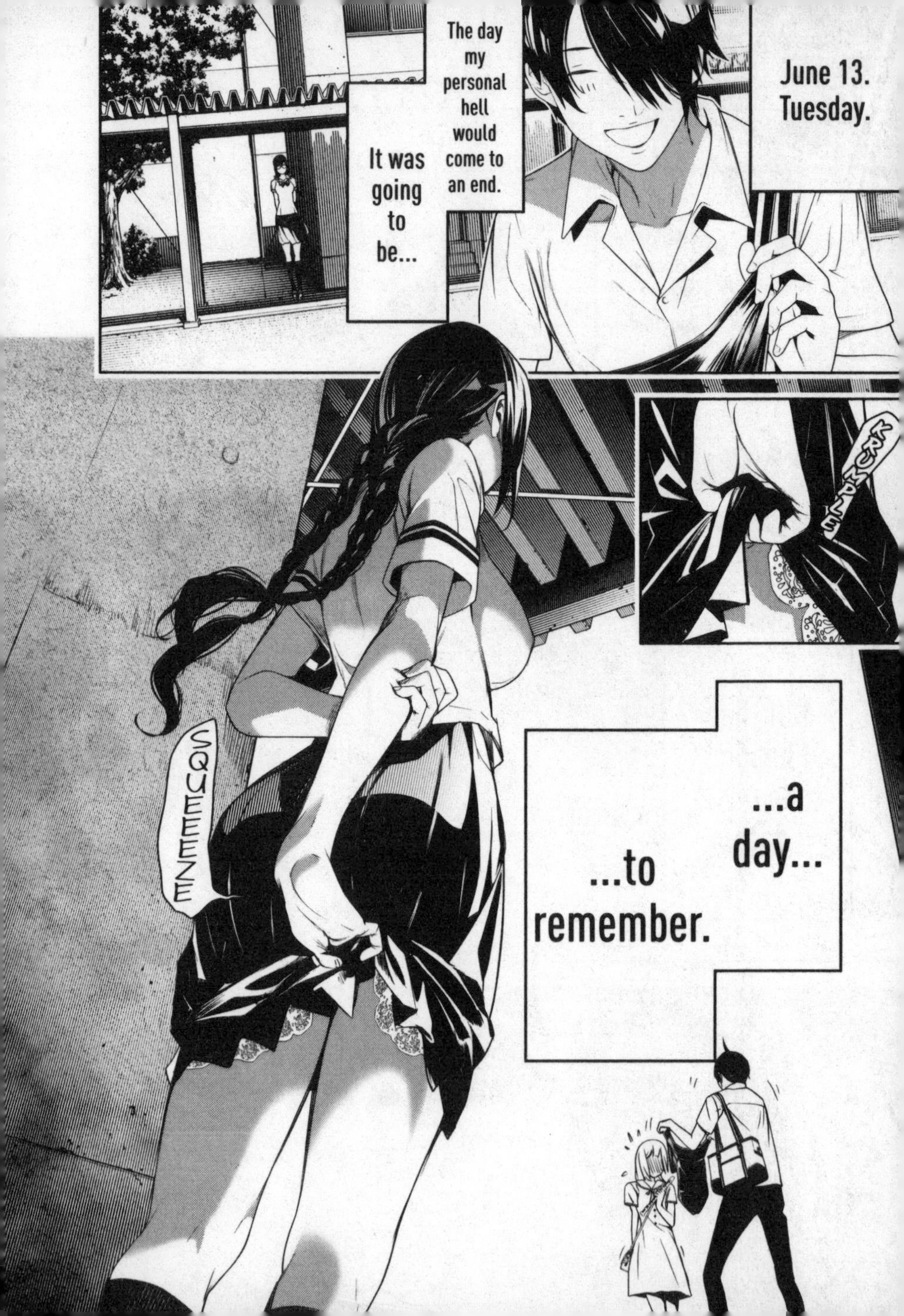
June 13. Tuesday.
The day my personal hell would come to an end.
It was going to be...
KRUMPLE
...a day...
...to remember.
SQUEEEEZE

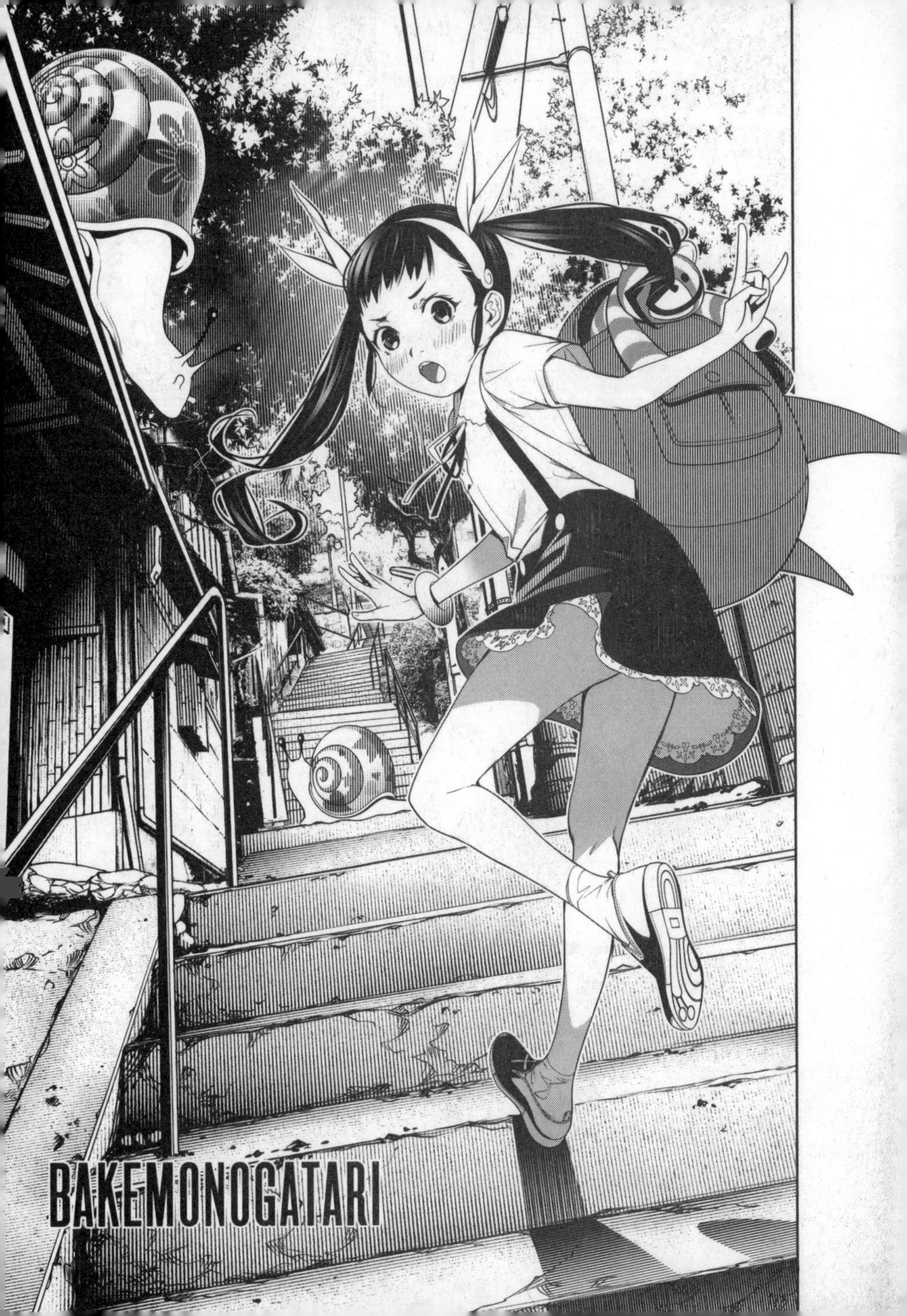
BAKEMONOGATARI

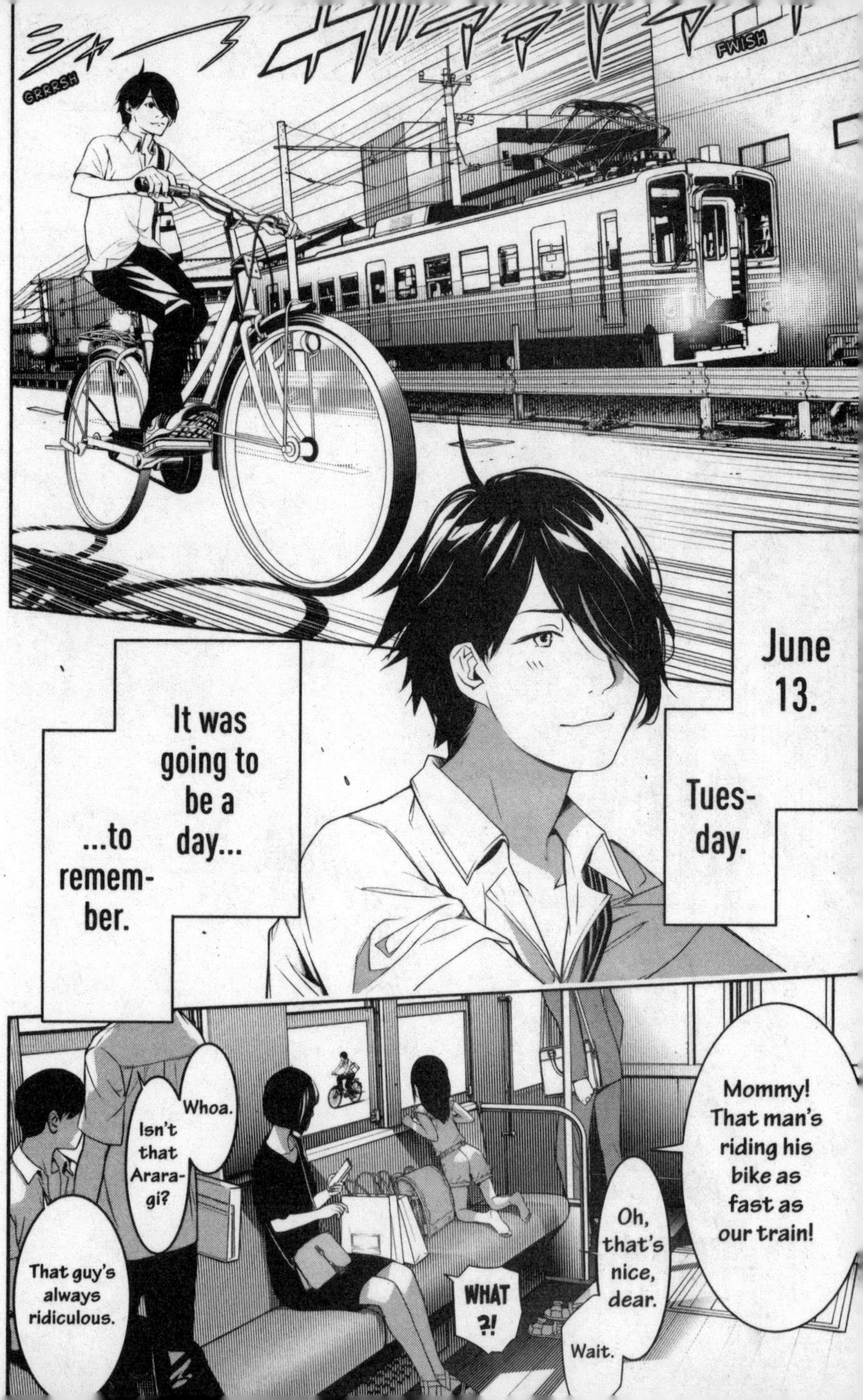
FWISH
GRRRSH
June 13.
Tues-day.
It was going to be a day...
...to remem-ber.
Mommy! That man's riding his bike as fast as our train!
Oh, that's nice, dear.
Wait.
WHAT ?!
Whoa.
Isn't that Arara-gi?
That guy's always ridiculous.

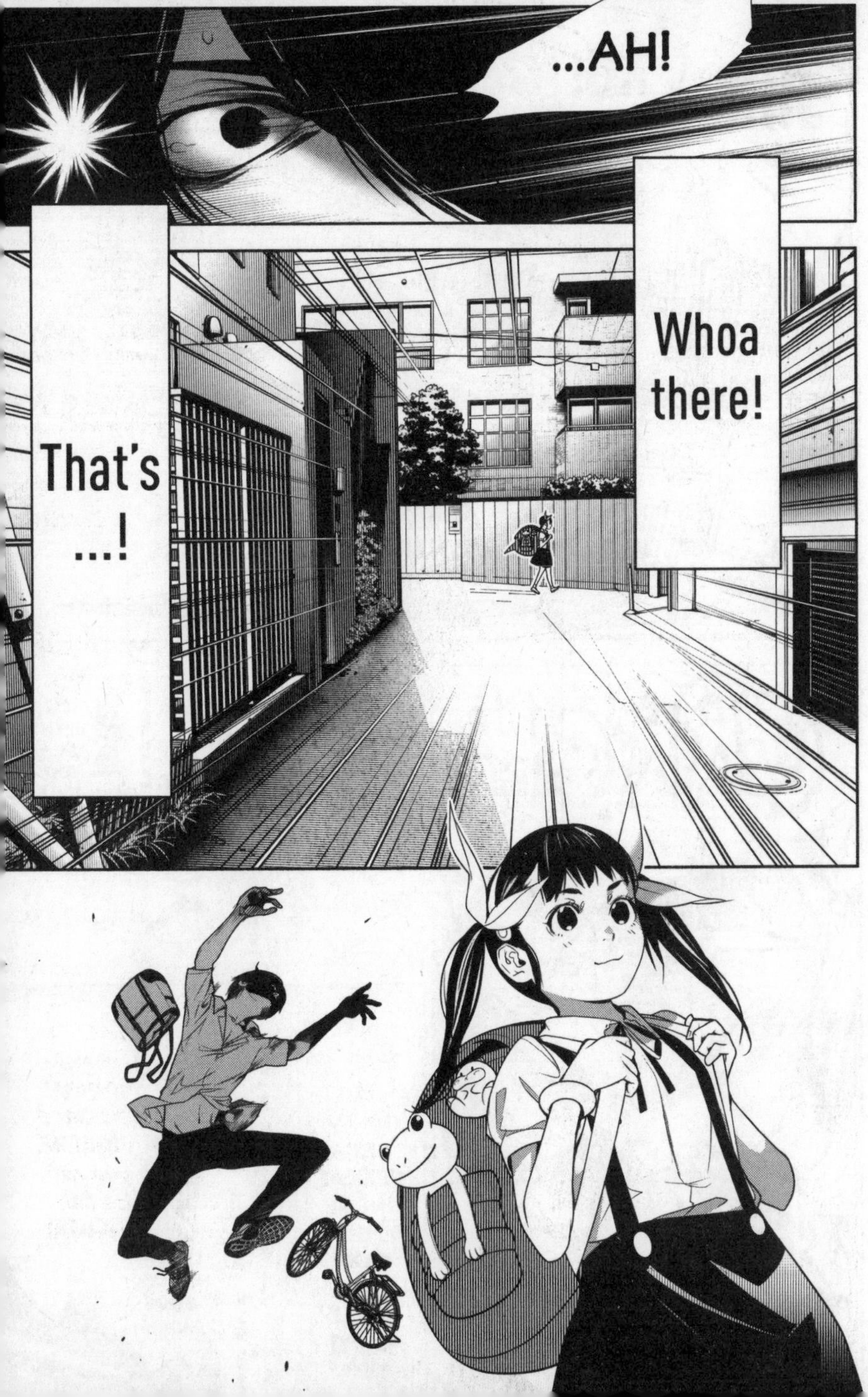
...AH!
Whoa there!
That's ...!

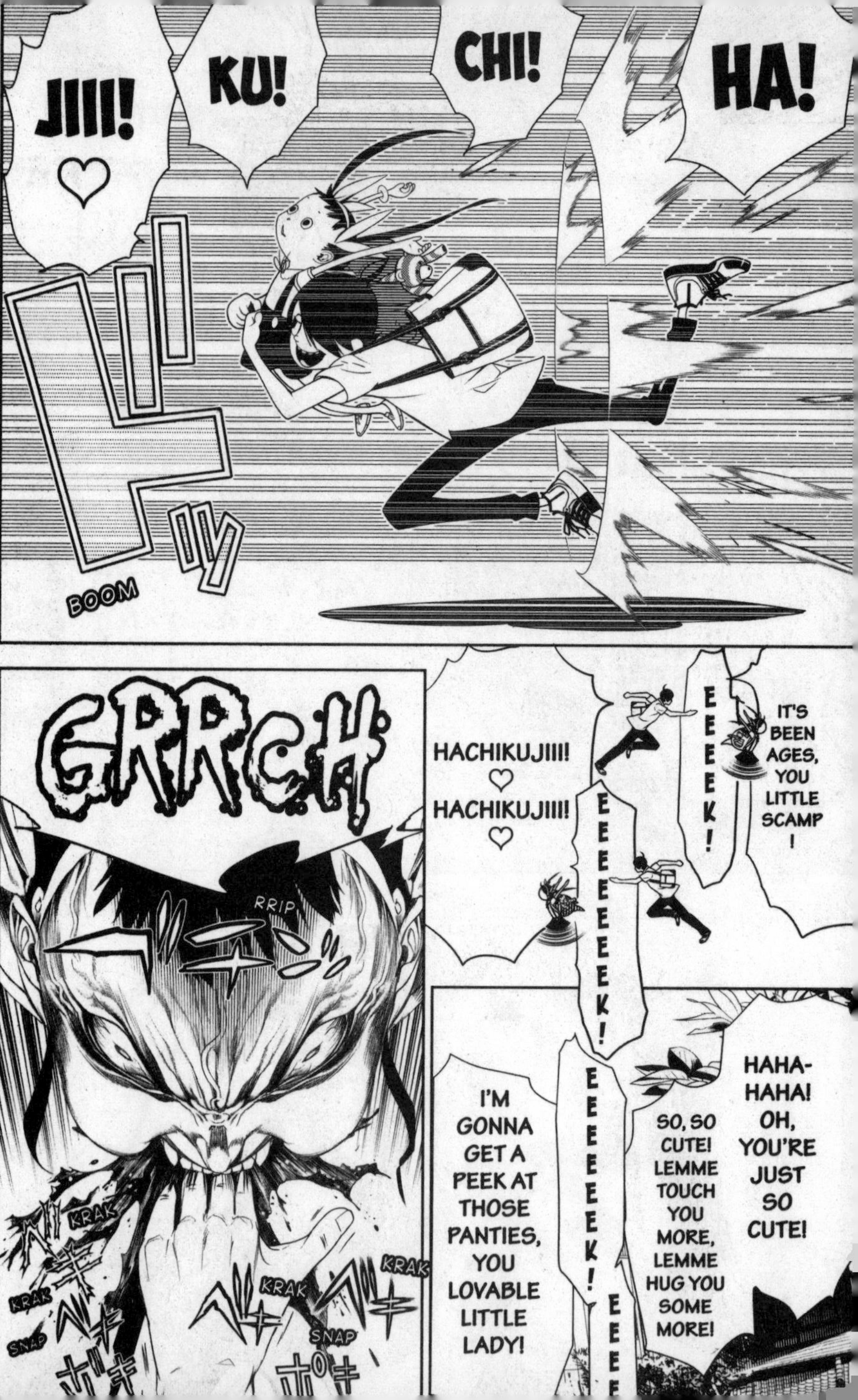
HA!
CHI!
KU!
JIII! ♡
BOOM
IT'S BEEN AGES, YOU LITTLE SCAMP!
EEEEK!
HACHIKUJIII! ♡ HACHIKUJIII! ♡
EEEEEEEEK!
HAHA-HAHA! OH, YOU'RE JUST SO CUTE!
SO, SO CUTE! LEMME TOUCH YOU MORE, LEMME HUG YOU SOME MORE!
EEEEEEK!
I'M GONNA GET A PEEK AT THOSE PANTIES, YOU LOVABLE LITTLE LADY!
EEEE
GRRCH
RRIP
KRAK
KRAK
KRAK
KRAK
SNAP
SNAP

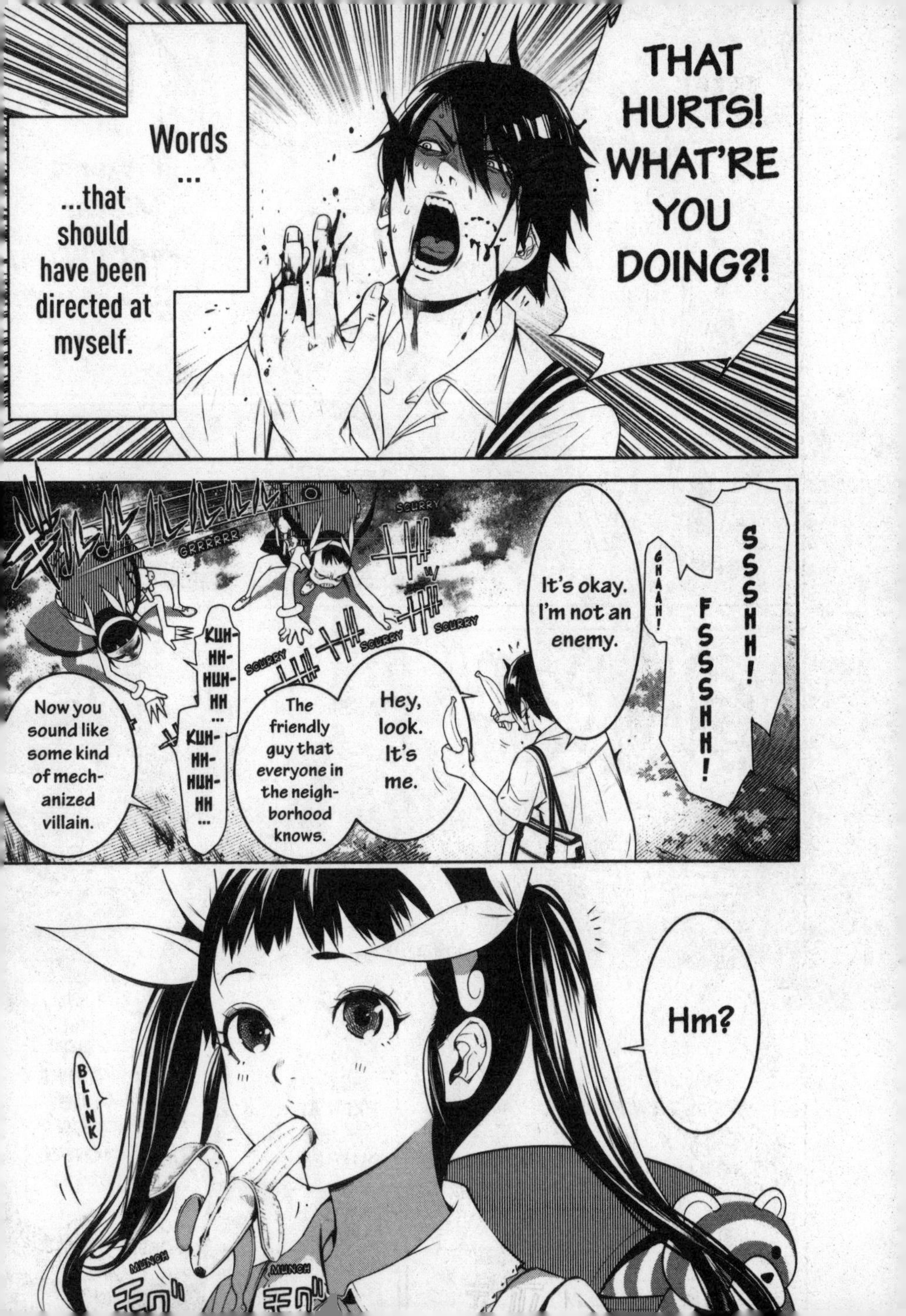
THAT HURTS! WHAT'RE YOU DOING?!
Words ...
...that should have been directed at myself.
SSSHH!
FSSSHH!
GHAAH!
It's okay. I'm not an enemy.
SCURRY
GRRRRRR
SCURRY
SCURRY
SCURRY
SCURRY
Hey, look. It's me.
The friendly guy that everyone in the neighborhood knows.
KUH-HH-HUH-HH ... KUH-HH-HUH-HH ...
Now you sound like some kind of mechanized villain.
Hm?
BLINK
MUNCH
MUNCH

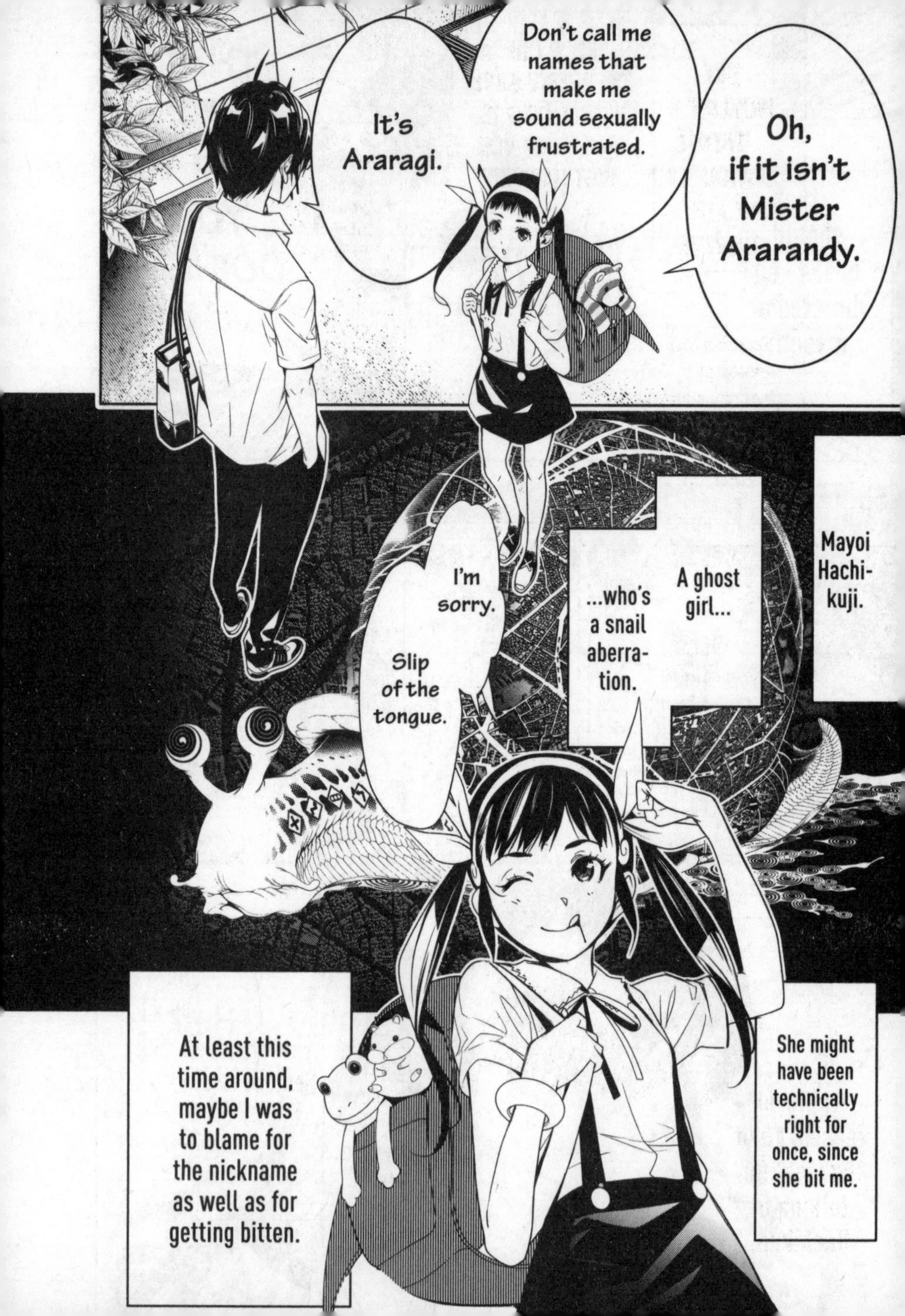

Oh, if it isn't Mister Ararandy.
Don't call me names that make me sound sexually frustrated.
It's Araragi.
Mayoi Hachikuji.
A ghost girl...
...who's a snail aberration.
I'm sorry. Slip of the tongue.
She might have been technically right for once, since she bit me.
At least this time around, maybe I was to blame for the nickname as well as for getting bitten.

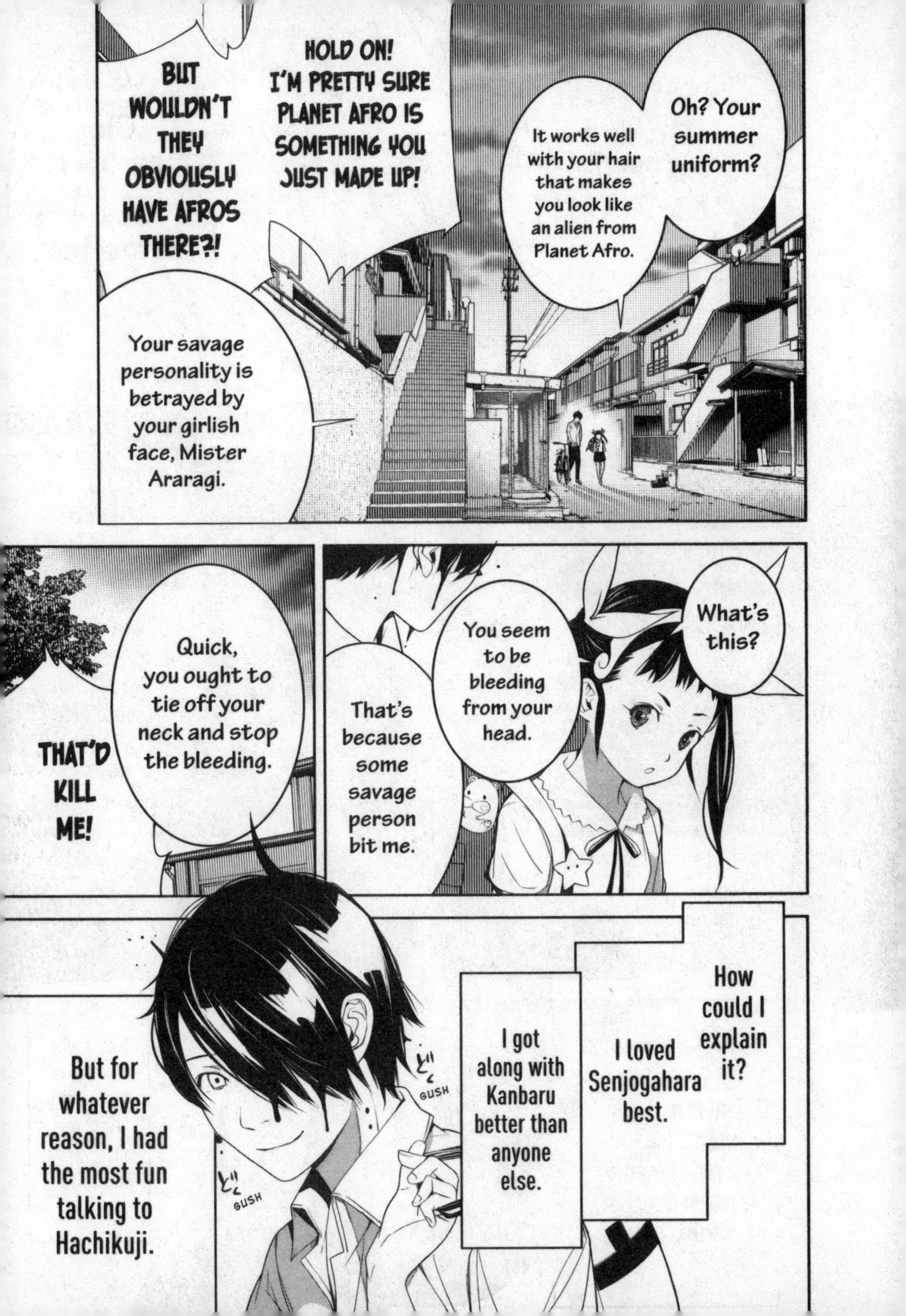
Oh? Your summer uniform?
It works well with your hair that makes you look like an alien from Planet Afro.
HOLD ON! I'M PRETTY SURE PLANET AFRO IS SOMETHING YOU JUST MADE UP!
BUT WOULDN'T THEY OBVIOUSLY HAVE AFROS THERE?!
Your savage personality is betrayed by your girlish face, Mister Araragi.
What's this?
You seem to be bleeding from your head.
That's because some savage person bit me.
Quick, you ought to tie off your neck and stop the bleeding.
THAT'D KILL ME!
How could I explain it?
I loved Senjogahara best.
I got along with Kanbaru better than anyone else.
GUSH
GUSH
But for whatever reason, I had the most fun talking to Hachikuji.

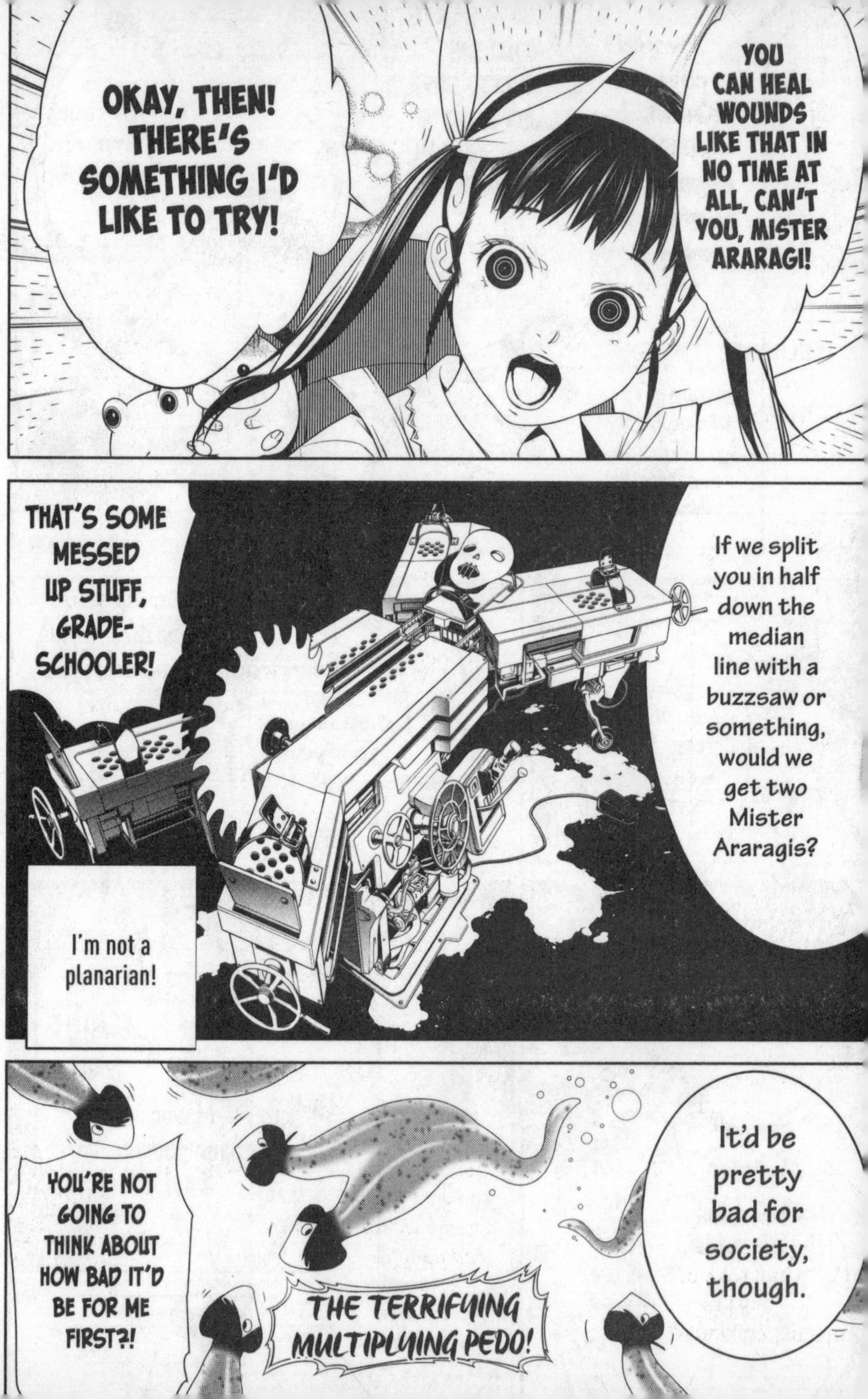
YOU CAN HEAL WOUNDS LIKE THAT IN NO TIME AT ALL, CAN'T YOU, MISTER ARARAGI!
OKAY, THEN! THERE'S SOMETHING I'D LIKE TO TRY!
If we split you in half down the median line with a buzzsaw or something, would we get two Mister Araragis?
THAT'S SOME MESSED UP STUFF, GRADE-SCHOOLER!
I'm not a planarian!
It'd be pretty bad for society, though.
YOU'RE NOT GOING TO THINK ABOUT HOW BAD IT'D BE FOR ME FIRST?!
THE TERRIFYING MULTIPLYING PEDO!

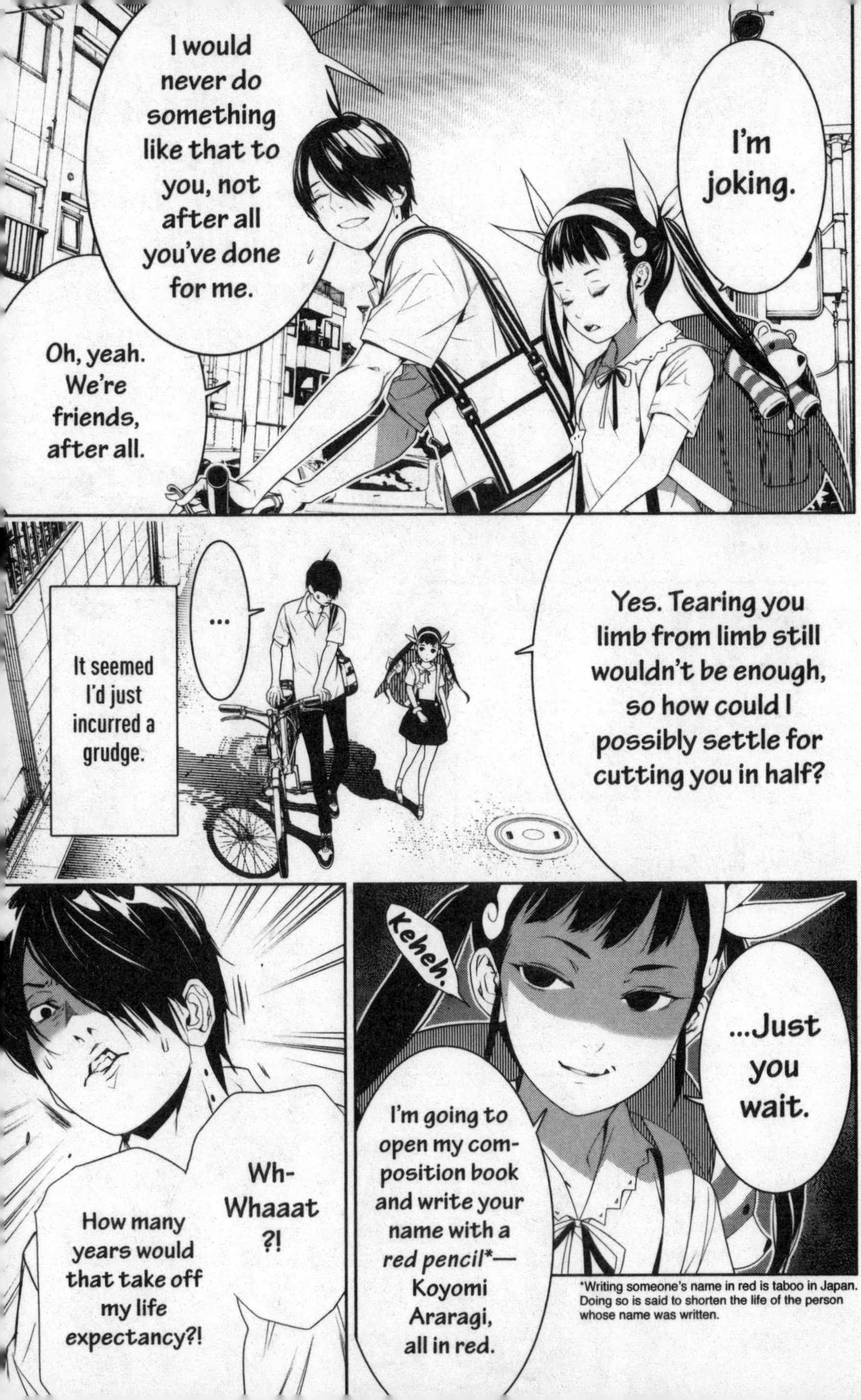
I'm joking.
I would never do something like that to you, not after all you've done for me.
Oh, yeah. We're friends, after all.
Yes. Tearing you limb from limb still wouldn't be enough, so how could I possibly settle for cutting you in half?
...
It seemed I'd just incurred a grudge.
Keheh.
...Just you wait.
I'm going to open my composition book and write your name with a *red pencil**— Koyomi Araragi, all in red.
Wh-Whaaat?!
How many years would that take off my life expectancy?!

*Writing someone's name in red is taboo in Japan. Doing so is said to shorten the life of the person whose name was written.

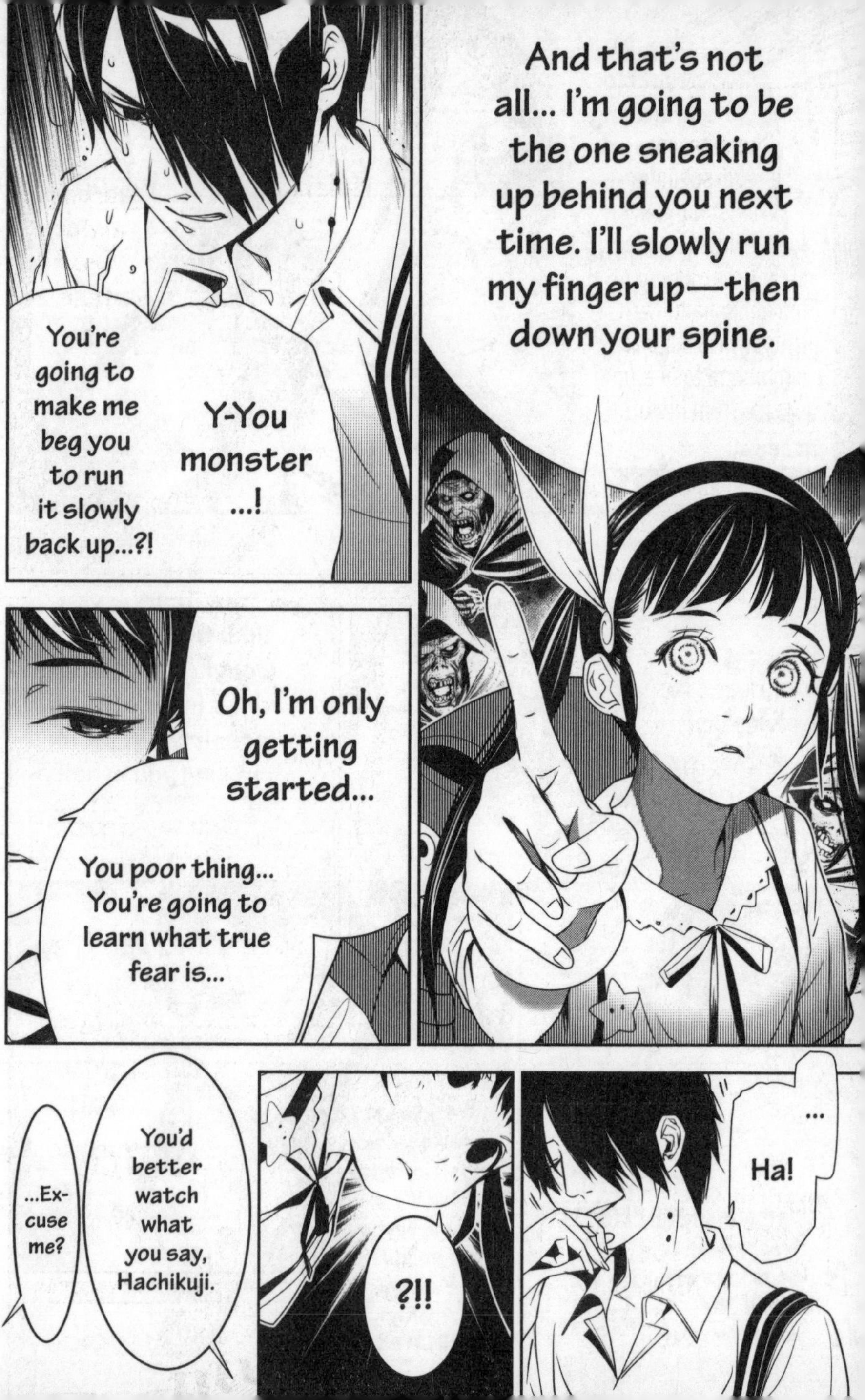
And that's not all... I'm going to be the one sneaking up behind you next time. I'll slowly run my finger up—then down your spine.
Y-You monster ...!
You're going to make me beg you to run it slowly back up...?!
Oh, I'm only getting started...
You poor thing... You're going to learn what true fear is...
...
Ha!
?!!
You'd better watch what you say, Hachikuji.
...Ex-cuse me?

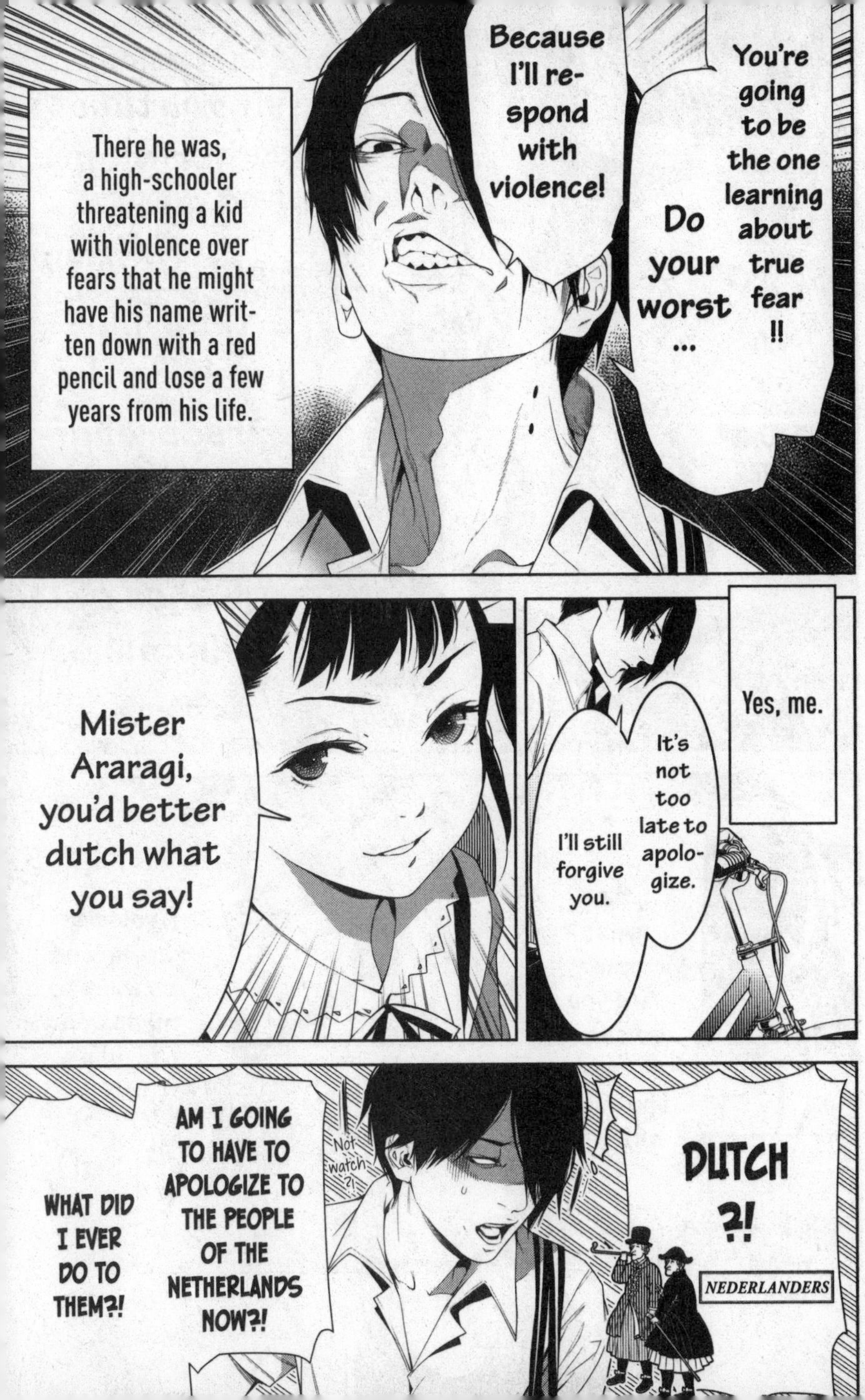
You're going to be the one learning about true fear!!
Because I'll re-spond with violence!
Do your worst...
There he was, a high-schooler threatening a kid with violence over fears that he might have his name writ-ten down with a red pencil and lose a few years from his life.
Yes, me.
It's not too late to apolo-gize.
I'll still forgive you.
Mister Araragi, you'd better dutch what you say!
DUTCH ?!
NEDERLANDERS
Not watch ?!
AM I GOING TO HAVE TO APOLOGIZE TO THE PEOPLE OF THE NETHERLANDS NOW?!
WHAT DID I EVER DO TO THEM?!

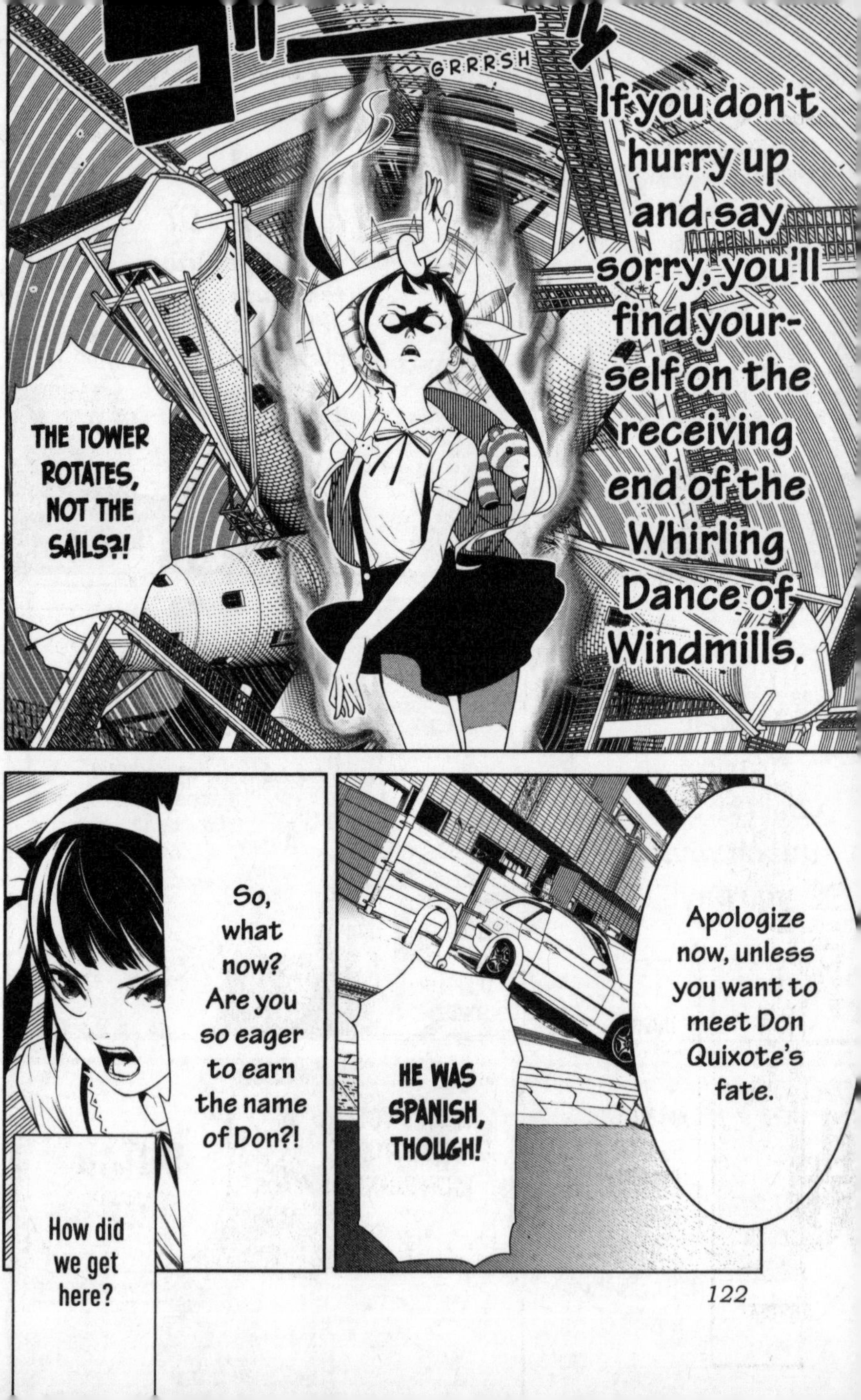
GRRRSH
If you don't hurry up and say sorry, you'll find your-self on the receiving end of the Whirling Dance of Windmills.
THE TOWER ROTATES, NOT THE SAILS?!
Apologize now, unless you want to meet Don Quixote's fate.
HE WAS SPANISH, THOUGH!
So, what now? Are you so eager to earn the name of Don?!
How did we get here?

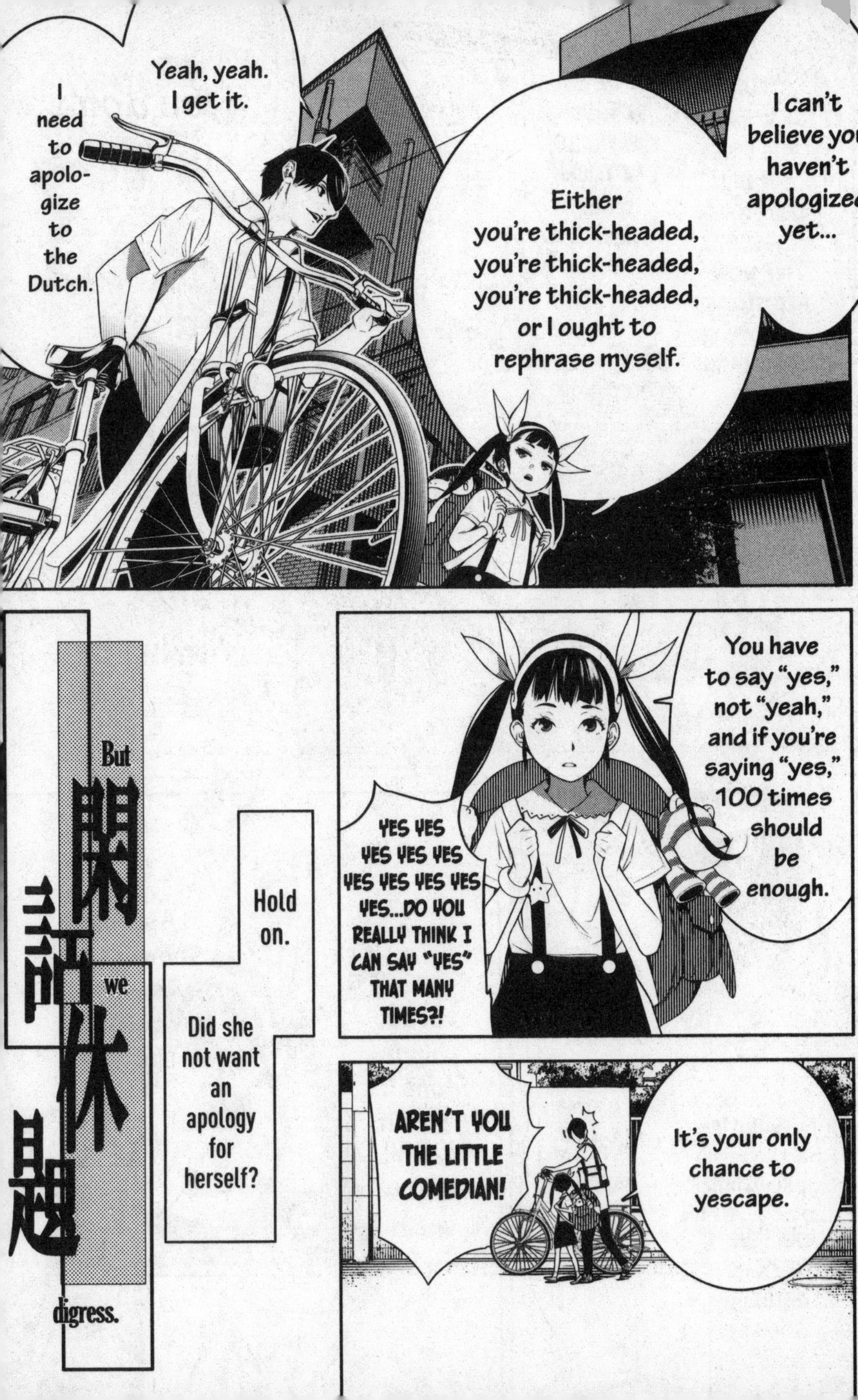
I can't believe you haven't apologized yet...
Either you're thick-headed, you're thick-headed, you're thick-headed, or I ought to rephrase myself.
Yeah, yeah. I get it.
I need to apologize to the Dutch.
You have to say "yes," not "yeah," and if you're saying "yes," 100 times should be enough.
YES YES YES YES YES YES YES YES YES YES...DO YOU REALLY THINK I CAN SAY "YES" THAT MANY TIMES?!
It's your only chance to yescape.
AREN'T YOU THE LITTLE COMEDIAN!
閑話休題
But we digress.
Hold on.
Did she not want an apology for herself?

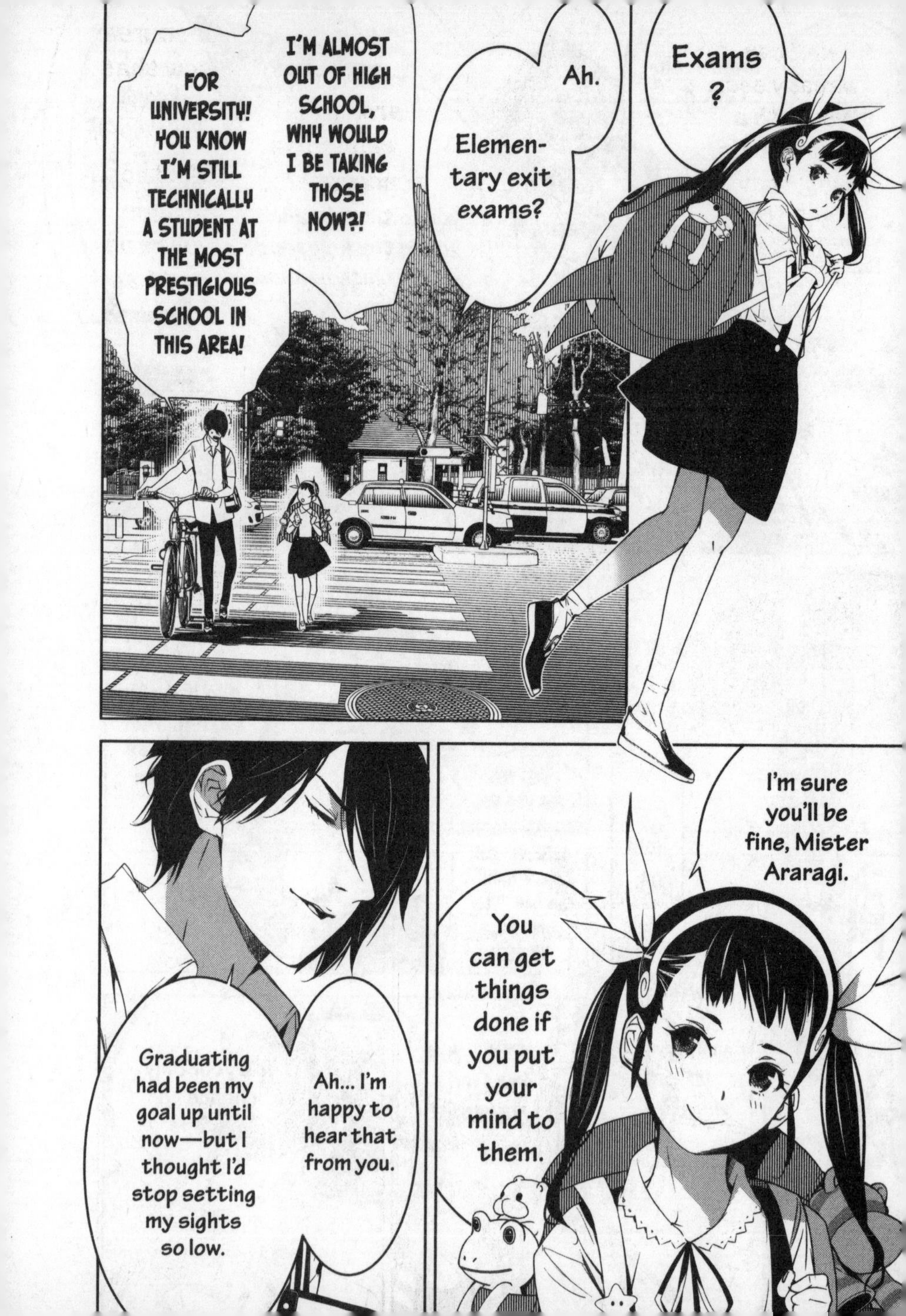
Exams ?
Ah. Elementary exit exams?
I'M ALMOST OUT OF HIGH SCHOOL, WHY WOULD I BE TAKING THOSE NOW?!
FOR UNIVERSITY! YOU KNOW I'M STILL TECHNICALLY A STUDENT AT THE MOST PRESTIGIOUS SCHOOL IN THIS AREA!
I'm sure you'll be fine, Mister Araragi.
You can get things done if you put your mind to them.
Ah... I'm happy to hear that from you.
Graduating had been my goal up until now—but I thought I'd stop setting my sights so low.

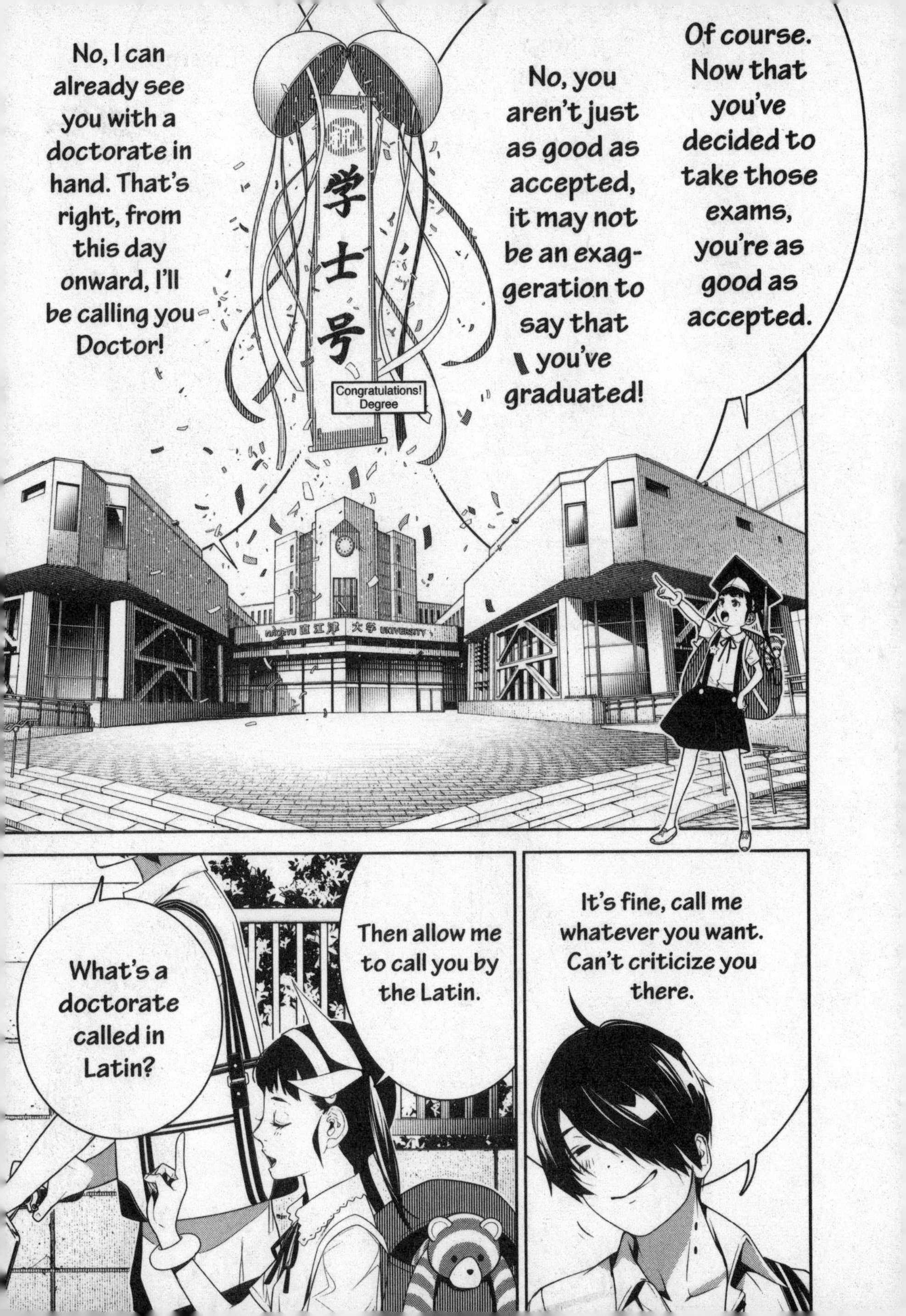
Of course. Now that you've decided to take those exams, you're as good as accepted.
No, you aren't just as good as accepted, it may not be an exaggeration to say that you've graduated!
No, I can already see you with a doctorate in hand. That's right, from this day onward, I'll be calling you Doctor!
祝
学士号
Congratulations! Degree
It's fine, call me whatever you want. Can't criticize you there.
Then allow me to call you by the Latin.
What's a doctorate called in Latin?

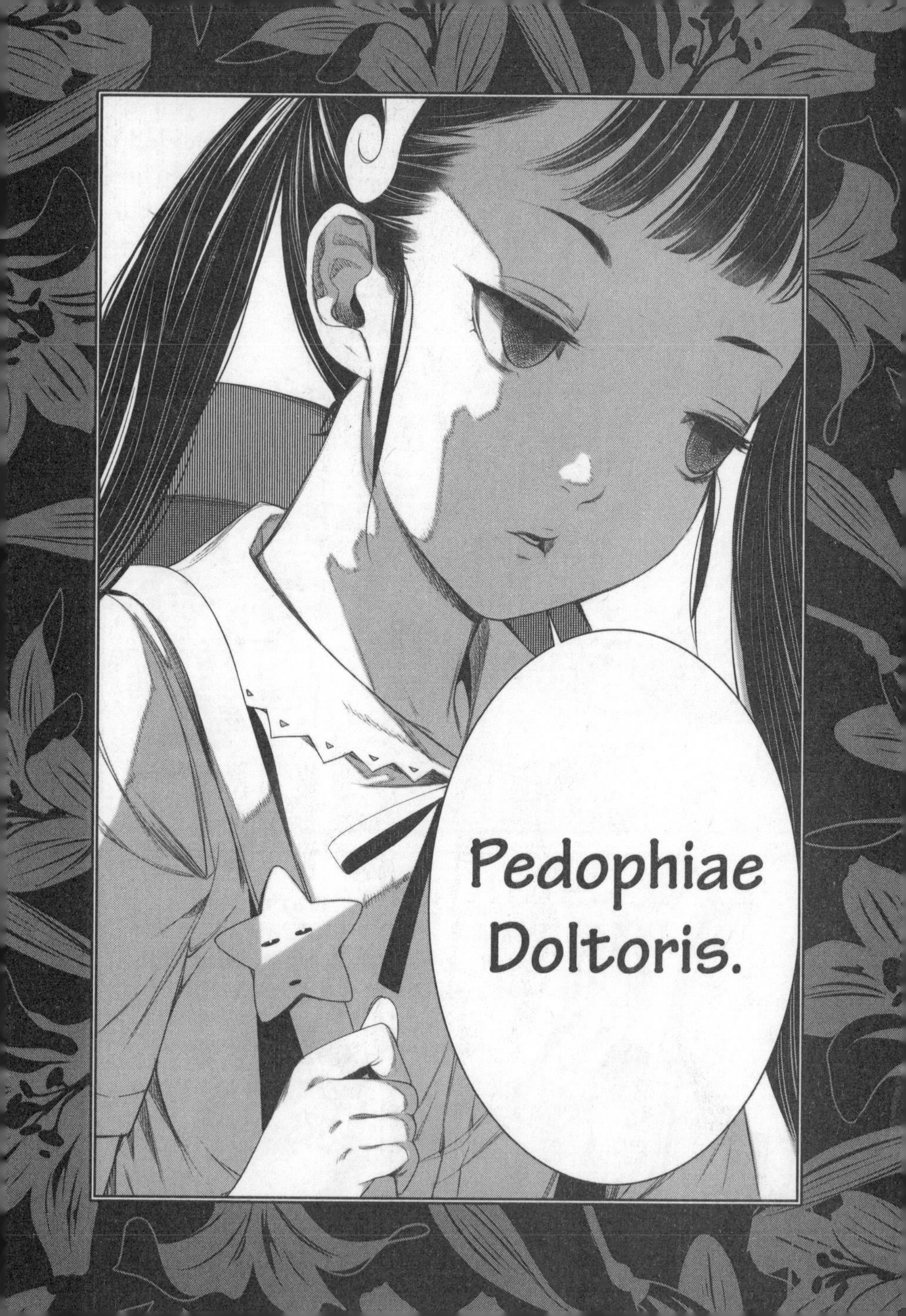
Pedophiae Doltoris.

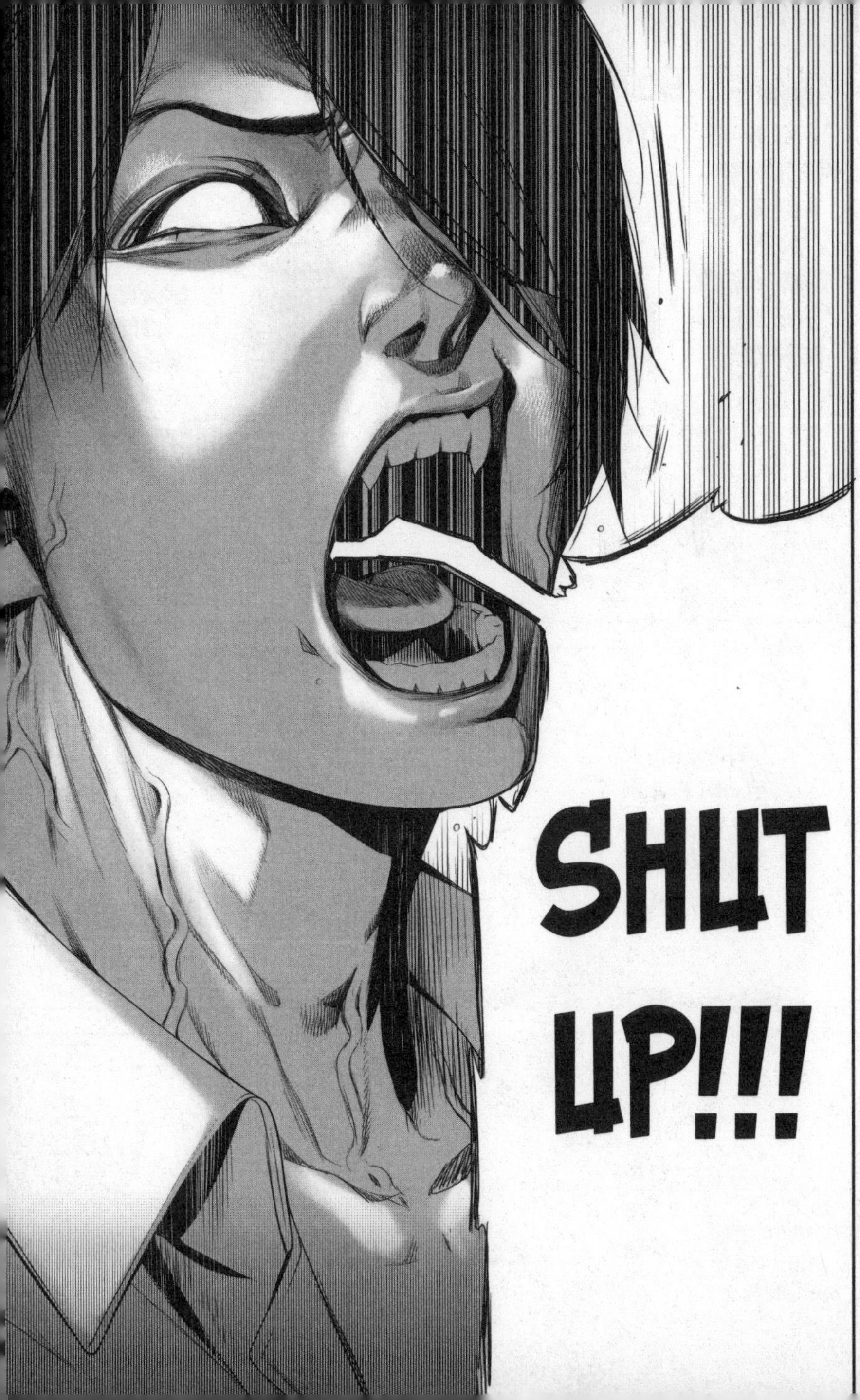
SHUT UP!!!

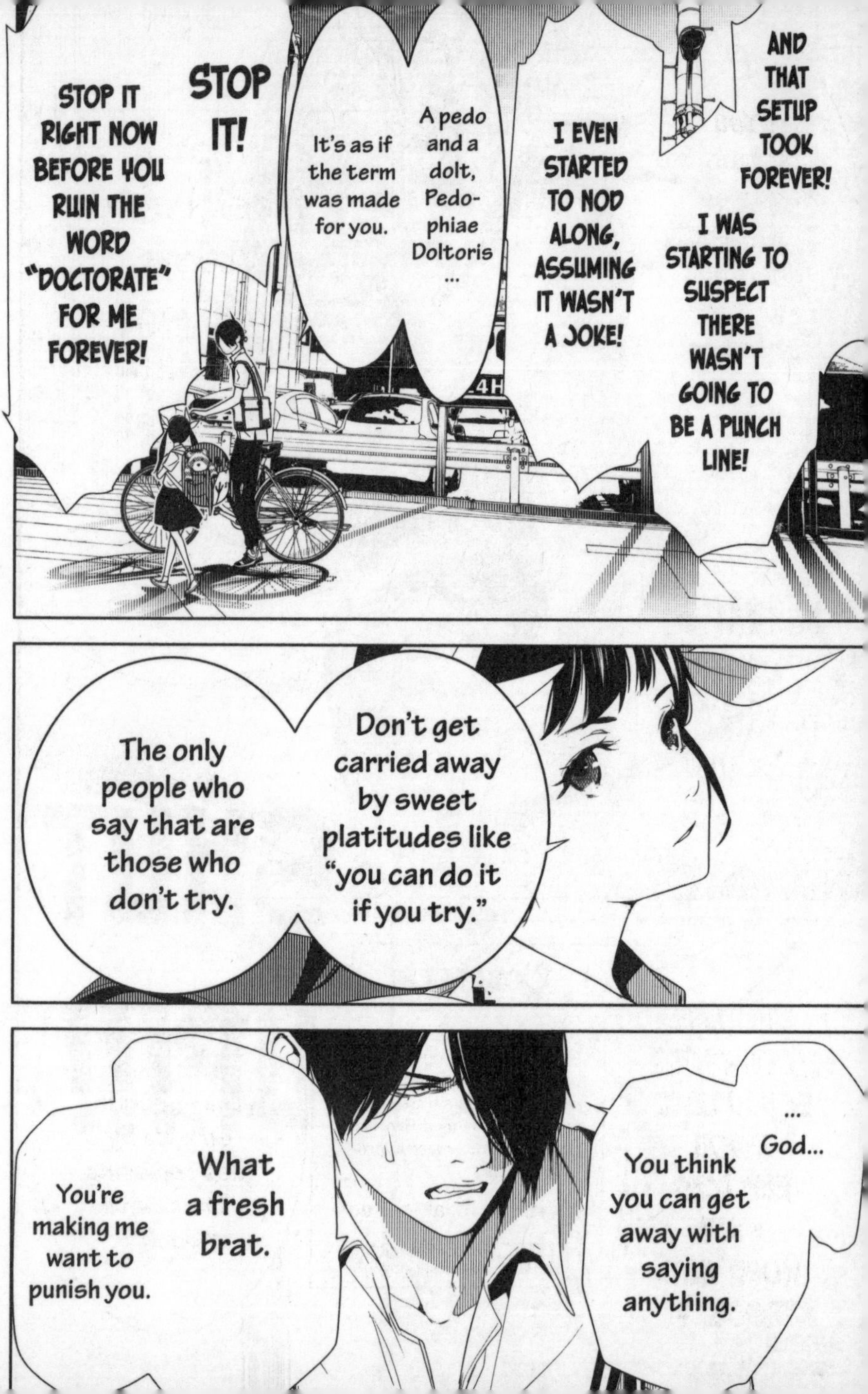
AND THAT SETUP TOOK FOREVER!
I WAS STARTING TO SUSPECT THERE WASN'T GOING TO BE A PUNCH LINE!
I EVEN STARTED TO NOD ALONG, ASSUMING IT WASN'T A JOKE!
A pedo and a dolt, Pedophiae Doltoris ...
It's as if the term was made for you.
STOP IT!
STOP IT RIGHT NOW BEFORE YOU RUIN THE WORD "DOCTORATE" FOR ME FOREVER!
Don't get carried away by sweet platitudes like "you can do it if you try."
The only people who say that are those who don't try.
... God...
You think you can get away with saying anything.
What a fresh brat.
You're making me want to punish you.

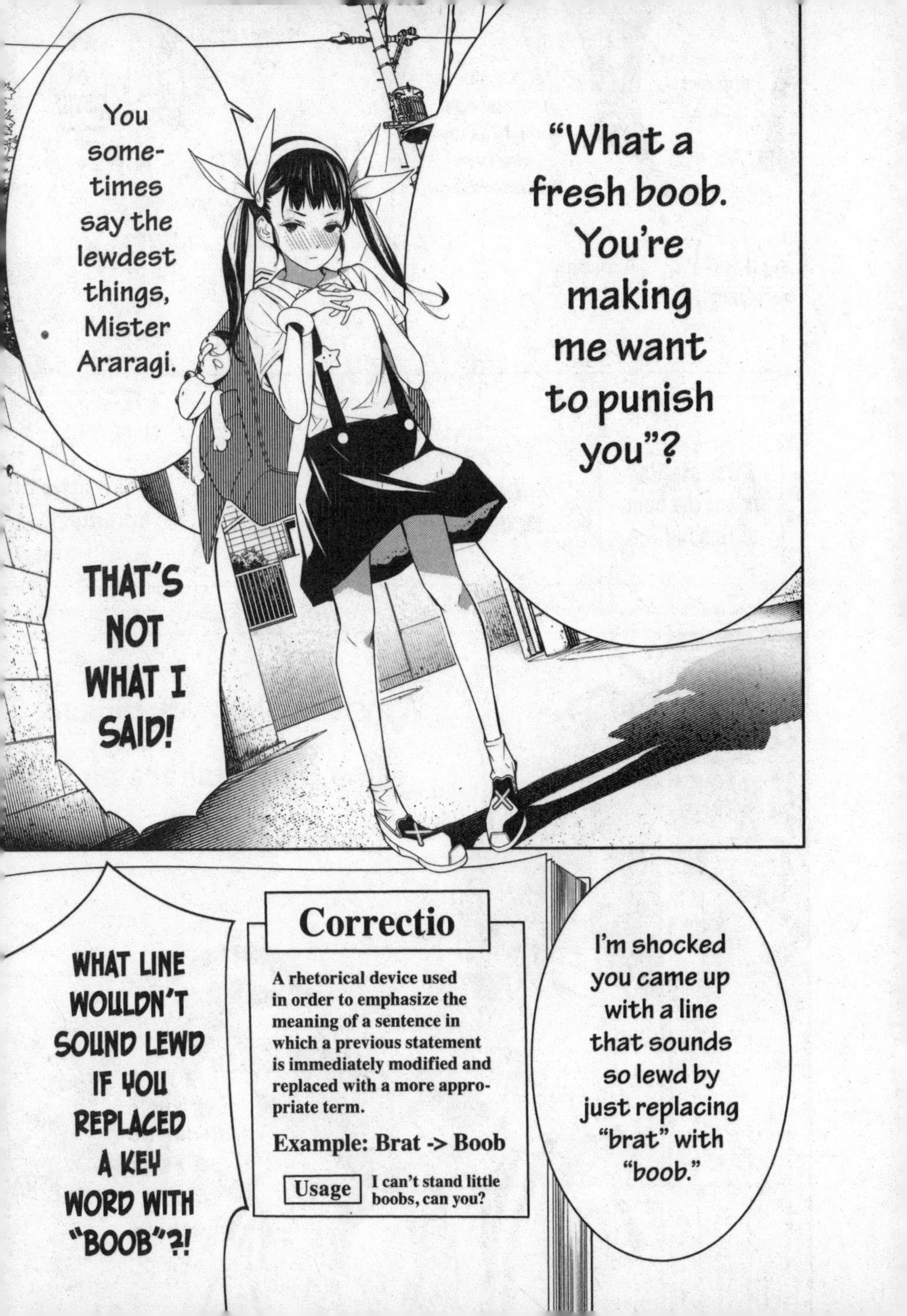
"What a fresh boob. You're making me want to punish you"?
You sometimes say the lewdest things, Mister Araragi.
THAT'S NOT WHAT I SAID!
I'm shocked you came up with a line that sounds so lewd by just replacing "brat" with "boob."
Correctio
A rhetorical device used in order to emphasize the meaning of a sentence in which a previous statement is immediately modified and replaced with a more appropriate term.
Example: Brat -> Boob
Usage
I can't stand little boobs, can you?
WHAT LINE WOULDN'T SOUND LEWD IF YOU REPLACED A KEY WORD WITH "BOOB"?!

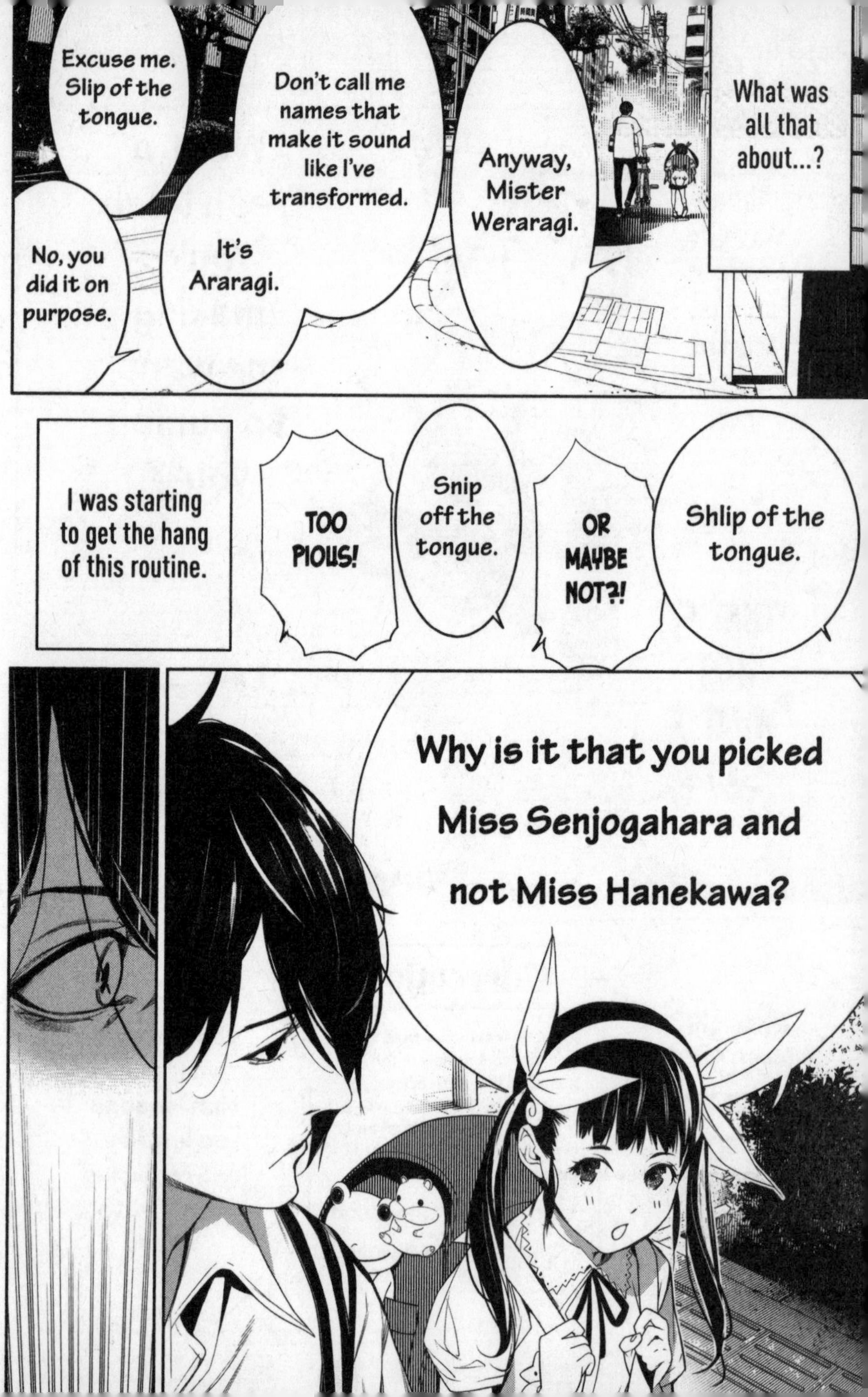
What was all that about...?
Anyway, Mister Weraragi.
It's Araragi.
Don't call me names that make it sound like I've transformed.
Excuse me. Slip of the tongue.
No, you did it on purpose.
Shlip of the tongue.
OR MAYBE NOT?!
Snip off the tongue.
TOO PIOUS!
I was starting to get the hang of this routine.
Why is it that you picked Miss Senjogahara and not Miss Hanekawa?

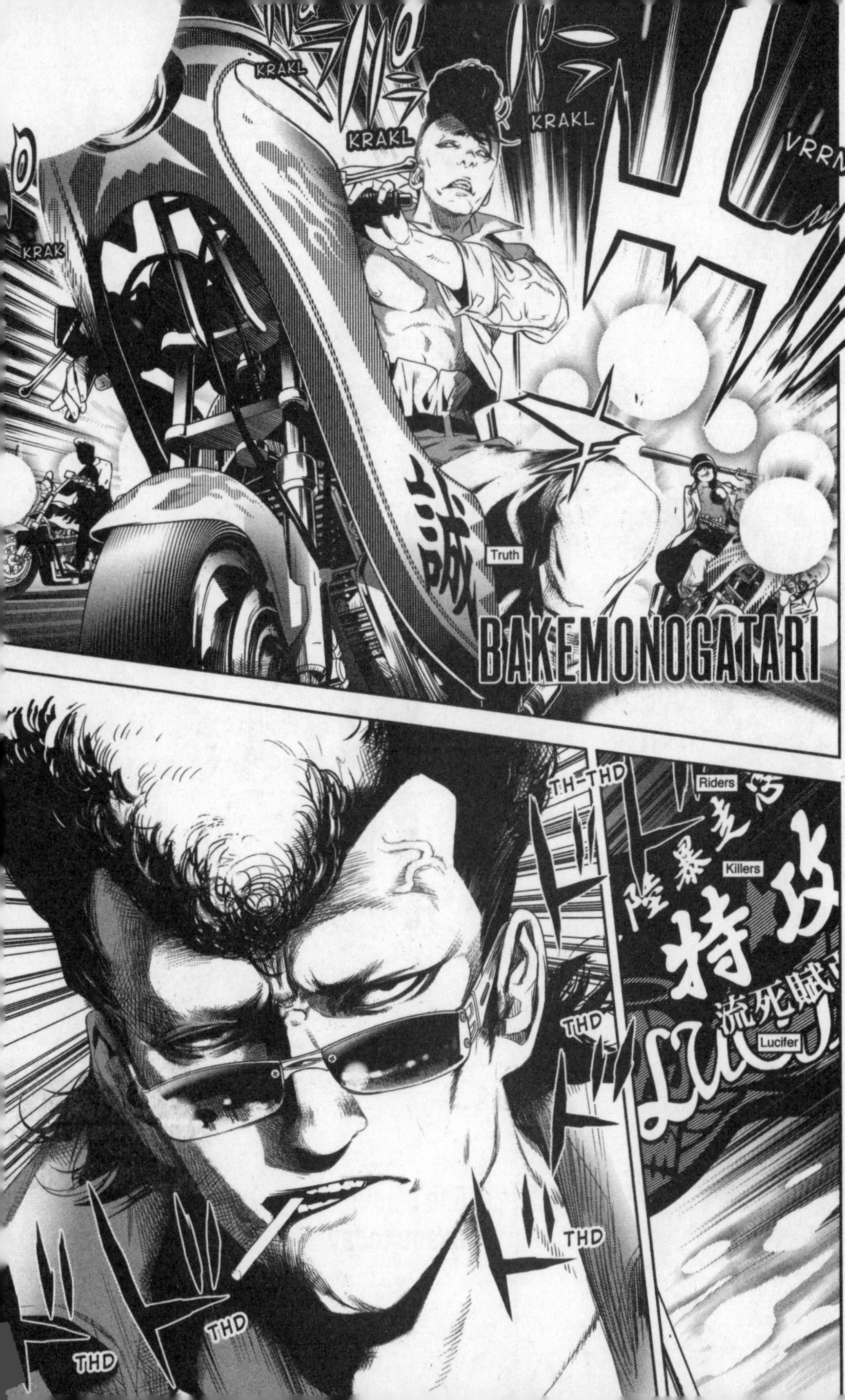
VRRM
KRAKL
KRAKL
KRAKL
KRAK
Truth
BAKEMONOGATARI
Riders
Killers
TH-THD
Lucifer
THD
THD
THD
THD

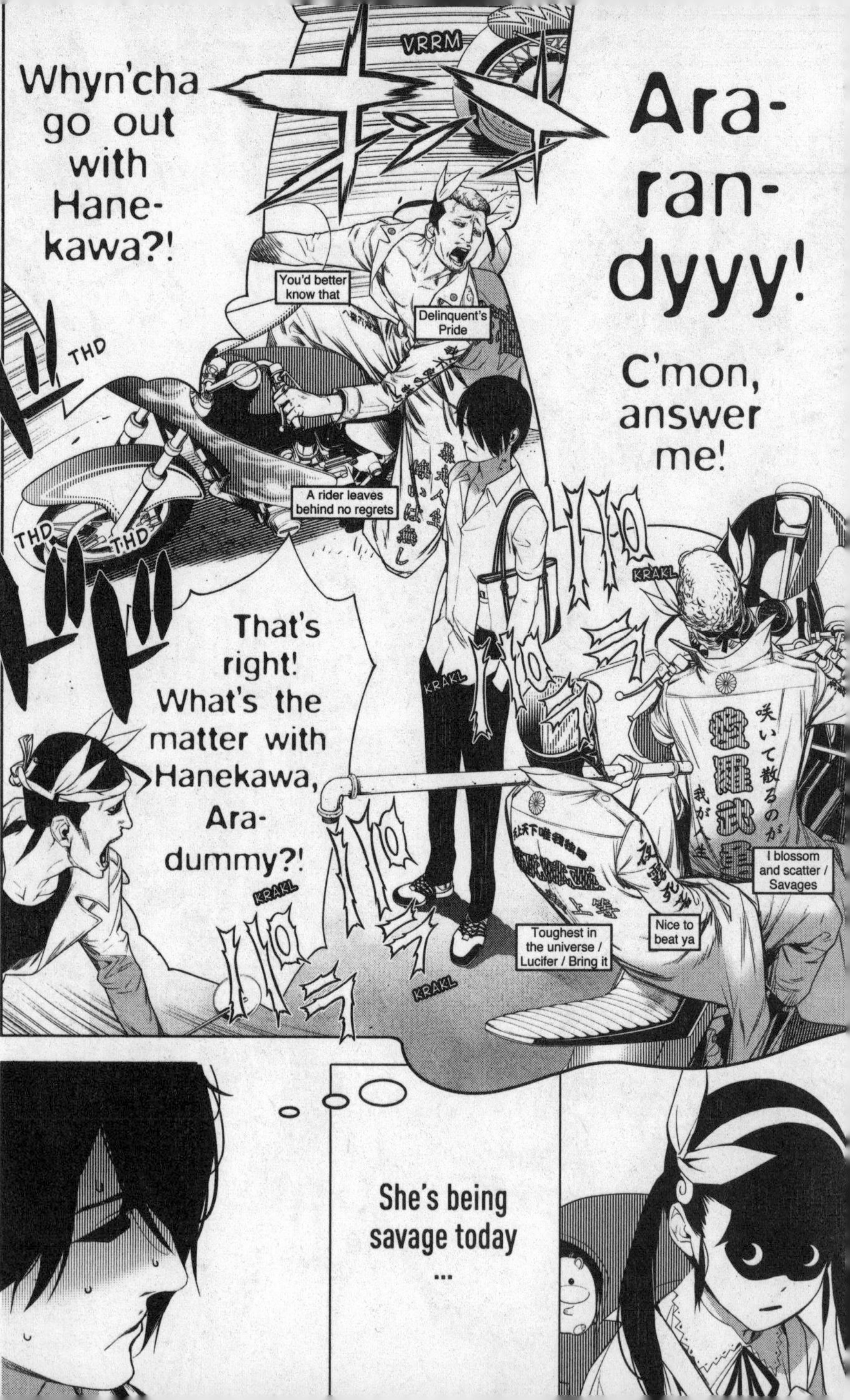
VRRM
Ara-ran-dyyy!
C'mon, answer me!
Whyn'cha go out with Hane-kawa?!
You'd better know that
Delinquent's Pride
THD
A rider leaves behind no regrets
THD
THD
KRAKL
I blossom and scatter / Savages
Nice to beat ya
Toughest in the universe / Lucifer / Bring it
KRAKL
That's right! What's the matter with Hanekawa, Ara-dummy?!
KRAKL
KRAKL
She's being savage today ...

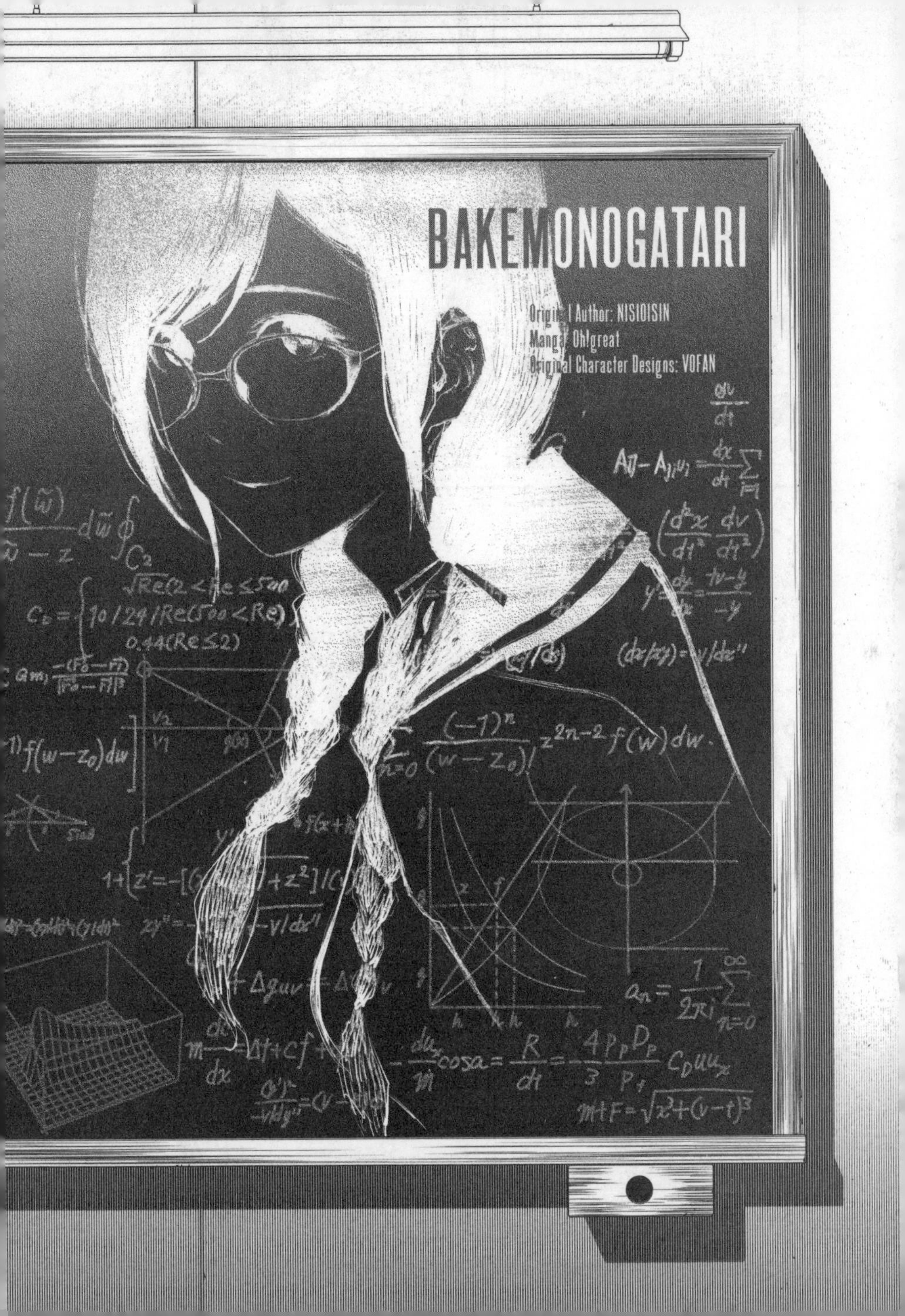
BAKEMONOGATARI
Original Author: NISIOISIN
Manga: Oh!great
Original Character Designs: VOFAN

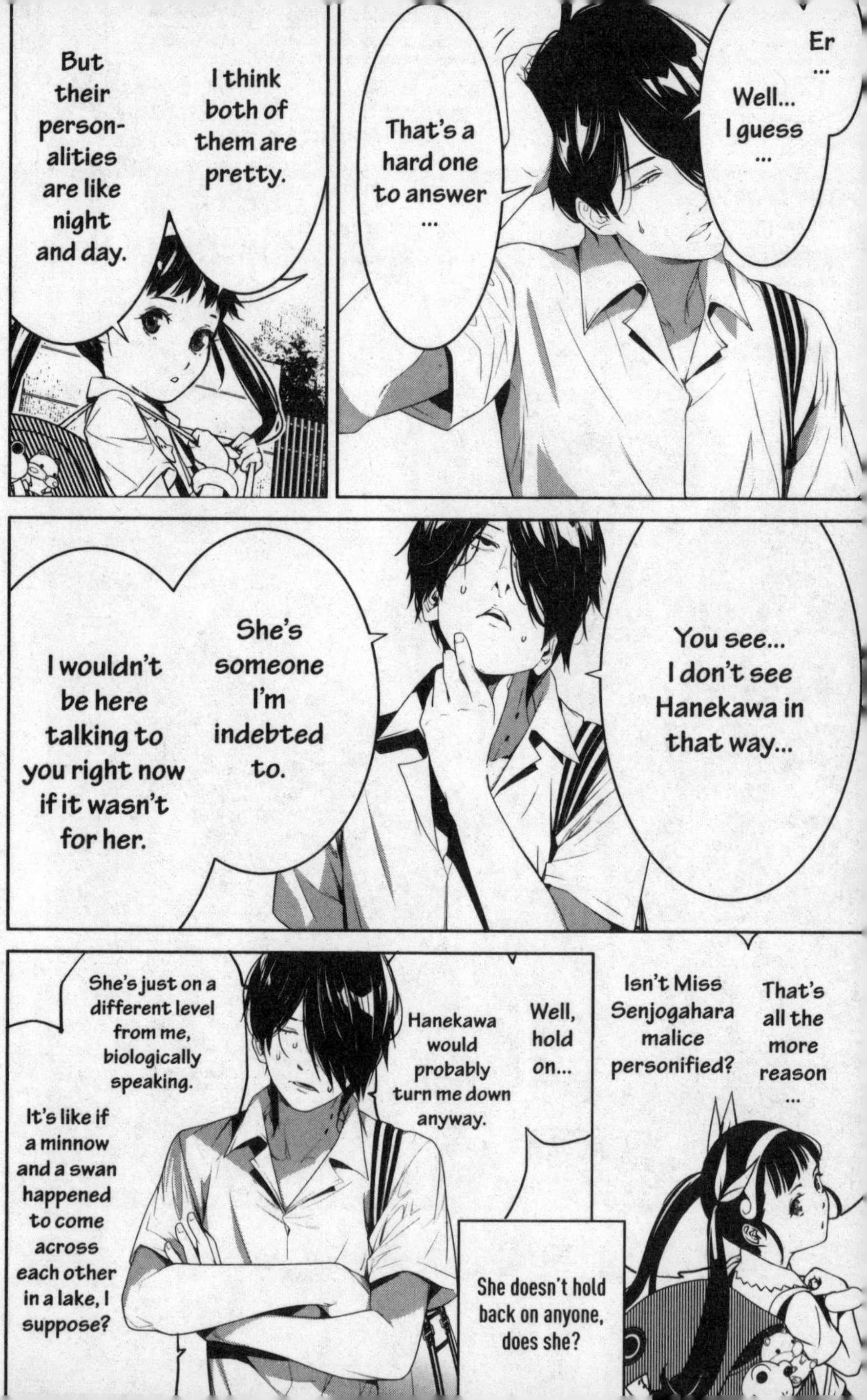
Er...
Well... I guess...
That's a hard one to answer...
I think both of them are pretty.
But their personalities are like night and day.
You see... I don't see Hanekawa in that way...
She's someone I'm indebted to.
I wouldn't be here talking to you right now if it wasn't for her.
That's all the more reason...
Isn't Miss Senjogahara malice personified?
Well, hold on...
Hanekawa would probably turn me down anyway.
She's just on a different level from me, biologically speaking.
It's like if a minnow and a swan happened to come across each other in a lake, I suppose?
She doesn't hold back on anyone, does she?

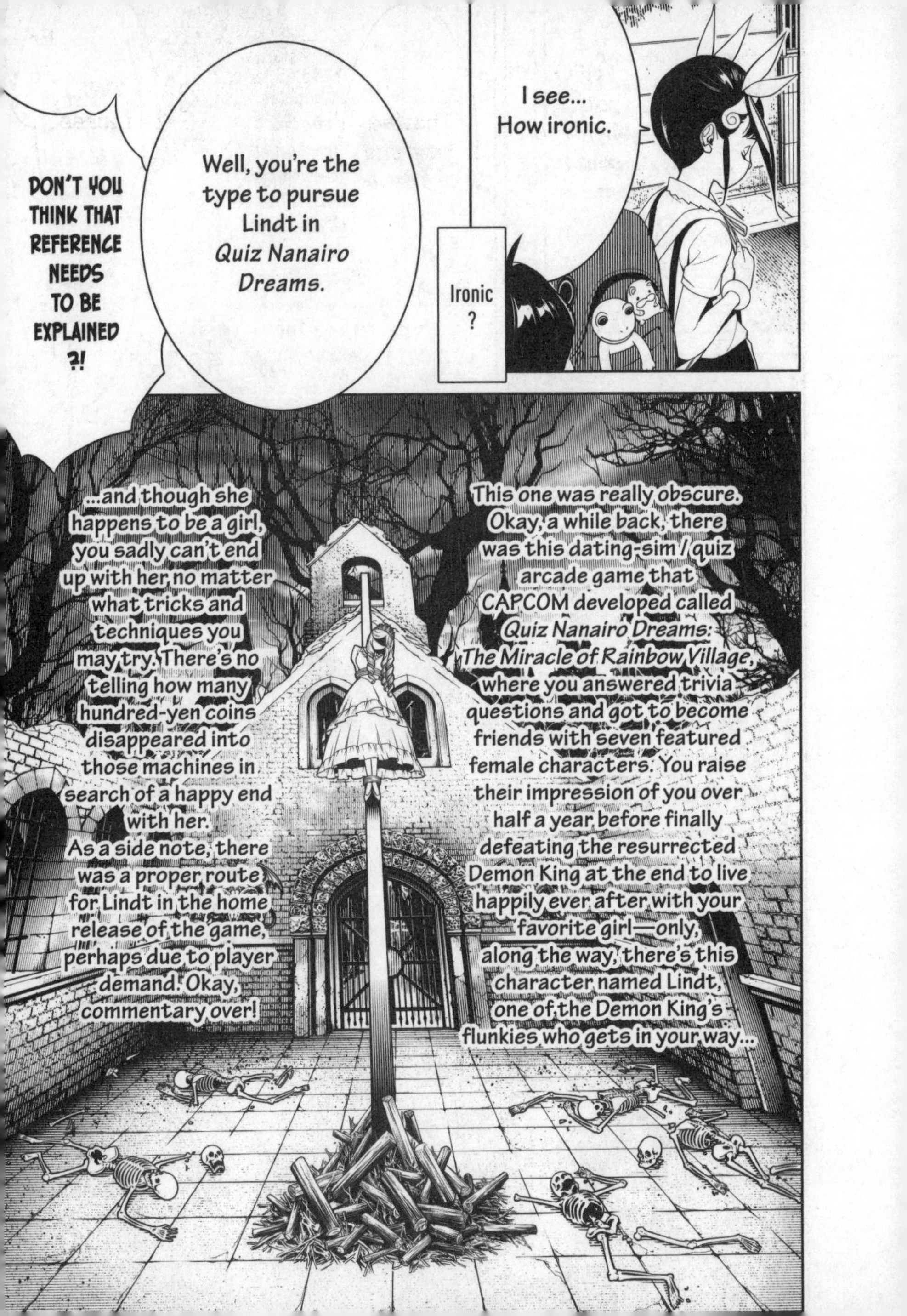
I see... How ironic.
Ironic ?
Well, you're the type to pursue Lindt in *Quiz Nanairo Dreams.*
DON'T YOU THINK THAT REFERENCE NEEDS TO BE EXPLAINED ?!
This one was really obscure. Okay, a while back, there was this dating-sim / quiz arcade game that CAPCOM developed called *Quiz Nanairo Dreams: The Miracle of Rainbow Village,* where you answered trivia questions and got to become friends with seven featured female characters. You raise their impression of you over half a year before finally defeating the resurrected Demon King at the end to live happily ever after with your favorite girl—only, along the way, there's this character named Lindt, one of the Demon King's flunkies who gets in your way...
...and though she happens to be a girl, you sadly can't end up with her, no matter what tricks and techniques you may try. There's no telling how many hundred-yen coins disappeared into those machines in search of a happy end with her.
As a side note, there was a proper route for Lindt in the home release of the game, perhaps due to player demand. Okay, commentary over!

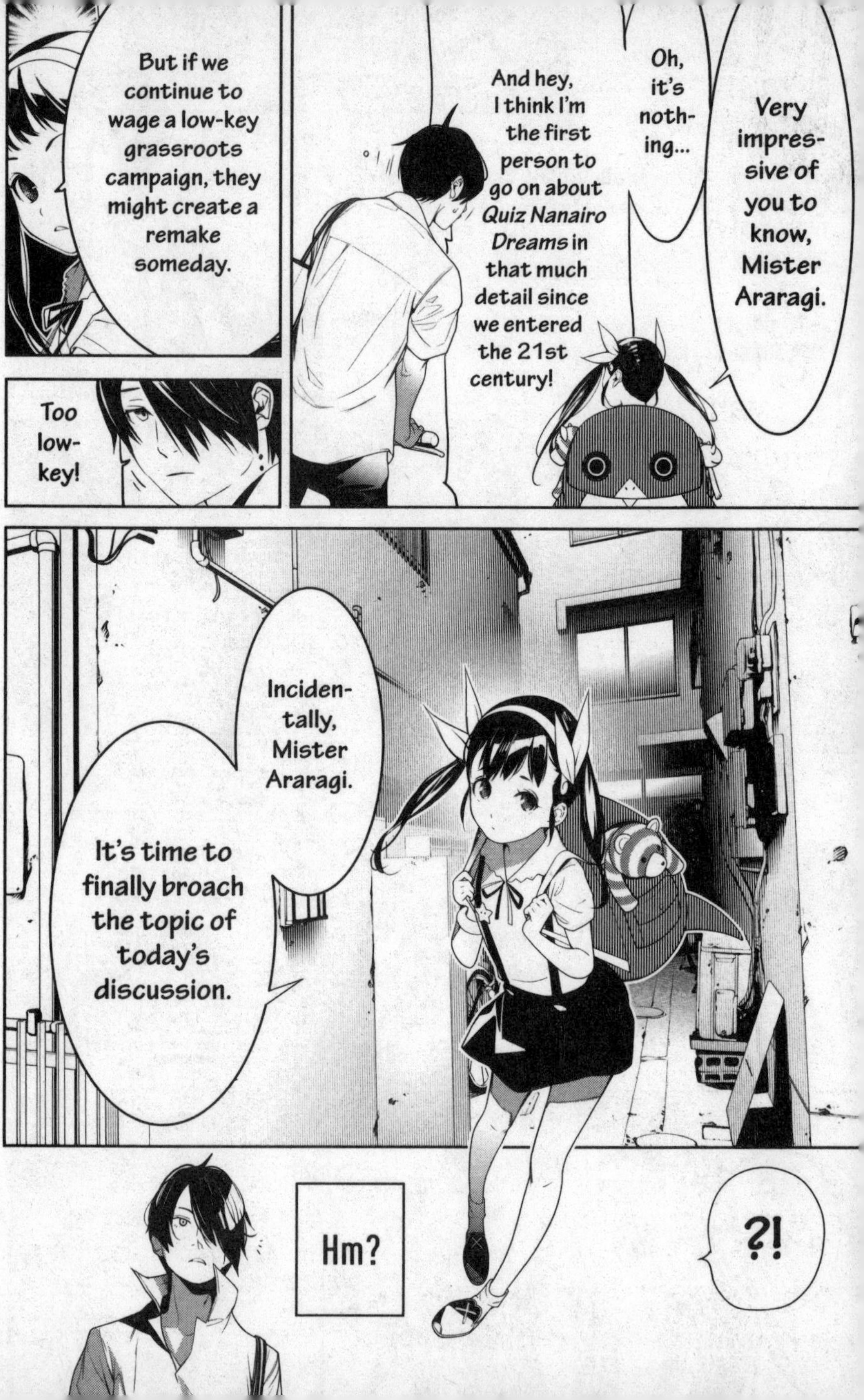
Very impressive of you to know, Mister Araragi.
Oh, it's nothing...
And hey, I think I'm the first person to go on about *Quiz Nanairo Dreams* in that much detail since we entered the 21st century!
But if we continue to wage a low-key grassroots campaign, they might create a remake someday.
Too low-key!
Inciden-tally, Mister Araragi.
It's time to finally broach the topic of today's discussion.
?!
Hm?

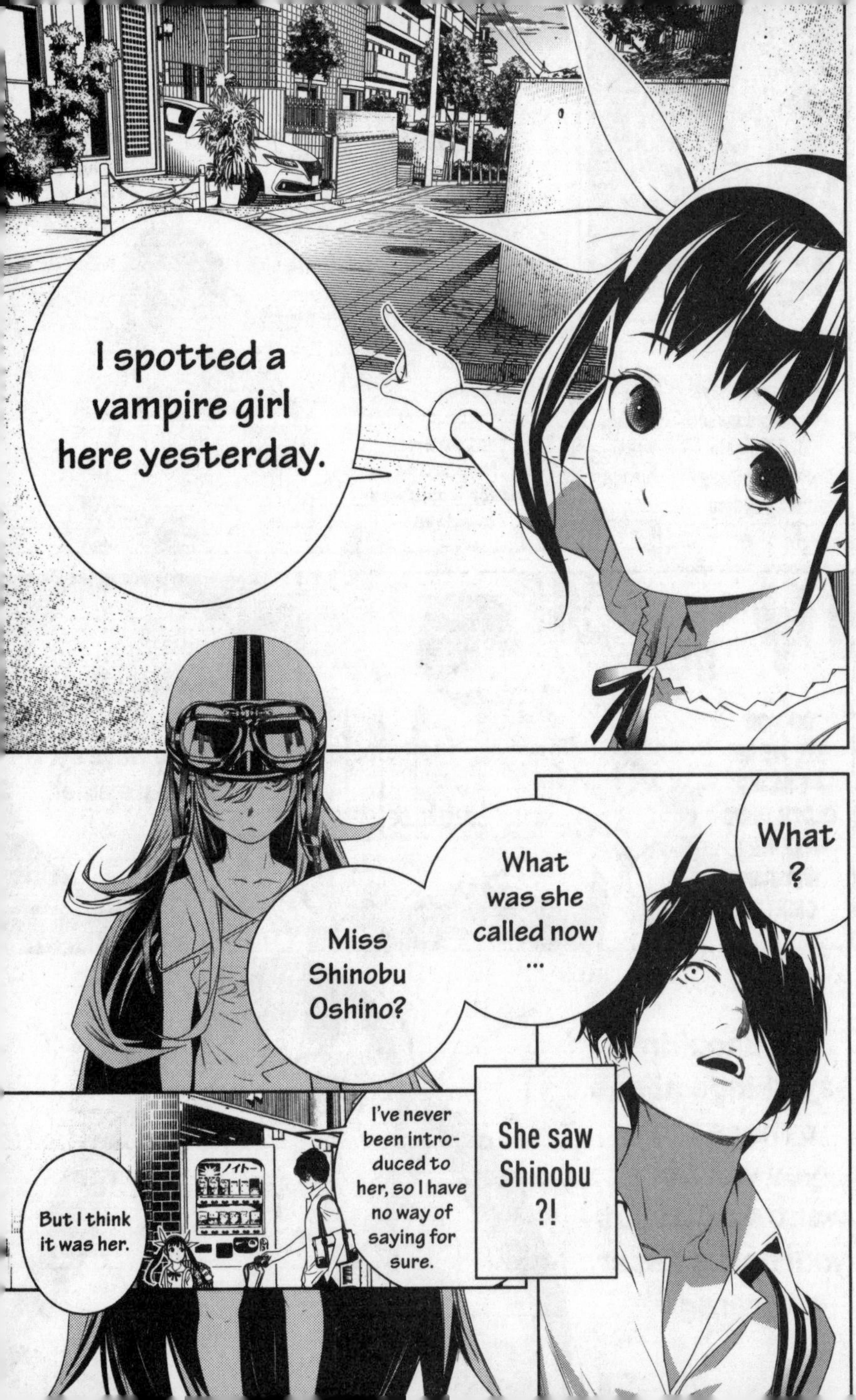
I spotted a vampire girl here yesterday.
What ?
She saw Shinobu ?!
What was she called now ...
Miss Shinobu Oshino?
I've never been intro-duced to her, so I have no way of saying for sure.
But I think it was her.

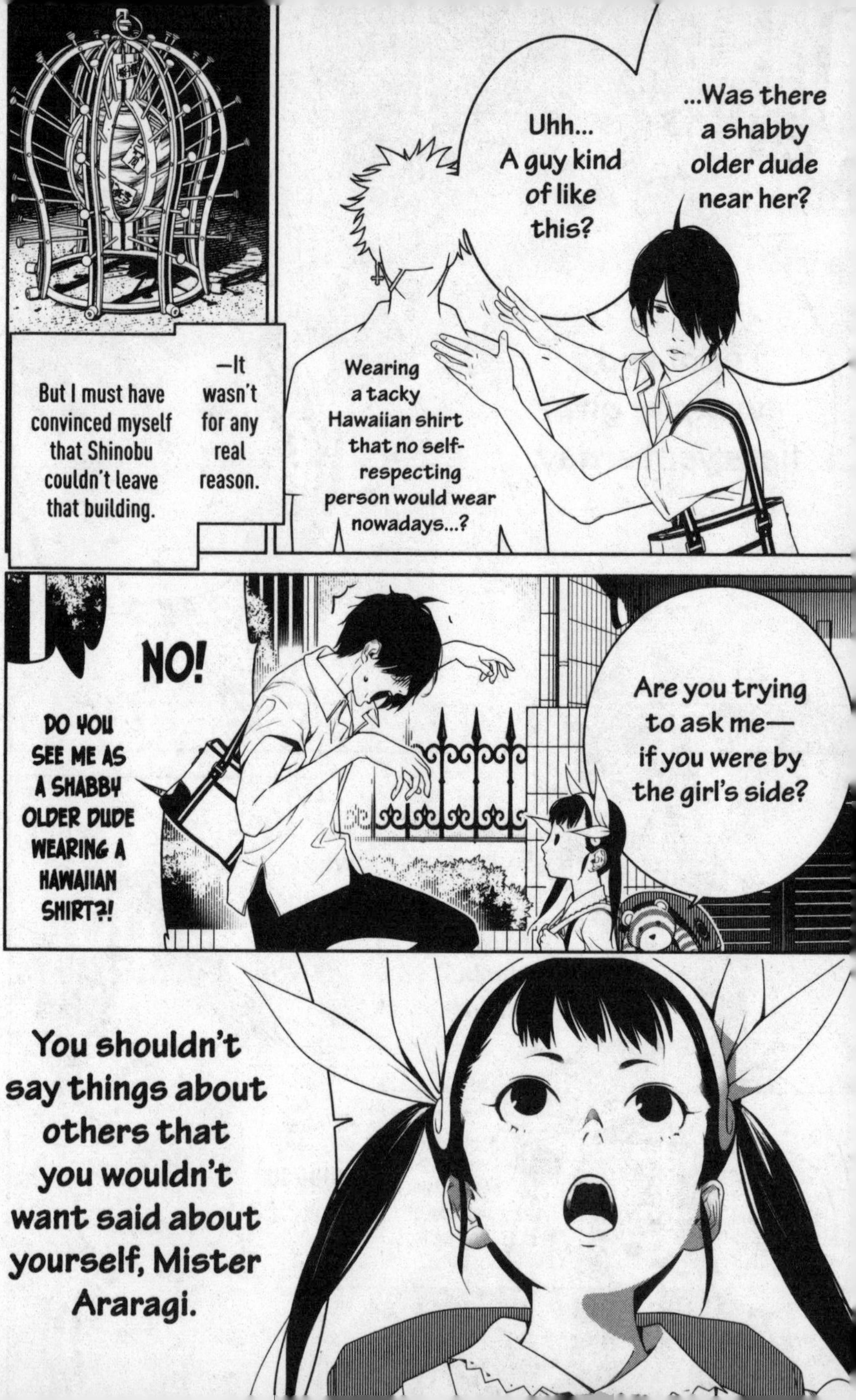
...Was there a shabby older dude near her?
Uhh... A guy kind of like this?
Wearing a tacky Hawaiian shirt that no self-respecting person would wear nowadays...?
—It wasn't for any real reason.
But I must have convinced myself that Shinobu couldn't leave that building.
Are you trying to ask me— if you were by the girl's side?
NO!
DO YOU SEE ME AS A SHABBY OLDER DUDE WEARING A HAWAIIAN SHIRT?!
You shouldn't say things about others that you wouldn't want said about yourself, Mister Araragi.

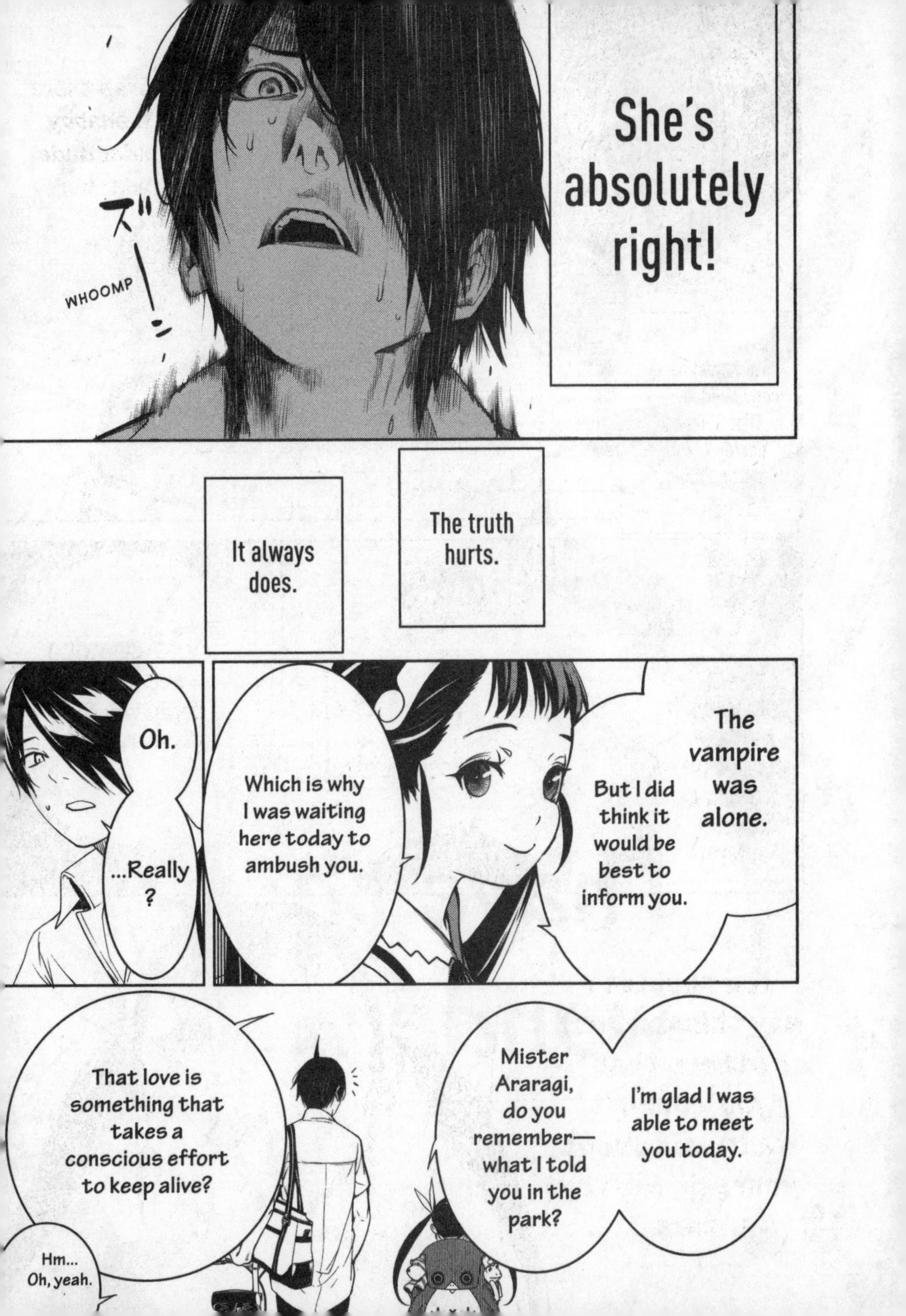
She's absolutely right!
ズー
WHOOMP
The truth hurts.
It always does.
The vampire was alone.
But I did think it would be best to inform you.
Which is why I was waiting here today to ambush you.
Oh.
...Really ?
I'm glad I was able to meet you today.
Mister Araragi, do you remember— what I told you in the park?
That love is something that takes a conscious effort to keep alive?
Hm... Oh, yeah.

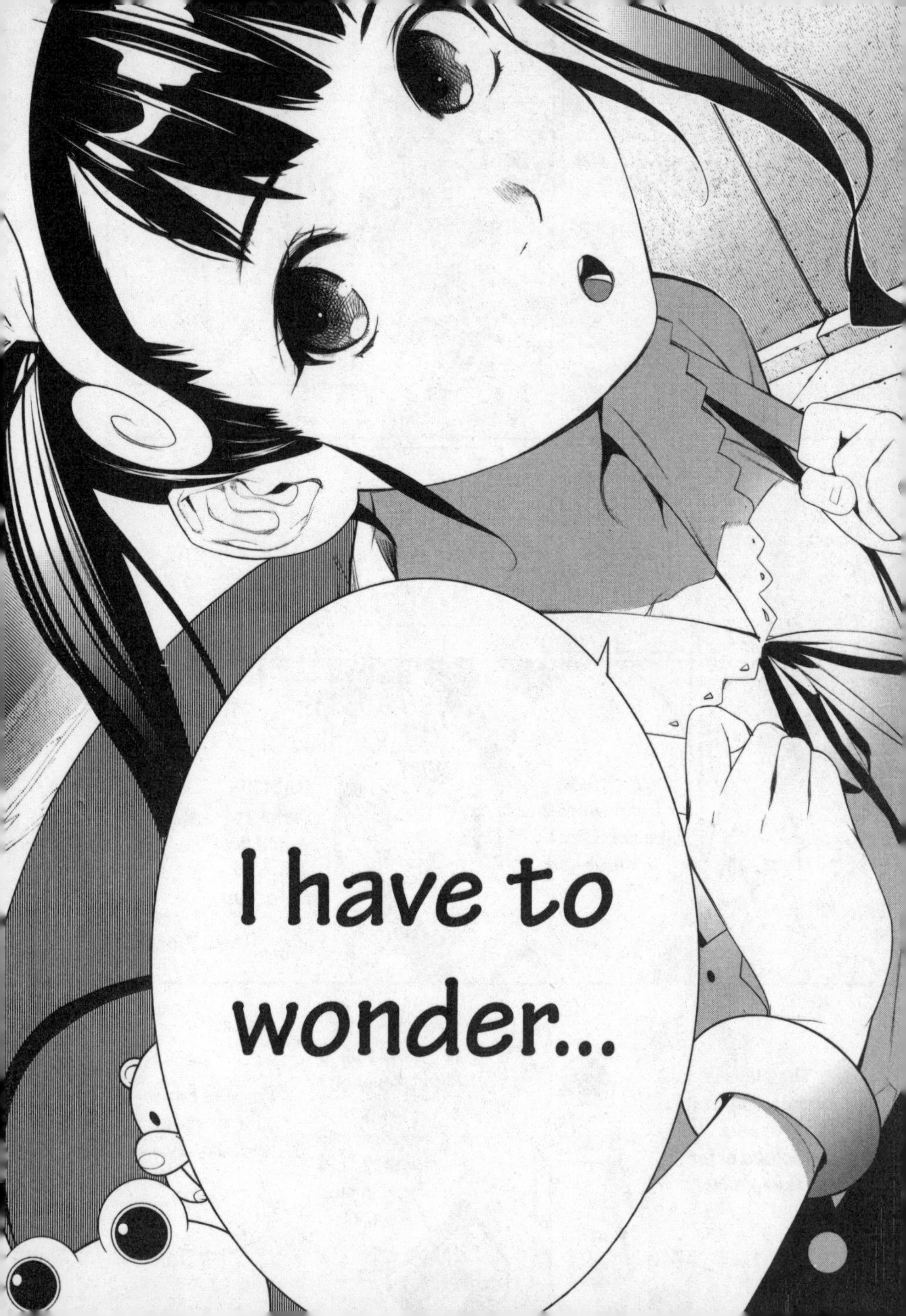
I have to wonder...

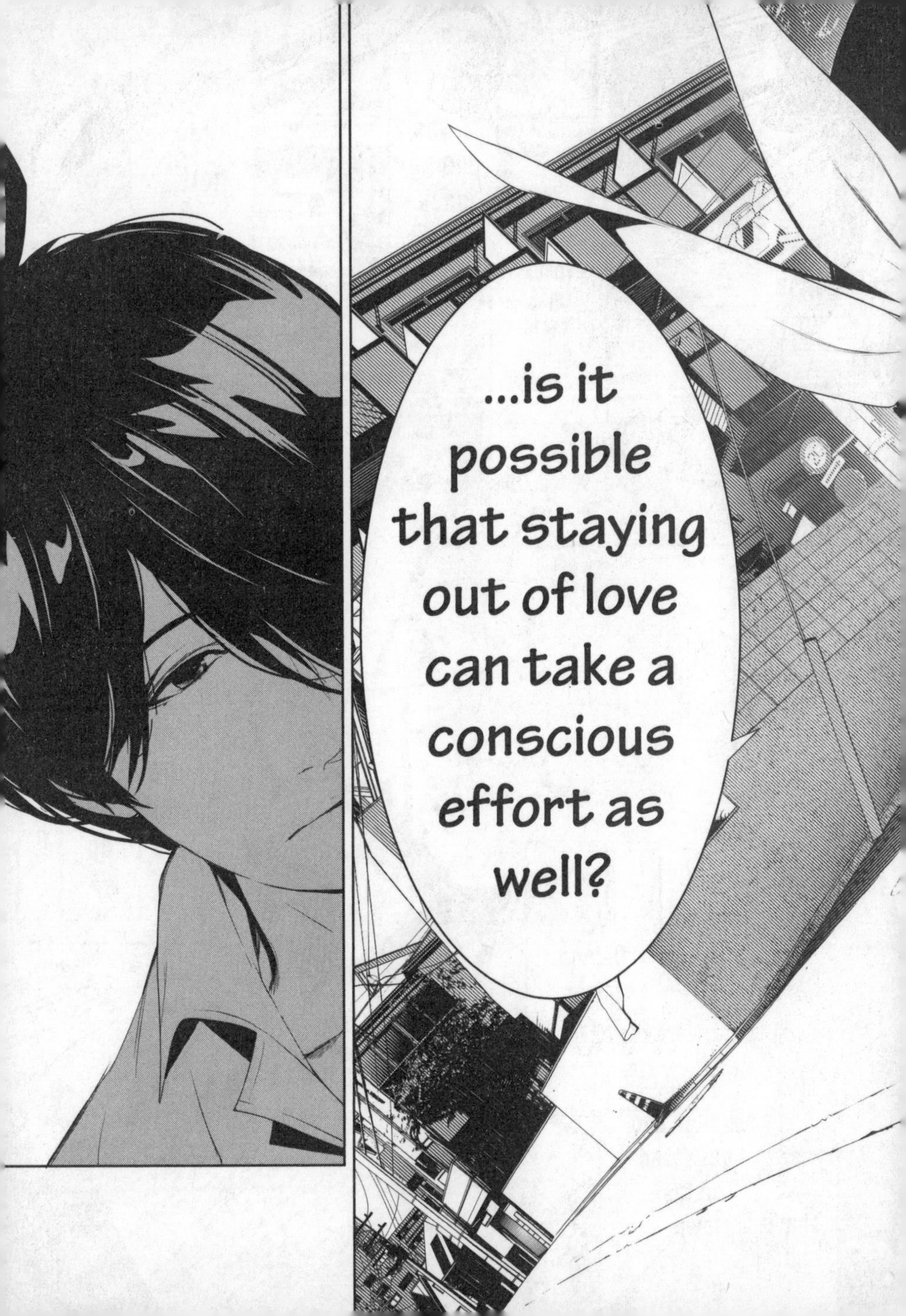
...is it possible that staying out of love can take a conscious effort as well?

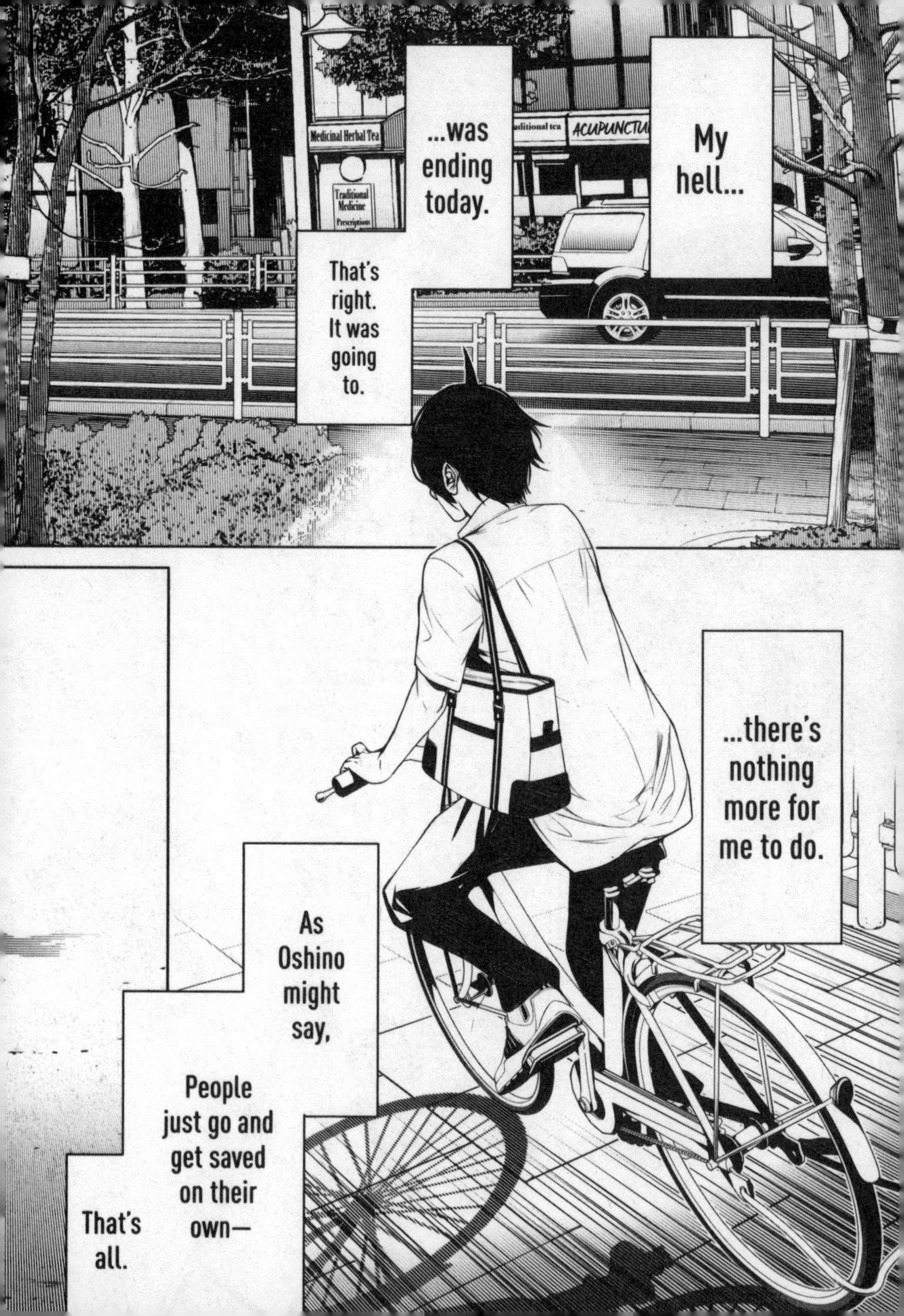
My hell...
...was ending today.
That's right. It was going to.
Medicinal Herbal Tea
Traditional Medicine Prescriptions
...there's nothing more for me to do.
As Oshino might say,
People just go and get saved on their own—
That's all.

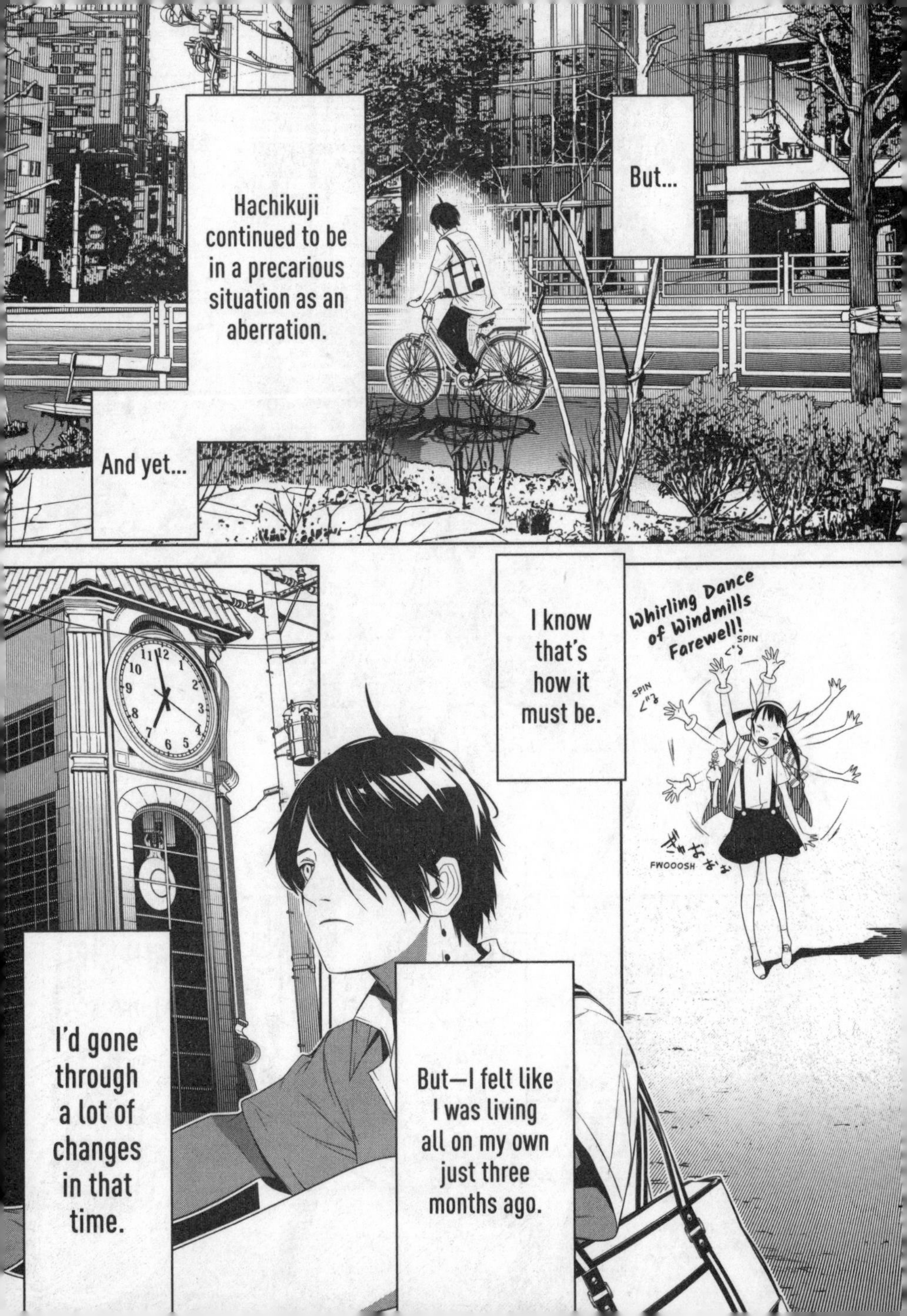
But...
Hachikuji continued to be in a precarious situation as an aberration.
And yet...
Whirling Dance of Windmills Farewell!
SPIN
SPIN
FWOOOSH
I know that's how it must be.
But—I felt like I was living all on my own just three months ago.
I'd gone through a lot of changes in that time.

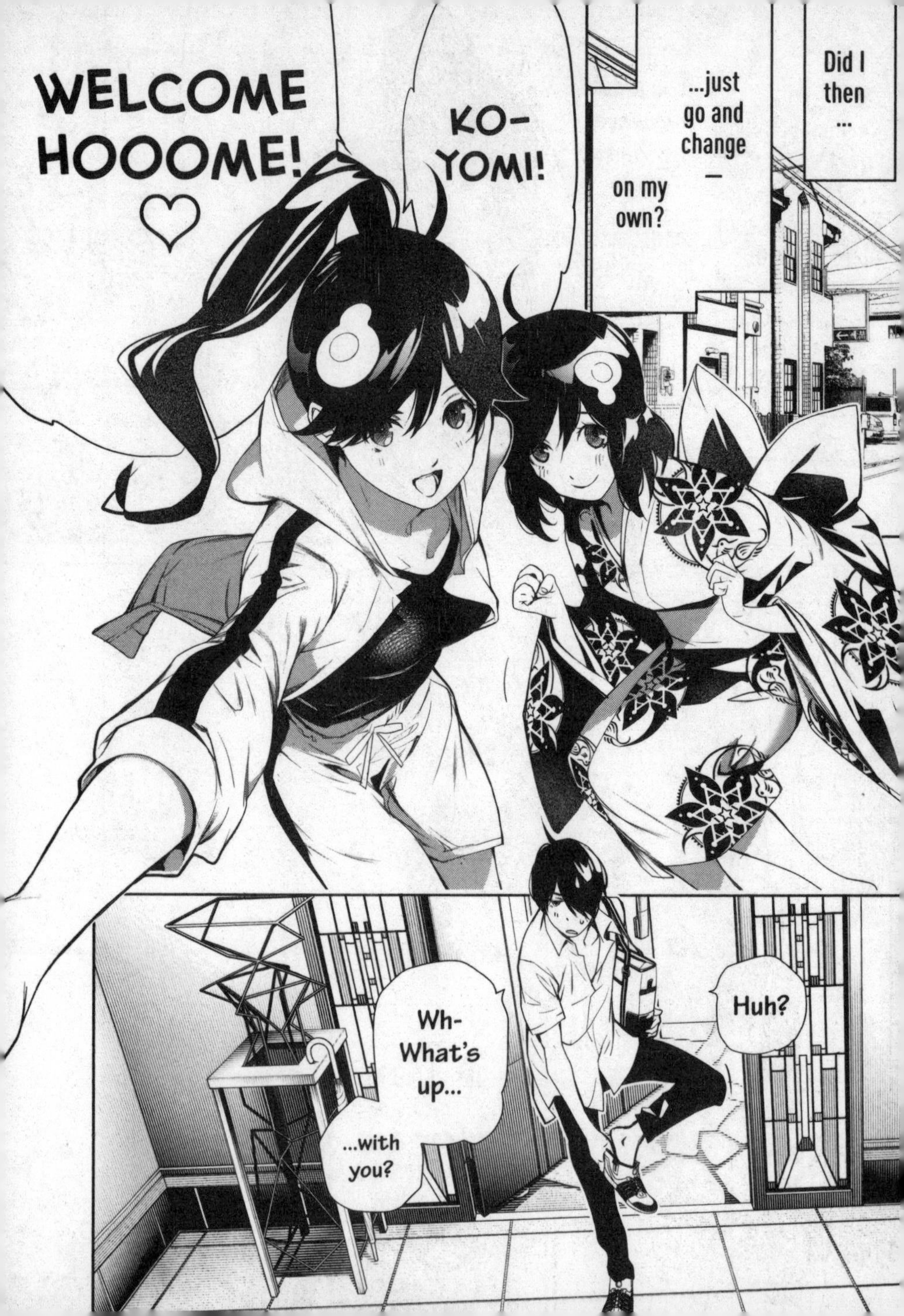
Did I then ...
...just go and change — on my own?
KO-YOMI!
WELCOME HOOOME! ♡
Huh?
Wh- What's up...
...with you?

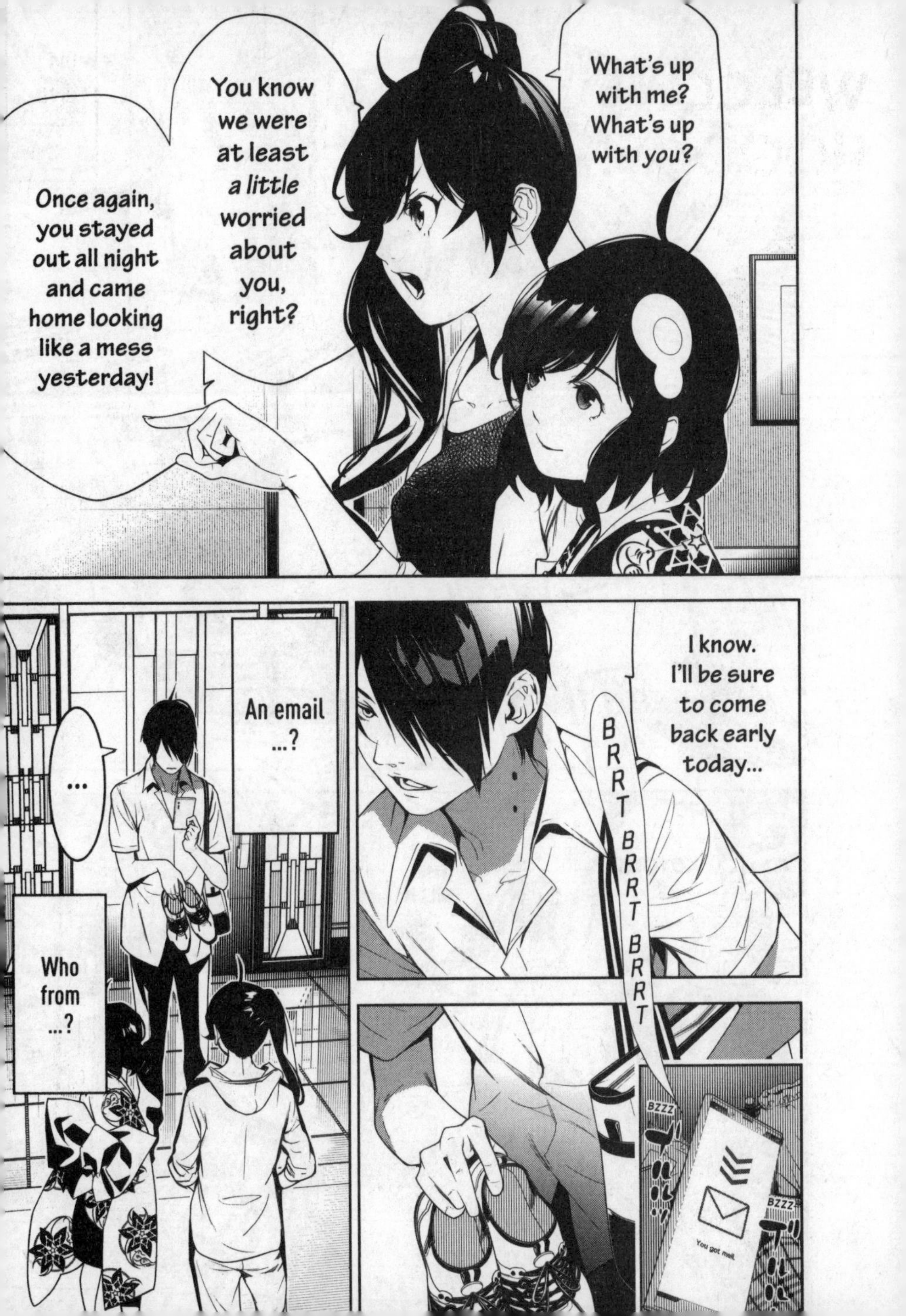
What's up with me? What's up with *you*?
You know we were at least *a little* worried about you, right?
Once again, you stayed out all night and came home looking like a mess yesterday!
I know. I'll be sure to come back early today...
BRRT BRRT BRRT BRRT
BZZZ
BZZZ
You got mail
An email ...?
...
Who from ...?

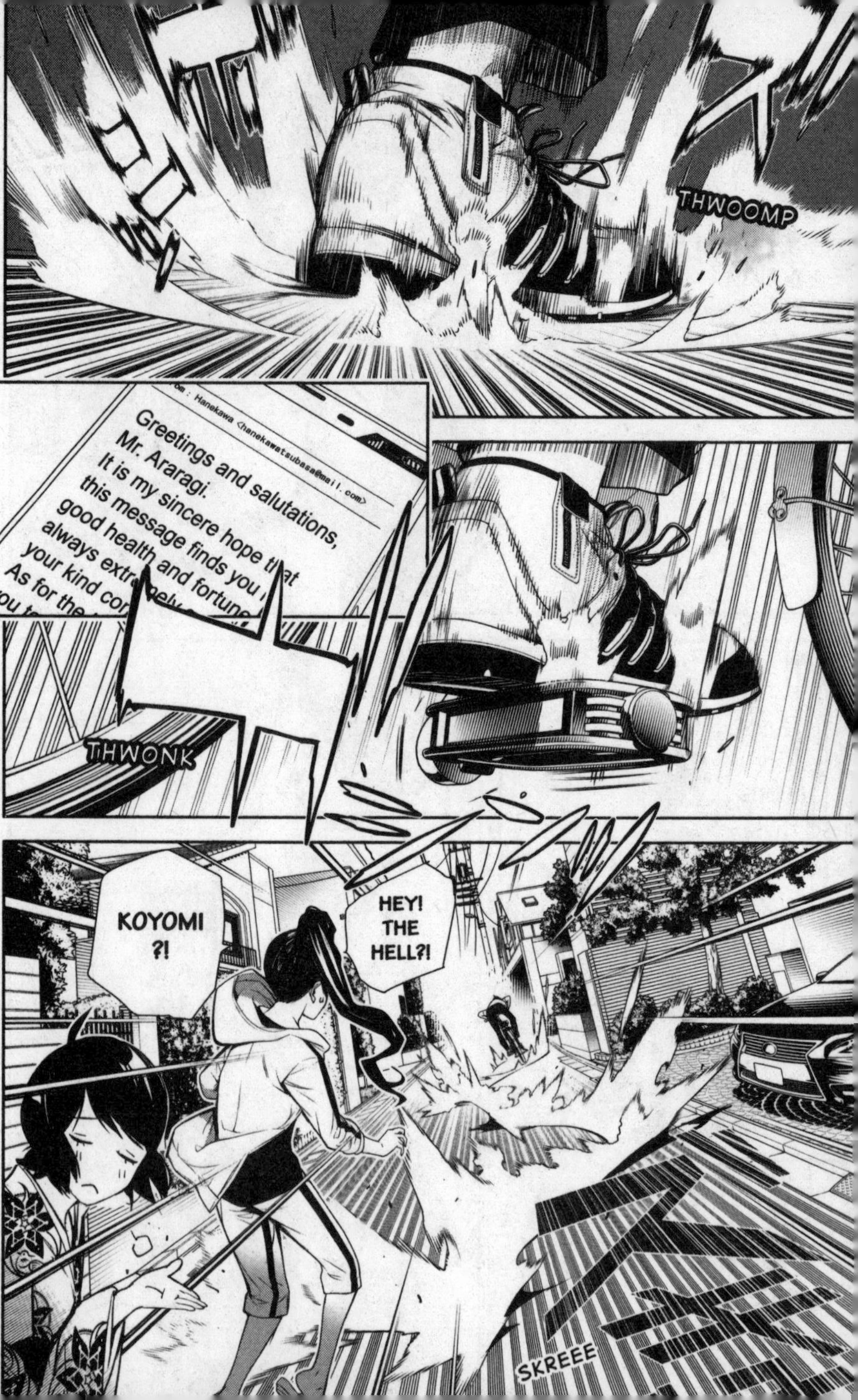
THWOOMP
THWONK
om : Hanekawa <hanekawatsubasa@mail.com>
Greetings and salutations,
Mr. Araragi.
It is my sincere hope that
this message finds you
good health and fortune
always ext
your kind co
As for the
HEY! THE HELL?!
KOYOMI ?!
SKREEE

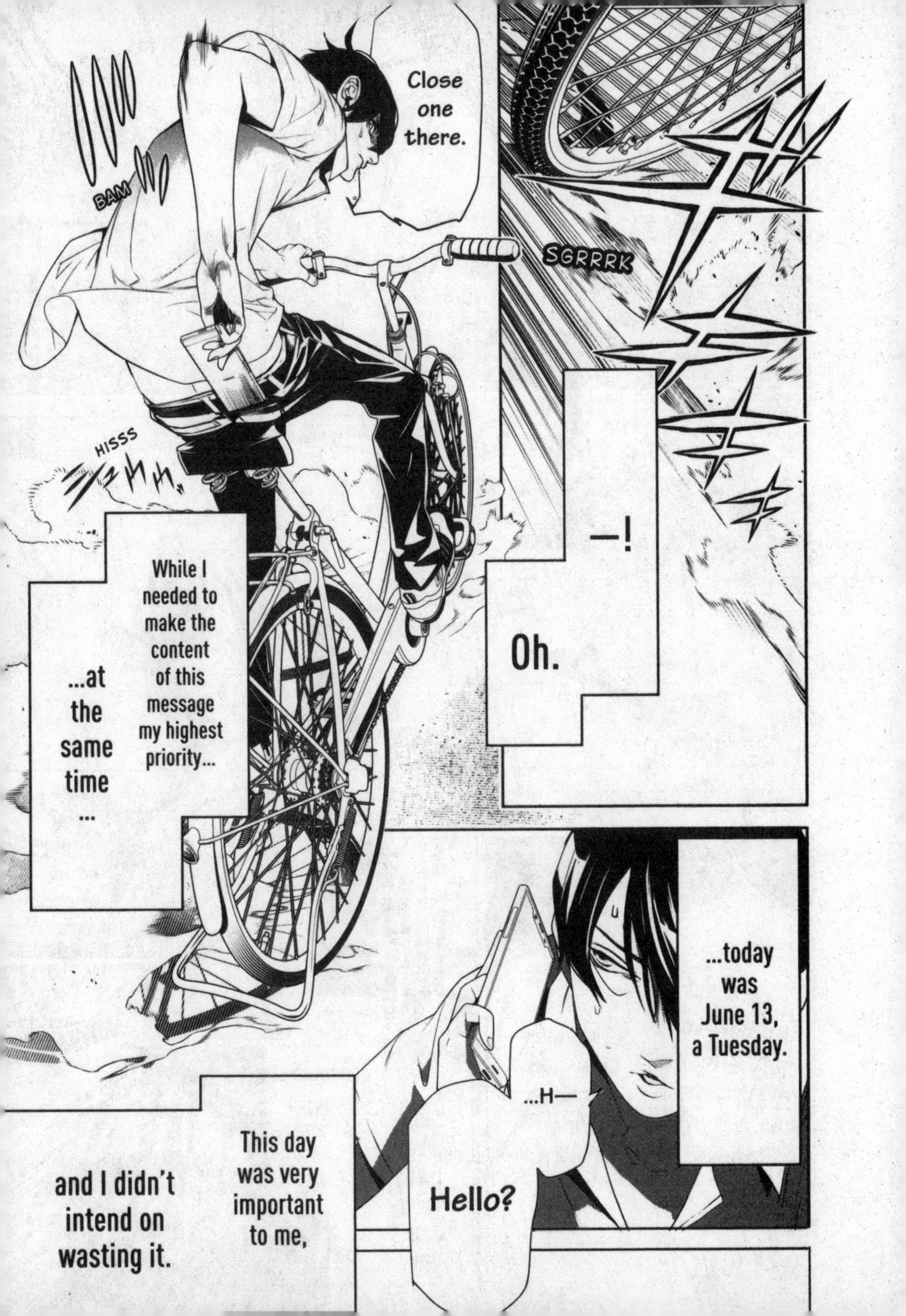
SGRRRK
—!
Oh.
Close one there.
BAM
HISSS
While I needed to make the content of this message my highest priority...
...at the same time...
...today was June 13, a Tuesday.
...H—
Hello?
This day was very important to me,
and I didn't intend on wasting it.

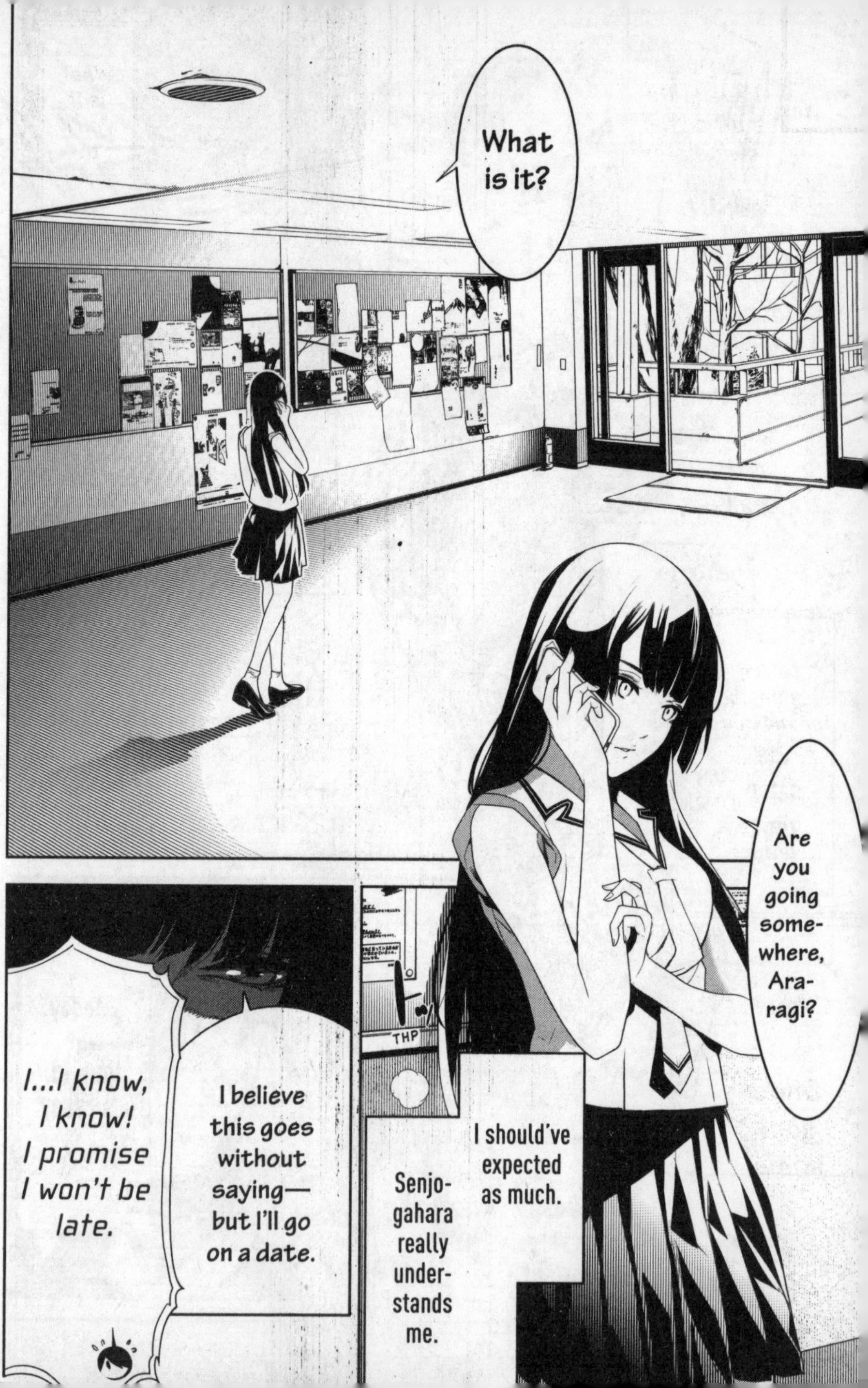
What is it?
Are you going somewhere, Araragi?
I should've expected as much.
Senjogahara really understands me.
I believe this goes without saying—but I'll go on a date.
I...I know, I know! I promise I won't be late.
THP

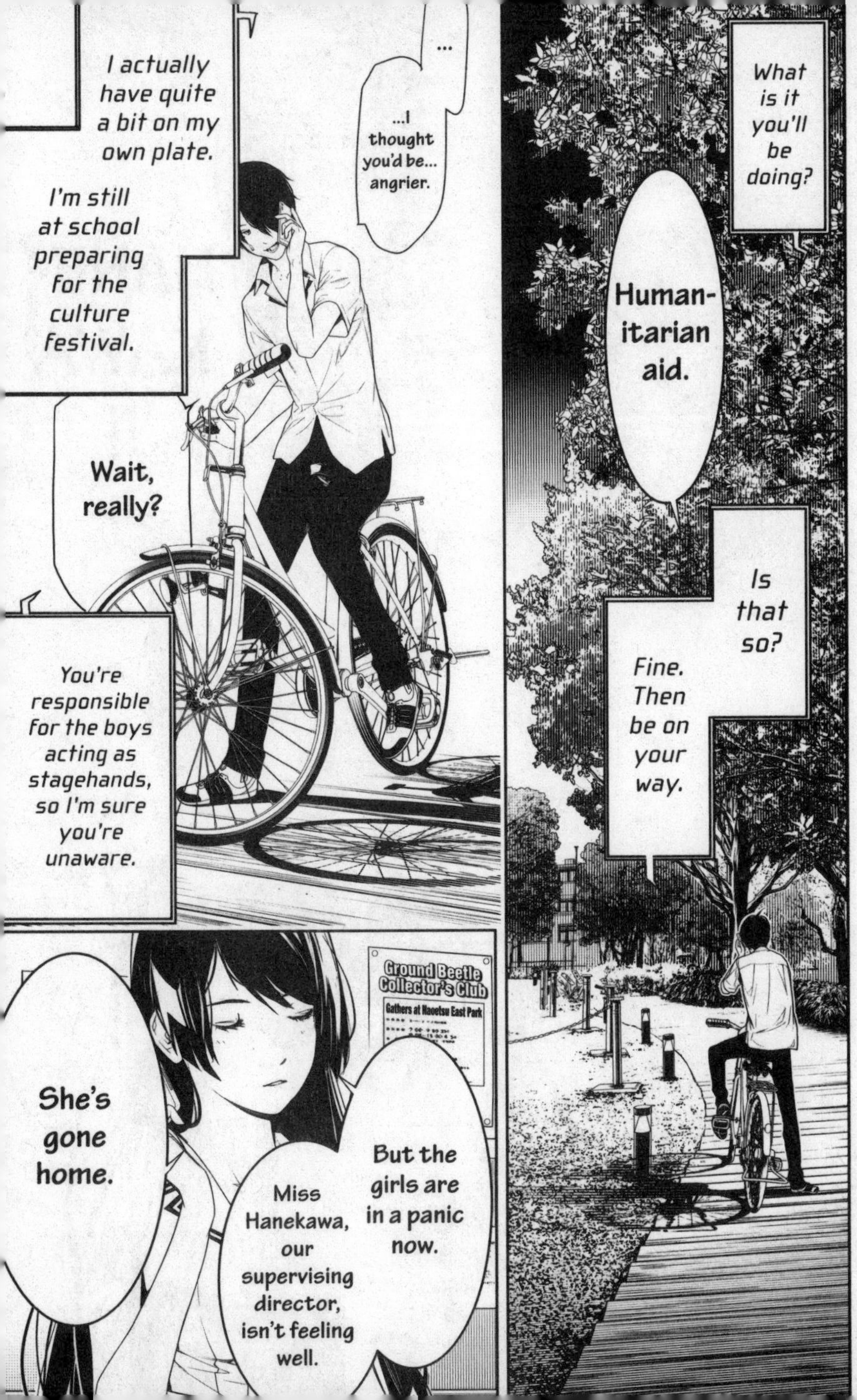
What is it you'll be doing?
Human-itarian aid.
Is that so?
Fine. Then be on your way.
...
...I thought you'd be... angrier.
I actually have quite a bit on my own plate.
I'm still at school preparing for the culture festival.
Wait, really?
You're responsible for the boys acting as stagehands, so I'm sure you're unaware.
Ground Beetle Collector's Club
Gathers at Naoetsu East Park
But the girls are in a panic now.
Miss Hanekawa, our supervising director, isn't feeling well.
She's gone home.

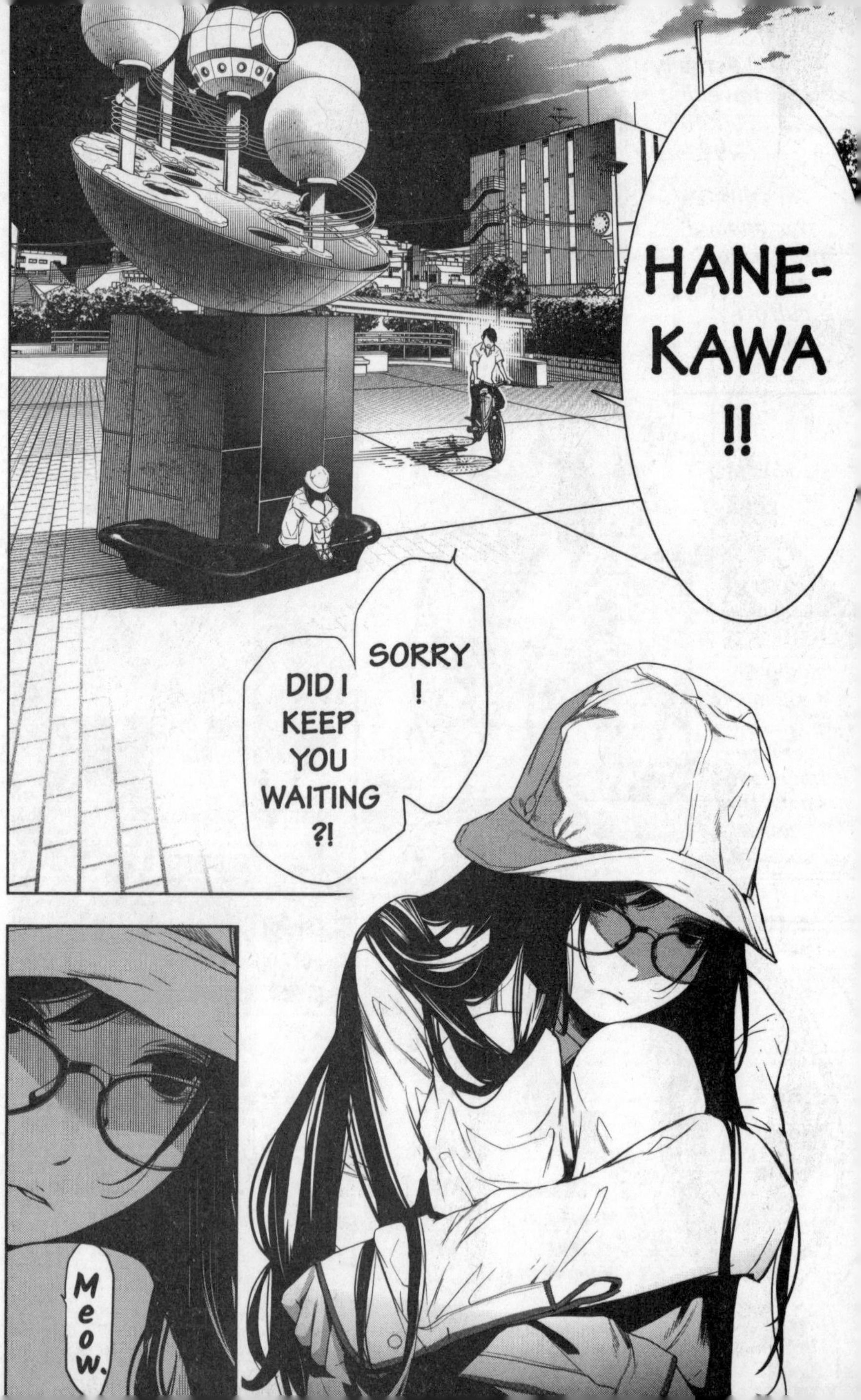
HANE-KAWA !!
SORRY !
DID I KEEP YOU WAITING ?!
Meow.

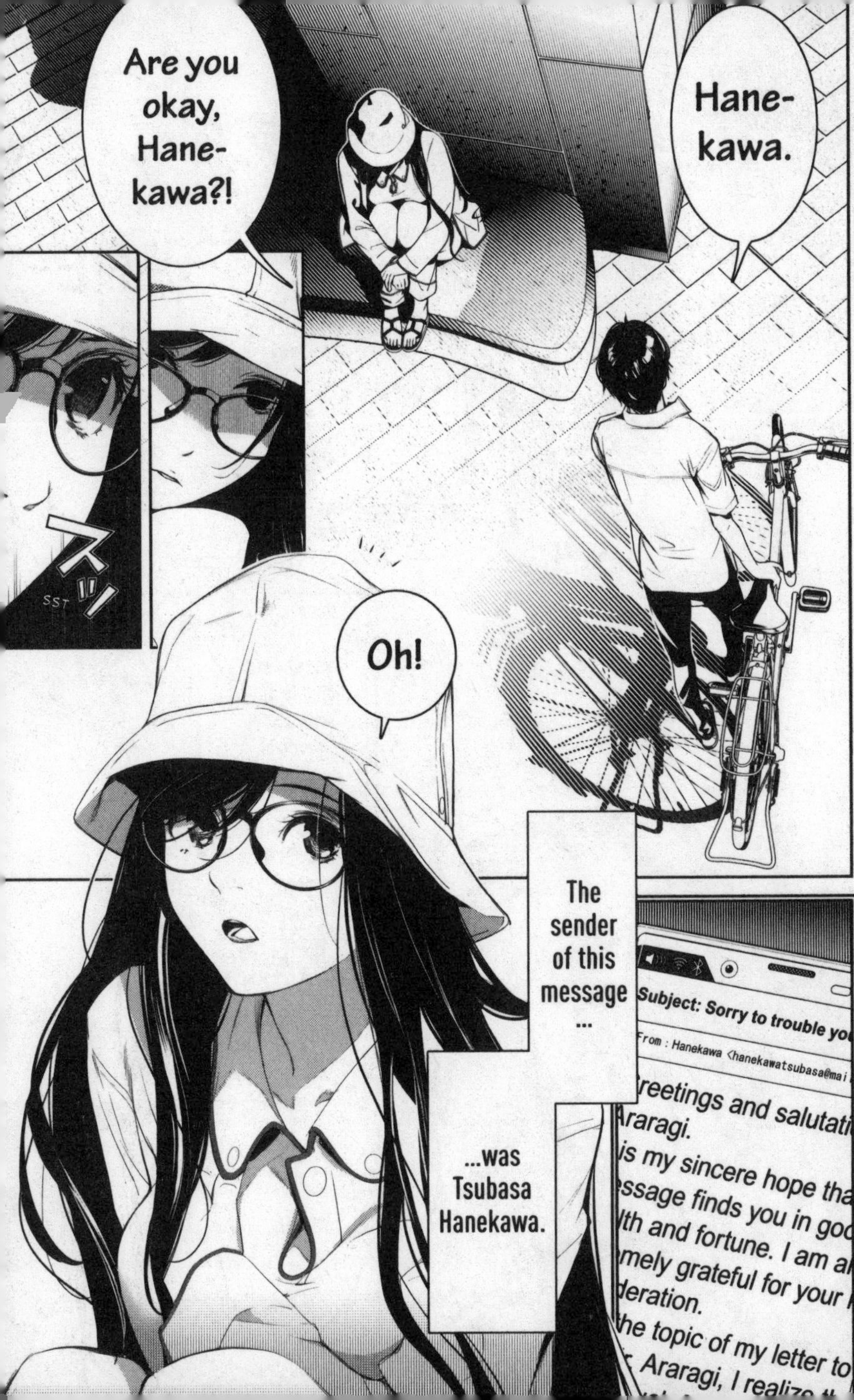
Hane-kawa.
Are you okay, Hane-kawa?!
SST
Oh!
Subject: Sorry to trouble yo
From : Hanekawa <hanekawatsubasa@mai
reetings and salutati
Araragi.
is my sincere hope tha
ssage finds you in goo
lth and fortune. I am a
mely grateful for your
deration.
the topic of my letter to
Araragi, I realize
The sender of this message...
...was Tsubasa Hanekawa.

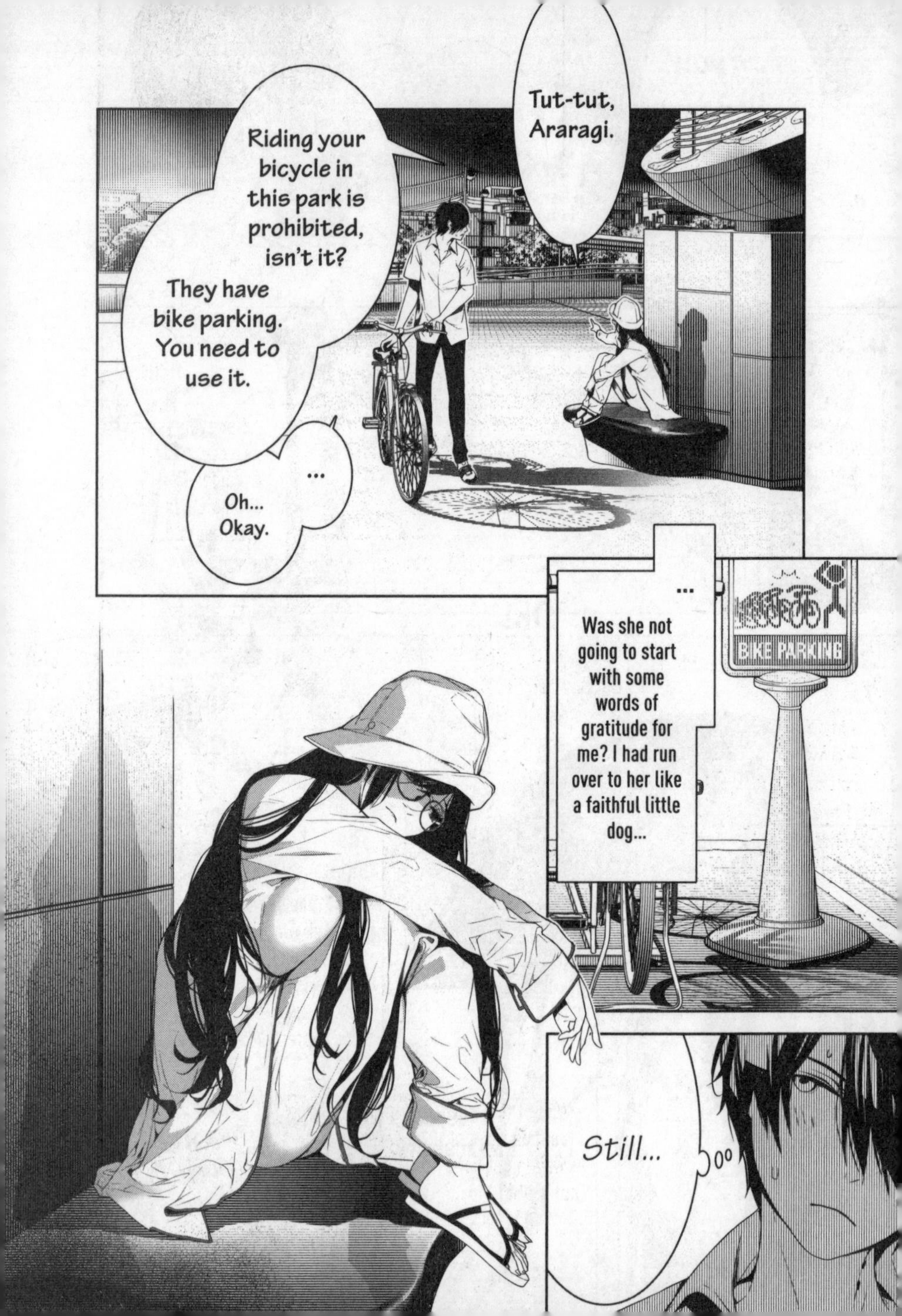
Tut-tut, Araragi.
Riding your bicycle in this park is prohibited, isn't it?
They have bike parking. You need to use it.
...
Oh... Okay.
... Was she not going to start with some words of gratitude for me? I had run over to her like a faithful little dog...
BIKE PARKING
Still...

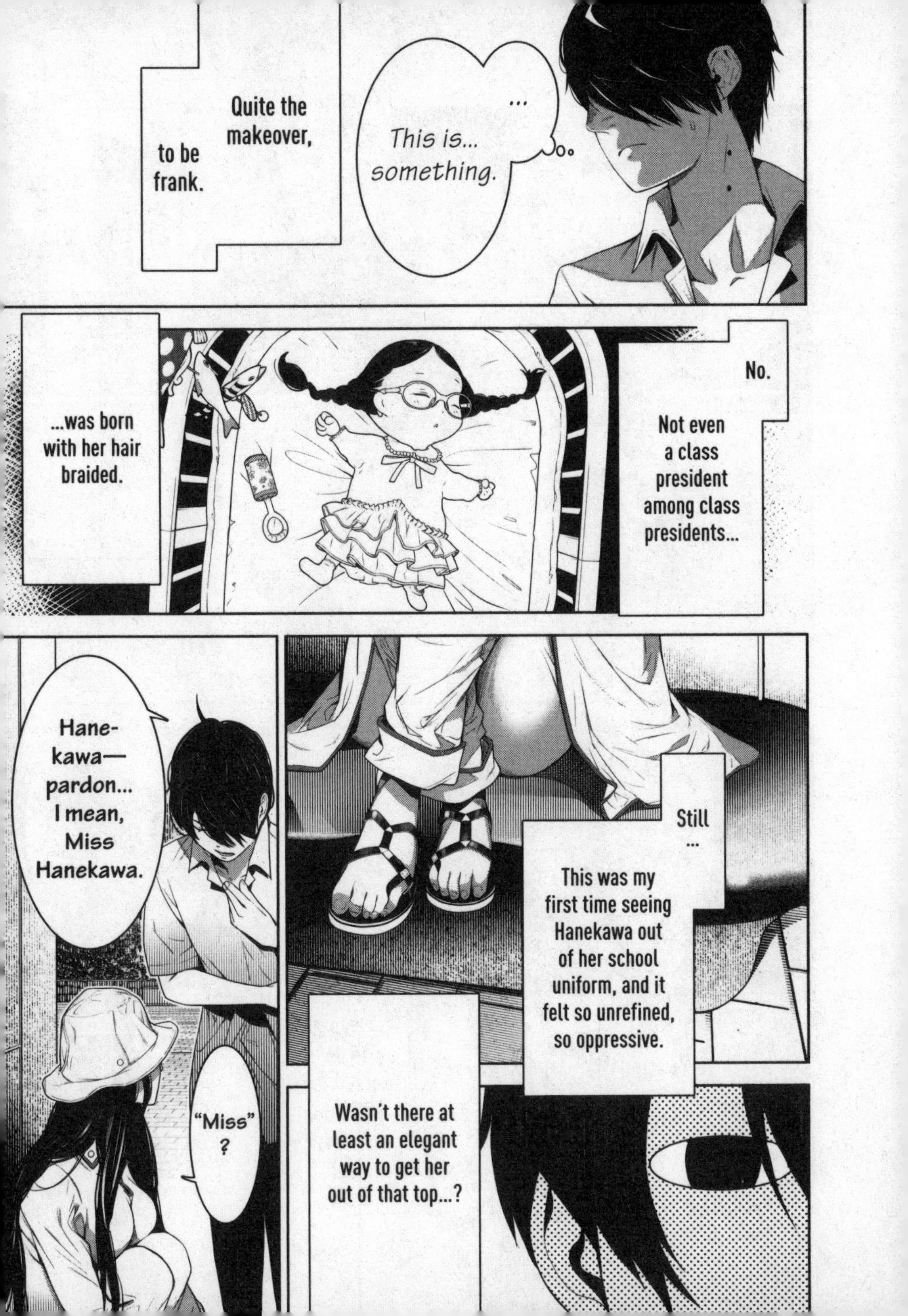
...
This is... something.
Quite the makeover, to be frank.
No. Not even a class president among class presidents...
...was born with her hair braided.
Still ... This was my first time seeing Hanekawa out of her school uniform, and it felt so unrefined, so oppressive.
Wasn't there at least an elegant way to get her out of that top...?
Hane-kawa—pardon... I mean, Miss Hanekawa.
"Miss"?

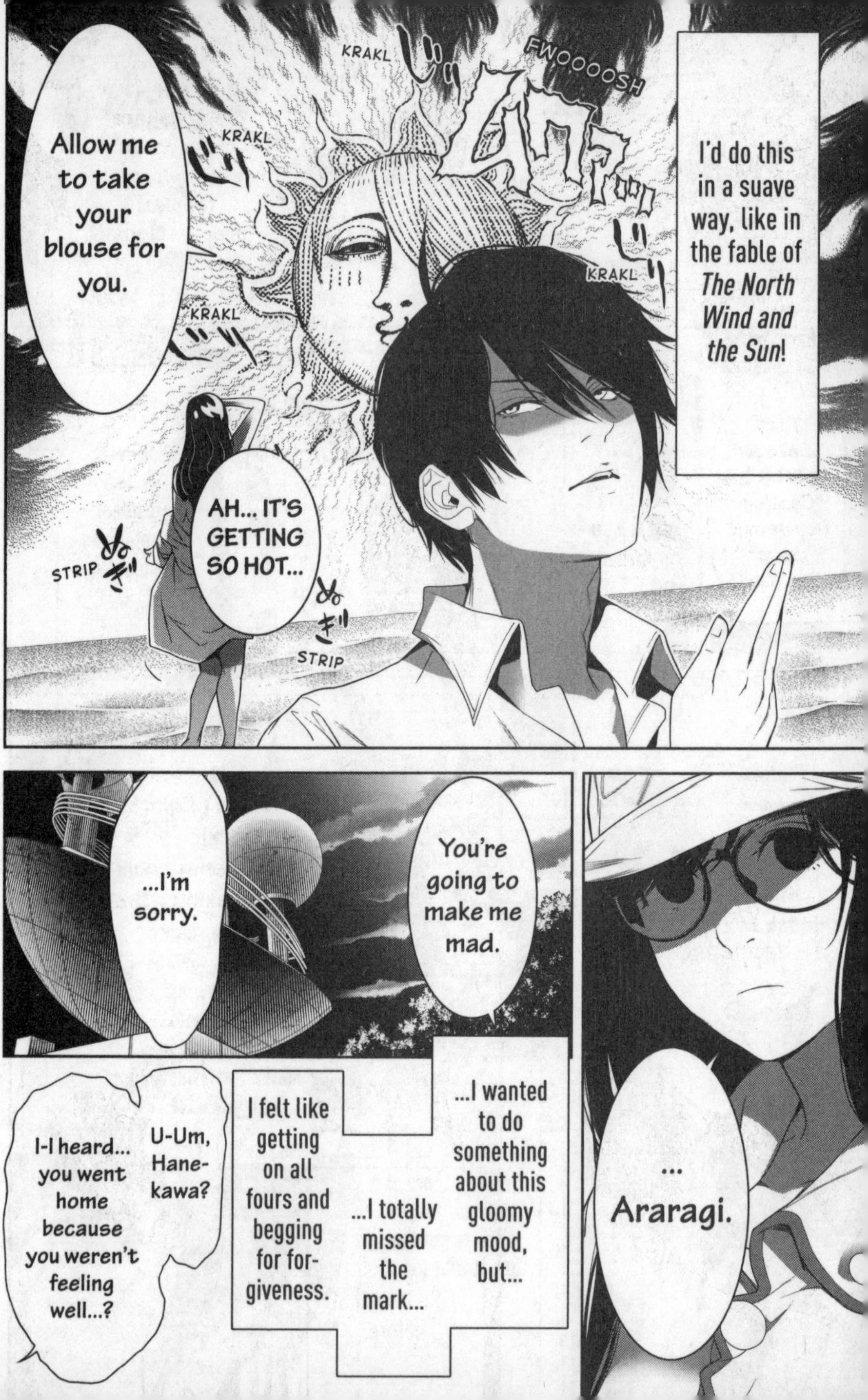
I'd do this in a suave way, like in the fable of *The North Wind and the Sun*!
FWOOOOSH
KRAKL
KRAKL
KRAKL
KRAKL
Allow me to take your blouse for you.
AH... IT'S GETTING SO HOT...
STRIP
STRIP
... Araragi.
You're going to make me mad.
...I'm sorry.
...I wanted to do something about this gloomy mood, but...
...I totally missed the mark...
I felt like getting on all fours and begging for for-giveness.
U-Um, Hane-kawa?
I-I heard... you went home because you weren't feeling well...?

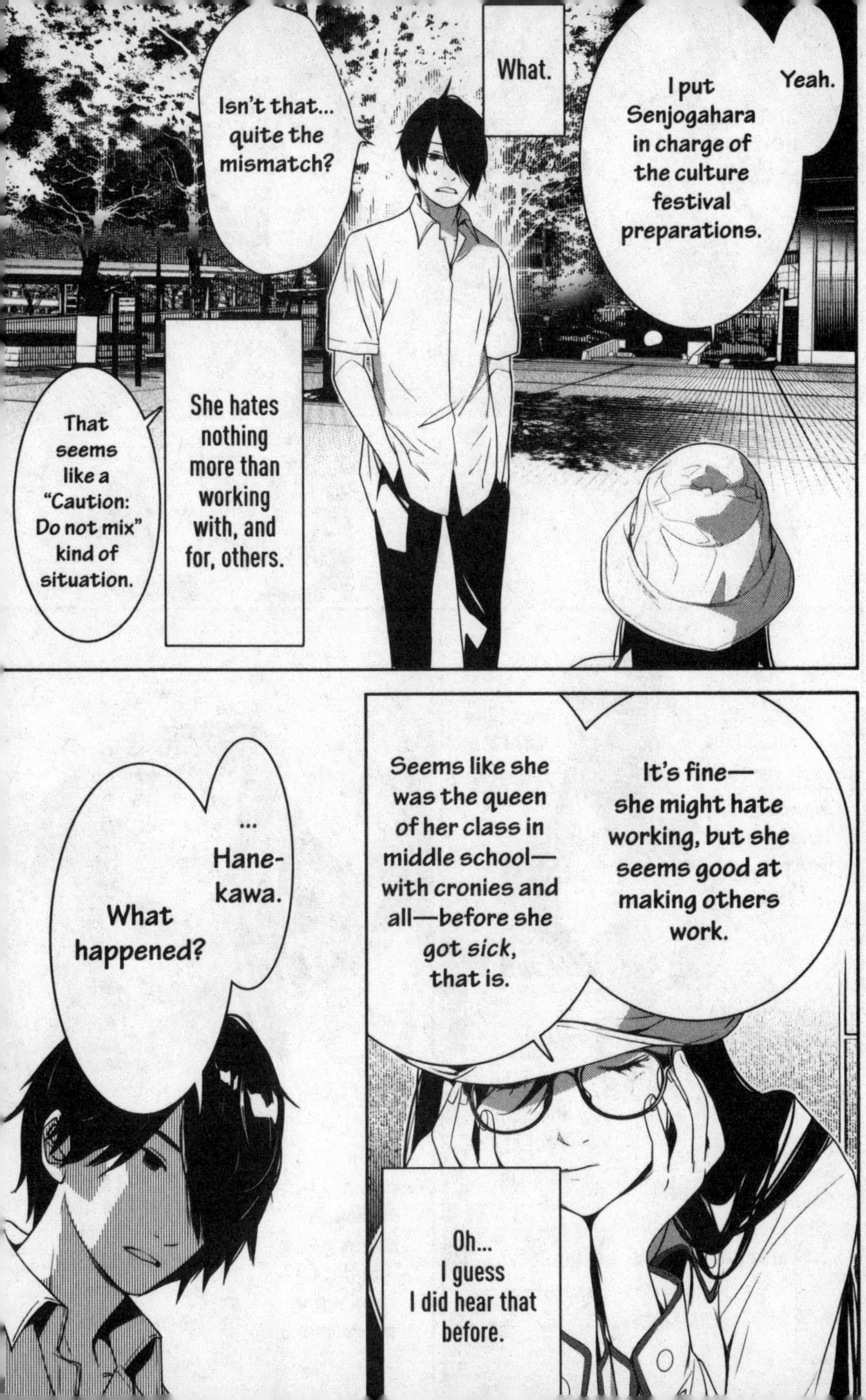
Yeah.
I put Senjogahara in charge of the culture festival preparations.
What.
Isn't that... quite the mismatch?
She hates nothing more than working with, and for, others.
That seems like a "Caution: Do not mix" kind of situation.
It's fine—she might hate working, but she seems good at making others work.
Seems like she was the queen of her class in middle school—with cronies and all—before she *got sick*, that is.
Oh... I guess I did hear that before.
... Hanekawa.
What happened?

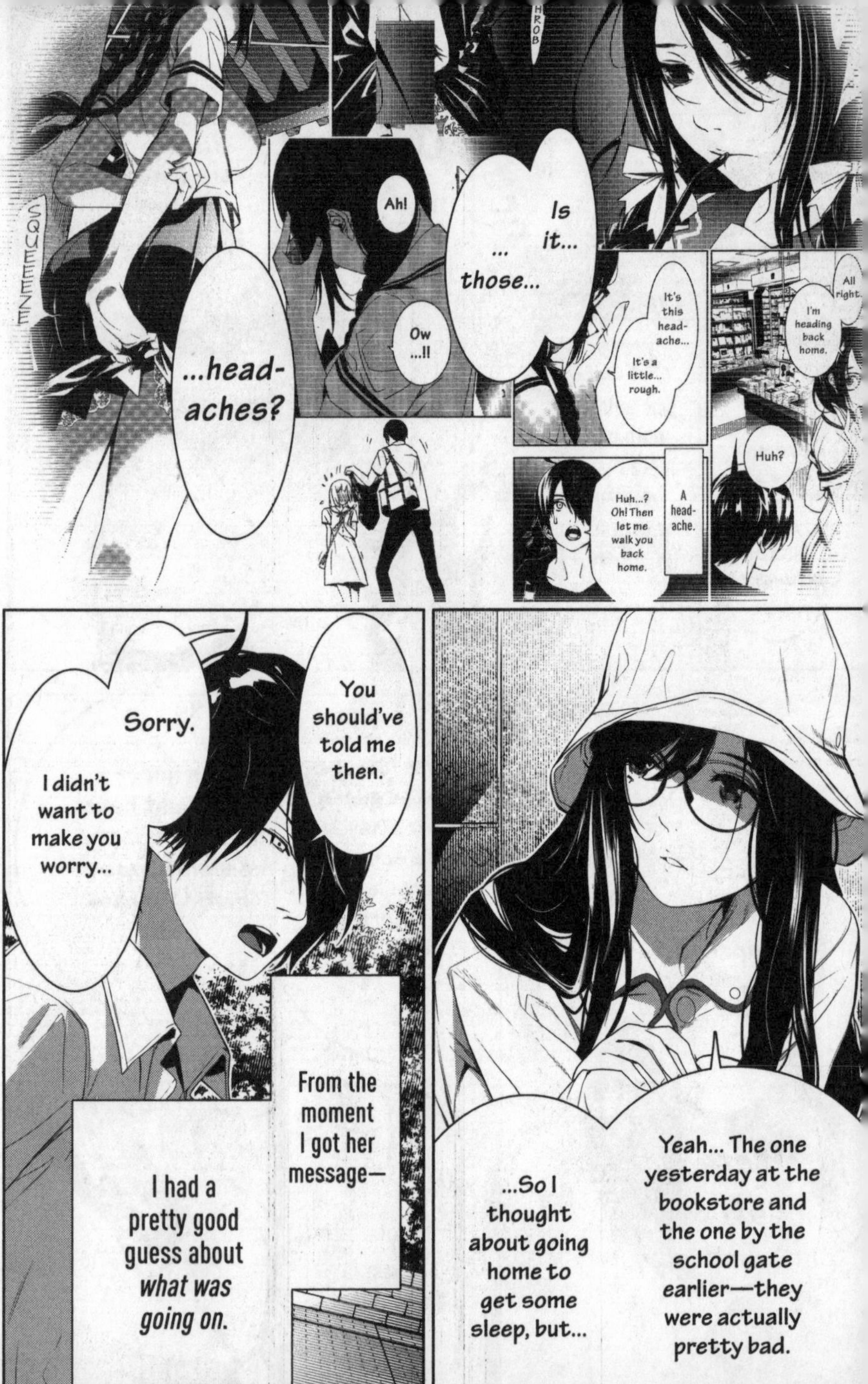
HROB
Is it... ...those... ...head-aches?
All right. I'm heading back home.
Huh?
It's this head-ache... It's a little... rough.
A head-ache.
Huh...? Oh! Then let me walk you back home.
Ah!
Ow ...!!
SQUEEEZE
Yeah... The one yesterday at the bookstore and the one by the school gate earlier—they were actually pretty bad.
...So I thought about going home to get some sleep, but...
You should've told me then.
Sorry.
I didn't want to make you worry...
From the moment I got her message—
I had a pretty good guess about *what was going on.*

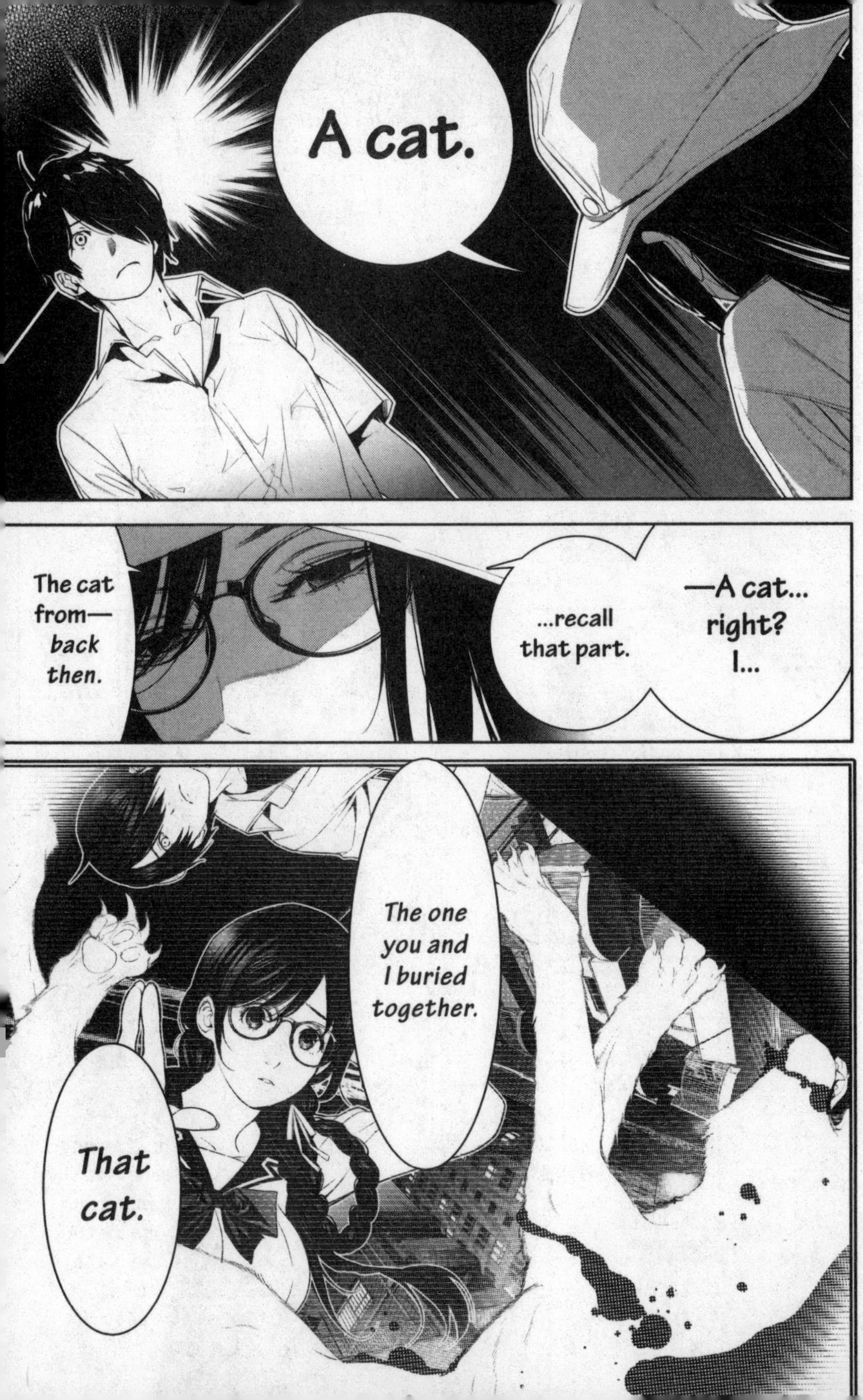
A cat.
—A cat... right? I...
...recall that part.
The cat from— back then.
The one you and I buried together.
That cat.

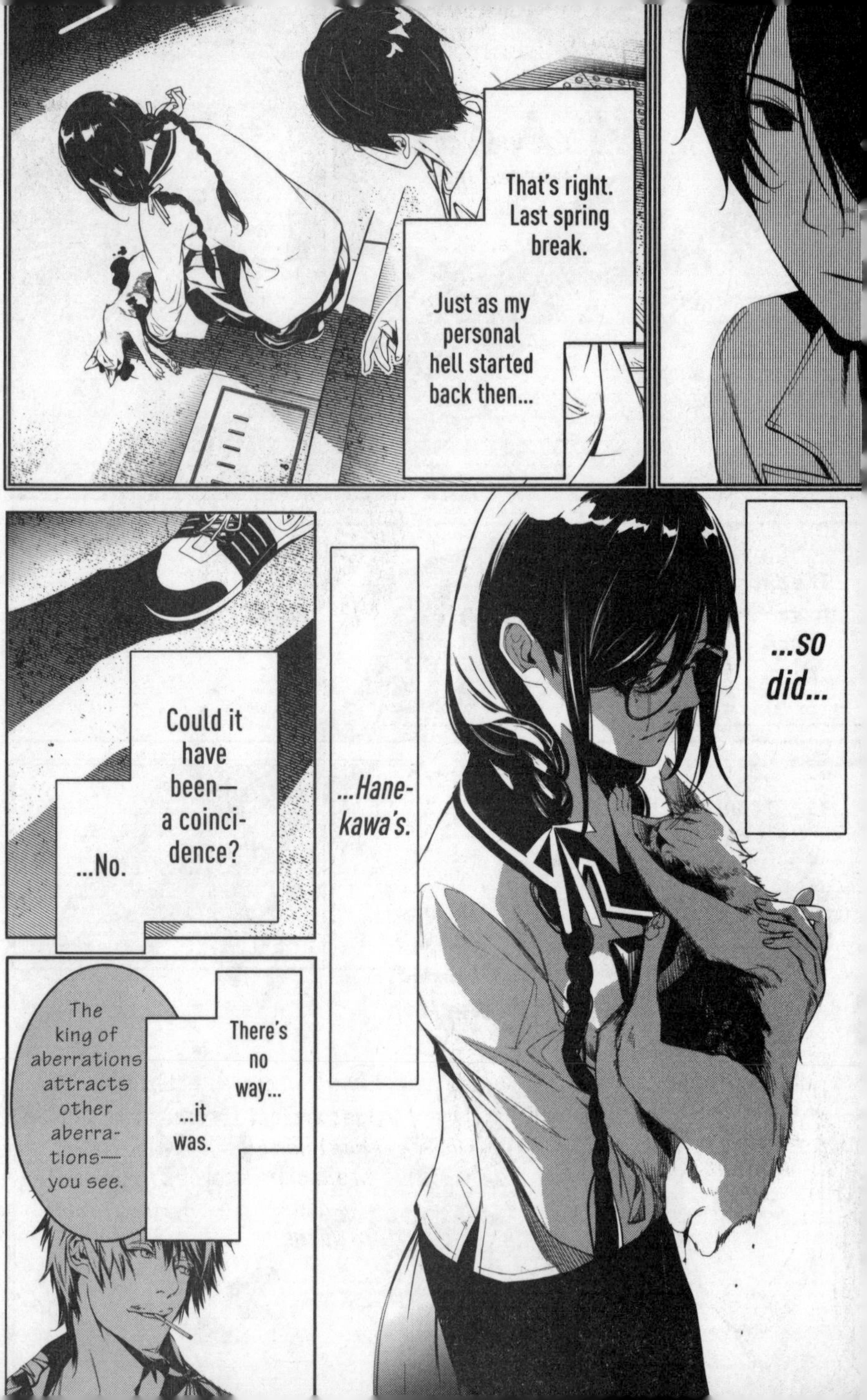
That's right. Last spring break.
Just as my personal hell started back then...
...so did...
...Hane-kawa's.
Could it have been— a coinci-dence?
...No.
There's no way...
...it was.
The king of aberrations attracts other aberra-tions— you see.

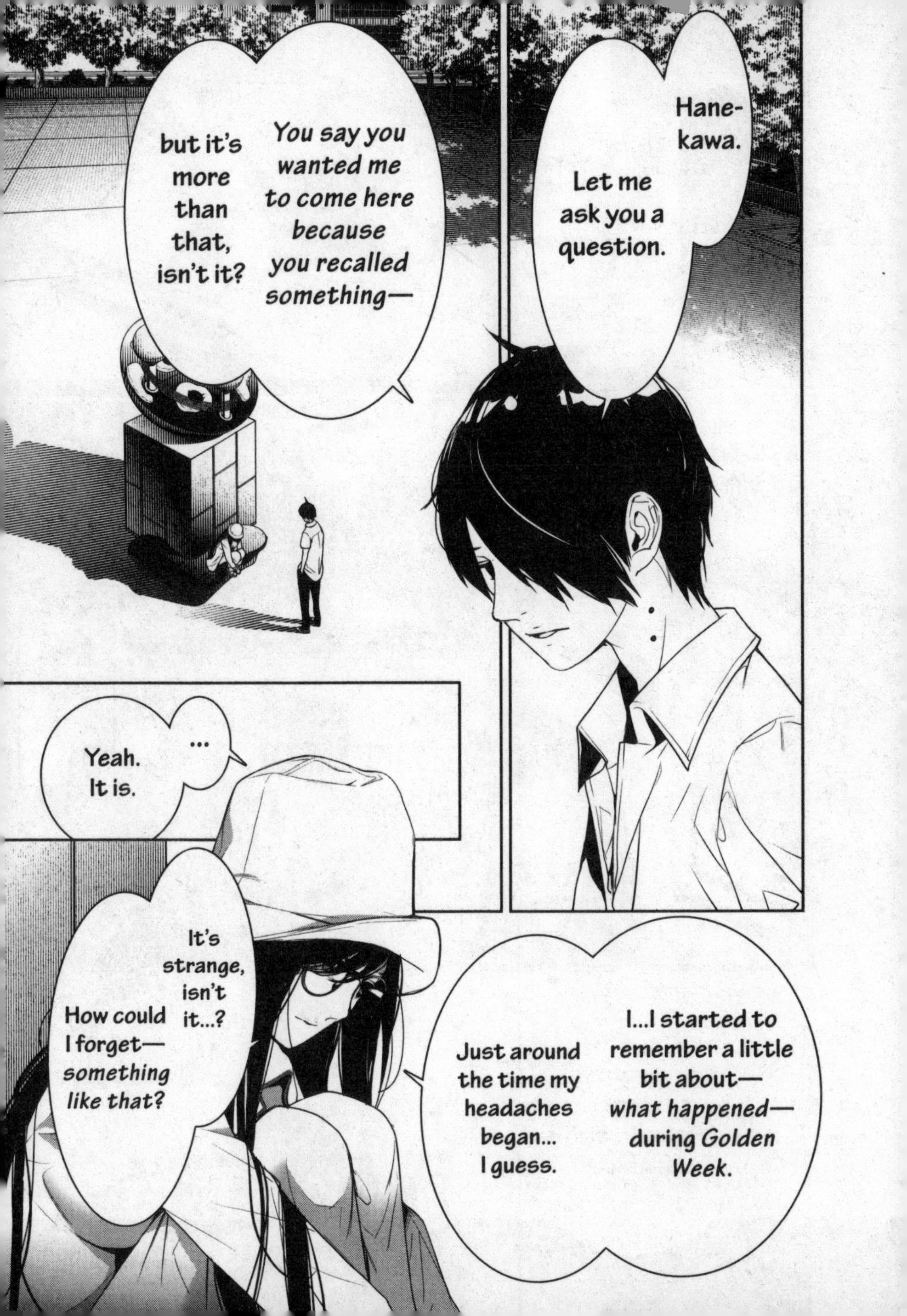
Hanekawa.
Let me ask you a question.
You say you wanted me to come here because you recalled something—
but it's more than that, isn't it?
...
Yeah. It is.
I...I started to remember a little bit about— *what happened*— during *Golden Week.*
Just around the time my headaches began... I guess.
It's strange, isn't it...?
How could I forget— *something like that?*

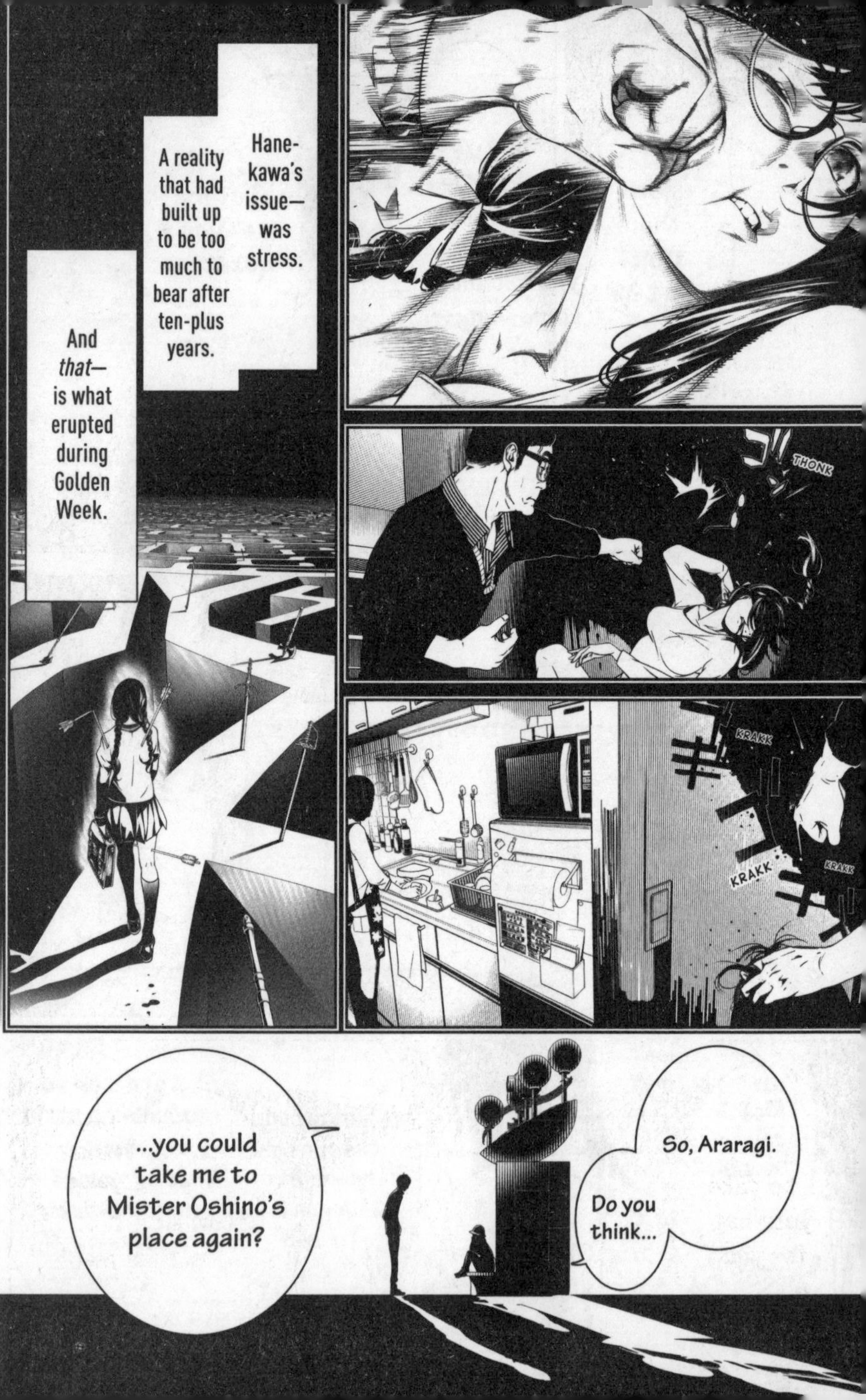
THONK
KRAKK
KRAKK
KRAKK
Hane-kawa's issue—was stress.
A reality that had built up to be too much to bear after ten-plus years.
And *that*—is what erupted during Golden Week.
So, Araragi.
Do you think...
...you could take me to Mister Oshino's place again?

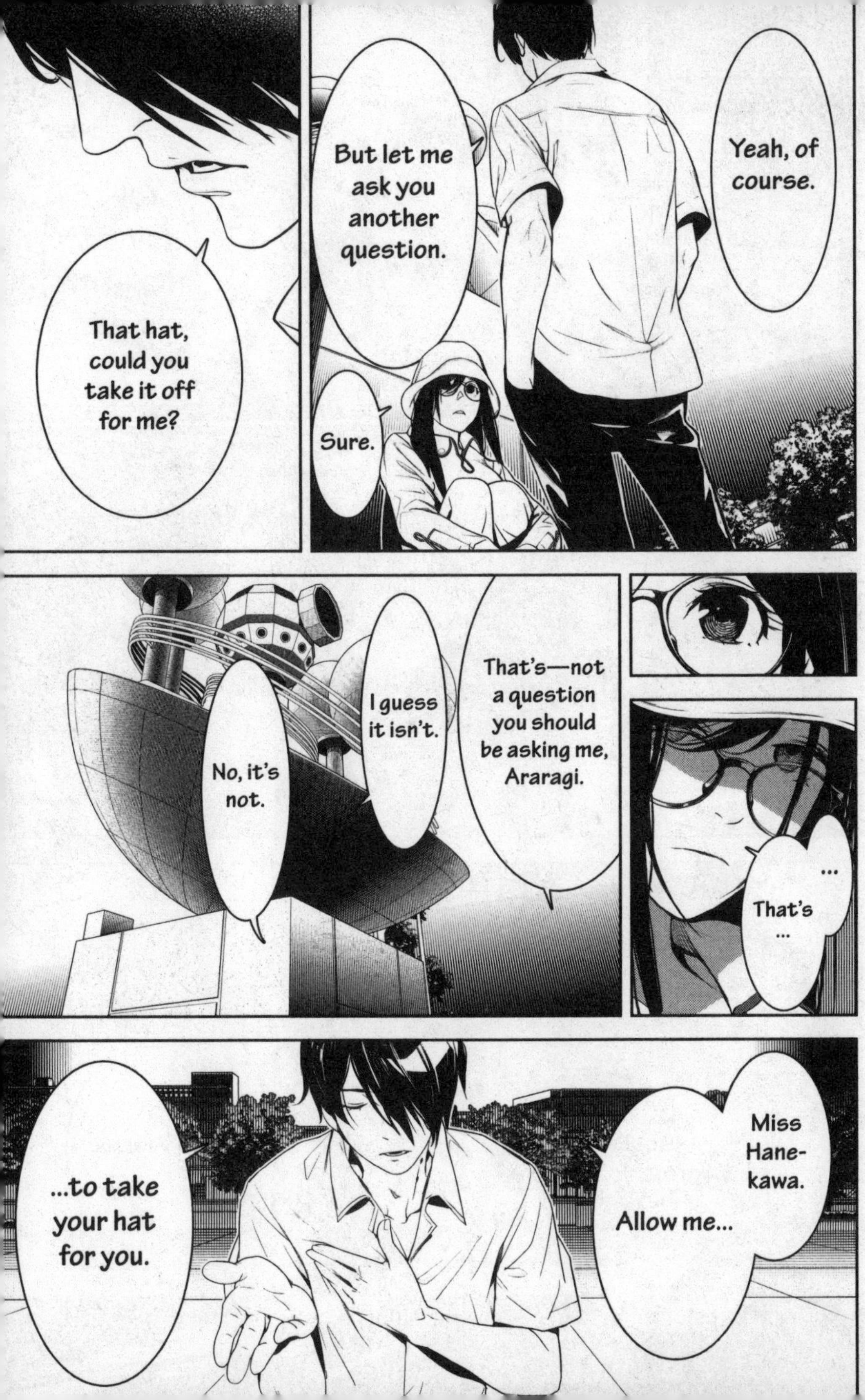
Yeah, of course.
But let me ask you another question.
Sure.
That hat, could you take it off for me?
... That's ...
That's—not a question you should be asking me, Araragi.
I guess it isn't.
No, it's not.
Miss Hane-kawa.
Allow me...
...to take your hat for you.

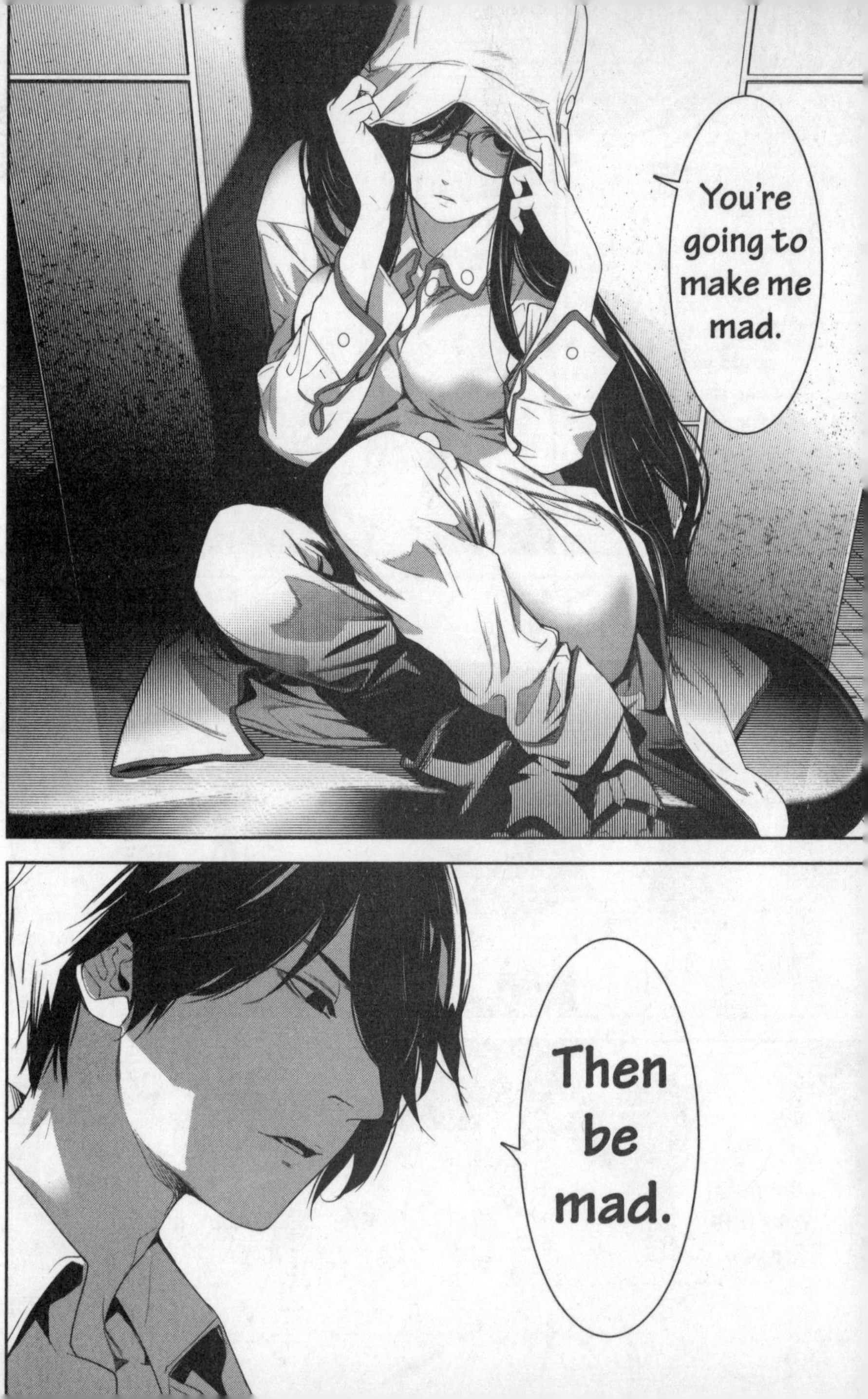
You're going to make me mad.
Then be mad.

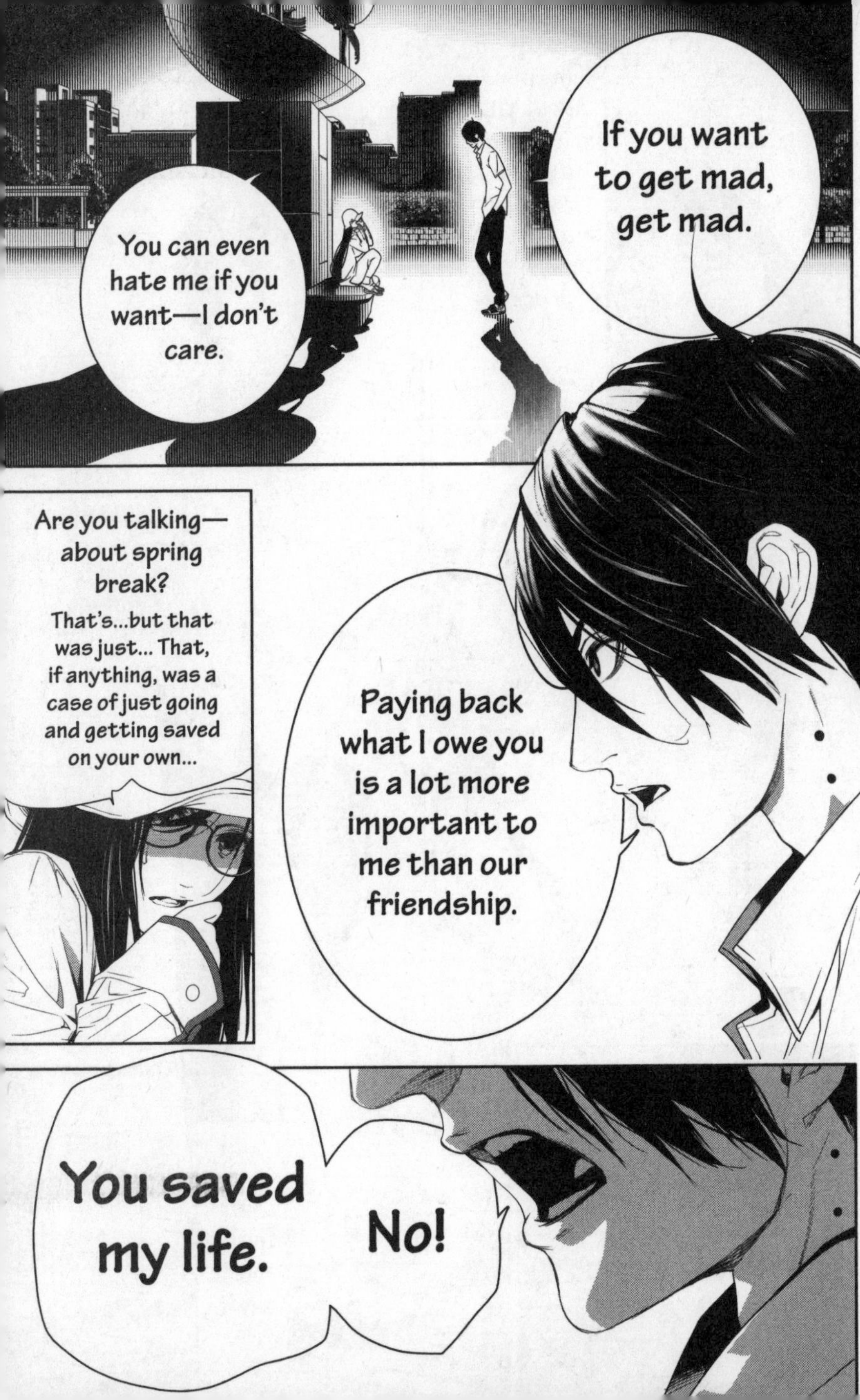
If you want to get mad, get mad.
You can even hate me if you want—I don't care.
Paying back what I owe you is a lot more important to me than our friendship.
Are you talking—about spring break?
That's...but that was just... That, if anything, was a case of just going and getting saved on your own...
No!
You saved my life.

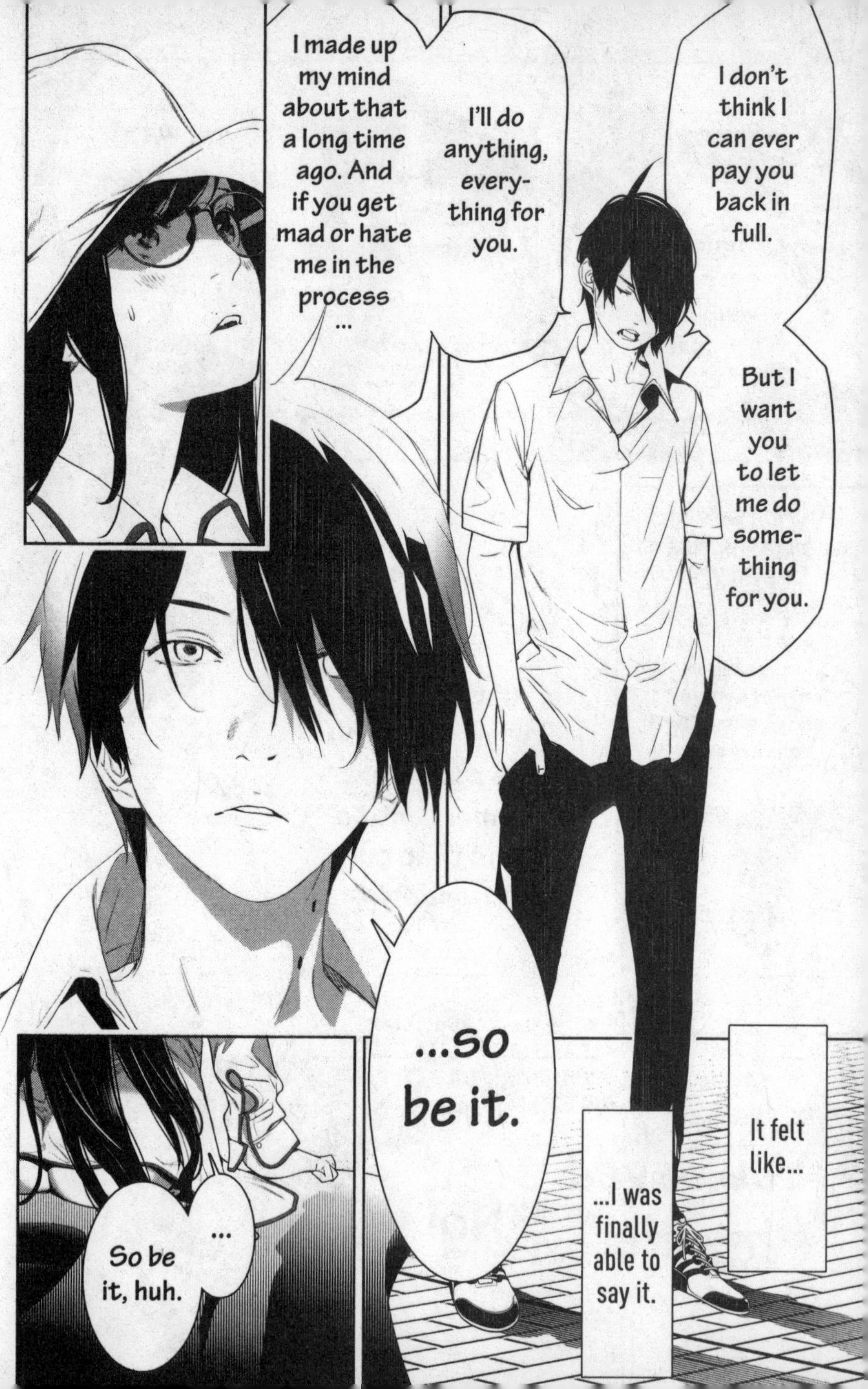
I don't think I can ever pay you back in full.
But I want you to let me do something for you.
I'll do anything, everything for you.
I made up my mind about that a long time ago. And if you get mad or hate me in the process...
...so be it.
It felt like...
...I was finally able to say it.
...
So be it, huh.

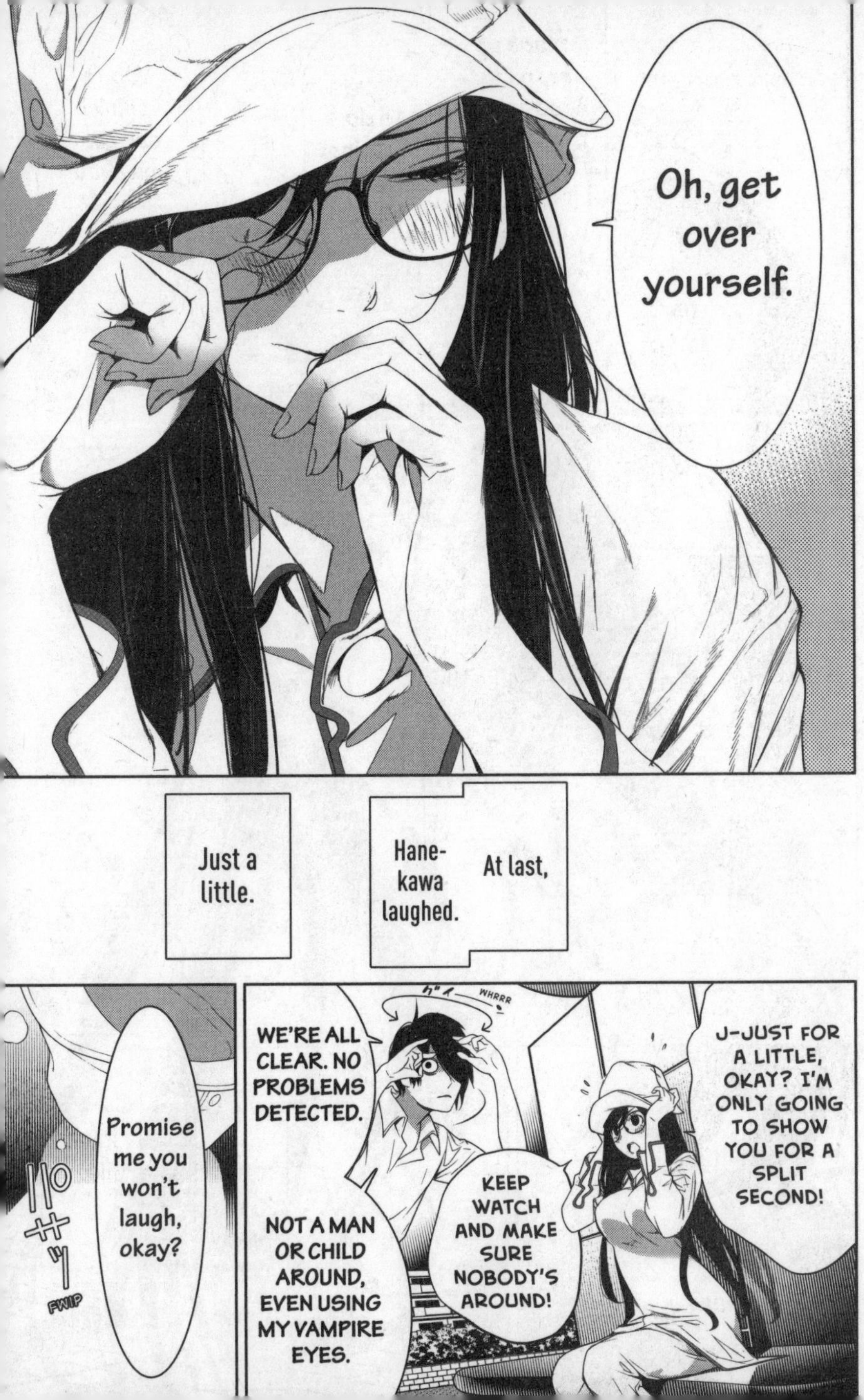
Oh, get over yourself.
At last,
Hane-kawa laughed.
Just a little.
J-JUST FOR A LITTLE, OKAY? I'M ONLY GOING TO SHOW YOU FOR A SPLIT SECOND!
WHRRR
KEEP WATCH AND MAKE SURE NOBODY'S AROUND!
WE'RE ALL CLEAR. NO PROBLEMS DETECTED.
NOT A MAN OR CHILD AROUND, EVEN USING MY VAMPIRE EYES.
Promise me you won't laugh, okay?
FWIP

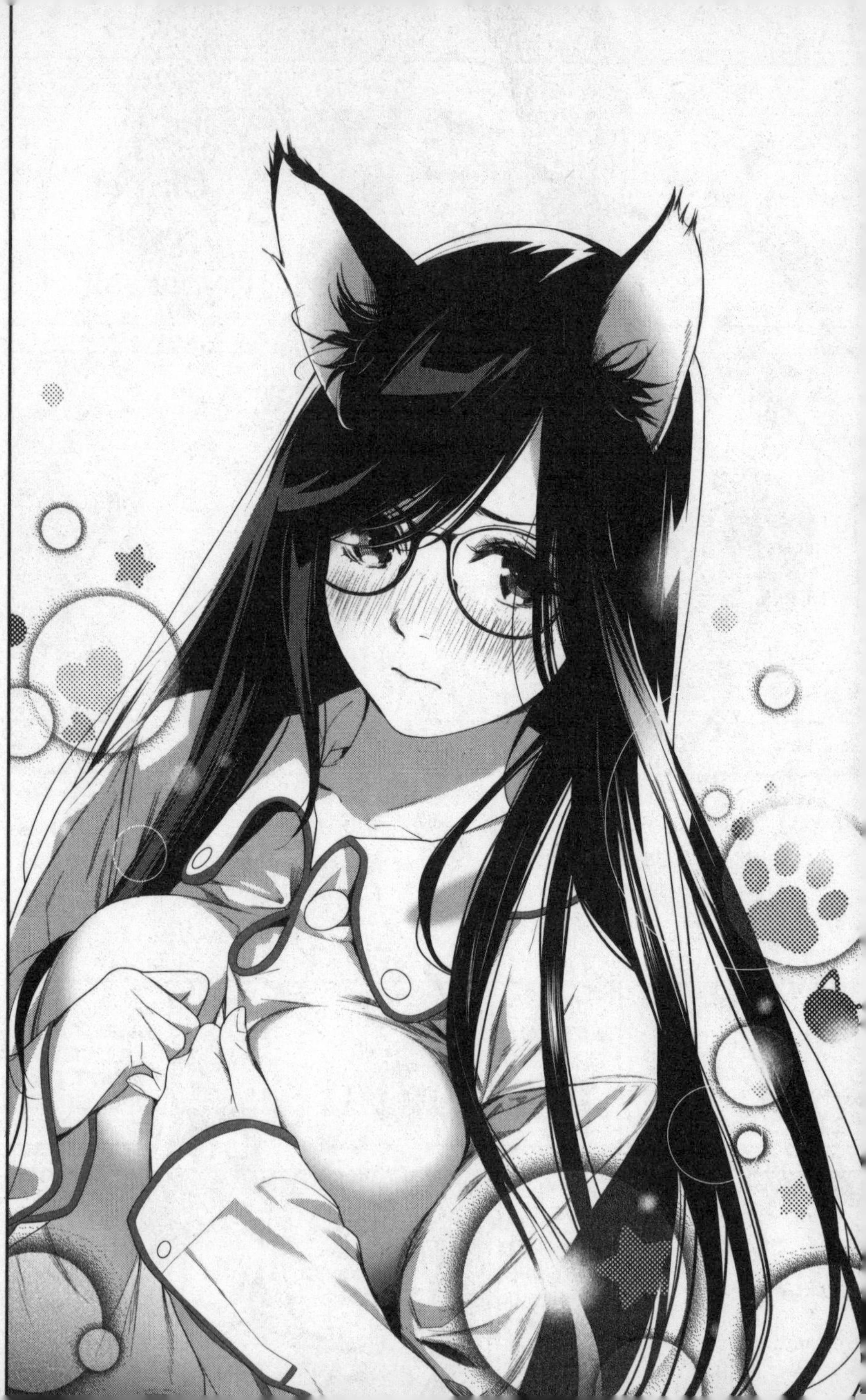

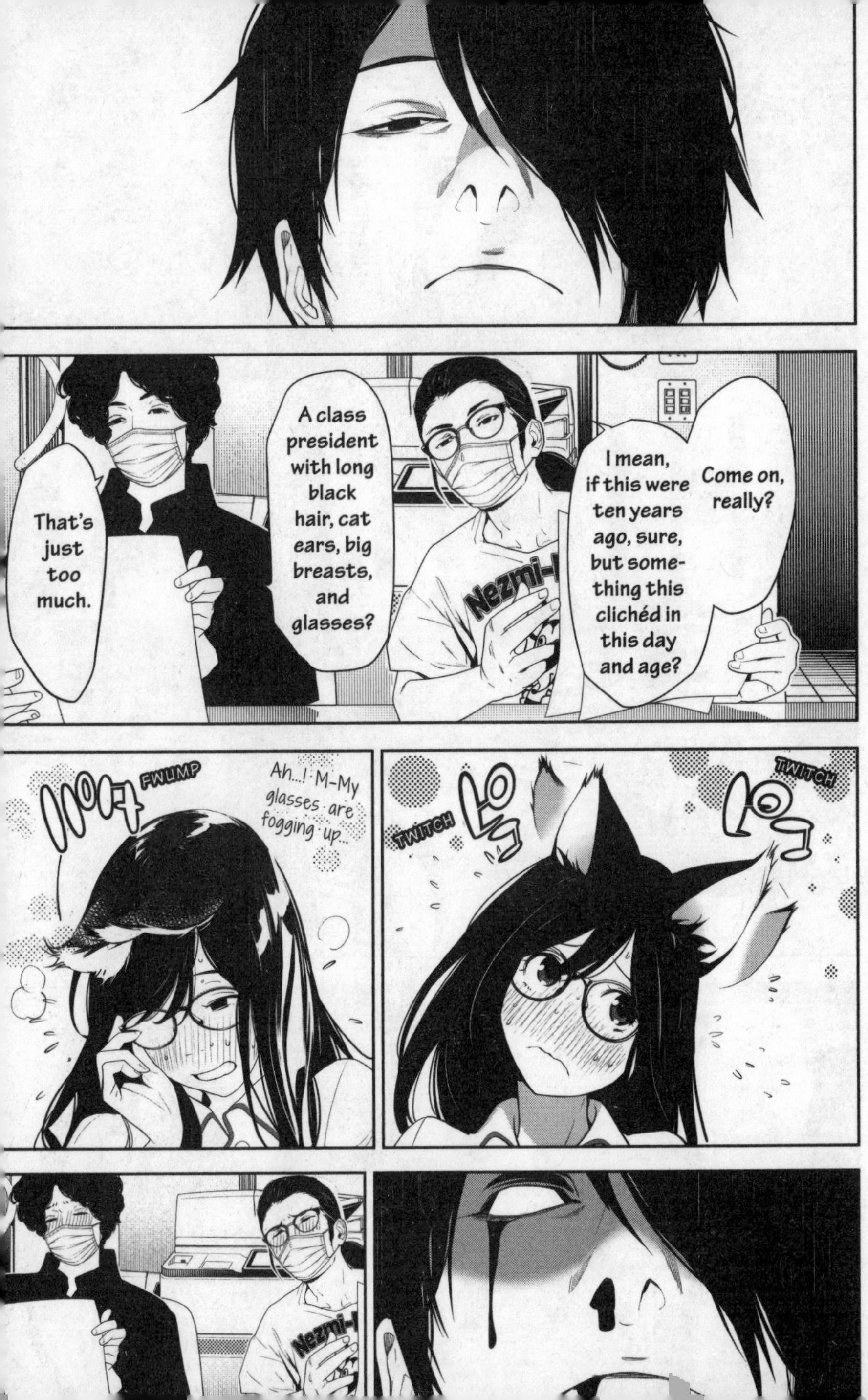
Come on, really?
I mean, if this were ten years ago, sure, but some-thing this clichéd in this day and age?
A class president with long black hair, cat ears, big breasts, and glasses?
That's just too much.
TWITCH
TWITCH
FWUMP
Ah...! M-My glasses are fogging up...

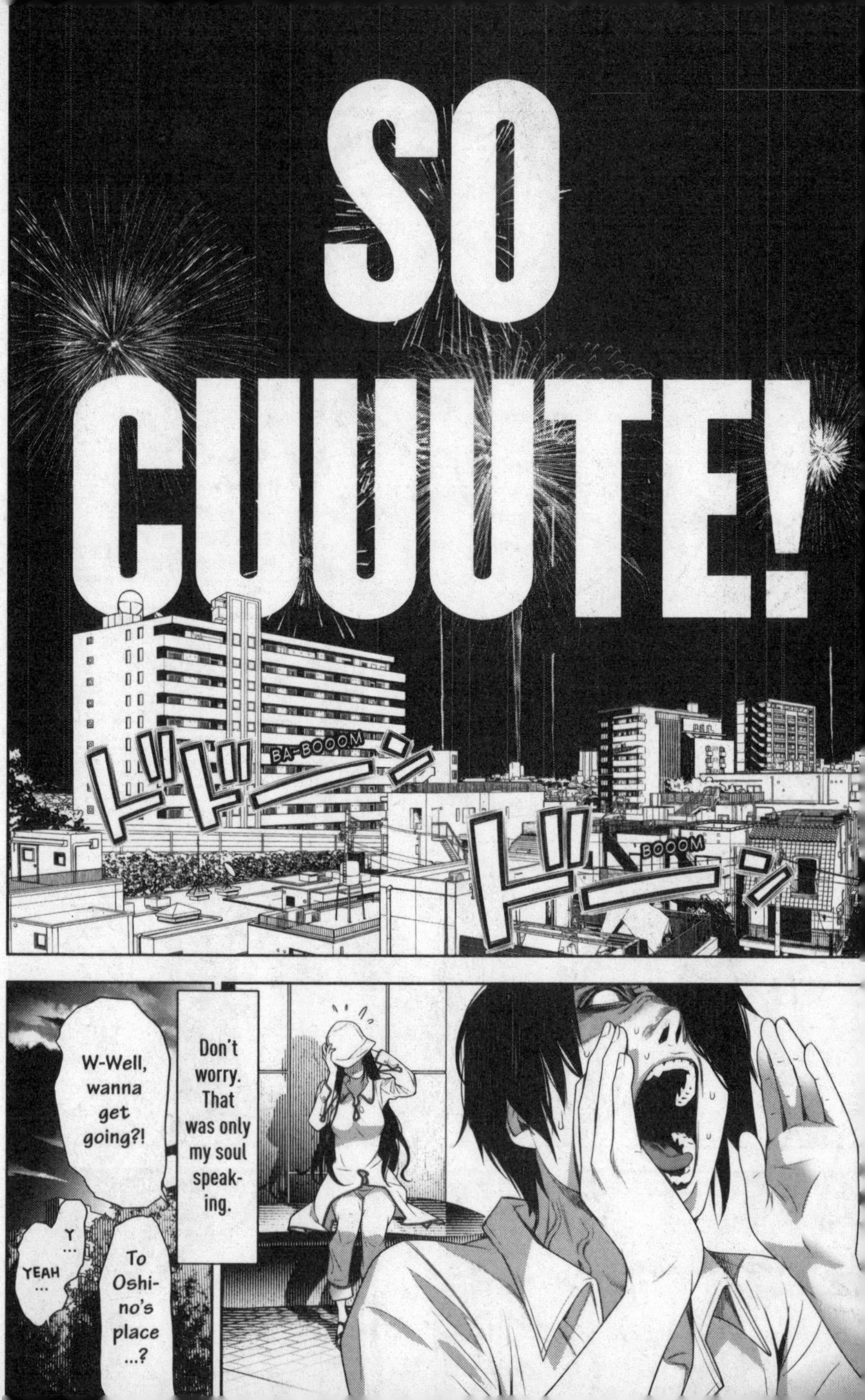
SO CUUUTE!
BA-BOOOM
BOOOM
Don't worry. That was only my soul speak-ing.
W-Well, wanna get going?!
To Oshi-no's place ...?
Y... YEAH...

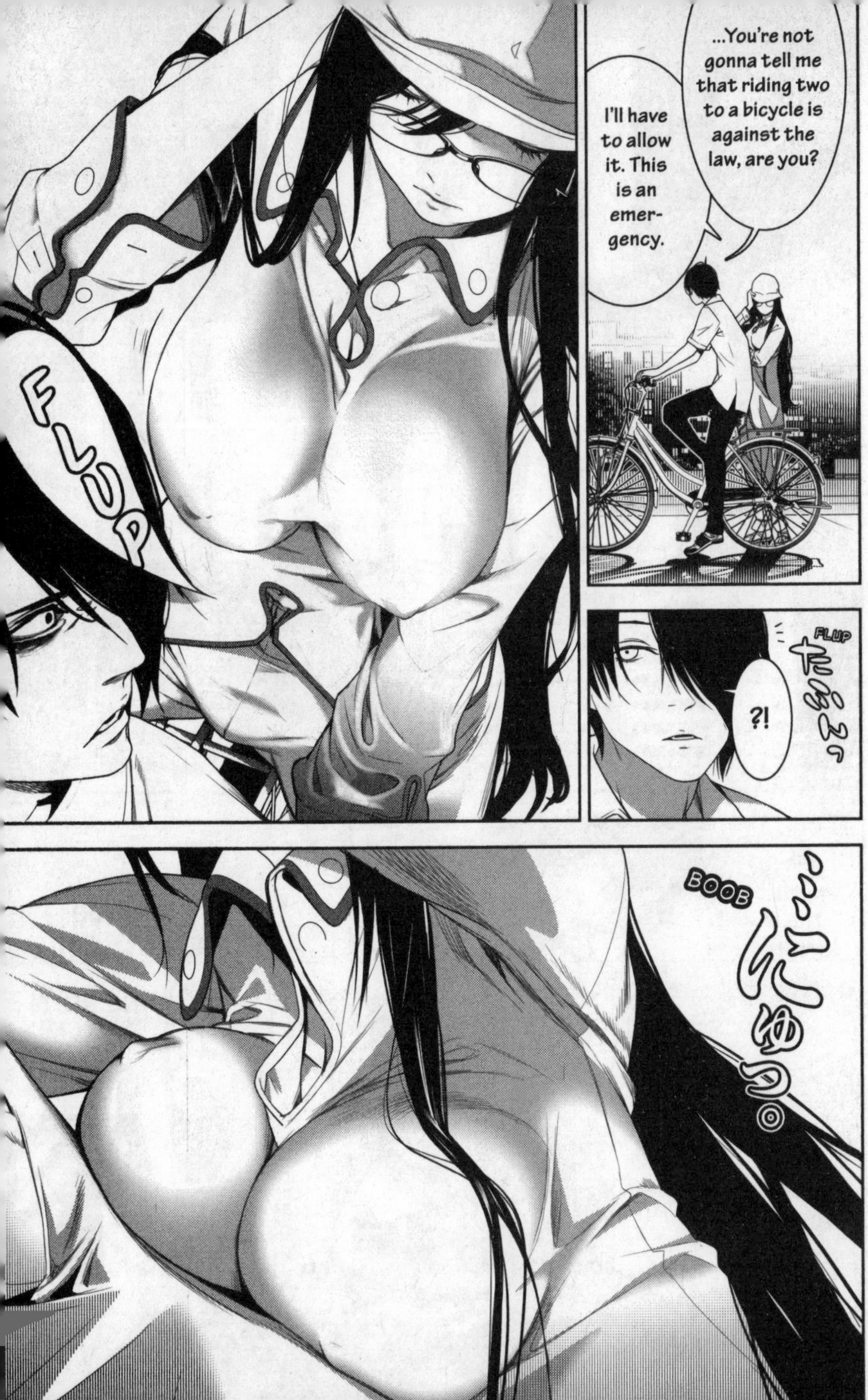
...You're not gonna tell me that riding two to a bicycle is against the law, are you?
I'll have to allow it. This is an emergency.
FLUP
?!
FLUP
BOOB

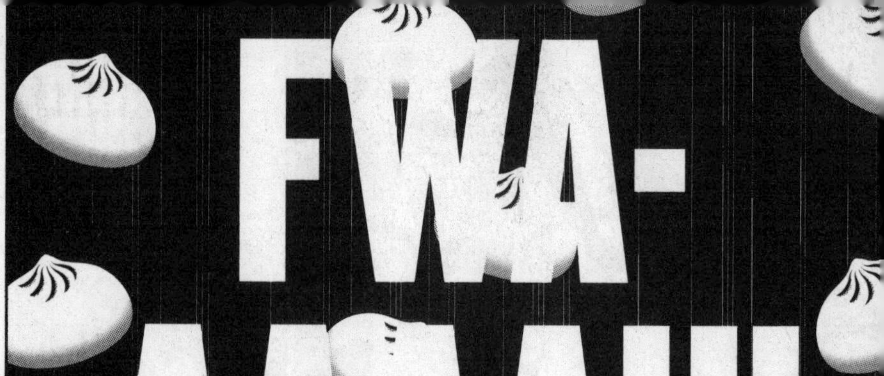
FWA-
AAAH!

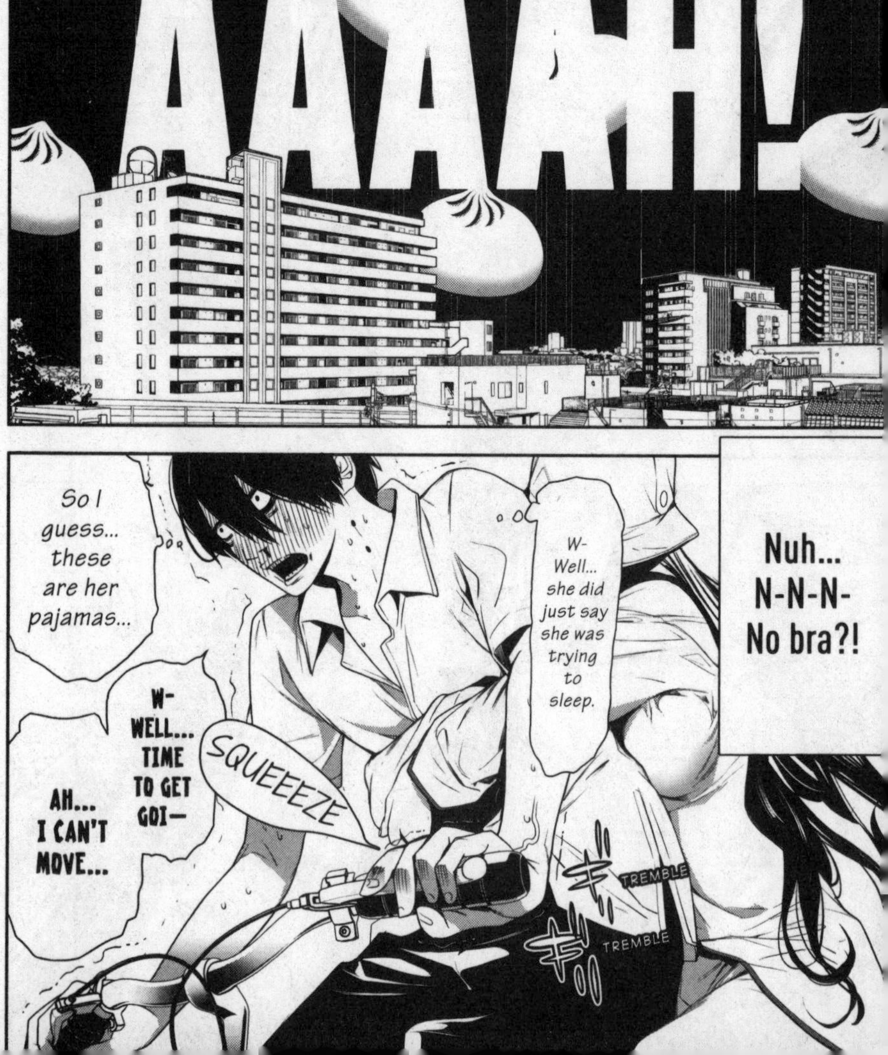
Nuh... N-N-N- No bra?!
W- Well... she did just say she was trying to sleep.
So I guess... these are her pajamas...
W- WELL... TIME TO GET GOI—
SQUEEEEZE
AH... I CAN'T MOVE...
TREMBLE
TREMBLE

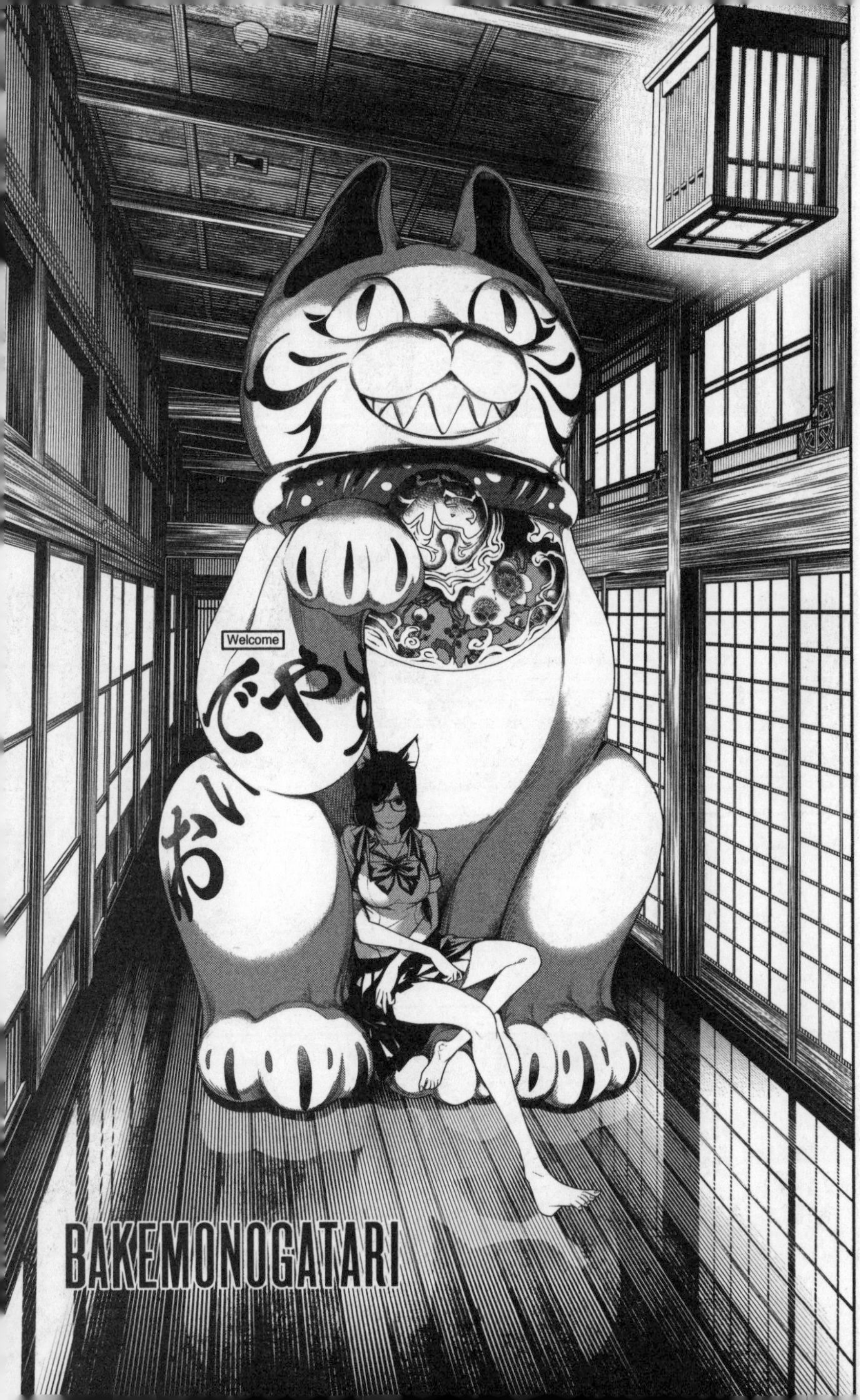
Welcome
おいでやす
BAKEMONOGATARI

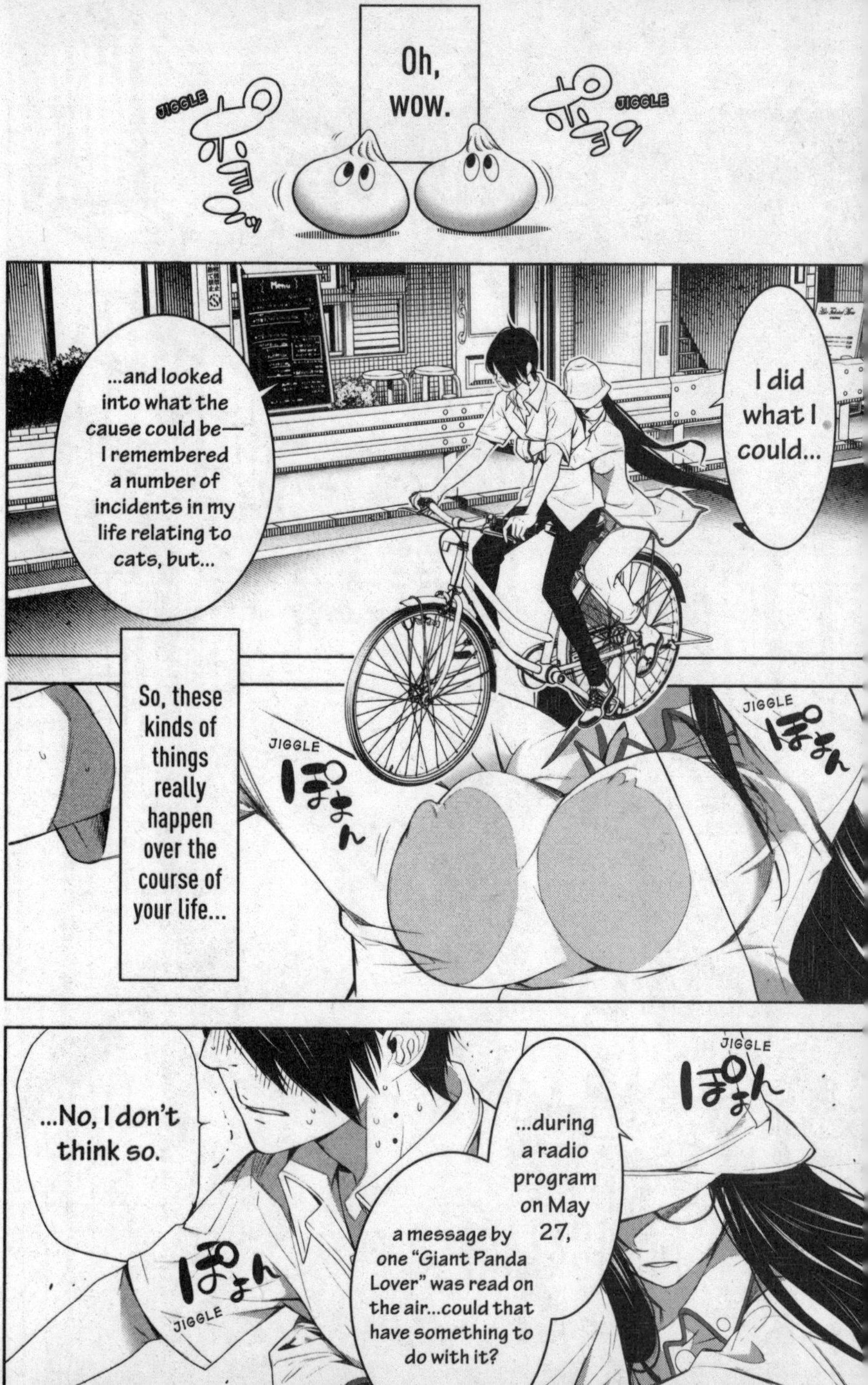
JIGGLE
Oh, wow.
JIGGLE
I did what I could...
...and looked into what the cause could be—I remembered a number of incidents in my life relating to cats, but...
JIGGLE
So, these kinds of things really happen over the course of your life...
JIGGLE
JIGGLE
...during a radio program on May 27, a message by one "Giant Panda Lover" was read on the air...could that have something to do with it?
...No, I don't think so.
JIGGLE

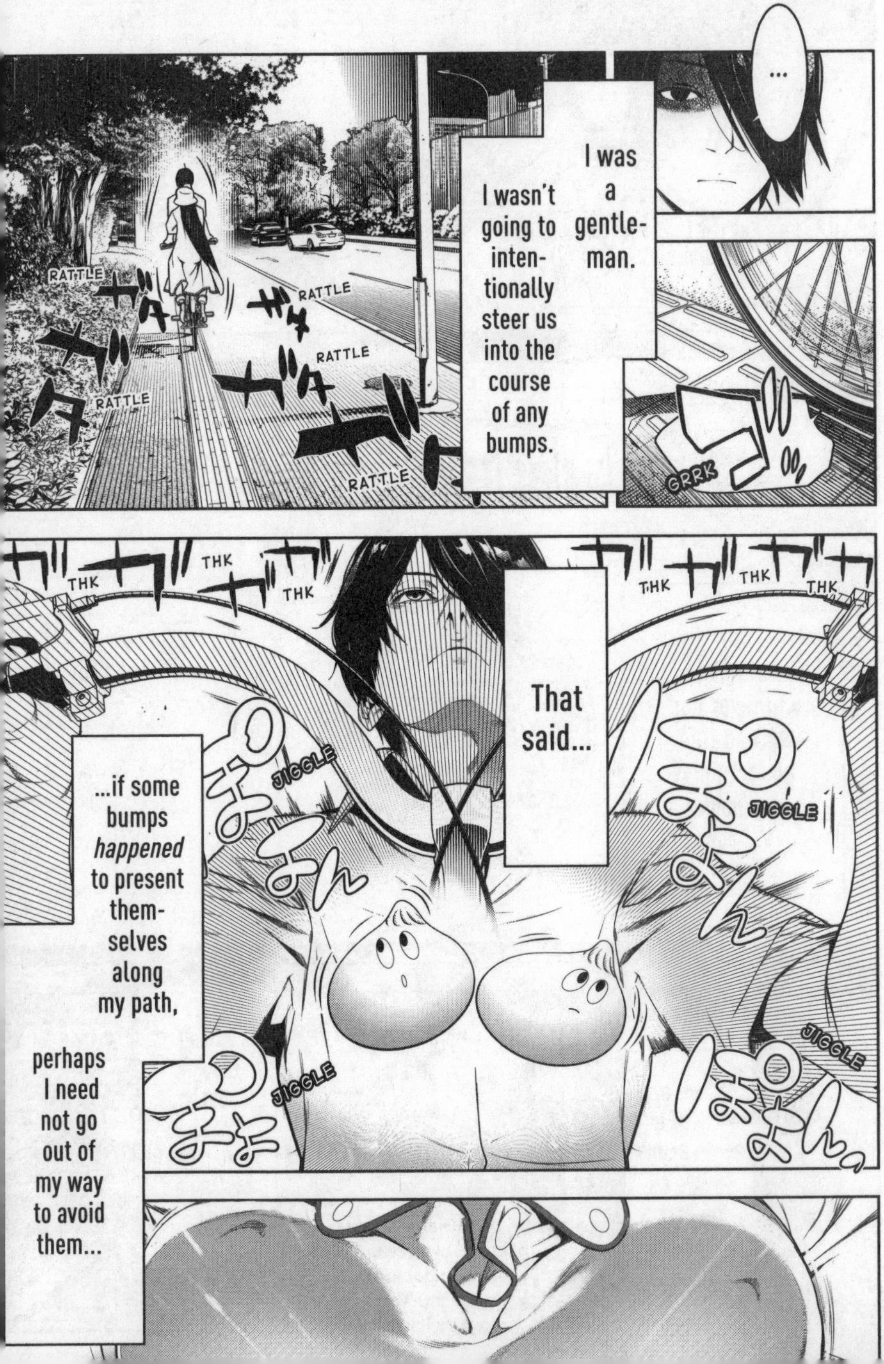
...
I was a gentleman.
I wasn't going to intentionally steer us into the course of any bumps.
GRRK
RATTLE
RATTLE
RATTLE
RATTLE
RATTLE
THK
THK
THK
THK
THK
THK
That said...
...if some bumps happened to present themselves along my path,
JIGGLE
JIGGLE
JIGGLE
JIGGLE
perhaps I need not go out of my way to avoid them...

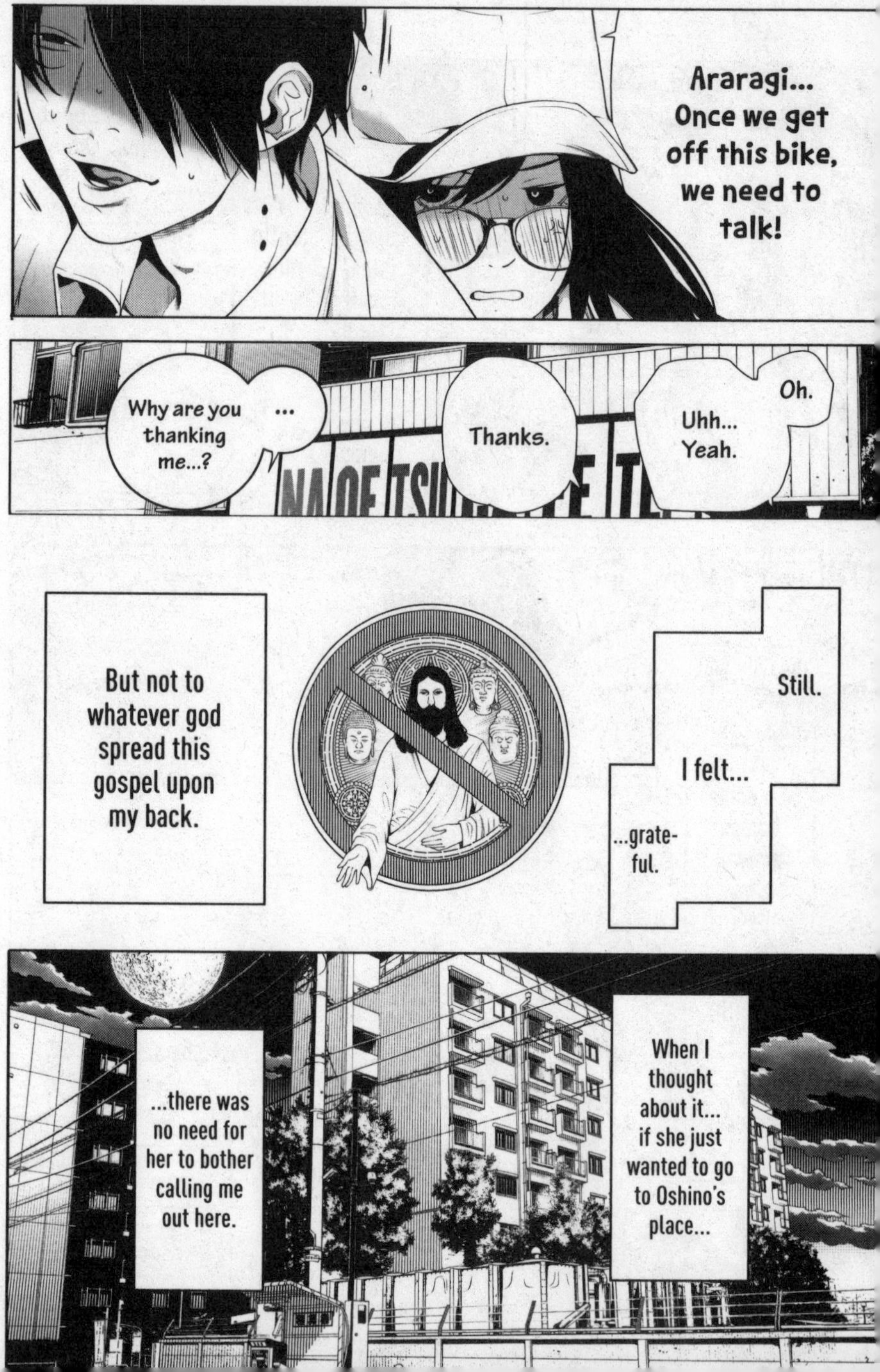
Araragi... Once we get off this bike, we need to talk!
Oh.
Uhh... Yeah.
Thanks.
...
Why are you thanking me...?
Still.
I felt...
...grate-ful.
But not to whatever god spread this gospel upon my back.
When I thought about it... if she just wanted to go to Oshino's place...
...there was no need for her to bother calling me out here.

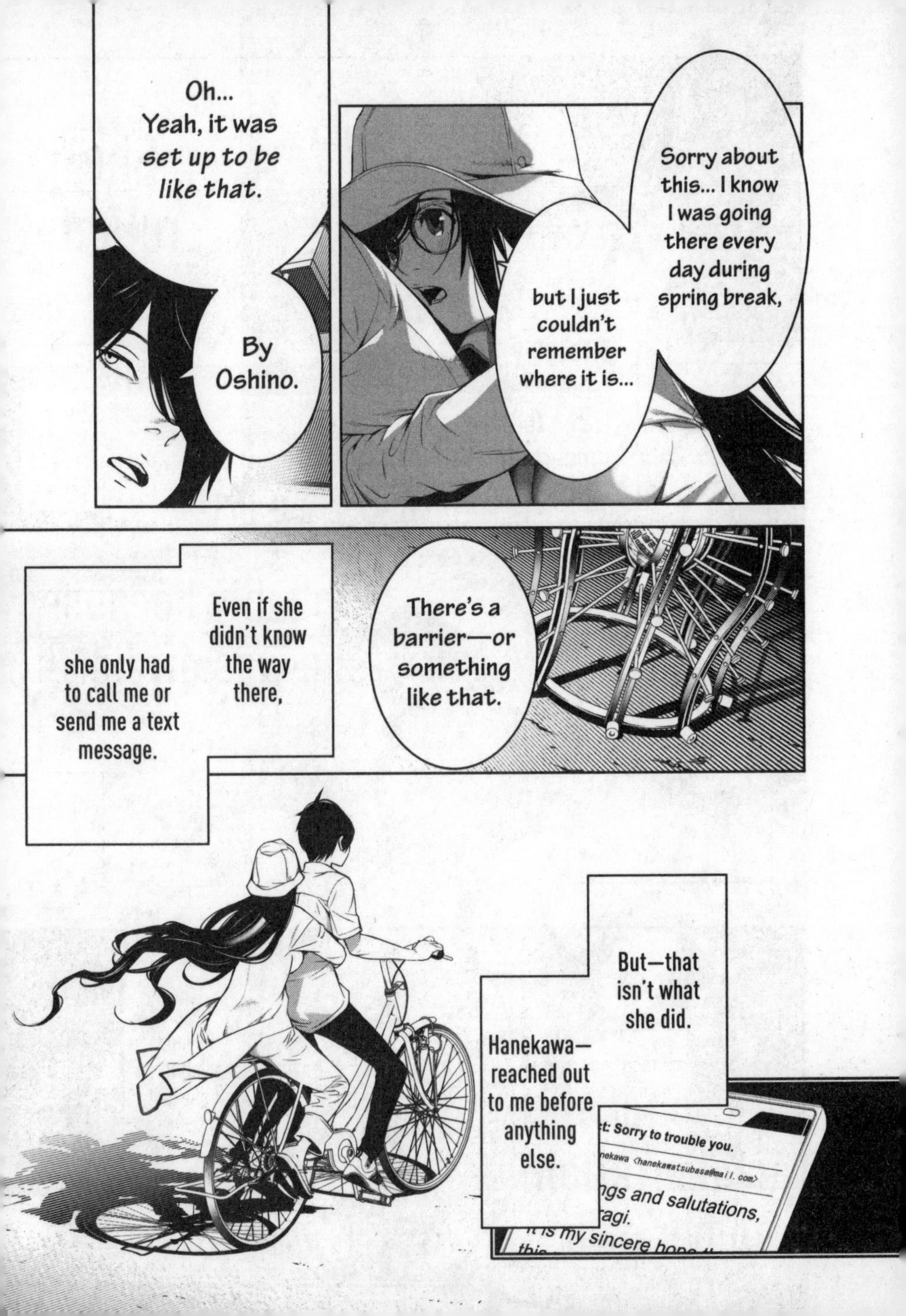

Sorry about this... I know I was going there every day during spring break,
but I just couldn't remember where it is...
Oh... Yeah, it was set up to be like that.
By Oshino.
There's a barrier—or something like that.
Even if she didn't know the way there,
she only had to call me or send me a text message.
But—that isn't what she did.
Hanekawa—reached out to me before anything else.
Sorry to trouble you.
<hanekawatsubasa@mail.com>
and salutations,

She
relied
on
me.

Probably—
because
she felt
uncertain.

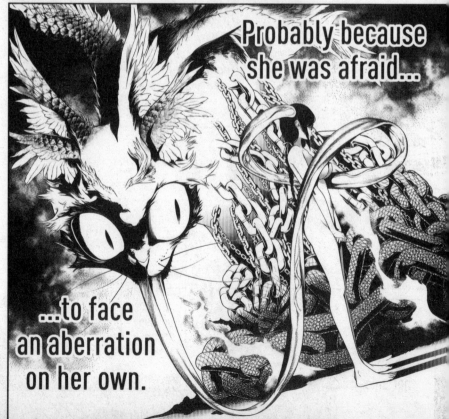

Probably because
she was afraid...

...to face
an aberration
on her own.

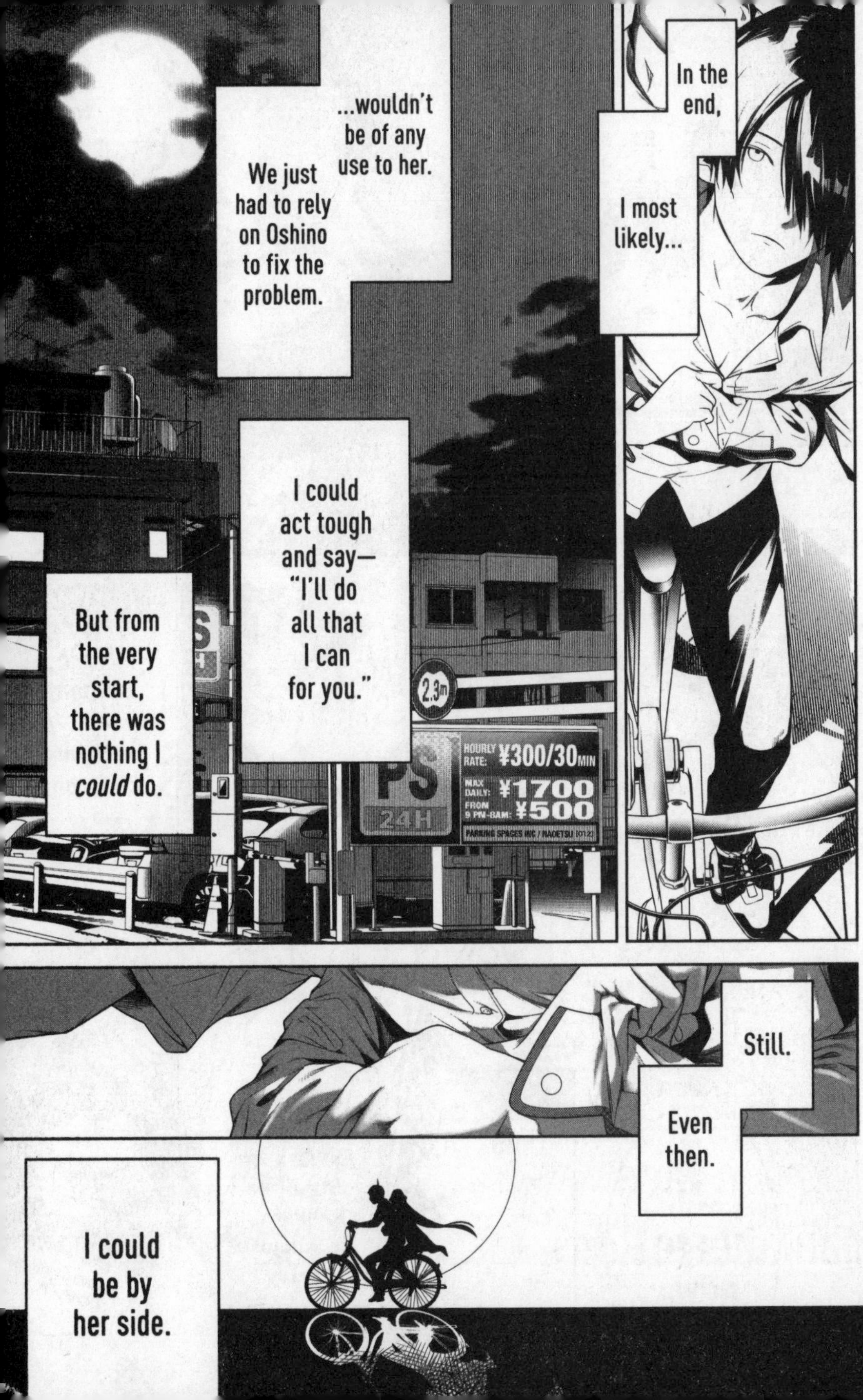
In the end,
I most likely...
...wouldn't be of any use to her.
We just had to rely on Oshino to fix the problem.
I could act tough and say—"I'll do all that I can for you."
But from the very start, there was nothing I *could* do.
2.3m
PS
24H
HOURLY RATE: ¥300/30MIN
MAX DAILY: ¥1700
FROM 9 PM-8AM: ¥500
Still.
Even then.
I could be by her side.

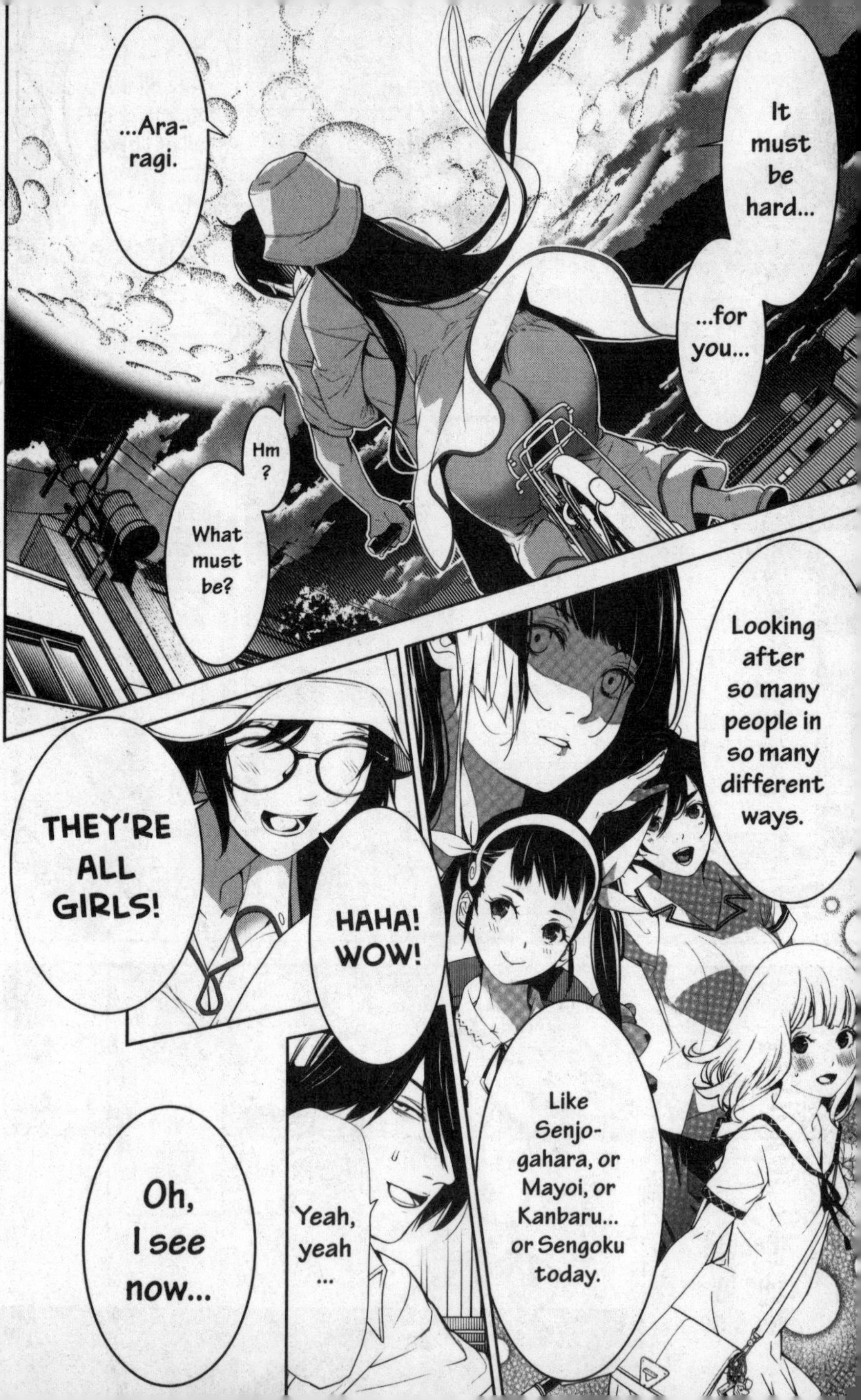
It must be hard...
...for you...
...Ara-ragi.
Hm?
What must be?
Looking after so many people in so many different ways.
Like Senjo-gahara, or Mayoi, or Kanbaru... or Sengoku today.
THEY'RE ALL GIRLS!
HAHA! WOW!
Yeah, yeah ...
Oh, I see now...

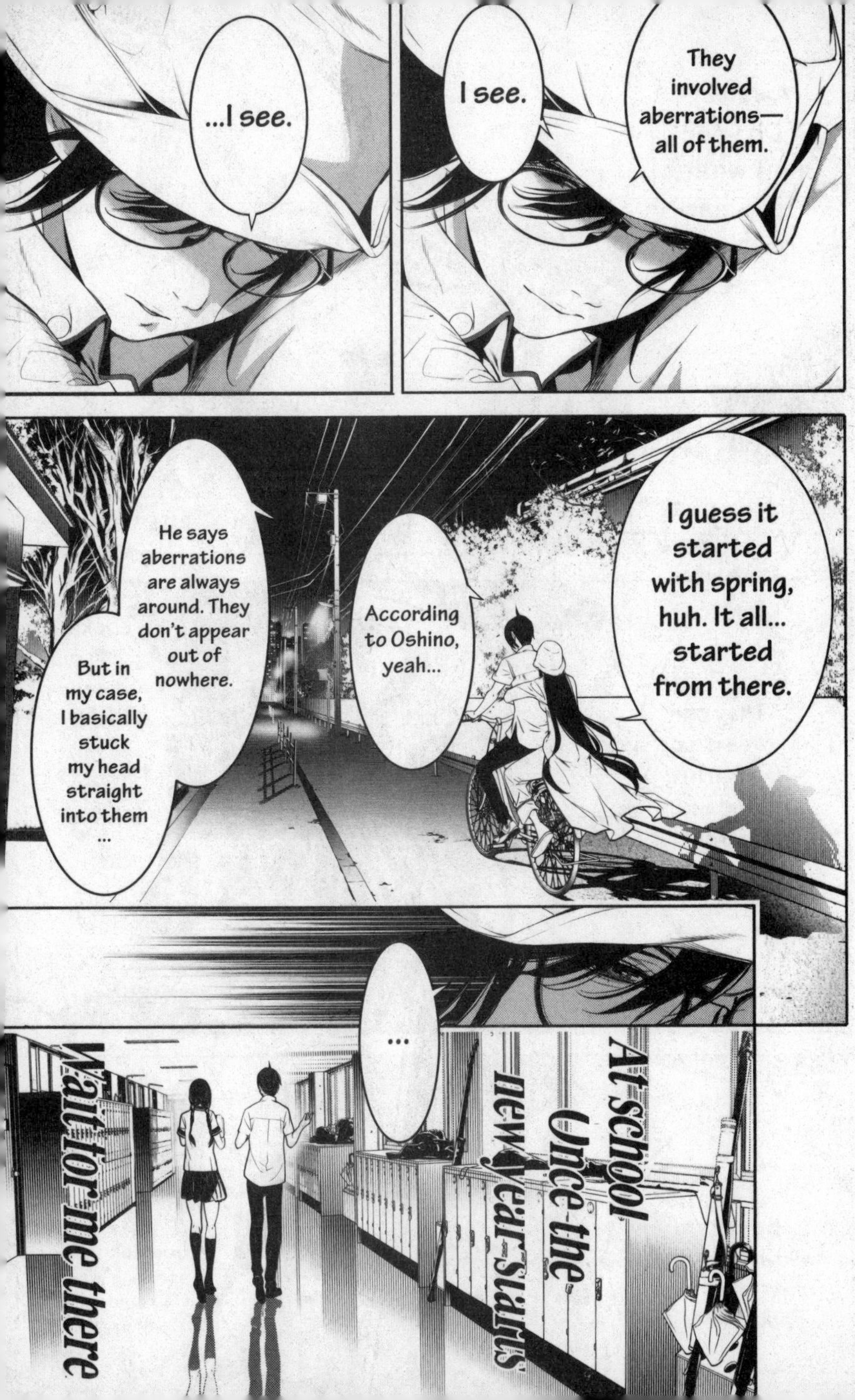
They involved aberrations—all of them.
I see.
...I see.
I guess it started with spring, huh. It all... started from there.
According to Oshino, yeah...
He says aberrations are always around. They don't appear out of nowhere.
But in my case, I basically stuck my head straight into them...
...
At school
Once the new year starts
Wait for me there

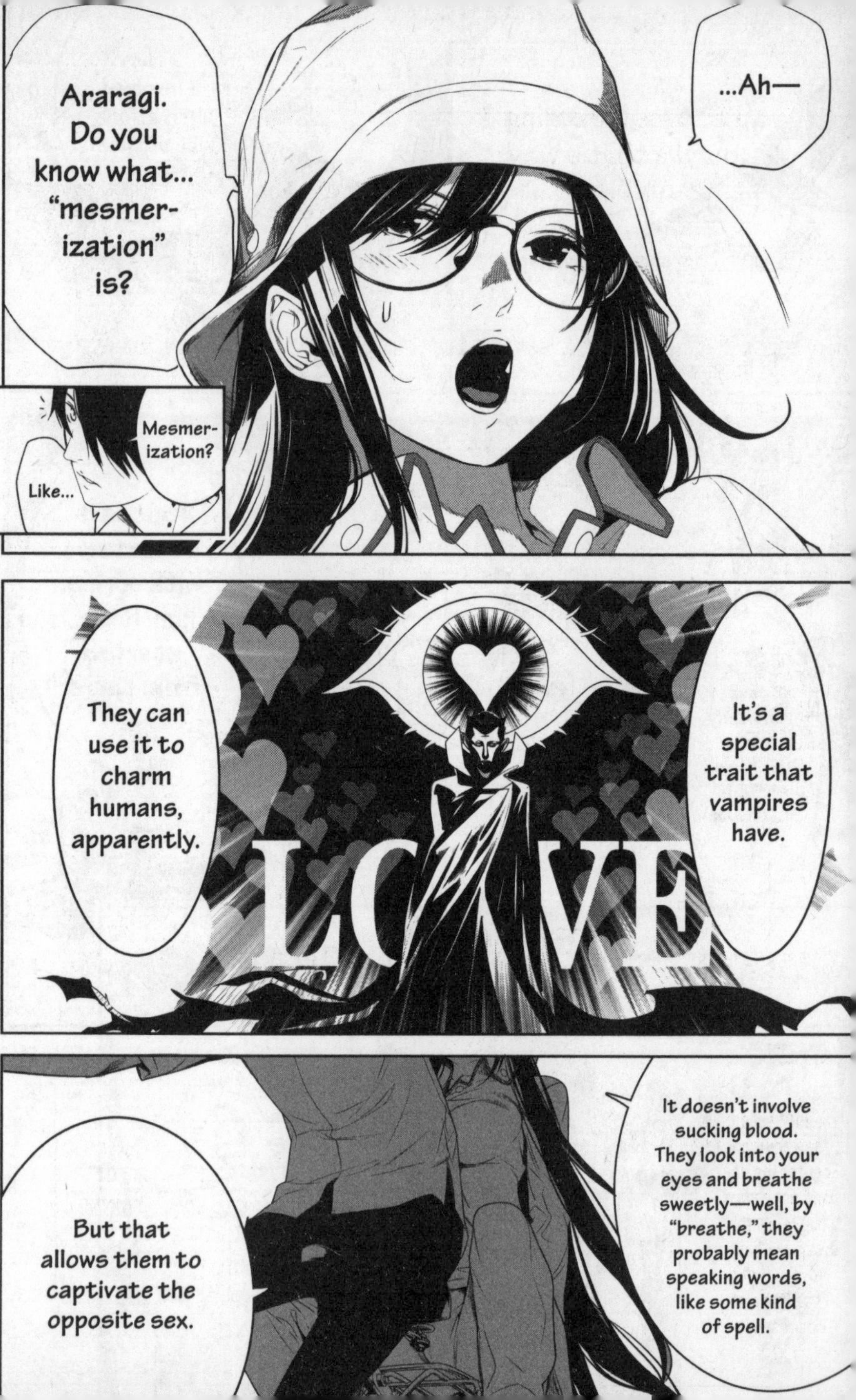
...Ah—
Araragi. Do you know what... "mesmer-ization" is?
Mesmer-ization?
Like...
It's a special trait that vampires have.
They can use it to charm humans, apparently.
LOVE
It doesn't involve sucking blood. They look into your eyes and breathe sweetly—well, by "breathe," they probably mean speaking words, like some kind of spell.
But that allows them to captivate the opposite sex.

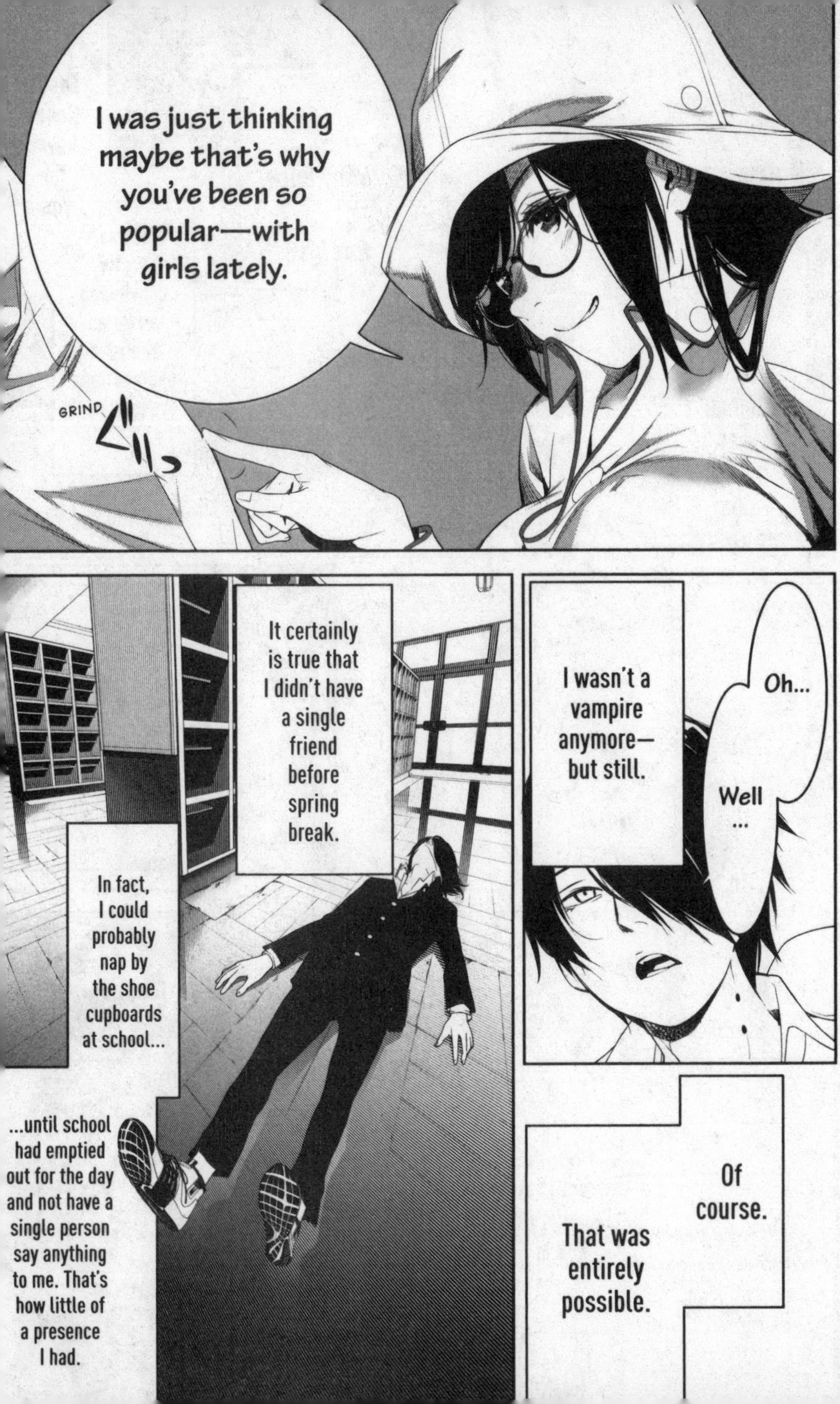
I was just thinking maybe that's why you've been so popular—with girls lately.
GRIND
Oh...
Well...
I wasn't a vampire anymore—but still.
Of course.
That was entirely possible.
It certainly is true that I didn't have a single friend before spring break.
In fact, I could probably nap by the shoe cupboards at school...
...until school had emptied out for the day and not have a single person say anything to me. That's how little of a presence I had.

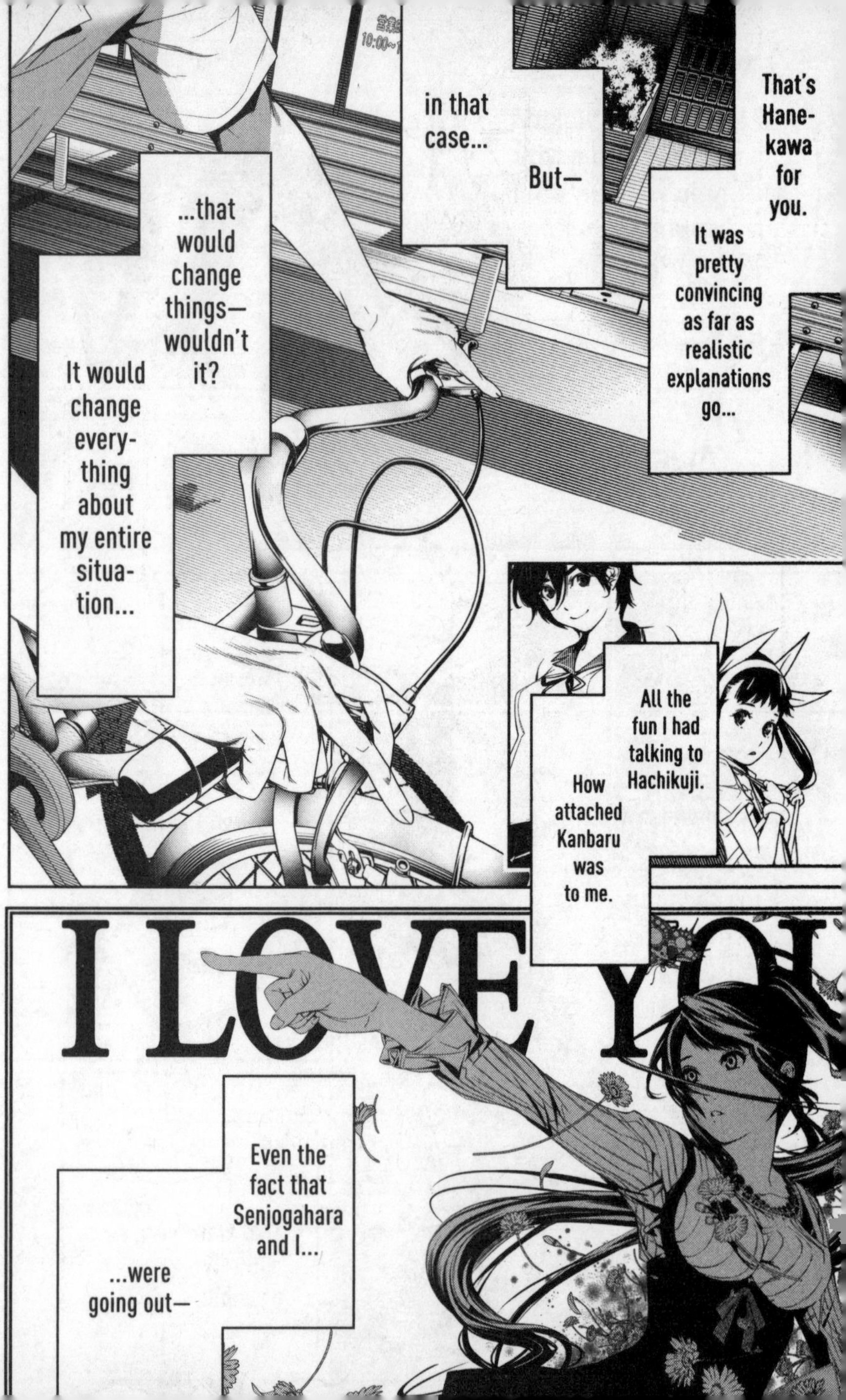
That's Hanekawa for you.
It was pretty convincing as far as realistic explanations go...
But—
in that case...
...that would change things—wouldn't it?
It would change everything about my entire situation...
All the fun I had talking to Hachikuji.
How attached Kanbaru was to me.
I LOVE YO
Even the fact that Senjogahara and I...
...were going out—

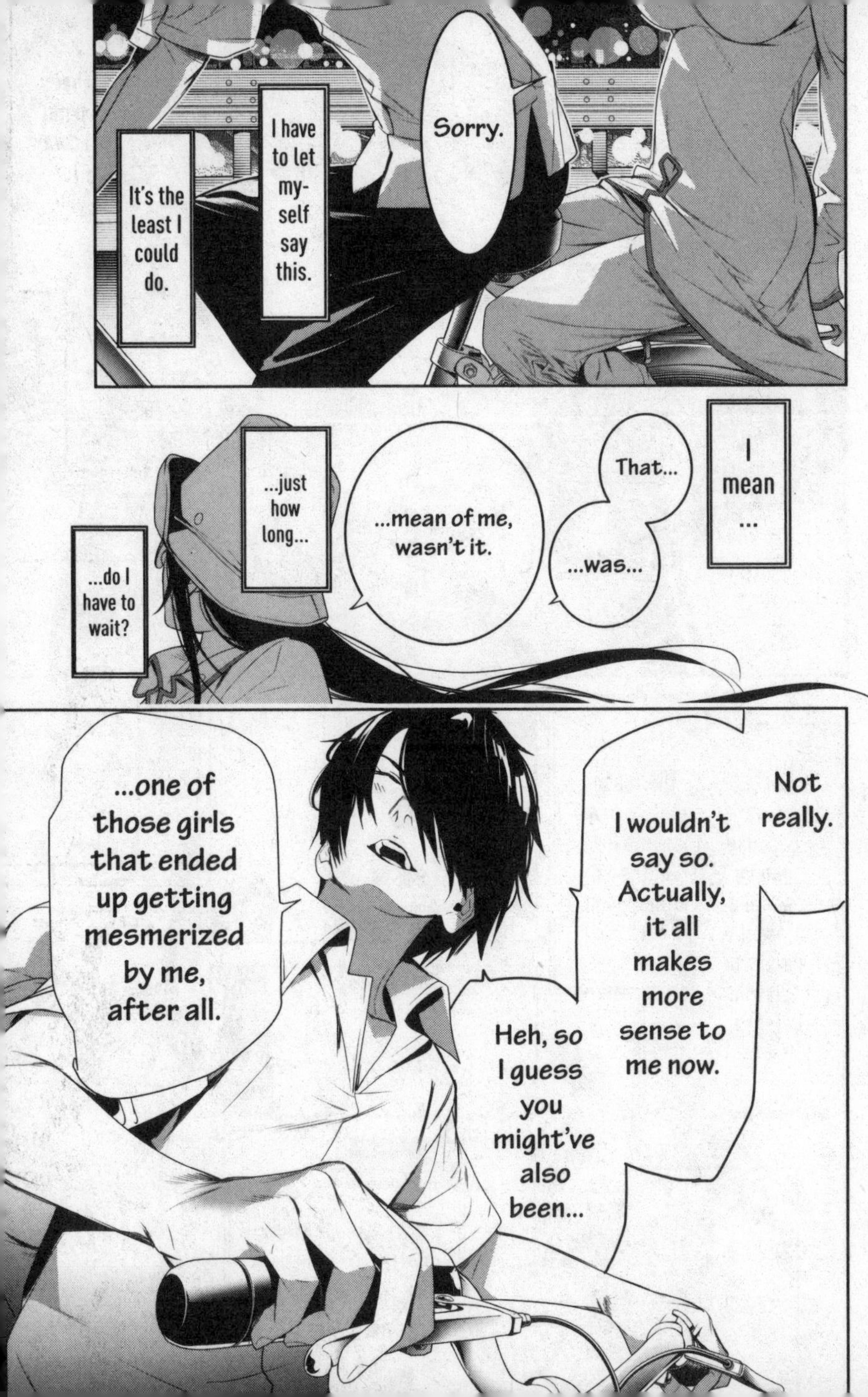
Sorry.
I have to let my-self say this.
It's the least I could do.
I mean...
That... ...was...
...mean of me, wasn't it.
...just how long...
...do I have to wait?
Not really.
I wouldn't say so. Actually, it all makes more sense to me now.
Heh, so I guess you might've also been...
...one of those girls that ended up getting mesmerized by me, after all.

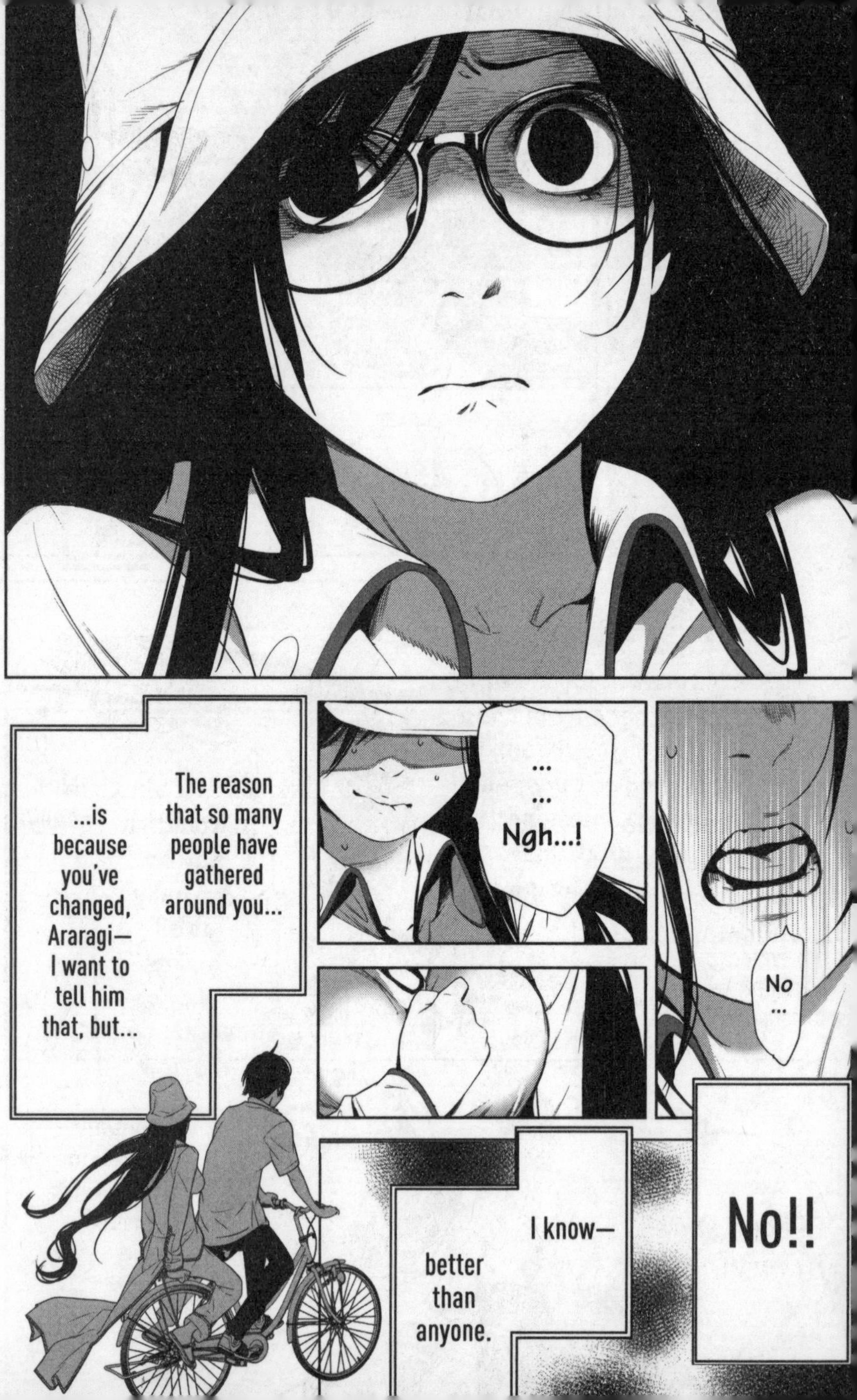
No
...
...
...
Ngh...!
The reason that so many people have gathered around you...
...is because you've changed, Araragi— I want to tell him that, but...
No!!
I know—
better than anyone.

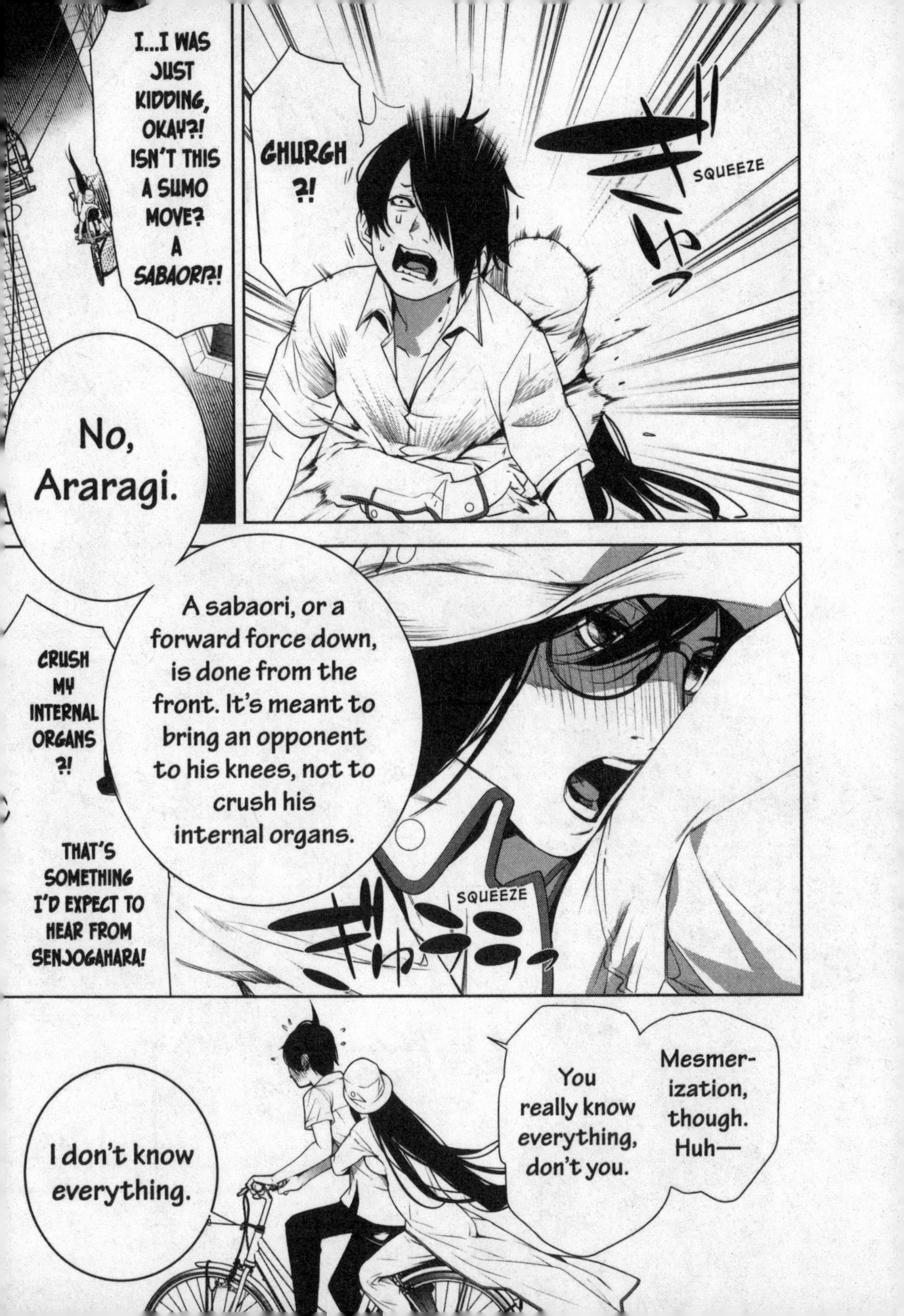
GHURGH ?!
SQUEEZE
I...I WAS JUST KIDDING, OKAY?! ISN'T THIS A SUMO MOVE? A SABAORI?!?!
No, Araragi.
A sabaori, or a forward force down, is done from the front. It's meant to bring an opponent to his knees, not to crush his internal organs.
SQUEEZE
CRUSH MY INTERNAL ORGANS ?!
THAT'S SOMETHING I'D EXPECT TO HEAR FROM SENJOGAHARA!
Mesmer-ization, though. Huh—
You really know everything, don't you.
I don't know everything.

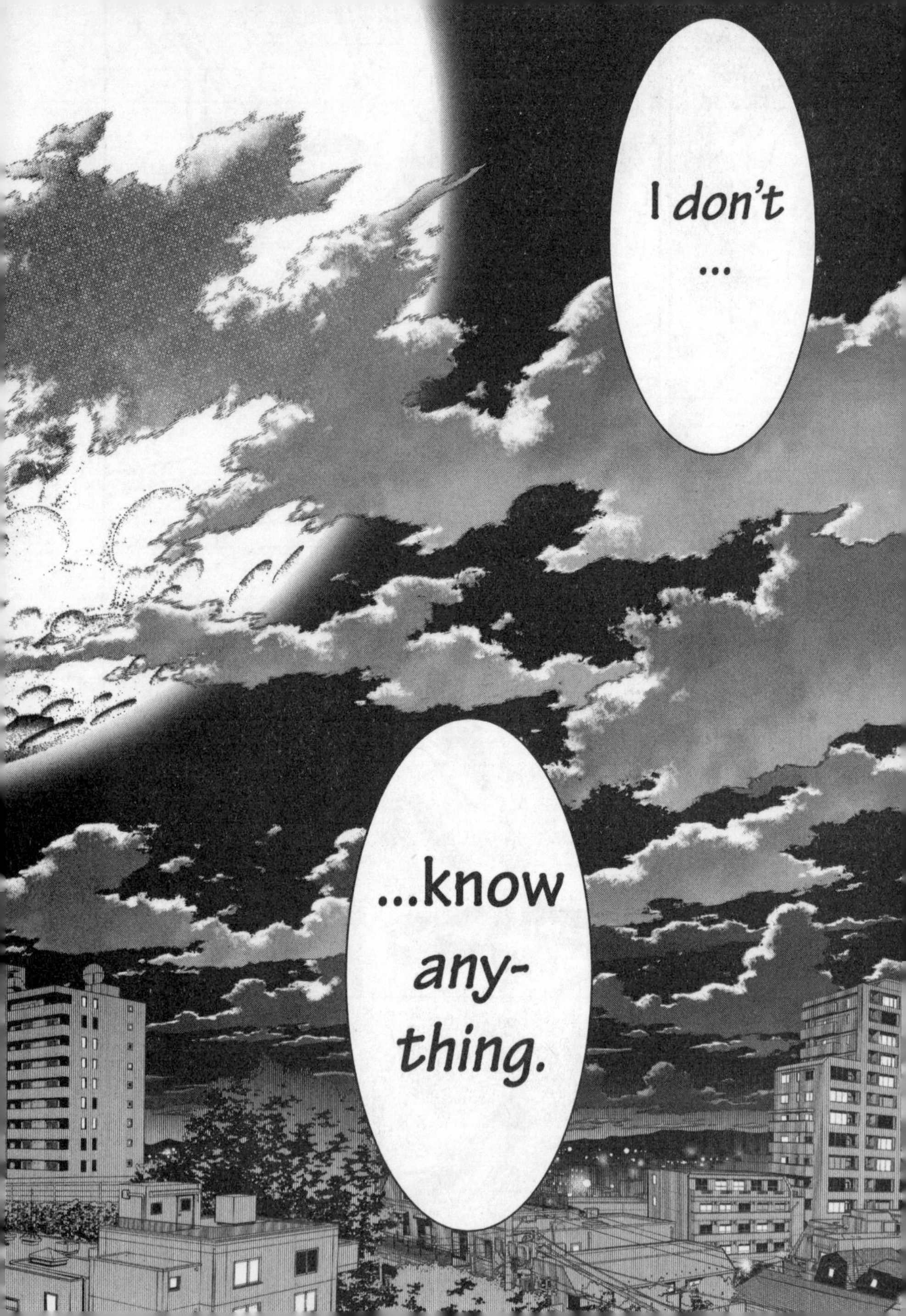
I don't ...
...know any-thing.

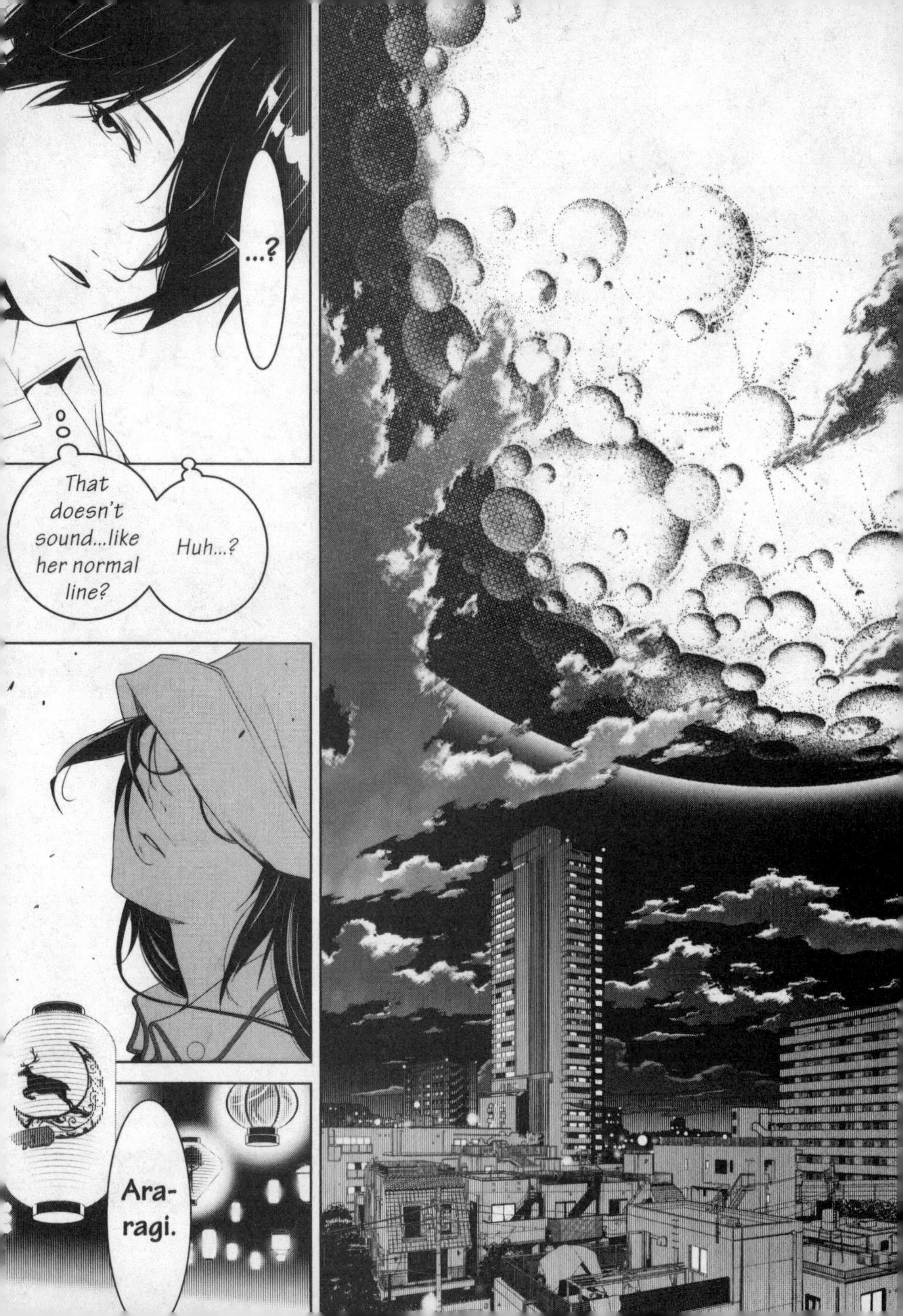
...?
Huh...?
That doesn't sound...like her normal line?
Ara-ragi.

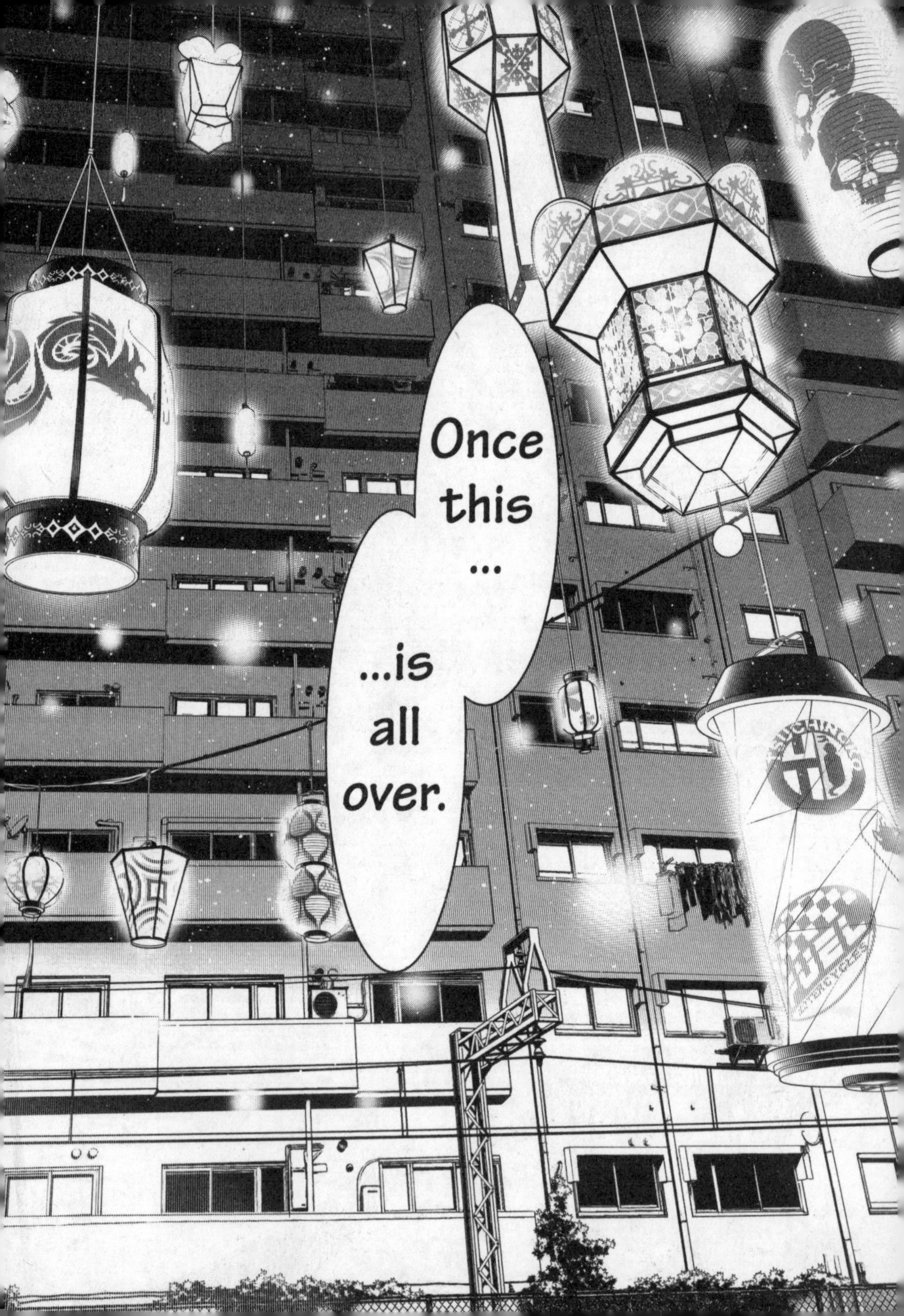
Once this ...
...is all over.

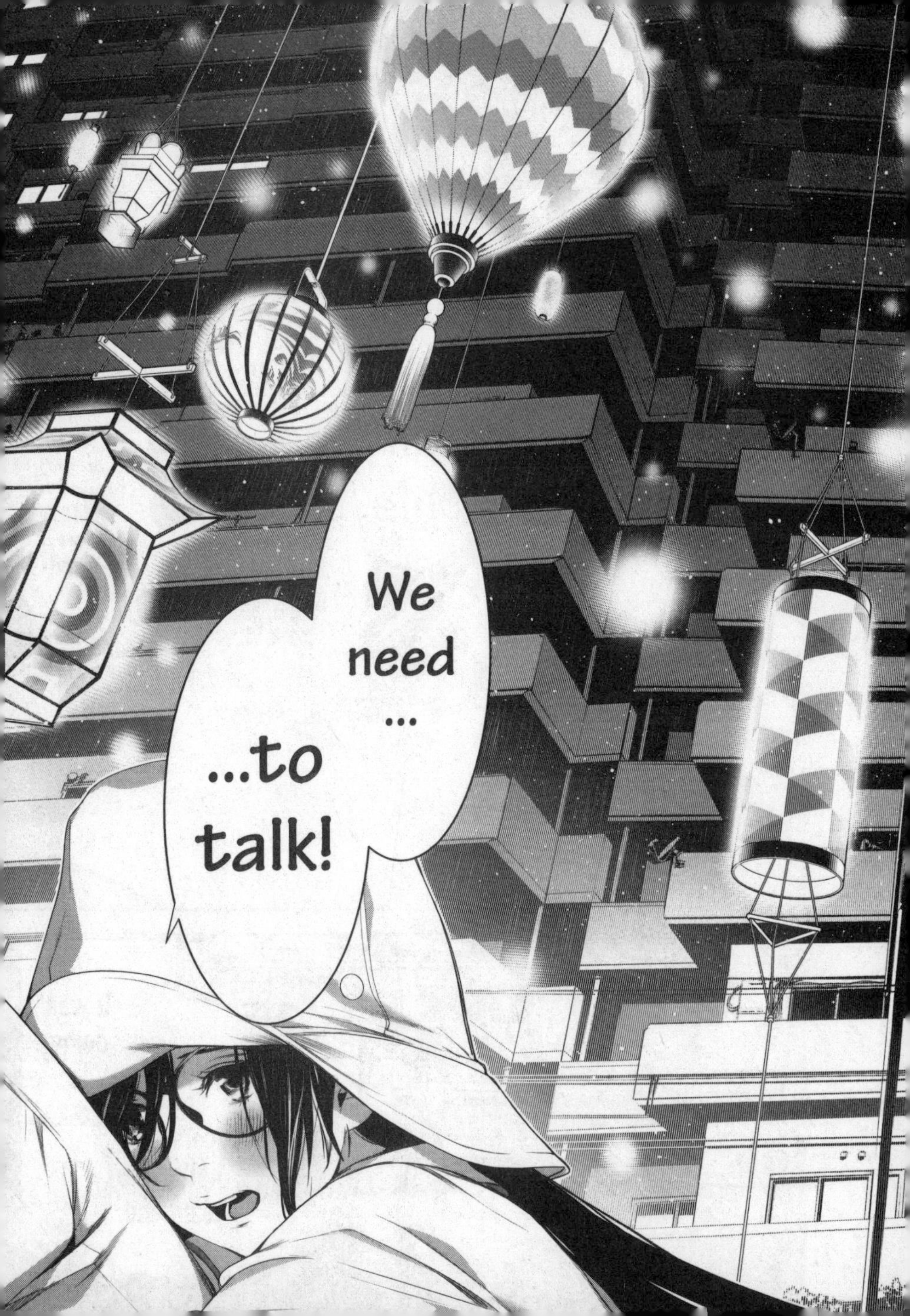
We need ... ...to talk!

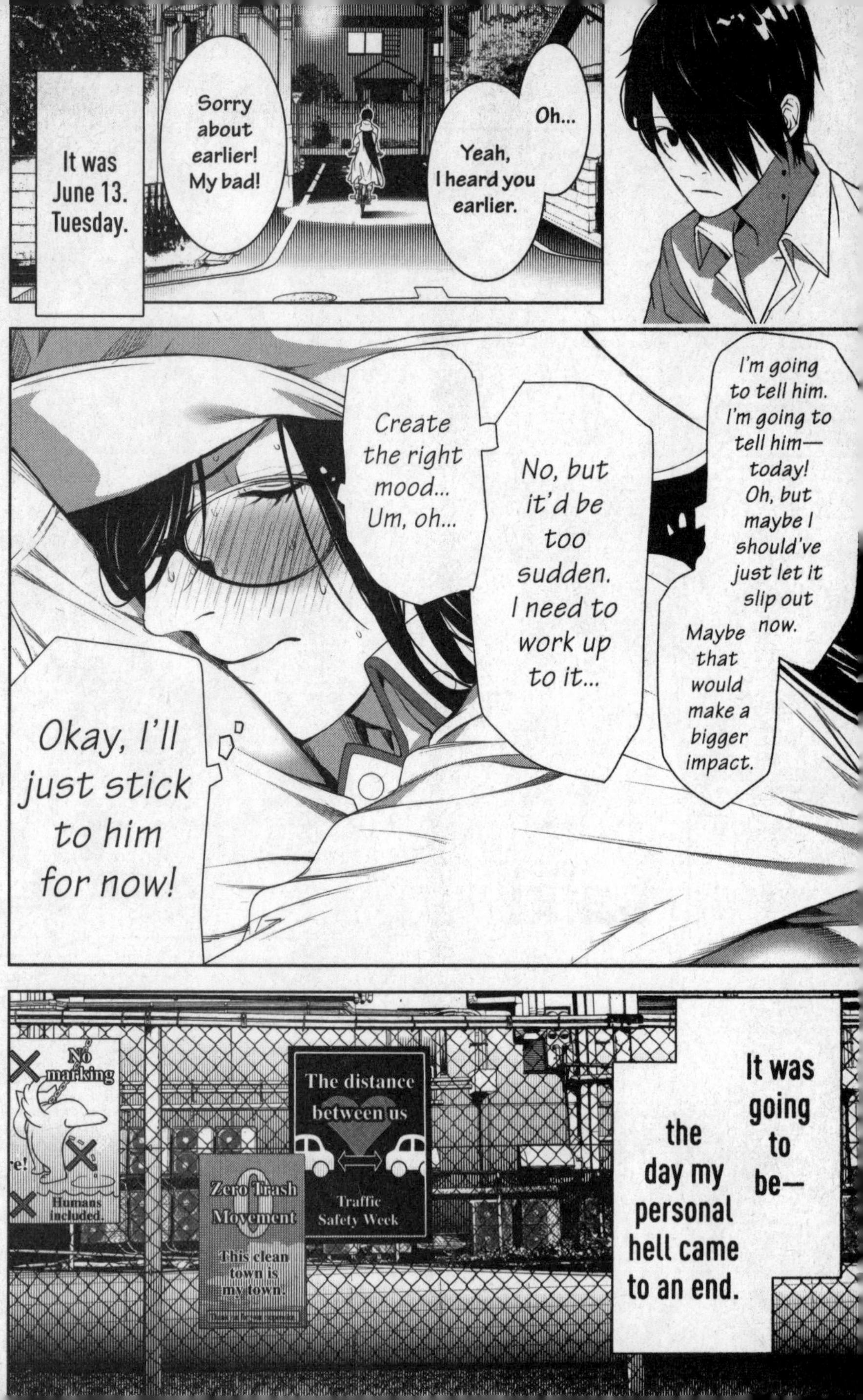
Sorry about earlier! My bad!
Oh...
Yeah, I heard you earlier.
It was June 13. Tuesday.
I'm going to tell him. I'm going to tell him— today! Oh, but maybe I should've just let it slip out now.
Maybe that would make a bigger impact.
No, but it'd be too sudden. I need to work up to it...
Create the right mood... Um, oh...
Okay, I'll just stick to him for now!
It was going to be—
the day my personal hell came to an end.
The distance between us
Traffic Safety Week
Zero Trash Movement
This clean town is my town!
No marking
Humans included.

Continued in Volume 16

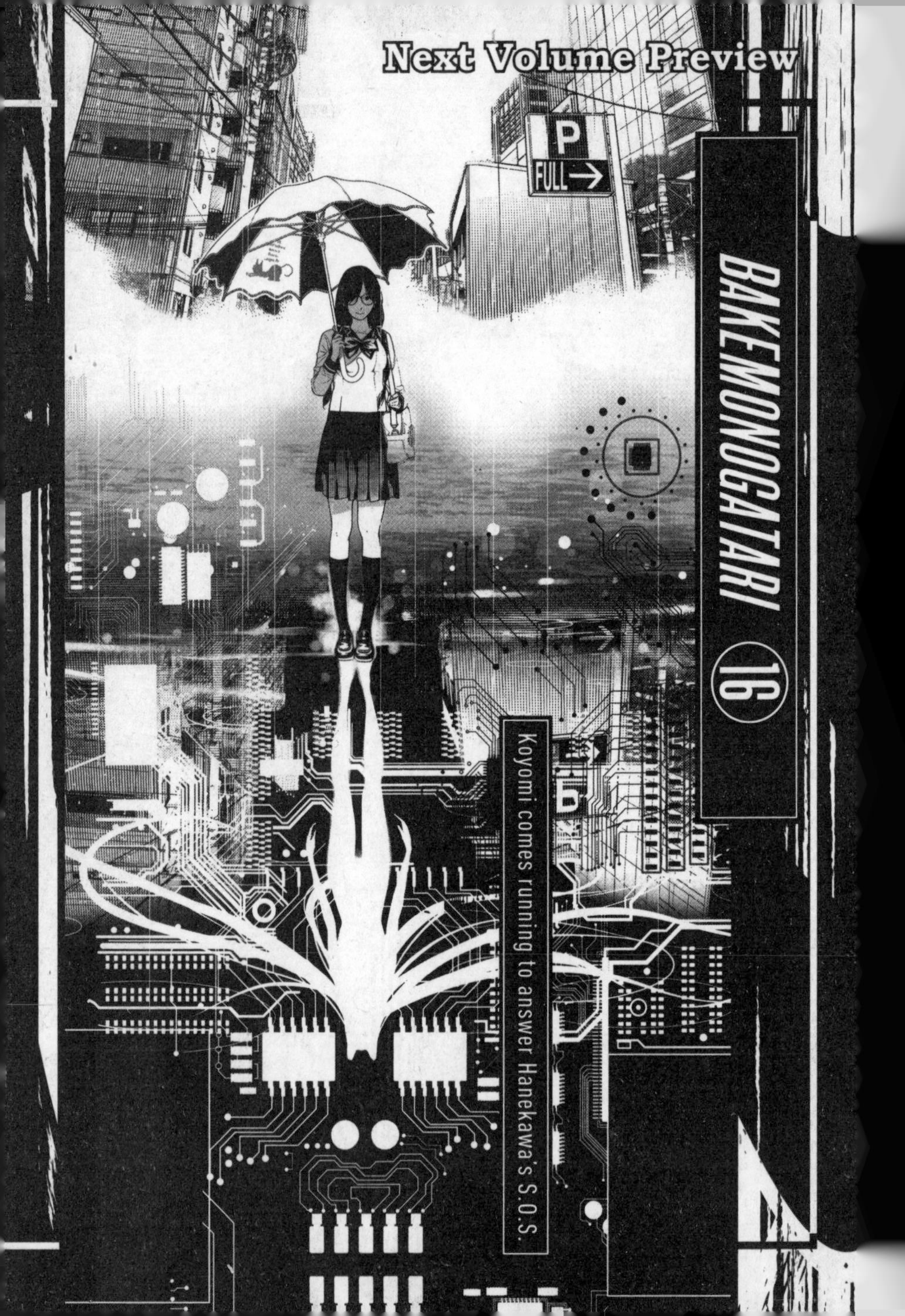
Next Volume Preview
P
FULL →
BAKEMONOGATARI 16
Koyomi comes running to answer Hanekawa's S.O.S.